THE FIFTH BORDER STATE

WEST VIRGINIA AND APPALACHIA
Edited by Ronald L. Lewis, Ken Fones-Wolf, and Kevin Barksdale

TITLES IN THE SERIES

A Union for Appalachian Healthcare Workers: The Radical Roots and Hard Fights of Local 1199
JOHN HENNEN

Wheeling's Polonia: Reconstructing Polish Community in a West Virginia Steel Town
WILLIAM HAL GORBY

Never Justice, Never Peace: Mother Jones and the Miner Rebellion at Paint and Cabin Creeks
LON KELLY SAVAGE AND GINNY SAVAGE AYERS

The Industrialist and the Mountaineer: The Eastham-Thompson Feud and the Struggle for West Virginia's Timber Frontier
RONALD L. LEWIS

Memorializing Motherhood: Anna Jarvis and the Struggle for Control of Mother's Day
KATHARINE LANE ANTOLINI

Working Class Radicals: The Socialist Party in West Virginia, 1898–1920
FREDERICK A. BARKEY

"They'll Cut Off Your Project": A Mingo County Chronicle
HUEY PERRY

An Appalachian Reawakening: West Virginia and the Perils of the New Machine Age, 1945–1972
JERRY BRUCE THOMAS

An Appalachian New Deal: West Virginia in the Great Depression
JERRY BRUCE THOMAS

Culture, Class, and Politics in Modern Appalachia
EDITED BY JENNIFER EGOLF, KEN FONES-WOLF, AND LOUIS C. MARTIN

Governor William E. Glasscock and Progressive Politics in West Virginia
GARY JACKSON TUCKER

Matewan before the Massacre: Politics, Coal, and the Roots of Conflict in a West Virginia Mining Community
REBECCA J. BAILEY

SCOTT A. MacKENZIE

THE FIFTH BORDER STATE

SLAVERY, EMANCIPATION, AND THE FORMATION OF WEST VIRGINIA, 1829–1872

West Virginia University Press / Morgantown

Copyright © 2023 by West Virginia University Press
All rights reserved
First edition published 2023 by West Virginia University Press
Printed in the United States of America

ISBN 978-1-952271-71-7 (paperback) / 978-1-952271-72-4 (ebook)

Library of Congress Cataloging-in-Publication Data
Names: MacKenzie, Scott A. (Scott Alexander), author.
Title: The fifth border state : slavery, emancipation, and the formation of West Virginia,
    1829–1872 / Scott A. MacKenzie.
Other titles: West Virginia and Appalachia.
Description: First edition. | Morgantown : West Virginia University Press, 2023. | Series:
    West Virginia and Appalachia | Includes bibliographical references and index.
Identifiers: LCCN 2022020004 | ISBN 9781952271717 (paperback) | ISBN 9781952271724
    (ebook)
Subjects: LCSH: Slavery—West Virginia—Public opinion—History—19th century. | West
    Virginia—History—To 1950. | West Virginia—History—Civil War, 1861–1865. |
    Border States (U.S. Civil War) | BISAC: HISTORY / United States / Civil War Period
    (1850–1877) | HISTORY / United States / State & Local / South (AL, AR, FL, GA, KY,
    LA, MS, NC, SC, TN, VA, WV)
Classification: LCC F241 .M13 2023 | DDC 975.4/03—dc23/eng/20220504
LC record available at https://lccn.loc.gov/2022020004

Material in chapter 5 previously appeared as "Forming a Middle Class: The Civil War in
Kanawha County, West(ern) Virginia, 1861–1865," *West Virginia History* 9, no. 1 (Spring
2015), 23–45.

Cover and book design by Than Saffel / WVU Press
Cover image: The new naval and military map of the United States, by John Calvin Smith,
Philadelphia, Pa., 1862. Library of Congress control number 99447095.

IN MEMORIAM

Roderick A. MacKenzie, BA, BComm (1976–2002)
Wishing you were somehow here again.

Stanley P. Hirshson, PhD (1928–2003)
For showing me the way.

Roderick I. MacKenzie, MD (1944–2007)
Thank you, Dad, thank you.

Bianca R. DiLorenzo, MSW (1977–2015)
For bringing out the best in me.

Carol Ann Bachl Dennis, PhD (1950–2018)
For guiding me along the way.

Vincent A. Rigg (1969–2020)
Father, brother, son, and cousin.

Contents

List of Illustrations ix

Acknowledgments xi

Introduction 1

1 Northwestern Virginia's Path 9
toward Reconciliation, 1829–1851

2 Northwestern Virginia on the Defensive, 1851–1860 39

3 Northwestern Virginia in the 63
Secession Crisis, January–July 1861

4 The Conservative Phase of the West Virginia Statehood ... 92
Movement, August 1861–February 1862

5 The Radical Phase of the West Virginia Statehood 117
Movement, March 1862–June 1863

6 West Virginia under Radical Rule, June 1863–December 1869 147

Epilogue: West Virginia's Redemption, 1870–1872 179

Appendix A 189
An Appeal of the People of West Virginia to Congress,
Suggesting for the Consideration of Members Material Facts

Appendix B 201
Report of the Minority to Lincoln's Border State
Emancipation Plan, July 15, 1862

Notes 203

Index 229

List of Illustrations

FIGURES

1. Map of Virginia in 1860	21
2. John S. Carlile, ca. 1855	46
3. West Virginia Independence Hall, Wheeling, ca. 2010	81
4. Waitman T. Willey, ca. 1860	95
5. Abraham Lincoln, ca. 1862	141
6. Arthur I. Boreman, ca. 1860	149

TABLES

1. White and Enslaved Populations of Northwestern Virginia, 1830–1850	19
2. Places of Birth of Adult Heads of Households in Three Northwestern Virginia Counties	20
3. Border State Slavery	23
4. Slaveholders' Share of Property by County and Head of Household, 1850–1860	24
5. Wheeling, West Virginia, Election Returns by Ward, 1864 Presidential Election	155

Acknowledgments

Many wonderful people gave me their time and interest while I wrote this book. I wish to acknowledge as many of them as possible here. Space limits me from including more, so I will thank other deserving family, friends, and colleagues individually.

The first grace the In Memoriam page. My brother and father passed away far too young and left enormous gaps in our family's life. The next generation will never enjoy their love. Professor Hirshson encouraged me to study the Civil War era. Without his inspiration, I do not know where I would be today. My dear friend Bianca came back into my life after a long absence. She also left too early but made me a better person. Carol Ann, my best friend at Auburn, guided me through those important years. Finally, my cousin Vincent passed suddenly as I finished the manuscript, leaving behind his loving family. I dedicate this book to their memories.

I next honor my beloved family. My mother Maryel constantly encouraged me to pursue my education. To my brother John, sister-in-law Brandi, nephew Noah, and niece Sara in Calgary, thank you. To my sister Karen, brother-in-law Erik, and nephews Samuel, David, and Malcolm, and niece Alexandra in Stockholm, tack så mycket. To my brother Bryan and his friend Chloe in Melbourne, thank you. To my numerous uncles, aunts, and cousins, thank you.

Third, I am grateful to my many friends. Jamie Afifi and Sarah Chalke, Philip and Maria Baker, Ainsley Bishop, Meredith Bocian, Jessica Broussard, Alex, Tawni, and Michael Brown, Tommy Brown, Dave Burke, Joshua and Mallory Carson, Carey Cauthen, David Champa, Jake Clawson, Ashley Coley, the late Don Dennis, Dick Denny and Sharon Hamilton, Linda and Rick Denny, Brett and Kim Derbes, Helena Nunes Duarte, Jonathan Epstein, Tom Feasby, Mary Margaret Fincher, Sabrina Fischer, Caylan Ford and Jared Pearman, Judy Goberdhan, Ashlee Graham, David Grebstad, Elizabeth Butcher Grinsted, Susan Moore Grizzard, Monique Buonocore Grossman, Laurence Halparin, Julian and Kay Hamilton, Sarah Hamilton and Mike Buxton, Ashley Hartt, Karen Hartt, John R. Heckman, Stephanie Horner, Rebecca Woodham Johnston, Bill King, John Klein, Chris Kluke, Cindy Kressler, Mary Lavigne, Cam and Leah MacArthur, Corey and Jenny Markum, Annie McCullough, Scott McFadyen, the late David McRae, Jennifer Mikkelson, Scott Monroe, Rudy Narvas, Robert xii / Acknowledgments

Nash, Kim Nguyen, Vanessa Moraes Pacheco, Meghan Emery Pan, Jason and Krissy Parrish, Tyler Paul, Tyler Peterson, Rebecca Eckstein Powell, Jennifer Zimmer Quigley, Lawrence Rebman, Misty Reynolds, Rolundus and Dana Rice, Teresa Riley, Hannah Riordan, Paola Rodriguez Ruah, Jarrett Ruminski, Joseph and the late Maryann Salvato, the late Dr. George Satran, Abby Sayers, Colin Shannon and Julia Portiz, Geoffrey Shaw, Trevor Sigmundson, Noah Skelton and his daughter Noelle, Noel Steele, Mercedes Swearingen, Thomas Csongor Szendry, Matt Vogeler, Bridget Warren, Darin J. Weeks, Ian Wilson, Roy "Tre" Wisecarver, Andy Wood, and Jeff and Emily Zvengrowski each deserve my eternal gratitude.

Fourth, I thank the following members present and past of the History Department at Auburn University. They include, in alphabetical order, Guy Beckwith, Morris Bian, Donna Bohanan, Kathryn Braund, Jennifer Brooks, David Carter, Alfreda Cosby, Ruth Crocker, Patience Essah, Larry Gerber, Cathleen Giustino, Boris Gorshkov, Reagan Grimsley, James R. Hansen, Charles Israel, Adam Jortner, Kelly Kennington, Joseph Kicklighter, Ralph Kingston, Angela Lakwete, Sharon Lewis, Matthew Malczycki, Alan Meyer, Aaron Shapiro, Mark Sheftall, Tiffany Sippial, Rod Steward, and William F. Trimble. I also thank the late Gerry Gryski from the Political Science Department and the International Student Services Office staff. To the thousands of students whom I served as a teaching assistant and/or studied alongside in joint classes, I thank you for a great experience. War Eagle!

Fifth, I also acknowledge the faculty and staff of the following institutions at which I studied. They include, in order of my attendance, Timothy E. Anna, Francis Carroll, Mary Margaret Johnston-Miller, John Kendle, Ian Kerr, Michael Kinnear, Leonard Kuffert, Geoffrey Lambert, Keith Sandiford, Douglas N. Sprague, Lea Stirling, T. E. Vadney, Vanessa Warne, and the late Larry Desmond of the University of Manitoba; Sylvia Coppi, Elena Frangakis-Syrett, Marilyn Harris, Francine Kapchan, Phyllis Proctor, Rolf Swensen, and Frank Warren, and the late Philip V. Cannistraro, the late Jay Gordon, the late Janet Hirshson, the late Jay Kinsbruner, the late Frank Merli, and the late David Syrett of Queens College of the City University of New York; Christon Archer, David J. Bercuson, Patrick Brennan, Hendrik Kraay, the late Marian McKenna, Francine Michaud, Jewel Spangler, and Frank Towers of the University of Calgary; and finally James Broomhall, Denise Messenger, Al Pejack, Mark Snell, and Tom White of the George Tyler Moore Center for the Study of the Civil War in Shepherdstown, West Virginia.

Sixth, I appreciate the following scholars from around the world for their input. They include Allison Abra, Bob Arrington, Aaron Astor, Kenneth R.

Bailey, Benjamin Bankhurst, L. Diane Barnes, the late Ed Bearss, Jonathan Berkey, Neil and Gail Besner, Glenn David Brasher, Stephen G. Brown, Victoria Bynum, Greg Carroll, Beau Cleland, Robert Colby, James H. Cook, Zac Cowsert, A. Glenn Crothers, Steve Cunningham, Luke Daly-Groves, Laura June Davis, Adam Domby, Andrew Duppstadt, Douglas Egerton, Niels Eichorn, Angela Esco Elder, Nathan Ellstrand, Cicero Fain, the late Michael Fellman, Matt Foulds, Allison Fredette, Barbara Gannon, Joseph Geiger, Joseph T. Glatthaar, David Gleeson, Randall Gooden, Michael B. Graham, Hilary Green, Michael Green, A. Wilson Greene, Mark Grimsley, Bruce Gudmundsson, Mark Guerci, Heather Haley, M. Keith Harris, Philip Hatfield, Jason Herbert and the #HATM crowd, Kathleen Hillard, Lucian Holness, Bob Hutton, John C. Inscoe, Ryan Keating, Tim Konhaus, W. Hunter Lesser, Kevin Levin, Terry Lowry, Scott A. MacKenzie of the University of California, Davis, Marko Manula, John Marszalek, Lawrence T. McDonnell, the late C. Stuart McGehee, Brian McKnight, John McMillan, Christian McWhirter, Keri Leigh Merritt, Jennifer Murray, Barton Myers, Steven Nash, Clayton R. Newell, Caroline Wood Newhall, Leopoldo Nuti, Tore Olsson, Billy Joe Peyton, Jason Phillips, Holly Pinhero, Stewart Plein, Paul Quigley, Ethan Rafuse, Darren Reid, Amelia Smith Reinhart, David Reynolds, Connie Park Rice, the late Otis K. Rice, Stephen Rockenbach, Donald Shaffer, John W. Shaffer, Amanda Shaver, Aaron Sheehan-Dean, Patrick Sheridan, Craig M. Simpson, Andrew L. Slap, John E. Stealey III, Randall Stevens, Bruce Stewart, Steven Straley, Philip Strum, Daniel Sunshine, Jacob Thomas, Jerry Bruce Thomas, Kathleen Logothetis Thompson, David J. Trowbridge, Jinny Turman, Susannah Ural, Pater Wallenstein, Cheryl Wells, LeeAnn Whites, Kristen L. Wilkes, John Alexander Williams, Tristan Williams, Richard A. Wolfe, Michael Woods, David Zimring, and Adam Zucconi.

Seventh, I am grateful to the West Virginia and Regional History Collection, the West Virginia State Archives, the Library of Virginia, the Mid-Atlantic Branch of the National Archives, the Library of Congress, and the Interlibrary Loan section of the Ralph Draughon Library of Auburn University for allowing me to access their resources. Without these fine institutions and their diligent staffs, this book would never have become a reality.

Finally, I recognize the hard work of the staff at West Virginia University Press. Kevin Barksdale, Elizabeth Catte, Joseph Dahm, Kenneth Fones-Wolf, Sara Georgi, Hal Gorby, Natalie Homer, Derek Krissoff, Ron Lewis, Sarah Munroe, Than Saffel, and the anonymous reviewer believed in this project from its inception and diligently aided its completion.

I take full responsibility for any errors in research and analysis in this work.

INTRODUCTION

The Fifth Border State

Every account of West Virginia's creation is wrong. For one hundred sixty years, historians have explained the transformation of the northwestern corner of Virginia into the Thirty-Fifth State in only one way. Long-standing and irreconcilable natural, ethnic, cultural, and economic differences between its western and eastern halves, it goes, created two distinct societies within Virginia's borders. The politically dominant plantations of the east neglected the small, independent, free-laboring farmers of the west, it follows. From these circumstances, the latter rejected Virginia's secession when the Civil War began in 1861. Siding with the Union, the west's long-desired independence came inevitably two years later. This idea has permeated every history book and article on the matter ever since. The earliest accounts come from the wartime generation. Union Army veteran Theodore Lang called his home state "a child of the storm" in his *Loyal West Virginia from 1861 to 1865* (1895). He argued that by "every natural association West Virginia was allied to Ohio and Pennsylvania, and therefore to Northern sentiments and institutions." Granville Davisson Hall, a firsthand witness to and recorder of the statehood movement, similarly stated in *The Rending of Virginia* (1902) that "if Eastern Virginia and Western had been separate commonwealths, there could hardly have been less business and social intercourse than there was." Little has changed since these scholars penned their works. Books published in the 2010s say the same things. This thesis is, unfortunately, totally wrong. By constantly retelling this account, this mixture of wartime propaganda and old and bad history went unchallenged for over a century.[1]

A sample of some general works on the Civil War era shows its durability. Eric Foner grouped West Virginia with the other border states in his *Reconstruction* (1988) but like everyone else called its creation "both the culmination of deep-rooted sectional divisions within Virginia and the overthrow of the western region's own antebellum elite, which had generally supported secession." James M. McPherson dedicated seven full pages to western Virginia in his classic *Battle Cry of Freedom* (1988). "Slaves and slaveowners were rare among these narrow valleys and steep mountainsides," he wrote, and the "region's culture and economy were oriented to nearby Ohio and Pennsylvania rather than towards the faraway lowlands of Virginia." Likewise, William Link argued in *Roots of Secession* (2003) that as the east experienced increasingly disturbing events such as John Brown's raid on Harpers Ferry in 1859, the northwest developed a "new political consciousness" that "offered an aggressive critique of the politics of slavery" that led to the area's separation. Allen Guelzo reached perhaps the nadir of the state's experience when he inaccurately described the transformation of "the non-slaveholding counties" in a single sentence in his *Fateful Lightning* (2012). James Oakes's *Freedom National* (2013) gave more space than Guelzo to the state's formation but shared the same view as the rest. Western Virginia, he claimed, "chafed under the rule of aristocratic eastern planters." He, more than any other previous scholar, pushed the thesis to its limits when he declared the northwest's revolt was against "anti-slaveholder politics—but it still wasn't abolitionism." Elizabeth Varon repeated this view in her *Armies of Deliverance* (2019). Finally, Aaron Astor's two paragraphs on West Virginia in the *Cambridge History of the American Civil War* (2019) stated that its creation "completed one of the more extraordinary and permanent political developments in the Border States." Like his counterparts, however, he changed little about the subject. These top-flight scholars are blameless in maintaining this thesis. They studied dated secondary works that repeat the same old story.[2]

West Virginia's historians unintentionally caused the problem. Almost all research on the subject comes from people from the state or associated with it. The only two graduate history programs in the state, at West Virginia University in Morgantown and Marshall University in Huntington, prefer more pressing subjects such as the effects of resource extraction. The handful of amateurs, moreover, focus on military topics. The first professional scholar on the subject, Charles Henry Ambler, merely codified the views of Lang and Hall mentioned above. In *Sectionalism in Virginia from 1776 to 1861* (1910), he argued that two distinct societies lived within the Commonwealth, with the eastern planters oppressing the western proletariat. He found these differences in the state's political history from the start of white settlement in the colonial period. The arrival of Scots-Irish and German migrants to the Trans-Allegheny region, he stated, "constituted an important epoch in Virginia's history. The westward advance of her peculiar institutions was thereby interrupted, and a new society, naturally hostile to all things Virginian, was planted." Eastern refusal to grant universal male suffrage and internal improvements, he continued, drove deep wedges into the state's unity. When the planters tried to secede in 1861, the long-suffering westerners arose united for their inevitable independence. His book served as the standard text on West Virginia for the next half century. Its influence was so strong that Ambler's only contemporary rival, James C. McGregor, all but copied his work. The first half of his *Disruption of Virginia* (1922) reads like his colleague's book. The remainder, on the other hand, countered Ambler by pointing out extensive opposition to the new state. He argued that the separation of West Virginia was "an unnecessary wrong" that was both unconstitutional in its behavior and "not desired by more than a small minority of the people of the new state." He was more right than he knew, but sadly McGregor's work never influenced the field as Ambler's did. The latter's students carried on his legacy despite changing attitudes toward race after the Second World War. One of them, George Ellis Moore, crafted the first full political history of slavery in West Virginia in 1956. Its argument could have been written half a century earlier.[3]

The only significant challenger to Ambler barely changed a thing. In *A House Divided: Statehood Politics and the Copperhead Movement in West Virginia* (1964), Richard Orr Curry revealed significant divisions within the statehood movement on separation. Using the region's newspapers, he compiled a tally of election returns to better understand the "quantum relationship between Unionists and secessionists." His figures revealed severe limits to Ambler's unified population idea. As little as 60 percent of the white population opposed secession, and almost all of those lived in counties along the Ohio and Pennsylvania borders. Curry then identified widespread factions in the statehood movement. Despite these powerful insights, however, he agreed with many of Ambler's observations. They still shared the influence of regional variations dividing the state along with minimizing slavery's role in the statehood movement. He lightly touched on the slavery issue, saying that it "did not, indeed could not, thrive in the northwest." The topic appears only once in his book, when it merely "clouded" the drafting of the new state's first constitution. He also unfortunately ended his work with statehood in June 1863, although he covered later events with an article in his edited collection of essays titled *Radicalism, Racism, and Party Realignment* (1969). Despite these shortcomings, Curry's book remains the most cited work on the topic due mainly to limited alternatives. The few authors since have made little effort to reassess his work. Neither John A. Williams, William A. Link, and Mark Snell nor Eric J. Wittenberg, Edmund Sargus, and Penny Barrick offered many new insights. The Ambler-Curry thesis, as I call it, remains the standard interpretation of West Virginia's formation.[4]

Much of the problem stems from limited source materials. Researchers have so far tapped only three sources. The first is the Ruffner Pamphlet of 1847. In it, a northwestern slaveholder asked the region to expunge the institution from their midst to remove its perceived economic harm. The next is the *Wheeling Daily Intelligencer*, the most extensive surviving newspaper in the region from the Civil War and statehood eras. Historians of the Ambler-Curry school took its editorial criticisms of slavery as the dominant voice of the region. The third is the congressional debates on statehood in 1862. For decades, scholars argued that the radical Republicans in Washington forced the new state to accept a gradual emancipation plan as a condition for statehood. Loyal West Virginians, they concluded, fell into line. Historians since have failed to sufficiently critique these three sources to discern the state's responses to slavery and emancipation. The experiences of the enslaved themselves, moreover, rarely appear in these sources, but to be fair, few slave histories ever survived. Booker T. Washington described his enslaved experiences in his memoir *Up from Slavery* (1901). A handful lived into the 1930s to be recorded by Works Progress Administration interviewers. Previous histories have not only continued to argue that the region opposed slavery but also neglected to find additional sources that may counter this view. At present, a Wikipedia page on slavery in the state provides the most extensive coverage of the subject.[5]

Only in the past thirty years has any scholar investigated the subject. The main student here, John Stealey, first examined the institution's impact in the Kanawha Valley salt business. He concluded that its leading figures preferred slave to free labor and "did not hesitate to make the choice." Few have applied his thesis, although groundbreaking, to the rest of West Virginia. One historian, Wilma Dunaway, wrote several books on enslavement in Appalachia. She included northwestern Virginia in her world-systems analysis of the Mountain South, arguing that the institution exerted vast influence on the larger region's economic ties to the world economy. Dunaway expanded her view so widely, however, that the northwest appears as one part of many, neglecting its pivotal influence along slavery's border. Few studying the state have followed in her footsteps. John Shaffer argued that Virginia nativity affected Barbour County's Confederate enlistments more than slave ownership. On the other hand, Kenneth Fones-Wolf placed anti-Republican sentiment as the prime motivator behind Wheeling's few rebel soldiers' choices. My two articles on Kanawha County supplement Stealey's work in analyzing the area's internal responses to the Civil War. I discovered that its secessionists came almost exclusively from slaveholding families, occupations, and communities. Unionists, on the other hand, lacked such connections. In a subsequent article, I searched for similar patterns in six other counties. Men from Virginia backgrounds as well as slaveholders sided with the Confederacy in Ohio, Monongahela, Hampshire, Jefferson, Wayne, and Cabell counties. Their Union soldiers, surprisingly, mostly came from neighboring loyal states. West Virginia, I concluded, possessed more proslavery opinion than previously believed, and not just due to a particular community, economic activity, or heritage but due to all of the above. More recently, Michael Woods published a fine article arguing that statehood and emancipation went together. West Virginia's resistance to secession started to unhinge slavery in the area due to the actions of Union soldiers and Black self-liberation. At the same time, white Unionists used the occasion to overcome northern fears that they sought to make another slave state. This inspiring article, unfortunately, underestimated the power of proslavery opinion in West Virginia. The previous research taken together, no serious scholar of the state's formation can ignore this issue anymore, but more work is needed.[6]

If slavery during the war remains underappreciated, few understand the influence of emancipation on the state's tortured first decade. Early writers barely mention the period, possibly due to its intense controversy surrounding the replacement of its wartime constitution in 1872. Ambler and his student Milton Geofsky both viewed the radical Unionists turned Republicans as villains for employing barely legal measures to restrain their conservative and former rebel opponents. Richard Orr Curry's 1969 article, previously mentioned, changed little from Ambler's earlier work. The Republicans, he argued, rose to power due to "an accident of history" and needed to use multiple measures to keep their opponents at bay. Gordon McKinney's work on Appalachian Republicans said the same thing. Stephen Engle's more recent article sought to bring African Americans into the discussion but followed in the same mold where Blacks became pawns between two white parties. Randall Gooden's dissertation omitted race entirely. He maintained that Reconstruction failed in West Virginia until moderates in the two main parties sought common ground on economic issues. Once they were strengthened, the Democrats turned on the Republicans once in power in 1872. John Stealey's *West Virginia's Civil War–Era Constitution* (2013) at last brought race to the debate. He argued that the state's second constitution came from conservative retaliations after the war, calling the "counter-revolution, not reconstruction." Race, which he termed "Banquo's Ghost," played a big role in the conservative efforts to erode radical rule. Like the specter in Shakespeare's *Macbeth*, the issue bedeviled the Republicans by forcing them to defend Black citizenship and suffrage in a thoroughly racist state. Adding race, however, merely perpetuated the Ambler-Curry thesis. Stealey still saw West Virginia as a special experience of the Civil War era. He warned readers against that "temptation [which] exists to compare the Mountain State with Kentucky, Maryland, Missouri, or Delaware, but significant differences emphasize the exceptional and unique West Virginia experience." His statement reveals that the study of the state's formation stands at an impasse as well as suggesting the answer to its relief. I offer this book as a solution to this problem.[7]

My work provides the first new interpretation of West Virginia's creation since the event itself. Within these pages, I argue that *the region experienced the Civil War in the same ways as the border states of Missouri, Kentucky, Maryland, and Delaware.* Proving this thesis requires me to approach the topic along two axes. First, I compare northwestern Virginia and West Virginia to four other slaveholding states along the border with the free states, namely Missouri, Kentucky, Maryland, and Delaware. Historians of the American Civil War call this quartet the border states. They also rejected secession in 1861, albeit with major internal divisions, from a common belief that the federal Constitution protected African slavery better than the slaveholding Confederate States of America could. Although plagued with battles large and small, unrepentant secessionists, stubborn conservative Unionists and radicals, and vicious guerrillas, the border states remained with the Union throughout the war. Second, I show how deeply white northwestern Virginians supported the institution of African slavery. Historians wrongly remember the region for having antislavery views. The proof for such opinions comes from narrow and unrepresentative sources. My use of previously neglected evidence and reassessment of existing materials permits me to offer a new interpretation. Although the region never held more than a few thousand enslaved persons, whites in the region supported the practice as much as those in any part of the slaveholding states. Their commitment to white supremacy and enslavement proved so strong that the northwest separated from Virginia to protect it and dogged the new state for years afterward. Only one difference separated northwestern Virginia and the others in 1861: it was not a state *yet*.

The examples set by the other border states grant me the opportunity to offer a new interpretation of West Virginia's formation. President Abraham Lincoln's famous if possibly apocryphal statement "I would like to have God on my side, but I must have Kentucky" still perfectly sums up his border state policy. Histories of their experiences have tended to exclude West Virginia from this group. The initial study by Edward C. Smith in 1931 included the region among the western borderlands but omitted Maryland and Delaware. He argued that the border was pro-Union but also proslavery, if angry about federal war policies. Decades passed before new state-specific works appeared to ask why those areas rejected secession and endured the war and its aftermath. Barbara Fields's study of Maryland, Patience Essah's of Delaware, and Aaron Astor's of Kentucky and Missouri revealed the devotion of whites to slavery, as Smith argued decades before. Yet subsequent authors omitted West Virginia entirely. William C. Harris even excluded Delaware from his seminal 2011 study. The latest scholarship by Christopher Phillips and Matthew Stanley sought to expand the border area's boundaries northward to include Ohio, Indiana, and Illinois. Robert Sandow and David G. Smith discovered similarities in Pennsylvania. Steven Rochenbach, Matthew Salafia, and Bridget Ford followed suit with their comparisons of communities straddling the Ohio River. While these are important and useful works, the Ambler-Curry thesis still makes them see the Mountain State as unique and special. So far, only Stanley Harrold's 2010 examination of slave catching along the antebellum border and Allison Fredette's 2020 study of marriage between West Virginia and Kentucky have connected the former to the broader borderlands.[8]

This book is divided into six chapters and an epilogue. The first covers the first half of the nineteenth century as northwestern Virginia reconciled with the rest of the state. Despite furious opposition from the eastern planter class along the way, the region used the common ground of slavery to unite the Commonwealth. Chapter 2 shows how the events of the 1850s further sealed the breach. Rising tensions with the northern states led the region to confront every real or perceived antislavery threat to Virginia. By the time of John Brown's raid and the 1860 presidential election, northwestern whites reacted as strongly as the east in defense of slavery. In chapter 3, we will see that secession forced the region to make some awful choices. Leaving the Union meant, in their eyes, undermining the institution. As such, they formed a new loyal government to preserve the status quo. The notion of creating a new state was not inevitable but rather floated to the top of preferred options. The Lincoln administration, as part of its appeasement of the border states, encouraged their idea to keep southern Unionists on his side. Chapter 4 shows this policy at work as northwestern men drafted their constitution in what I call the conservative phase of the statehood movement. Those proceedings succeeded by keeping the slavery issue off the table and rebels under control. The convention delegates barely triumphed. Chapter 5 details the radical phase, when Lincoln's offer to the border states for compensated and gradual emancipation ran across the West Virginia statehood process. The other four border states famously rejected his plan, but the proto-state supported it. They did so not from a paucity of enslavement in the area or partisan allegiances but from the ruling radicals needing federal assistance to overcome their conservative rivals. Lincoln happily rewarded the region by signing the statehood bill in December 1862 for their support of his controversial plan. Their experience preceded the same processes later occurring in Maryland and Missouri. In chapter 6,

I detail the consequences of emancipation for the new state. Conservatives and former rebels retaliated against the radicals for collaborating with Lincoln and Congress. The latter, like many others in the border states, needed voting proscriptions to suppress their enemies. These succeeded until 1870, when changes in federal law undermined their legality. The epilogue concludes this book by examining how conservative Unionists and former Confederates redeemed West Virginia just as Maryland and Missouri experienced at the same time. By then, my readers will see how West Virginia was not a rogue appendage of its parent state but instead was *the fifth border state*.

I must make one special acknowledgment. Gary Gallagher used my title term as early as 2000 in his Great Courses lecture series on the American Civil War. He and Joan Waugh later referred to West Virginia joining the Union in 1863 as "in effect, a fifth border state" in *The American War* (2015). He has otherwise followed the same thesis as every other historian has for the past century. I use the term for my book, but with one modification. Instead of using the indefinite article "a," I refer to the state using the definite article "the." The northwestern counties started acting like a border state from the moment that Virginia announced its secession from the Union and just as the other four responded to the outbreak of the war. The only difference between that quartet and West Virginia is that the latter was simply not a state *yet*. It became one because of the same behaviors of the federal and state governments during this period. I pray that my adoption of Gallagher's term does justice to his solid contributions to the study of the Civil War era.[9]

CHAPTER 1

Northwestern Virginia's Path toward Reconciliation, 1829–1851

In January 1803, John G. Jackson of Harrison County explained northwestern Virginia's political frustrations to the eastern readers of the *Richmond Examiner*. Writing as "A Mountaineer," he described the disenfranchisement of most whites in his region as "so impolitic a measure, and so subversive of natural right, that if the constitution were perfect in every other part, it would demand a prompt interference and a decisive change." He denounced that only those able to pay the "tax on slaves, horses, taverns and peddlers license, of those owning land" could vote. His sentiments accurately described his white neighbors' dissatisfaction with Virginia's affairs despite his personal status. Jackson, as a prominent slaveholding businessman, easily met the suffrage requirements. Few others around him, however, could afford land, livestock, businesses, or slaves that would have granted them the right to vote and hold office. Nowhere did he mention differences in culture, desires for internal improvements (which were in their infancy anyway), or ties to neighboring states, as historians continued to claim two centuries later. He understood that suffrage, and no other issue, divided the state in the antebellum period. At the same time, Jackson also pointed out why eastern Virginia limited the franchise to property-owning white men. They trusted power only to individuals and by extension regions with strong commitments to slavery. This practice disadvantaged most western Virginians. Yet, in 1851, a new state constitution removed these restrictions and healed the breach. Although Jackson died in 1825 before any change occurred, he would have liked that appeals by his neighbors to support slavery granted that relief.[1]

This chapter deals with the northwest's reconciliation with Virginia in the first half of the nineteenth century. I argue that the region's support for slavery provided the means to bring Virginia's sections together. My approach counters previous claims by the Ambler-Curry school that long-standing cultural, economic, and regional differences separated the northwest from the rest of the state. These do not stand up to historical scrutiny. Instead, only one issue divided the state—suffrage. For the first five decades of the century, eastern Virginia's planter class stubbornly refused to grant political equality across the state. They distrusted anyone not as fully invested in slavery as themselves with power. Northwestern Virginia bore the brunt of their suspicion, despite supporting the practice of enslaving persons of African descent far beyond their actual numbers. It took a sectional crisis and some compromising to bridge these gaps at midcentury. This chapter traces how eastern and western Virginia came together from the 1820s through to the constitutional debates of 1850–1851. Reconciliation, not division, therefore, best describes antebellum Virginia affairs.

I first critique the several causes cited for the creation of West Virginia. Historians have claimed that cultural distinctions divided the state from the start of white settlement. In the first half of the eighteenth century, Scots-Irish and German-speaking migrants heeded promises of cheap land to move to the Shenandoah Valley and the Trans-Allegheny region. Their presence created a region, scholars have argued, ethnically distinct from the English- and African-dominated eastern counties. Ambler stated that this aspect made the west "naturally hostile to all things Virginian." McGregor, Curry, and others uncritically repeated his view. It is, however, complete fiction. None of these authors dedicated more than one or two paragraphs to the topic. None provided a single contemporary source. Later scholars merely cited the earlier works. All expected their readers to believe that northwestern Virginia changed little between the start of white settlement and statehood in 1863. On the contrary, a century of Americanization and Virginiaization via the American Revolution and practice of slavery turned those white people from migrants into citizens. I can find no convincing proof in the primary or secondary literature that mid-nineteenth-century northwestern Virginians spoke of themselves as anything but white Americans. A minor exception could exist in Wheeling's larger foreign-born population around 1850. The factories of that city attracted Irish and German immigrants fleeing the Great Famine in Ireland and the failed 1848 European revolutions for the United States, almost a century after the first settlers arrived. Ambler and McGregor appear to have borrowed this idea from a then current trend in history writing around 1900. Grady McWhiney and Forrest MacDonald revived it in the 1980s, but all these works apply poorly to northwestern Virginia. What may have been true in 1750 was obsolete a century later. I must conclude that the cultural aspect of the Ambler-Curry school is historically unprovable and therefore has no place in my analysis.[2]

The issue of internal improvements likewise has little relevance to West Virginia's formation. Historians borrowed claims from the state makers in 1861 that eastern Virginia neglected the west's economic development by denying them construction of roads, turnpikes, canals, and eventually railroads.

McGregor claimed that "a good system of canals and railroads" would have united the two halves of the state. Curry, likewise, wrote that the existing improvements that directed trade to Ohio and Pennsylvania exacerbated intrastate tensions. They are wrong. In fact, the northwest possessed as many connections to the outside world as any area west of the Appalachian Mountains before the Civil War. Nature provided the earliest transportation routes. The mighty Ohio River stretched for a thousand miles from Pittsburgh, Pennsylvania, to Cairo, Illinois. Its waters served as the main highway for westward migration. Many communities grew up along the river, including Marietta, Ironton, and Cincinnati in Ohio and New Albany in Indiana, while older ones such as Louisville, Kentucky, found new life, especially after locks and canals allowed boats to cross the Falls of the Ohio in 1830. The towns of Wheeling, Parkersburg, and Guyandotte (the last destroyed during the Civil War and replaced by Huntington) arose much like the others mentioned above. River linkages placed these communities in competition with each other. Parkersburg and Marietta, for example, squared off for years. So did Guyandotte and Gallipolis, Ohio. Neither rivalry came close to that between Wheeling and Pittsburgh. For the first half of the nineteenth century, those cities competed for control over trade on the Upper Ohio River. The latter succeeded because Wheeling had neither the strength nor the numbers to prevail.[3]

Tributaries of the Ohio further connected the northwest to the world. The Great Kanawha penetrated one hundred miles into the interior, through Cabell, Wayne, Kanawha, and Fayette counties, especially after river clearances in the 1840s. This important area of Appalachia developed another early industrial economy in the 1810s—salt production. Starting in small skiffs and progressing to steamships in later decades, barrels of salt headed down the Kanawha to the Ohio River, bound for the meatpacking markets of Cincinnati, St. Louis, and New Orleans. Many Charleston salt makers grew wealthy from this trade. As John Stealey argues, the Kanawha salt business influenced politics and economics both within the region and across the rest of the country. The need for laborers led early manufacturers to import enslaved Africans to toil alongside whites in the dangerous salt factories, in coal mines, or on the river. By 1850, Kanawha had the largest slave population in northwestern Virginia. The Little Kanawha served the same purpose for Parkersburg, although it had nowhere near the reach of its southerly counterpart.[4] The headwaters of the Monongahela River linked the central northwest to Pittsburgh. Its tributaries, the Tygart, the Cheat, and the West Fork rivers, offered alternatives to difficult overland travel. These branches were not mere creeks or streams. Steamboats plied these waters as early as the 1820s. Virginia made several unsuccessful attempts to dam and control the West Fork in the early nineteenth century. Many towns sprang up along these rivers, including Morgantown, Philippi, Fairmont, and Clarksburg. Few parts of the northwest, therefore, lacked a natural transportation route to the outside world before the Civil War.[5]

Artificial means emerged in the early nineteenth century, but only for certain areas. In the wake of the War of 1812, the federal government constructed a road to link the new western territories to the east. The National Road passed through the northwestern part of Virginia, connecting Cumberland, Maryland, to Vandalia, Illinois. Passing through southwestern Pennsylvania, it reached Wheeling in 1818. Once finished, it produced mixed effects. On one hand, it encouraged urbanization in that city, and immigration and trade increased as a result. Yet, as Billy Joe Peyton showed, calling the Cumberland or National Road a success strains credibility. Railroads, he wrote, overtook it in Maryland within a decade. Still, his conclusion that the highway left an important mark on American society still stands. By 1820, the National Road tied the Northern Panhandle to the Atlantic coast and to the western states. The remainder of northwestern Virginia soldiered on with lower quality turnpikes. The Winchester to Parkersburg Road opened in 1838, linking the Shenandoah Valley to the Ohio through the region's center. The Staunton to Parkersburg Road ran farther south a decade later. The northern parts of the region, therefore, possessed numerous ties to Virginia, Ohio, and Pennsylvania by 1840. Counties below the Kanawha Valley had to wait a little longer.[6]

Developments in neighboring states further connected northwestern Virginia to the rest of the country. Canal building marked the early nineteenth century's first attempt at rapid, regular communications. From the late 1810s up to the Civil War, several states constructed artificial waterways. The most famous was the Erie Canal in New York, which linked the Hudson River and the Great Lakes in 1823, a mere seven years after digging started, an incredible technical feat for the time. Pennsylvania's canals, constructed between 1826 and 1834, likewise cut across that long state. Opened in 1833, the Ohio and Erie Canal ran north to south to tie the Great Lakes to the big river. The riverine portions of northwestern Virginia benefitted from these canals by linking the Monongahela to the Atlantic Ocean. While expensive and restricted by the elements, canals improved trade and movement throughout these states. George R. Taylor has rightfully argued that they should not be rejected as failures. High construction costs aside, he pointed to their continued use later in the century. Moreover, turnpikes and even railroads also lost money over time. Sean Patrick Adams offered some insights as to why. He argued that a superior legal, business, and government arrangement allowed the Keystone State to build its canals and turnpikes faster than the Old Dominion's. Both views are valid, but they each point to the same conclusion. Efforts in other states helped to connect parts of the northwest with the outside world, but with one exception their state never denied them improvements.[7]

Virginia's failure to complete a similar canal constituted no substantial obstacle to the northwest's economy. Indeed, the combined James River and Kanawha Canal represents the sole shortcoming in the region's otherwise tight external connections. Encouraged and even personally surveyed by George Washington himself, the canal never reached its intended terminus in northwestern Virginia. Technology was never the issue. While it came short of the Ohio River destination, by 1851 the canal covered a respectable two hundred miles from Richmond to Botetourt County at the foot of the Appalachians along the modern state boundary. Instead, political complications over its funding impeded its progress more than the digging.[8] Westerners must have chafed under such constraints, which did not make them feel any less Virginian. An account of southwestern Virginia maintains that a railroad that brought slavery and its attendant economic effects to the region in the 1850s made the area closer to its parent but applies poorly to the northwest. The latter area had already attained a high degree of integration within the state and the rest of the world, yet its white population remained as committed to the state before its railroad appeared. In fact, Virginia made good its promises of improvements to the west in remarkably little time. The Baltimore and Ohio Railroad reached Wheeling and the Northern Panhandle in 1853. The Pennsylvania Railroad, by comparison, connected Pittsburgh in the year before. Likewise, the railroad arrived in Parkersburg in 1857 around the same time as did in Marietta, Ohio. A river ferry connected the two cities. The Civil War interrupted plans for more railroads. By any measure, therefore, northwestern Virginia possessed as many internal improvements as any part of the eastern United States by the middle of the nineteenth century. I therefore reject the Ambler-Curry thesis's claims that Virginia's neglect of improvements caused the northwest's separation in 1861.[9]

A third claim about closer ties to neighboring northern states causing West Virginia's separation also falls short of logic. Starting with Lang and Hall mentioned above, historians claimed that the region had more in common with Ohio and Pennsylvania than with Virginia. Whites certainly traded with their neighbors, and many early West Virginia leaders came from those states. Yet escaping slaves caused considerable friction along the Ohio River. In the 1830s and 1840s, northwestern Virginians defended their human property against menaces in adjoining states. The attempted pursuit by two Morgantown men of a suspected slave in Uniontown, Pennsylvania, in 1833 resulted in the man grievously wounding one of his pursuers. John J. Jackson held a rally in Parkersburg in Wood County in 1837 to demand "immediate, united and active exertions on the part of every Virginian" to stop "the aggressive interference of unauthorized associations of individuals in . . . the State of Ohio, called Abolition Societies," combined with the "recapture [of] decoyed and runaway slaves." Vigilantes from Guyandotte in Wayne County entered Ohio in pursuit of a local man who they believed was luring slaves across the river in December 1838. A few months later, in mid-1839, Adna van Bibber from Kanawha County brought an escaped slave named William Mitchell before a judge in Marion, Ohio. The jury released him, but van Bibber and some allies tried to seize him again. The judge threatened the whites with kidnapping charges. By 1845, the jailing of three white Ohio men in the Parkersburg jail prompted strong reactions from their home state. Public meetings compelled Governor Mordecai Bartley to intervene. The report of the *Parkersburg Gazette* in April 1850 that four escapees who returned to their masters "perfectly disgusted with their abolition friends" places a nice seal on the region's proslavery beliefs. These few examples demonstrate the valuable point that northwestern Virginia had less in common with its neighbors than the state makers and historians believed. They acted for and reacted against threats to the institution of slavery. They belie the antislavery reputation bestowed on them by eastern Virginia planters and subsequent accounts. I will return to this issue in the next chapter where I discuss the sectional tensions of the 1850s that exacerbated relations between northwestern Virginia and its northern neighbors.[10]

Suffrage thus constituted the only real issue dividing Virginia in the antebellum period, but it was a big one. Colonial aristocrats from Bacon's Rebellion in 1676 until the American Revolution a century later distrusted poorer whites with political power. The first state constitution enacted in 1776 perpetuated this policy by limiting suffrage to property holders. This feature granted the eastern half of the state most of the seats in the Virginia General Assembly, which held the House of Delegates and the Senate, while reducing the governorship to a mere appointment. Over the next thirty years the white population, and their enslaved Blacks, spread westward to the Shenandoah Valley and beyond to the state's western border along the Ohio River. Once there, these whites found themselves at a major political disadvantage. This situation compelled westerners to press collectively for greater equality. In August 1816, delegates from the Shenandoah Valley, the northwest, and the southwest, pressed for constitutional amendments at a congress in Staunton. Their convention took issue with the government of the Commonwealth remaining in the "hands of a minority." Tidewater delegates represented less than one-half of the state's white population yet held most of the seats in both houses of the legislature. The constitution gave thirteen seats to the eastern and southern sections of Virginia, while the larger western portion had only four. A more just distribution on the whites-only basis, the westerners argued, would grant nine senators to the west and seven to the east. The convention asked that the legislature "alter and amend the defects of the constitution" to allay "the excitements existing in the State." This appeal to numbers indicates another tactic in the struggle for reconciliation. These attempts to use population figures, however, failed to convince the eastern-dominated legislature to change the constitution. Another decade of frustration occurred before Virginians met again to discuss the divisions within their state.[11]

Demographic changes over the next decade influenced the next round of constitutional change. In the 1820s, white westerners matched the combined free-unfree population in the Tidewater and Piedmont areas. The representation in the legislature did not change despite these influxes. A decade of agitation for change ensued. A depression in the eastern counties caused by falling tobacco values scuttled the idea of a convention in 1825. After much debate, the Assembly approved a referendum in 1828. The result endorsed a convention by a vote of 21,896 (56.8 percent) in favor to 16,646 (43.2 percent) opposed. Most of the dissent came from the Tidewater, at least half of the Piedmont, and even some western counties.[12] Nonetheless, the convention took place in 1829. The chairmanship of former presidents James Madison and James Monroe and federal Supreme Court chief justice John Marshall added great dignity to the occasion. The convention demonstrated the huge gulf between the two sections. Eastern leaders demanded that the state protect their investment in slaves. In the process, they expressed little faith in the ability of westerners, whether slaveholders or not, to help them. Abel Upshur of Northampton County on the Eastern Shore (and later the secretary of the Navy who died in the famous accident on the USS *Princeton* in 1844), decried any bargain with the west. "It must be manifest to all," he said to the convention, "that the slave-holder of the east cannot calculate on the co-operation of the slave-holder of the west, in any measure calculated to protect that species of property, against demands made upon it by other interests, which to the western slave-holder, [and] are of more importance and immediate concern." This intransigence threatened westerners' hopes that appeals to patriotism would lead to political equality.[13]

In response, western delegates changed tactics to meet their opponents directly on the slave question. Philip Doddridge of Brooke County in the

Northern Panhandle claimed that such laws violated both the basic rights of westerners and their proslavery beliefs. "It is feared," he said, "that forsaking the example of their fathers, they will become freebooters; not that they will plunder their immediate neighbors, nor that they will have courage enough to attack the minority with open force." He continued that slavery had a future in the west as neighboring northern states tightened up their enforcement rules. As examples, he cited a recent decision by the Supreme Court of Ohio to order stricter measures to keep slaves out of the state. Pennsylvania, moreover, had always been friendly to masters retrieving their property. "I have no doubt," Doddridge argued, "that there are many western citizens who will purchase slaves again, when the causes before mentioned shall render their property secure." Ultimately, Upshur and the eastern planters prevailed with the help of the Shenandoah Valley. The 1830 constitution continued to restrict the franchise to white males twenty-one years or older who held twenty-five dollars' worth or more in property. This limit affected the entire state, including the many whites in the eastern counties. Yet their region's control over the legislature benefitted them. The west's situation changed little. The 1830 census reported only population, not wealth figures. Historians cite a voting discrepancy where only 31,000 of 76,000 white male voters in the western counties, defined as the Shenandoah Valley, the southwest, and the northwest, received suffrage. These numbers are likely skewed toward the more prosperous and wealthier Shenandoah. If these values are true, only 40 percent of the white population of Virginia could vote or hold office. Moreover, representation remained based on a mixture of whites and Blacks as per the federal Constitution, against western desires for a whites-only calculation. Despite Doddridge's proslavery appeals, 84 percent of the northwest voted against the new constitution. The rest of the state ratified it to maintain the status quo.

Northwestern frustration over eastern neglect led some observers to suggest separation. Abner Maxwell of Harrison County used the pages of the *Clarksburg Enquirer* to appeal to his fellow freeholders. He denounced "the new constitution" that "has been palmed on us by our eastern friends (if I am right in so calling them)" for being "so irrepublican in its principles and so hostile to the best interests of the West that it must meet with my most decided vote to reject it." He could not support a government that "consigns one portion of the Commonwealth to perpetual slavery to the other." A letter printed in the *Wheeling Gazette* denounced the failure of the delegates to redress the western counties' limited suffrage. "The west," it read, should unite in order to "treat with the eastern nabobs for a division of the state—peaceably if we can, forcibly if we must!" The editor of the *Wheeling Compiler* echoed this sentiment. If the western counties could act unanimously, he wrote, "we still have one chance left, and that is separation." Ambler and his followers have used these sentiments to demonstrate the inherent problems between eastern and western Virginia. These passions, however, dissipated quickly. No one ever petitioned either the state or the federal government to form a new state out of western Virginia.[14] Northwestern secessionism, therefore, amounted only to an angry dream in this period. The region's whites may have been frustrated with their Commonwealth in 1830, but they made no effort then to leave it.

The enslaved drove an even bigger wedge into Virginia's troubles. Between August 21 and 23, 1831, Nat Turner and many other enslaved men killed sixty whites in Southampton County near Richmond. Immediate reprisals added as many as two hundred Blacks to that total. The ensuing debate among whites raised the question of ending slavery. Two options emerged: either gradual emancipation or immediate colonization. Many even in eastern Virginia entertained the idea of ridding the state of slavery, an act that Allison Freehling called unthinkable even a few months before. The debate fell along geographic lines. Western delegates voted nearly unanimously for a resolution sponsored by William Ballard Preston of Montgomery County in the Shenandoah asking for the immediate and uncompensated removal of all slaves from the state. Some Trans-Allegheny members made overtly antislavery statements. Rising star George W. Summers of Kanawha County called slavery "the fountain of all of Virginia's ills" that harmed the development of "a wise and extensive system of internal improvements." Many easterners reeled in horror at this suggestion. Yet the delegates disagreed only on how to end slavery. Some sought a gradual and compensated approach followed by removal from the state, while others urged slaves' immediate departure. A virtually equal number of westerners and easterners split on the issue; the measure failed by a mere ten votes. Despite that result, northwestern Virginians' willingness to oppose slavery confirmed the east's worst fears.[15]

The statements from a pair of delegates reveal how widely Nat Turner's raid had split white Virginians. Thomas Dew of King and Queen County in the Tidewater questioned the west's reliability on slavery. A celebrated professor at the College of William and Mary, he also started an alternative career as a proslavery author. In *Review of the Debate in the Virginia Legislature of 1831 and 1832*, he called the situation "degrading" for eastern slaveholders to "fear losing that property which they had been accumulating for ages," to submit "with fearful anxiety for the capricious edict of the West" to give up their slaves. A Piedmont slaveholder, Benjamin Watkins Leigh, agreed. Writing as "Appomattox," even though he lived nearly one hundred miles to the east in

Dinwiddie County, he attacked westerners for encouraging abolition while professing to support slavery. They treated eastern concerns over slave security as "idle fears, and even as mere pretenses, and made the most solemn assurances, that their constituents respected the right of slave property as highly as any other kind and held them absolutely inviolable." He knew from experience not to trust such men. Those who, he argued, "vainly undertake to regulate affairs and to direct events, are themselves so much the creatures of circumstances, the mere effects of causes, that none but the most vigorous minds are capable even of making an effort to resist them, much more rising above them, or know to-day what sentiments they shall entertain to-morrow." Leigh particularly attacked Summers for using the immortal words of Thomas Jefferson to support his antislavery views. These statements exemplify the lack of faith that most eastern delegates shared about the ability of westerners to preserve the institution of slavery.[16]

The feeling was mutual, but not for the commonly believed reasons. Contrary to notions of the Mountain South having antislavery views—derived from post–Civil War beliefs—slavery was secure in northwestern Virginia. With a steadily rising white population and a stagnant number of enslaved persons, the institution showed no signs of ending. The demographics of the region sustain this observation. In the counties that made up northwestern Virginia between 1830 and 1850, the overall population nearly trebled.[17] As table 1 indicates, the white population increased from 92,292 around the time of the convention to 129,067 a decade later, a jump of 50 percent. It would increase by a further 50,000 by 1850. An additional 70,000 lived in the area by the eve of the Civil War. These are remarkable rates of increase given the westward expansion of the United States during this time. The lure of lands in the Ohio Valley and across the Mississippi brought far larger numbers of people beyond the northwest. Yet enough whites stayed in the area to increase the total population.

The census also indicates the kinds of people who lived in the region. Table 2 shows the nativity of three northwestern Virginia counties between 1850 (the first census to record that information) and 1860 changed little during that decade. In the mixed industrial- agricultural Harrison County, more than 80 percent of the white population consisted of native-born Virginians. The remainder of foreign-, northern-, and southern-born people changed little and never amounted to more than 10 percent of the population. The enslaved numbered about 4 percent. Kanawha County, home to the prosperous salt industry, had similar white demographics, but with around 20 percent enslaved in 1850. Ohio County, on the other hand, had a foreign- and northern-born majority.

Table 1. White and Enslaved Populations of Northwestern Virginia, 1830–1850

Year	1830	1840	1850
Total	98,411	135,584	189,061
White	92,292 (93.8%)	129,067 (95.2%)	185,188 (98.0%)
Enslaved	6,119 (6.2%)	6,581 (4.9%)	6,686 (2.0%)

Source: These figures come from the 1830, 1840, and 1850 federal censuses. US Department of the Interior, Bureau of the Census, Manuscript Census Returns, Fifth Census of the United States, 1830; the Sixth Census of the United States, 1840; and the Seventh Census of the United States, 1850.

Immigrant wage laborers came to work in Wheeling's factories. Virginians there amounted to only a quarter of the population, while the enslaved numbered no more than an invisible 1 percent or less. This county, therefore, had a greater ability to attract immigrants than other parts of the region. Whites were free to leave and move around and tended to go for the wage labor in an industrial town with few slaves.

Despite their best efforts to escape, many of the enslaved could not leave. The same census figures show that the number of slaves remained steady throughout the antebellum period. In 1830, whites held a total of 6,119 enslaved persons in the area. That number increased by a few hundred a decade later. Over the course of the next twenty years, that figure changed little if the percentage of the population dropped to 2.5 percent by 1860. In the three more closely examined counties, only Kanawha's statistic fell, from 20 percent in 1850 to 14 percent a decade later. John Stealey's observation that attributes this decline solely to market conditions appears correct.[18] Harrison and Ohio counties must have had little if any need to import more enslaved persons. Indeed, the proximity of Wheeling to the free states of Pennsylvania and Ohio must have made slave escapes a constant concern for masters and the legal authorities. Harrison, which lay over a hundred miles from either border, could exert greater control over its bondspeople. Loose frontiers and economic factors, therefore, kept the northwestern Virginia slave population in check. The notion held by eastern Tidewater planters that the region could not be trusted to protect slavery is unfounded, but also deceptive. Northwestern masters did not face a Black majority that could have risen at any time to slay them as Nat Turner did in the east. Instead, their stable enslaved population and even

Table 2. Places of Birth of Adult Heads of Households in Three Northwestern Virginia Counties, 1850–1860, in Percentages

County	Ohio		Harrison		Kanawha	
Year	1850	1860	1850	1860	1850	1860
Virginia	23	24	86	82	85	83
Foreign	38	50	1	4	5	6
North	30	22	8	9	6	7
South	7	4	3	4	4	1
Enslaved	1	>1	4	4	20	14
Total	98	100	98	99	100	97

Source: I counted adult heads of household, who constitute the most likely voters, from the census schedules for Ohio, Harrison, and Kanawha counties in 1850 and 1860. The 1840 census did not list nativity. US Department of the Interior, Bureau of the Census, Manuscript Census Returns, Seventh Census of the United States, 1850, and Eighth Census of the United States, 1860.

smaller numbers of free Blacks made whites feel comfortable with slavery-based status quo.

Numbers aside, the public then and historians since have underestimated the power slavery held over northwestern Virginians. Virtually all from Charles Ambler onward claimed that the environment precluded slavery from having much influence in the mountains. Even Ambler's biggest critic Richard Curry agreed on this point. The accompanying map, created to support a soldier's charity in 1861, appears to support their arguments. Using figures from the 1860 census, it contrasts the large population of enslaved persons in the eastern half of Virginia with the nearly slaveless west. These works, however, dismiss the institution too easily. My research instead investigates who owned these slaves, what they did with them, and what effect slavery had upon their communities.[19] For decades, historians placed slaveholding within a limited dichotomy between masters and non–slave owners. They neglected to mention the diversity of ownership in the former. They included large landowners, urban professionals, wealthy artisans, and even some plain folk. I base my observations on the 1850 and 1860 free and slave schedules of the federal census. From this I determined who owned slaves, how many they owned, the owners' occupation and wealth, and whether they lived in an urban or rural

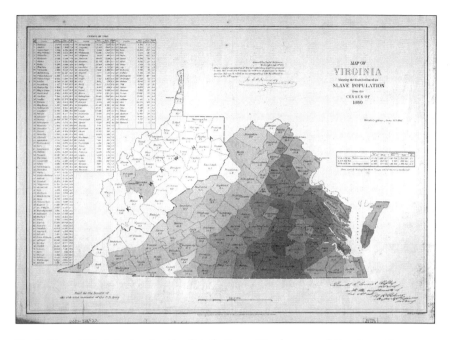

Fig. 1. Map of Virginia showing the distribution of its slave population from the census of 1860 (Library of Congress). This map shows that northwestern Virginia had less enslavement than the east, but it fails to indicate how strongly its white population supported the institution.

environment. I argue that slaveholding marked owners of their higher status, even though fewer retained or could attain across the period. Yet despite this limitation, non-slaveholders showed little if any opposition to this situation. From this, I derive a clearer understanding of how strong an influence slavery exerted on a place where most believe it had little or none.[20]

Every part of northwestern Virginia had a connection with slavery. At some point from the start of white settlement until 1860, masters and the enslaved existed in every county in Virginia except for two special cases. Neither Hancock at the very top of the Northern Panhandle nor McDowell at the very bottom of the future state had any slaves in 1860. Yet, this was true only of that year's census. A decade earlier, the former had three slaves and two masters. The latter did not exist at the time, but its parent Logan County had 87 slaves that year and 148 in 1860. In 1860, the largest was Kanawha with 2,187 slaves, which itself declined from over 3,000 ten years before. The counties with the fewest enslaved persons that year included Webster with only three, Calhoun with nine, Pleasants with fifteen, and Brooke with only eighteen. The census includes only masters who owned slaves in a specific county. They could hold them elsewhere. Alexander Campbell Jr. of Brooke County may have owned only one slave at home, but he held eighteen more slaves in Sabine Parish, Louisiana, along the Texas border. It is unclear how many northwestern Virginia masters owned slaves elsewhere or how many absentees did the same there. Slaveholding, therefore, had a substantial range throughout the northwest, from large to small populations. This observation comes from the census depicted in table 3, which compares the free and enslaved populations in the other border states. The northwest showed the largest decline among its unfree, but not by much—a mere 4 percent to 2 percent between 1850 and 1860. Maryland's enslaved population shrunk by the same amount, while Delaware's and Kentucky's dropped by a single point. Missouri's did not change despite its white population nearly doubling. Slavery in the border states therefore showed slight declines in its proportion of the population but otherwise had no signs of ending anytime soon. Yet this tells us nothing about how whites used the enslaved.[21]

Northwestern Virginia slaveholders topped the region's social hierarchy. The image of the noble mountaineer living on a self-sufficient farm isolated from the rest of the world is post–Civil War propaganda perpetuated by popular culture. Appalachian scholars such as John Inscoe demonstrate slavery's role in the great social stratification in the Mountain South. His arguments apply well to northwestern Virginia, which had the full range of classes among its white population. The landholding elites who owned six or more slaves and more than a hundred acres topped the list. The yeomen or smaller farmers with one hundred acres or less and who held up to five slaves stood below them. The region's few towns held its middling class of professionals and merchants. Most of the white population, the landless laboring plain folk, rested below them. The enslaved formed the bottom. The lines between whites sometimes blurred. Merchants and yeomen, for example, intermingled based on wealth patterns alone. Lawyers and landholders built strong relationships too. Slaves and some poor whites sometimes worked side by side at the same jobs. Family connections may have also bridged some gaps. The number of slaveholding households declined somewhat in the 1850s. In Ohio County, only 1.6 percent of heads of households owned slaves. A decade later, that number had halved. Kanawha, which had the largest enslaved population in the region, also showed a big decline. In 1850, 13.8 percent of households held slaves; in 1860, the figure stood at 7.1 percent. Those two marked the extreme points of comparison. Harrison stands in the middle. A total of 7.7 percent of households

Table 3. Border State Slavery

	Delaware	Kentucky	Maryland	Missouri	NWVA
1850 total	91,532	982,405	583,034	682,044	203,941
1850 enslaved	2,290	210,981	90,368	87,422	7,889
1850 free Black	18,073	10,011	74,723	2,618	1,374
1850 enslaved (%)	3	21	15	13	4
1850 free Black (%)	20	1	13	>1	1
1860 total	112,216	1,155,684	687,049	1,182,012	264,669
1860 enslaved	1,798	225,483	87,189	114,931	6,457
1860 free Black	19,829	10,684	83,942	3,572	1,045
1860 enslaved (%)	2	20	13	10	2
1860 free Black (%)	18	1	12	>1	>1

Source: Data compiled from Historical Census Browser, University of Virginia, Geospatial and Statistical Data Center, http://mapserver.lib.virginia.edu/collections/stats/histcensus/index.html (site now discontinued).

possessed slaved in 1860. In 1860, the number dropped to 6.6 percent, a small change compared to the other counties. While these figures indicate that the number of slaveholding households declined, they are misleading. The overall number of households increased in each county in the 1850s by an average of 20 percent. Slaveholding, therefore, became more concentrated among the wealthier white residents in the 1850s. Yet the institution showed no signs of ending.[22]

A statistical evaluation reveals that slaveholders held extensive social and economic authority throughout the northwest. Overall, they possessed a large amount of personal and real estate wealth far above their numbers, despite increasing concentration into fewer hands. The census for 1850 included amounts for real estate held by free people in each county in the country. The 1860 schedules added personal wealth, which included slaves as chattel property. The census sample used here includes only adult heads of household but excludes dependents, spouses, or others who may have owned property. Including those few people would not significantly alter the overall total. The numbers varied throughout the region, as table 4 indicates.

24 / Chapter 1

Table 4. Slaveholders' Share of Property by County and Head of Household, 1850–1860

County	1850 Real Estate ($)	Slaveholder Amount ($)	Percentage
Ohio	6,124,132	1,074,380	18
Harrison	2,663,881	865,988	33
Kanawha	2,305,002	1,794,645	78

County	1860 Real Estate ($)	Slaveholder Amount ($)	Percentage	1860 Personal Wealth ($)	Slaveholder Amount ($)	Percentage
Ohio	8,014,099	1,253,650	16	3,851,985	392,540	10
Harrison	4,862.326	1,909.467	39	2,019,538	1,145,666	56
Kanawha	2,733,722	1,520,924	56	2,281,184	1,631,836	72

Source: Source: US Department of the Interior, Bureau of the Census, Manuscript Census Returns, Seventh Census of the United States, 1850, and Eighth Census of the United States, 1860.

In Ohio County, the fifty-two slaveholders held 18 percent of all real estate in 1850. Ten years later, the thirty-five remaining still held almost the same rate at 16 percent. They also owned 10 percent of the county's personal wealth. Ohio appears to be typical for the Northern Panhandle and constitutes one extreme in this comparison. In the middle came Harrison's 117 owners in 1850, who alone held one-third of its real estate. A decade later, that amount increased to nearly 40 percent. They owned a remarkable 56 percent of the county's personal wealth. Kanawha represents the other extreme. Its 277 owners in 1850 held 78 percent of its real estate. In 1860, its 192 owners still held 56 percent of all real estate in the county. They also possessed 72 percent of its personal wealth. These figures point to the power slavery held in the northwest. For most there, it meant a huge gap between themselves and everyone else. The Panhandle had the lowest figures, indicating slavery's lesser economic grasp in the area. Kanawha, on the other hand, shows the virtual hegemony the master class had over the population, free and enslaved alike. Farther south, their control made it harder to accumulate more property. Harrison stands between the two. Its small master class held an excessively high amount of wealth, yet some room existed for advancement. In short, Ohio County's slaveholders exerted the least power of the three, but still held disproportionate amounts of wealth there. Kanawha's masters in contrast held the most authority. Harrison's masters stood between them in wielding economic and political influence. While the number of slaveholders declined, the master class retained their power in their communities all the same.

The middling ranks of white northwestern Virginia society also purchased their way into slaveholding. Roughly one-third of whites in each county came from the middling class of urban professionals. Historians such as Jonathan Dean Wells, Jennifer Green, and Frank Byrne have debated the exact definition of this class. I choose to apply Green's interpretation of a nonagricultural professional living in an urban area, including lawyers, merchants, grocers, and the like. Lawyers deserve special mention here. They had a special interest in the slave system. Westward expansion after the American Revolution brought slaves from the east to aid landholders in staking their claims. Lawyers founded the court systems and secured the land titles from which the former, including many absentees, grew wealthy. In time, the elites and their lawyers controlled political offices in the northwest, generously aided by the eastern planters and their undemocratic constitutions. John Alexander Williams called these lawyers a "buckskin elite," but often they held as much wealth as their patrons. They also, he continued, formed connections with a wide variety of people in their home counties and elsewhere. These ties made them important and vital figures in local politics. As will be seen later, they played substantial roles in the creation and later redemption of West Virginia.[23]

Although rare, slaveholding still influenced Ohio County's social and political life. The original landholders, those with the last names Zane and McCullough, tended to have large property holdings amounting to thousands of dollars. Mary L. Zane had $100,000 in real estate in 1850. Samuel McCullough, a farmer, held about $12,000 that year. Interestingly, neither owned slaves. The largest holder was Virginia-born Lydia S. Cruger, who owned thirteen. Living outside Wheeling, she had no stated employment but possessed some $32,000 in real estate, making her a prosperous woman and possibly a widow. Behind her was Daniel Steenrod, a New York–born farmer and another early settler also living in Ohio County. His $100,000 in property included nine slaves. In 1850, half of Ohio's masters lived in the countryside and/or farmed. The rest lived in Wheeling or a neighboring village and held nonagricultural positions. By 1860, the number of urban dwellers increased to one-third, or eleven of thirty-five. In 1850, eighteen of Ohio County's fifty-one owners consisted of middling-class heads of households. They included the

Pennsylvania-born S. Brady, a bank cashier who owned four slaves. John J. Yarnall, a Virginia-born hotelkeeper, also owned four. Some, like merchant William Paxton from Ireland, owned one slave.[24]

A decade later, the number of slaveholders in Ohio County stayed the same. Sherrard Clemens, a lawyer, politician, and owner of two slaves, typified the master class. Others included a grocer, a lottery vendor, a steamboat captain, and one laborer, the Virginia-born Mason Foreman of the town of West Liberty. It is not clear how he, who held no other property, acquired a slave. It is possible that he inherited him or her. In 1860, only two artisans, carpenter Alex Pannell and miller Isaac Kelley, owned slaves. Regardless of their numbers, masters clung tightly to their bondspeople. The absence of any slave houses in the census indicates that they lived near their owners. Escape occurred, but not as often as one may think. The census lists eleven fugitives of the listed one hundred. In January 1861, the *Wheeling Daily Intelligencer* reported the sensational case of an enslaved woman named Lucy Bagby. She fled the captivity of William and James Goshorn for Cleveland, Ohio.[25] On the other hand, the paper lists only a single manumission, a legally difficult process in 1850s Virginia. It must have been hard to keep slaves in a county surrounded on two sides by free states. Conceivably, few if any slave traders risked sending more to the Panhandle and fewer potential owners wishing to acquire more only to easily lose them. Slaveholding existed mostly among the older first generation of settlers and to a smattering of professionals and artisans. Those same people still held influential positions that most whites respected.

Harrison County embraced slave labor more extensively than Ohio. Its founding family, the Davissons, no longer ruled it. Just two heads of household bore that name in 1850. Granville, a clerk, owned one slave and held $1,600 in property. Its master class included two-thirds farmers and landholders and one-third urban professionals, with a handful of artisans. It had a much larger slave population than Ohio. In 1850, 145 masters owned a total of 482 enslaved persons there. A decade later, that number had risen to 163 masters and 575 slaves, most likely due to the coming of the Baltimore and Ohio Railroad in 1857. The 1850 census does not separate out towns from the countryside, so it is impossible to delineate where anyone lived. Based on the county's two census districts, a total of 341 slaves lived in District 21, while 141 lived in District 22. In 1860, more masters owned more slaves. Contrary to a 1910 history of Harrison County, most slaves were not urban or domestics. Of that number, ninety-four lived in the country, listed as "not stated." A further forty lived in Clarksburg, while the remaining seven came from the surrounding communities of Bridgeport, Lumberport, Milford, and West Milford. Fully half, or eighty-four, of those owners are listed as farmers or combined farming with another activity. The rest varied in occupation from doctors to merchants, bankers, ministers, lawyers, clerks, and other officials. The largest owner was Judge George H. Lee, who held thirteen slaves. Lawyer and future state maker John S. Carlile owned no slaves when he lived in Barbour County in 1850 but had one in Harrison a decade later. A handful of artisans such as blacksmiths, carpenters, cabinet makers, hatters, saddlers, tailors, tanners, and a wagon maker owned one or two slaves. For these men, slave ownership provided the means for social advancement, as Diane Barnes and Michele Gillespie have argued, but few could afford it.[26]

Harrison's lack of both a free Black population and an immigrant community indicates a firmer connection with slavery than in Ohio County. More than 85 percent of adult heads of household came from Virginia alone in 1850. A further 13 percent were northern-born, mostly Pennsylvanians. Only 4 percent, mostly Marylanders, came from elsewhere in the South. Just 2 percent immigrated from another country, largely Ireland. Little changed by 1860. Virginians made up 82 percent of the heads of household, northerners constituted 9 percent, and other southerners remained at 4 percent. Immigrants now numbered 5 percent, many of them Irish laborers who helped to build the Baltimore and Ohio Railroad in previous years. Only one nonwhite headed a household in the 1860 census. Mary Robinson, a Virginia-born mulatto with only ten dollars in personal property, lived outside of Clarksburg. Their median age was twenty, but one enslaved woman may have been 106 years old. With few free Blacks or immigrants available as laborers or domestics, social mobility depended on slaves. As shown above, numerous artisans and middling-class professionals owned slaves. If they could own slaves, many others could have leased or rented slaves to work with or for them. Harrison County, therefore, supported slavery like many other northwestern counties would have.[27]

Kanawha County's dependence on enslaved labor stands at the opposite end of the region's spectrum. With more than three thousand slaves in 1850 and about twenty-two hundred in 1860, the county's situation more closely resembled eastern Virginia than Ohio or Harrison. Unlike the others, its original white settlers retained vast political authority and economic power. The Ruffner family owned both slaves and large amounts of real estate. James Ruffner, a farmer, owned twelve slaves and $4,000 in real estate. His kinsman David held eight slaves and $4,600 of real estate. These examples do not include family members who had different last names. It would take a significant genealogical study to determine those connections. Most of Kanawha's wealthy elite came later in the nineteenth century. Many ventured there to produce salt, a profitable commodity in antebellum America whose production depended on slave labor. Whereas Ohio and Harrison County masters held between one and three slaves, the median for Kanawha in both 1850 and 1860 was ten slaves. Some individual Kanawhans owned more slaves than whole northwestern counties. Lewis Ruffner owned forty-seven for his salt business in 1850 and twenty-three in 1860. John D. Lewis held an astonishing 152 slaves in 1850 and 85 a decade later. Likewise, John N. Clarkson owned 127 in 1850 and 71 in 1860. Free Blacks and or mulattos headed thirty-seven households in 1850. A decade later, the number declined to a still strong thirty. Few of these had any property, and women headed a disproportionate number of them. The census lists few free domestics, possibly due to the large number of slaves available in the county, whose commitment to slavery was therefore almost absolute.

The master class of Kanawha County used enslaved labor in many ways. They included professionals and artisan alike, and even a few poorer folks. Of 277 heads of slaveholding households in 1850, 75 farmed and 51 listed no profession. Salt makers numbered a further 23 owners, each of them averaging about fifteen slaves. Professionals such as physicians, lawyers, agents, merchants, tavern keepers, and managers owned many more slaves. Yet artisans such as coopers, carpenters, well borers, grocers, and tailors also held a few. The census listed four laborers owning slaves. A decade later, slaveholding had become a more elusive goal. The 1860 census listed 188 slaveholders heading households. Almost half, or 90, farmed. Salt makers continued to hold the largest numbers, with a median of thirteen slaves per owner. Physicians, merchants, lawyers, and hotelkeepers made up the next largest group. Artisans appeared less often than before. Many coopers, engineers, grocers, a miller, a millwright, a printer, and a saddler owned at least one slave each. One farm laborer, James Sisson of Sissonville in the northern part of the county, owned three. As with Mason Foreman of Ohio County, he may have received his slaves by inheritance. Slaveholding may have become rarer for artisans, most likely due to rising slave costs and a declining need in the Kanawha salt economy, but it was still an option. The problem lay in the inability for most to plant their first step on that social ladder.

Slaveholding brought political success to northwestern Virginia owners if they sought it. James Oakes recently argued that the region adopted "an anti-slaveholder politics" in this period. His thesis applies better to the highest level of intrastate relations than to its local political behaviors.[28] Masters of even a single slave held a disproportionate number of its offices. A comparison of lists of officeholders from local elections to the census reveals clear wealth patterns of whom northwestern Virginians choose from among themselves to govern them. Candidates for governor, president, and Congress are excluded here, but I will use them in chapter 2. Lists for Ohio County are not available, but they exist for the city of Wheeling. A mix of upper- and middling-class men rotated through civic offices, including mayor, city sergeant, treasurer, and clerk. The fifteen men found in the 1850 census had a median wealth as $5,900. Only four owned slaves, but even that number indicates a gross overrepresentation among the population. Five of Wheeling's twelves lawyers served in these positions, mostly as mayor. Middling men such as physician James Tanner, bank cashiers S. Brady and Daniel Lamb, and pork packer William W. Shriver also served. Interestingly, non-Virginians held almost all these offices. Only Henry Chapline, who served as a city sergeant from 1854 to 1855, was born in the Old Dominion. The long-standing city treasurer, Richard W. Harding, came from Ireland. The remainder came from Pennsylvania, Maryland, and Ohio. Little changed by 1860. The median income stayed high at $3,000 in real estate and $2,000 in personal property. None owned slaves by that time, even among those listed in the 1850 census. More Virginians held the offices. Yet, the only foreigners to do so were Irish. No Germans did so despite their large presence in the community. Slaveholders had less control over Ohio County and the Northern Panhandle by the time of the Civil War as the industrial economy took its place in that area. The middling class there had taken charge, but they remained committed to slavery's preservation.[29]

Harrison County's officers had a similar experience. Its sheriffs, clerks, and delegates to Richmond each came from wealthy or middling-class backgrounds according to the 1850 census. The nineteen men who held these offices from 1830 to 1860 had a median wealth in real estate of $5,000. Eleven of them owned slaves, each holding a median of five each. As mentioned above, Judge George Lee had thirteen slaves. Waldo Goff, a New York–born "gentleman" and head of a prominent family, had eight. Joseph Johnson, owner of six slaves in 1850, served as a state delegate as well as in Congress. Like in Ohio County, Virginia-born men held few of these officers. Despite numbering more than 80 percent of the total Harrison population, Virginians made up fewer than half of all officers. Only nine of them held office. The remaining ten included New Yorkers, Pennsylvanians, Marylanders, a Connecticut man, and a New Jerseyan. The professionals held as many offices as farmers or wealthier men. Augustine J. Smith and William A. Harrison practiced law. Others included physician Jesse Flowers, engineer Luther Haymond, merchant Charles Lewis, and Daniel Kinchloe whose occupation is "not stated." Six men farmed, while three others had previously held office such as judge or clerk. Saddler Cyrus

Vance (the ancestor and namesake of a future secretary of state) and tailor Charles Holden represented the artisans in the sample who acquired slaves. The prosperous middling class, many of whom owned enslaved people, therefore ruled Harrison County.[30]

If beneficial in Harrison or Ohio, officeholding required slaveholding in Kanawha. Only the richest held office there. The sample's overall median property value was a $13,500, higher than the other two combined. The twelve men who served as delegates to Richmond between 1830 and 1850 included ten slaveholders. Combined, they had ten slaves each. Their masters sent almost all of them to work in the salt business. Two of the three salt makers, John D. Lewis and Lewis F. Donnally, owned more than one hundred slaves each, making them among the wealthiest men in the entire northwest. The other salt maker, James H. Fry, had thirteen slaves. All held an elite or professional occupation. Four of them, George W. Summers, Benjamin H. Smith, R. A. Thompson, and James M. Laidley, officially practiced law, but their huge slave holdings indicate that they earned a substantial part of their income by leasing their bondsmen to the salt business. One of the two farmers in the group, Charles Ruffner, must have done the same with his eight slaves given his family's connections to the salt industry. The other farmer, James Welch, owned no slaves. Doctor Spicer Patrick owned thirty-five slaves but, according to the 1850 census, employed five in the city for his personal use. The remainder, the census continues, lists them as working in the country, again presumably for the salt business. The other physician, Daniel Smith, lists no real property but leasing his thirteen slaves could have sustained a comfortable lifestyle for him and his wealthy wife. The slaveholders, therefore, ruled Kanawha almost absolutely, far beyond the experiences of Harrison or Ohio counties.[31]

Northwestern Virginia produced its future leaders from these ranks of slaveholding men. By the 1840s, the earlier generation who tried and failed to bridge Virginia's gaps—the Doddridges, the Jacksons, and the like—had passed away. In their place came new men who wholeheartedly embraced the Second Party System started by Andrew Jackson in 1828. Their ranks included, as William G. Shade has put it, "a new breed of professional politicians whose adherence to partisanship contrasted sharply with the disavowals of their predecessors." Their appearance, he continues, made the rise of parties more powerful and articulate.[32] The figures listed below exemplify their power, but they represented both Whigs and Democrats. One has already been mentioned. George W. Summers of Kanawha (1807–1868) served in the state legislature during the emancipation debates. Born in Fairfax County, he headed to the valley to live with his older brother, Lewis Summers, a prominent figure in his own right. After receiving a thorough education for the time, including a rare master's degree from Ohio University, George embarked on a legal career. The law led him to politics. He served many terms in the Virginia Assembly and in Congress as a Whig. He also, as mentioned above, owned over a dozen slaves. By 1850, Summers had become one of the region's most important leaders.[33]

Many other younger slaveholders rose to prominence in the 1840s. The previously mentioned John Snyder Carlile (1817–1878) hailed from Barbour and later Harrison counties. As a lawyer, he served in the Virginia Assembly between 1847 and 1850, which led him to become a delegate to the Constitutional Convention that year. Along the way, he found sufficient prosperity to acquire at least one slave.[34] Likewise, Sherrard Clemens (1820–1881) practiced law in his hometown of Wheeling as well as serving in Congress as a Democrat and owning two slaves. Whigs also rose to prominence in the 1840s. Waitman Thomas Willey (1811–1900) of Monongalia County studied law under the venerable Philip Doddridge. He had less success in politics. A Whig, he lost a race for the Virginia Assembly in 1840, but later served in county positions. Like Carlile and Clemens, he bought some slaves during his lifetime. He followed in his mentor's footsteps by serving in the 1850 Constitutional Convention.[35] As James Oakes has argued, slaveholding gave these professional men the leisure time to participate in politics. That said, non-slaveholders could attain public offices. Arthur Ingram Boreman (1811–1896) of Tyler County never owned a slave. Also practicing law, he served for many years in the Virginia Assembly. The true outlier among this group is Francis Harrison Pierpont (1814–1899) of Marion County. His biographer attributes his antislavery views to the horrors that he personally witnessed while traveling in Mississippi and Louisiana as a young man. Perhaps due to these opinions and his Whiggish leanings, Pierpont also never held elected office in this time. Instead, he became a prominent attorney, particularly for the Baltimore and Ohio Railroad, in the next decade. Few could have predicted before the Civil War that Pierpont would rise as high as he did. Despite constituting around 2 percent of the white population, slaveholders were overrepresented as officeholders in antebellum northwestern Virginia.[36]

The changing context behind the rise of these new leaders prompts a reassessment of one of the most cited antislavery statements to come out of northwestern Virginia. In 1847, Henry Ruffner of Kanawha published the *Address to the People of West Virginia* to encourage the gradual abolition of slavery there. Ruffner cited census figures to compare the western counties to other states to show how slavery retarded trade, the development of industry, and even of education. His treatise attacked abolitionists and the eastern master class in equal measure. The actions of the former, he wrote, threatened "the Federal Constitution which guarantees the rights of slaveholders, and the Federal Union which is the glory and safeguard of us all." Doing so, moreover, put themselves against every American and, ironically, "from the opposite extreme, those Southern politicians and ultra-proslavery men . . . who so often predict and threaten a dissolution of the Union. Thus, it is that extremes often meet." His goal was a compromise between the two poles. Ruffner, scion of a slaveholding family, defended the rights of masters and of whites at every turn. While he intended his tract to balance the security of Virginia with his home region's future prosperity, his views were out of step by the time of its publication. Had it appeared in 1832 during the emancipation debates, it would have been more popular with westerners. A decade and a half later, its white population had more fully embraced the institution. Instead of being symbolic of the region's antislavery views, Ruffner's *Address* deserves comparison to other white southern antislavery tracts like Hinton Rowan Helper's *The Impending Crisis*, published a decade later. It is simply not representative of the region's views on slavery.[37]

The political choices of white northwestern Virginians instead provide more reliable proof of their proslavery beliefs. They continually selected leaders who possessed a personal investment in slavery to guide them through the state's next constitutional debates. Many efforts at redressing the flaws in the 1829–1830 constitution occurred in the succeeding two decades. The Assembly was supposed to recommend a convention every decade, but 1840 came and went without one. A large bipartisan meeting held in Charleston in August 1841 demanded a new constitution in which "individual suffrage should be equal without respect to the disparity of individual fortunes, so an equal number of voters are entitled to equal representation, without regard to the disparity of their aggregate fortunes." Not doing so degraded white western Virginians to the level of the enslaved. "That the slaves," the meeting resolved, "and the honest, industrious and respected farmers of the west, can hold any analogy to each other, in the distribution of political rights and power, can only be rendered plausible by extending our southern principle; that it is utterly impossible, consistent with safety to extend equal rights to different races of men."[38] Similar meetings took place in Clarksburg and in Lewisburg in Greenbrier County around the same time, but to no avail. The Assembly rejected them all. A brief alignment of two rival factions in the state legislature, the Richmond Junto and the Valley-dominated Tenth Legion, brought some temporary relief to intrastate issues. Indeed, northwesterners felt such gratitude to the Junto that they named a new county after its leader, Thomas

Ritchie.[39] A more permanent resolution continued to elude the state until early 1850. National tensions brought by the sudden expansion of the United States after its victory over Mexico compelled the Virginia Assembly to agree to a convention. The slaveholding states wanted to expand into the new territories, but the remaining states sought to keep them free from slavery. Northwestern Virginia, like those along the border, chose the former.

The delegation sent to the constitutional debates in Richmond in October 1850 contained men deemed safe on slavery. After a brief preliminary session, the convention suspended itself until January to await the latest census figures. Discussions then resumed until August. None of the western delegates had previously attended the 1829–1830 meeting. Summers, Carlile, and Willey were there along with seventeen others. According to the 1850 census, their median real estate wealth was eight thousand dollars. A dozen delegates owned a total of seventy-three slaves, including Willey who owned five, Carlile one, and Summers five. They included twelve lawyers, a merchant, a doctor, a millwright, a court clerk, and a saddler, but only two farmers. William G. Brown of Preston County both farmed and practiced law. Only two owned no property, while the rest held substantial amounts of land. Fourteen of these twenty were native-born Virginians; two each came from Maryland and Pennsylvania, and one from New York, Peter G. Van Winkle of Wood County. Theirs was also a youthful group, with a median age of forty-four years, compared to fifty-five overall. One of those men was James Harvey Ferguson, a shoemaker from Cabell County who bettered himself by studying law. The *Kanawha Republican* felt "every confidence" in his support for the white basis for suffrage. "He has abilities—his constituents appreciate them—they have picked their flint well. At the same time, the *Republican* also said that western Virginians will on that question will be shot, that's for certain." They fit in well with Shade's arguments about the 1850 convention delegates. The presence of so many figures with close connections to Virginia and to slavery indicated where the region stood on both.[40]

The northwestern delegates faced an uphill struggle against deeply entrenched eastern leaders. Anti-western opinion reared itself from the beginning over suffrage. Most westerners supported the white basis, which granted the vote only to white men. The mixed basis, favored by eastern delegates, combined the free and enslaved population to give Tidewater and Piedmont districts more Assembly seats than the west. On January 6, 1851, Robert G. Scott of Richmond City scolded the western delegates over the convention's main venue. In a choice between two churches, an African and a Unitarian, he said that his "western friends might not be willing to go" to the former since

34   /   Chapter 1

it was "connected with the mixed basis." This implied that his opponents may not be familiar with slavery. The northwestern men wanted none of this. Willey attacked that perception. He turned the tables on Robert G. Scott's comment about the African church. "I say to him," he retorted, "that some of us come here with very strong instructions to carry the war right into the center of Africa and that location may be appropriate for us on that ground." The other delegates laughed at this statement. He then presented a memorial from his home of Monongalia County. Its signers "respectfully but earnestly remonstrate against the introduction of the principle of property-representation into the organic law of this Commonwealth. We would regard it as subversive of our proper political equality." They cited how these disabilities rendered their sacrifices in the War of 1812 meaningless. Virginia's unfair constitution not only belied its legacy to the nation as bestowed in the Declaration of Independence but undermined their status as equals. "The lessons of political equality taught us by our fathers from Eastern Virginia, even to acknowledge an inferiority, either personally or politically," it read. The signers believed that "any other element of representation which would stifle the voice of the majority of the community would be degradation of that majority to a state of political slavery, we appeal in the name of the 100,000 of the Western majority of the white population of Western Virginia." Samuel Watts of Norfolk City suggested that the convention move to his hometown to reduce sectional animosity. No other state, he says, "whose people know so little of each other, as those of Virginia; especially of the Eastern and Western portions of the State." Hosting in Norfolk would "bring together extremes which never before met. It would bring about a community of feeling which would be no less advantageous than happy." It was wishful thinking.[41]

The eastern delegates locked shields to repel the western offensive. One of the main issues was the new governorship. Westerners sought the office to be popularly elected for a single term, while their opponents preferred to keep it appointed. On February 4, Carlile spoke in favor of the amendment initially forwarded by John Minor Botts of Henrico. He drew immediate criticism. Walter Daniel Leake of Goochland County derided him for having "democracy . . . too much of northern origin." Carlile fired back that as "a Virginian by birth" and "claim[ing] to be a Southern man," he saw no "necessity of referring to Northern States or to Northern sentiments." He supported the measure out of his constitutional liberties and status as a man. "In the exercise of my rights as a freeman at the polls," he said, "I might not be disposed to elect any man for more than one term, yet I am willing the people of the State should have the same liberty that I claim for myself, and I would permit them to determine for themselves whether one elected by them should be retained in office in preference to those who might be his competitors." His response, which dragged on for an unnecessarily long time, drew attacks from others. Hector Davis, a prominent Richmond slave trader, said on the following day that Carlile's words caused him pain. He, not Botts, was "the real father of the bantling." The measure was "not as I supposed, of eastern origin, but claims its paternity, I believe, in the extreme north-west of the State." Davis retorted that had he "known on that occasion, as I know now, the true origin of this proposition, I should not have felt altogether the pain which I expressed on that occasion." Some westerners jumped to Carlile's defense. On February 10, Elisha McComas of Cabell criticized Davis for having "so poor an opinion of western members," and that when he voted against a measure, he "will not do it because of eastern origin." The debate reached an impasse.[42]

More issues clogged the convention. Westerners complained about their taxation system that burdened them unfairly. George W. Summers took the lead here. On February 17, he challenged Robert Eden Scott, a planter from Fauquier County, on why the proposed taxation provisions in the constitution favored the east over the more populous west. "Let us hear by what process of ratiocination you expect to establish a proposition by which, while you have a majority of 100,000 of your people in the western portion of the State," he said. Placing political power into the hands of a minority, he continued, implied that Scott intended to "import from South Carolina a principle of representation, and to seek to plant it in the Commonwealth of Virginia." John R. Chambliss of Greensville in the Tidewater had no time for such antics. His constituents alone, he argued, contained many slaveholders who refused to trust anyone with their property. He dismissed western grievances. "Our western brethren may be dissatisfied, but certainly they will have suffered no injury," he said. Giving westerners equal treatment would arouse "the fears of the whole of eastern Virginia . . . that their property would not suffer from cupidity, not because the western people were disposed to grind us by oppression, but they would distrust it." The convention remained stuck on the issue of equality.[43] As February dragged on, the battles continued. Richard L. T. Beale of Westmoreland County, the leader of the Richmond Junto, which some westerners supported in years past, declared his "happiness" when his canvass of western delegates revealed their reliability on protecting slavery. Yet he refused to budge after reading about the west's stances during the 1831–1832 emancipation debates. Giving them power, he concluded, "where would have been the destiny of eastern Virginia; and not alone of eastern Virginia, where would have been the destiny of the entire State?" In response, William G. Brown of

Preston County defended western reliability on slavery. When, he asked, "have western men manifested any disposition to burn down eastern temples, or disturb eastern society? Never, sir—never. It is empty declamation without one particle of foundation to support it." He concluded by boasting how the "honest and generous sons of the Valley of Virginia" stood side by side with the "noble sons of the east, who might possibly gain political power by the adoption of the mixed basis, have arrayed themselves on the side of principle." As fine as these sentiments were, western delegates still talked past the easterners. A new tactic was needed.[44]

With appeals to equality and tax relief going unheeded, the northwestern delegates adopted the same strategy that Philip Doddridge used in 1830. Instead of evading the slavery issue, they appealed to their region's reliability on the issue, exactly what Chambliss and others derided. Willey took the lead here. Much like his mentor Doddridge two decades before, he argued that their region also had both an interest in slavery and a solid track record on defending it. He began on February 24 by requesting how the existing constitution was established. "Was it your lands, your slaves, your property? No. It was the voice and the will of the majority of the community—at least of the qualified voters." Citing the recently concluded war with Mexico, Willey pointed to the sacrifices made by non-slaveholders in service to their country. "Was it our landlords, our slave owners, or the wealthy proprietaries of the country? No, sir, no. I hazard nothing in saying that few, very few, of the common soldiers were property holders of any kind to any considerable extent. And yet they were true to the death." He saved his best for last. In a fiery statement, Willey claimed that the east risked antagonizing potential allies in their need to protect the institution. It is worth quoting in whole:

> Can it be expected that men will ardently and cordially support negro slavery when by doing so they have virtually cherishing the property which is making slaves of themselves? What will be the result? It is impossible that the morbid, pseudo-philanthropic spirit of northern abolitionism should ever find a resting-place in Virginia. But will not hostility to slavery be engendered by the incorporation of such a principle into the Constitution? Your slaves, by this principle, drive us from the common place of civil rights, and usurp our place. Will the spirit of free men endure it? Never! Either the principle must be abolished, or you will excite a new species of political abolition against property itself. You will compel us to assume an attitude of antagonism towards you, or

towards the slave, and like the man driven to the wall; we shall be forced to destroy our assailants to save our own liberty.

Willey here learned from the shortcomings in early western strategies. Carlile, Summers, Brown, and others assumed that white unity was enough to convince eastern delegates to change the constitution. Tidewater and Piedmont planters and their allies saw the mixed basis as essential to securing their investment in slavery. Willey had to prove that westerners were as proslavery as they were. It almost worked. He gained enough ground to even the sides. The deadlock proved so stubborn that the *Parkersburg Gazette* suggested peaceful separation. If "the west cannot be justly expected to abandon the principles for which our fathers fought, in mere deference to the arrogant pretentions of an aristocracy whom neither birth, wisdom, nor prowess entitles to the high prerogative they claim viz that of governing the majority. No, better, far better accept the other branch of the alternative and peacefully divide the state."[45] It is easy to read this statement as a premonition, but its sentiments indicate that northwestern Virginians still placed their allegiances with their state.

Willey's strategy ultimately prevailed in forcing compromises. While eastern and western delegates dug in, another figure stepped in to resolve the situation. Henry A. Wise of Accomac County in the Eastern Shore, a past congressman and US minister to Brazil, took the initiative to break the deadlock. He succeeded. The west—both northwest and southwest—would receive their long-desired railroads, universal male suffrage, white-basis voting in the Assembly, and direct election of the governor and lieutenant governor. In exchange, the east retained its control over the State Senate until 1865 and, most important of all, a tax system that privileged slaveholders. Richard Curry has argued that the new constitution changed little. "These concessions, he wrote, "were designed for the defense of slavery rather than for the promotion of democracy." He is largely correct, but he mixes the two as being exclusive. The northwestern delegates' appeals to slavery had their desired effect. Assuring the whole state that the west was trustworthy on that pivotal issue brought about the necessary compromises. The vote tally of 75,784 to 11,063 statewide, with only five eastern counties giving majorities against the new constitution, supports the new acceptance of the west as a full partner in Virginia.[46]

The best proof of this success comes from the first gubernatorial election under the new state constitution. In December 1851, the entire Commonwealth had to choose between not one but two northwesterners for their chief executive. Democrat Joseph Johnson of Harrison prevailed over Whig George W.

Summers of Kanawha in a close vote. Statewide, the former won by a tally of 64,315 (53 percent) to 57,987 (47 percent). Within the northwest, the margin was razor-thin. Johnson prevailed with 12,275 votes (50.2 percent) to Summers's 12,166 (49.8 percent), a difference of a mere 109.[47] Either way, the presence on the ballot of two candidates from a region until recently derided as unreliable on slavery shows that Virginia had healed its internal issues.

Fifty years after John G. Jackson lamented his region's frustrations, Abia Minor of Harrison County praised the changes brought about in Virginia's new constitution. In May 1852, the wealthy Pennsylvania-born farmer ran for county sheriff. In a public letter, he lauded the new constitution for allowing men to "go up to the polls and elect the makers and ministers of his laws without being questioned by the Sheriff, whether they owned a negro, a horse or a clock, intimating thereby that the possession of wealth was the only requisite qualification of a voter."[48] He won the office, but his victory demonstrates the basis on which white Virginians had united. All parts and their white populations now, southwestern, Tidewater, Piedmont, Valley, and especially the northwest, became equal partners. Contrary to previous accounts, neither separate culture, nor neglect of internal improvements, nor attachments to neighboring states divided the Old Dominion. In the first half of the nineteenth century, only one issue afflicted Virginia: suffrage. The east's refusal to equalize voting and office holding came from their mistrust of non-planters like themselves. The northwest chafed under this limit since they, like all white Virginians, supported slavery out of proportion to their numbers. Their leaders, almost all of whom personally owned bondspeople, proved to the state and that they and their non-slaveholding neighbors protected the institution. In the 1851 constitution, they overcame eastern prejudices to such a degree that the state had to choose between two northwesterners for the state's first elected governor. They achieved this goal by stepping harder on the enslaved than ever before. They would continue to defend their state and the institution of slavery in the pivotal decade of the 1850s.

CHAPTER 2

Northwestern Virginia on the Defensive, 1851–1860

Americans celebrated Independence Day in 1851 with special relief. Five years of sectional tensions begun by the war with Mexico had finally calmed. Compromises between the slaveholding and non-slaveholding states over the future of slavery made in the previous year restored a measure of peace to the country. At the same time, Virginia had healed its own internal divisions. Daniel Webster, the esteemed Massachusetts senator, cited the Old Dominion's example to the entire country as he laid the cornerstone of the new capital building in Washington. He praised white Virginians for unifying around their new state constitution despite their regional differences. He dared them to say whether they supported the breakup of the government. "Ye men of the Potomac," he cried, "dwelling along the shores of that river on which Washington lived, and died." He then called upon "ye men of the James River and the Bay, places consecrated by the early settlement of your commonwealth." He knew that "ye men beyond the Blue Ridge" would oppose disunion as strongly as if their mountain "would soon totter from its base." Finally, he especially praised the northwest for their allegiance to their state. "Ye men of Western Virginia," he began, "what course do you propose to yourselves by disunion?" Webster then asked, "If you 'secede,' what do you 'secede' from, and what do you 'accede' to? Do you look for the current of the Ohio to change, and bring you and your commerce to the tidewaters of Eastern rivers? What man in his senses can suppose that you will remain part and parcel of Virginia a month after Virginia should have ceased to be part and parcel of the United States?" Advocates of statehood in 1861 and adherents of the Ambler-Curry thesis since have used this quote to show the renown of the state's internal problems and the inevitability of West Virginia's separation. They are wrong. Webster meant it to show how the state united, not separated. White Virginians from all regions at the time agreed with him. The national crisis over the Union and the institution of slavery of the 1850s brought them closer to Virginia's parent than the "God-like Daniel" envisaged.[1]

This chapter deals with how northwestern Virginians responded to the turbulent 1850s. The state's historians give this decade little attention. Ambler and Curry each incorrectly called it a time of calm before the storm.

39

The 1850s contained much tension between the slaveholding and non-slave-holding states. Northwestern Virginia's responses to those issues serve as my focus here. I argue that instead of holding a middling or moderating stance between those camps, the region defended its state against the numerous internal and external threats of the time. The collapse of the Second Party System in 1853 introduced new political parties such as the Know Nothings and the Republicans that northwesterners, like other Virginians and residents of the other slaveholding states, believed risked the Union itself. They also contended with perceived antislavery elements within their borders. The election of a Know Nothing to Congress, the brief existence of the Kansas-style Ceredo Colony, and John Brown's raid on Harpers Ferry each prompted strong reactions from the staunchly proslavery white population in the decade. From these experiences, however, the region developed a strong conservative approach that preferred order over chaos. As in chapter 1, here I use newspapers and election returns primarily from Ohio, Harrison, and Kanawha counties, for which the greatest number of both have survived, to reveal the overlooked but intense debates on the events of the time. Previous histories cite evidence written after 1861 to show the northwest's troubles with its parent. I believe that secession and the statehood movement rendered them inherently unreliable. My views on the famed *Wheeling Daily Intelligencer* newspaper will shock readers. I found that, contrary to the paper's reputation as the main source of West Virginia's history, contemporaries hated its presence for its criticism of slavery and the state. Instead of drifting away from the Old Dominion, as previously claimed, the region moved closer toward it. This approach makes West Virginia's actions in 1861 even more surprising.

As the new decade began, white northwestern Virginians showed no signs of drifting away from their state. The Ambler-Curry school maintains that the region started to question its attachments around this time. This is not true. The best proof of this comes from its electoral patterns of the time. Its voters regularly chose the same political party as the rest of their state while its non-slaveholding neighbors began to support more radical parties. The two main national groups, the Democrats and the Whigs, enjoyed healthy support across the state and the region. Both differed in constituencies and philosophies, but each represented stability on the main issue of the period, slavery. The northwestern voters backed them in almost equal measure. The debates over the future of slavery and Union started by victory over Mexico made the 1848 election especially fierce. The region gave Democrat Lewis Cass a 300-vote margin of 7,890 (51.1 percent) to 7,560 (48.9 percent) over overall winner and Whig Zachary Taylor that year. The number represented a sizable portion of Cass's

Virginia-majority of 1,400 votes. Among the other border states, only Missouri voted for Cass the Michigander. Maryland, Delaware, and his home state of Kentucky backed Taylor. Pennsylvania also supported Taylor, while Ohio selected Cass. Congress was a different matter. Virginia regularly filled most if not all its offices with Democrats. In 1849, they won all fifteen seats, although Whig Thomas Haymond of Marion replaced the deceased Alexander Newman of Ohio County. Two years later, the state sent a record two Whigs (James F. Strother of Rappahannock and Charles J. Faulkner of Berkeley) along with thirteen Democrats to the federal House. By comparison, in both elections the two parties evenly split seats in Kentucky, Maryland, and Pennsylvania. The neighboring northern states experimented with the openly antislavery Free Soil Party, with the former sending two of its members to Congress in addition to nineteen Whigs and Democrats, while Indiana sent one from the new antislavery party. Only Illinois and Missouri sent all Democrats to Congress like Virginia did. The next election saw more of the same. In 1852, the region cast 15,181 (55.4 percent) votes for New Hampshirite Franklin Pierce, while giving 12,245 (44.6 percent) for native Virginian but Whig Winfield Scott, a tenfold increase over the previous race. The Free Soil Party won a mere 56 votes in Maryland, 63 in Delaware, and 264 in Kentucky. By comparison, it won over 30,000 in Ohio and still placed a distant third. Pierce won there, in Pennsylvania, and in three of the four other border states. Only Kentucky supported Scott. The party also won all of Virginia's seats in the 1853 congressional races.[2] Northwestern Virginia's white voters, therefore, preferred Democrats in almost all circumstances.

A new wave of newspapers emerged in the region to feed a newly enlarged electorate. While the northwest produced many journals before 1851, few have survived even in scattered runs. Those existing before the decade included the Democratic *Wheeling Gazette*, along with the Whiggish *Parkersburg Gazette and Courier* and the *Kanawha Republican* of Charleston. Those founded after 1850 are more numerous, if most survive in partial format. They include the Democratic *Cooper's Clarksburg Register*. Its editor, the New York–born printer William P. Cooper, intended to fill his columns "with all the current news of the day, foreign local and political, besides devoting a very liberal portion to literature and useful reading." Other papers strove for the same ends, including the new Whiggish *Wellsburg Herald* in Brooke County. In 1855, the Democratic *Kanawha Valley Star* began publication, first in Putnam County, before moving to Charleston the following year.[3] None of these papers would influence the region as much as the *Wheeling Daily Intelligencer* did. Started in August 1852 by Eli B. Swearingen and Oliver L. Taylor, who edited it with J. H. Pendleton, the *Intelligencer* aimed to reach the broadest possible audience. They boasted at having the latest Boston steam press machine "which cannot be excelled in the precision and neatness of its impressions by any in the country." The machine gave it the huge advantage over its rivals by appearing in daily and weekly formats as well.[4] While this responsive media culture kept the region's voters well informed about national, state, and local affairs in the years to come, it also divided them. The *Intelligencer* became the most controversial newspaper in the region as it oriented toward the new Republican Party after 1856. Its criticism of slavery belies its claims and those of later historians to be the true voice of northwestern Virginia.

The *Intelligencer* entered the region's strong and often vicious partisan political culture. The Democrats and Whigs left little space for alternative views. In the wake of the 1852 election, the editors of the Democratic *Wheeling Times* attacked their opponents for being weak on slavery and the Compromise of 1850. Pendleton and Taylor of the *Intelligencer* defended the party's record on these issues. "We are Union men all, we are compromise men all, and above all we are Virginians," they proclaimed. They pledged to "stand or fall with Virginia in defense of her Constitutional rights, so long will we advocate the fugitive slave law." In another editorial the following day, they attacked articles from the *Times* and another Democratic paper, the *Wheeling Argus*, as "most unfortunate and improper" for attacking the city's Whigs, who made up the local majority. Furthermore, they described the *Argus*'s stance, which resembled the *Times*'s, for attacking their party as "a most unjust and illiberal effort to identify the Whig with principles as foreign to its feelings and impulses, as they are suicidal to the interests of Virginia."[5] The Whiggish *Parkersburg Gazette and Courier* described the *Intelligencer*'s editors as having "down right disingenuous and jesuited reasoning" when it came to internal improvements. The Wheeling area, it claimed, had interests different from the rest of the northwest. Enos W. Newton, editor of the Whig *Kanawha Republican*, agreed. The failure of Wheeling and other Panhandle delegates to support the construction of the proposed Covington and Ohio Railroad that would run southward to the Kanawha Valley caused too much internal friction. The *Intelligencer* responded in kind. Newton was wrong, they wrote. In fact, the representatives in question voted for the railroad. Moreover, they pointed out that one of Kanawha's delegates, Spicer Patrick, a local doctor, had done more to stop the bill. "No one cause or person in our judgment," the *Intelligencer* opined, "are the true friends of the Covington bill more indebted for their defeat than to the impracticable and headstrong (or the opposite) course of one of her delegation, a man [Patrick] . . . whose general course of speech-making and meddling with what does not concern him is well calculated to drive off from the support of a bill which he supports, its warmest friends." Seeking peace between Ohio and Kanawha counties, the editors stated that our "sympathies and feelings as Virginians have always been with the Central Railroad and its connections. Its friends have been our friends, and we would gladly have them continue such and be such to them, but the *Republican* knows that the reciprocity is the basis of mutual good feeling."[6] The latter's response is unknown, but these condescending attitudes show the extensive divisions in the region's politics even in good times.

The collapse of the Second Party System in 1853 worsened the situation. Sectional divisions over slavery brought by the Kansas-Nebraska Act splintered the Whigs into northern and southern wings, and thence into collapse. While the Democrats remained mostly united, the resulting vacuum led to the creation of new opposing parties. A loose coalition of former Whigs, Free Soilers (which had also folded), and antislavery northern Democrats gathered in Ripon, Wisconsin, to form the Republican Party in 1854. Before that, however, a different group filled the gap. The American Party, better known as the Know Nothings for their pretenses at secrecy, rose first nationwide and within the state. They promised to curtail the influence of Catholics and immigrants, but their true strength lay in carrying the old Whig votes against the Democrats. The northwestern Virginia Democratic press had no such misgivings about their new opponents. Their editors used every chance they had to attack this upstart party. The *Register* took offense to the defection of longtime Democrat John S. Carlile to the new party. In April 1854, Cooper stated that he was "gratified that [Carlile] has secured the nomination [for Congress], because it is generally understood that he joined the order to obtain it and it would be a pity to disappoint him. The personal relations which exist between us make us regret that he could consent to place himself in his present position."[7] In time, Cooper accused the Know Nothings of being "the first secret political society that we have any knowledge of." Moreover, it was "antagonistic to the principles of this government, so peculiar for the free and public discussions of all political questions." Since white Americans descended from foreigners, the *Register* continued, the Know Nothings' nativist platform was "unwise, unjust, un-American and unbecoming any but an egotist and a bigot." Cooper later accused the party's secrecy of perverting the course of democracy in the North. The *Register* printed reports of local men disrupting a Know Nothing meeting in Buckhannon in Upshur County and the egging of a Marion County man, as well as events in New York, Pennsylvania, and Massachusetts. This hostility dogged new party in the region from its inception.[8]

The *Intelligencer* bore the brunt of this response. It had an unusual relationship with the Know Nothings. Some of its stories claimed that it opposed the party, yet in others it gave qualified support. In February 1855, the editors rebuffed an accusation from the Democratic *Wheeling Argus* that it supported the new party: "We are decidedly inclined to the opinion that we have not struck our colors to the Know-Nothings or to any other party faction or men. We are also decidedly inclined to the opinion that we are advocating no principle inconsistent with the uniform course of this paper and that our colors are now flying where they have always been." A few weeks later, the newspaper called for unity among the parties to obtain more improvements for the northwest. "Let us, then, one and all, Whigs, Democrats, and Know-Nothings, look to this common end, namely, the good of the country," it opined, "to attain it we must have a strong delegation in Richmond this winter; men who can comprehend and advocate great State questions." In June 1855, the *Intelligencer* reprinted the party's platform but with a proviso that it assumed no responsibility for the content. "The apparent difference between the two papers is that the editors of the *Intelligencer*," it said, "approve the principles but oppose the order, whilst Wharton [the other editor of the *Gazette*] approves the order but hates the principles." The *Intelligencer* denied having any anti-Catholic or antiforeign attitudes. It claimed to have supported the American Party in the state and congressional elections "because we thought it to be the best State ticket." The paper went on to state saying that it did not "advocate the State ticket as blindly as did the editor of the *Gazette*." The proof of the accusations came from the newspaper's support for schools. These editors took few punches in this petty journalistic war. Rather, the party's stance on slavery lay behind this odd statement. Its platform condemned pro- and antislavery forces for threatening national unity. This middling stance suited the *Intelligencer*'s approach to the issues of the day, but it also encouraged its opponents' beliefs that it was an antislavery paper.[9]

The state elections in May 1855 fulfilled the Democrats' worst fears. The Know Nothings stunned Virginia by winning one-third of the seats in both the House of Delegates, including a victory by Arthur I. Boreman of Wood County, and the State Senate. Democrat Henry Wise of Accomac, the forger of the compromises behind the 1851 constitution, won the governorship, but his opponent Thomas Flournoy managed to take one-third of the state's counties. Even more ominous for Cooper and other Democratic editors, the northwestern counties gave the latter a thin four-hundred-vote majority over Wise. The biggest shock came in one of the region's congressional races. John S. Carlile managed to beat Charles S. Lewis by an identical margin to win the Eleventh Congressional District to become the only member of his party to win federal office from Virginia. Upon his arrival in Washington, he arranged to have a photograph taken (figure 2). While his sole speech failed to distinguish his time in Congress, the shock of this new party making such major gains disturbed their opponents. The *Register* tried to justify their defeat. They claimed that Democrats seldom succeeded in Harrison County, having voted for Summers for governor in 1851 and expected to support Flournoy in the same way. They were mistaken in both cases. In the first, the county sent its native son Joseph Johnson to Richmond by a vote of 893 (60.3 percent) to 588 (39.7 percent). The second disappointed them too, as Wise received 1,017 (52.5 percent) of Harrison's votes to his opponent's 921 (47.5 percent), a respectable showing for the new and controversial party.[10] Their ability to carry over the Whig vote made them a potent threat to Democrats. When compared to neighboring states, Virginia was the only one to resist the Know Nothing wave. Maryland, Delaware, and Kentucky split their congressional seats among the parties, and the latter two elected their governors from the new party. The northern neighbors rejected the nativists in favor of an opponent. The Democrats prevailed in congressional races in Pennsylvania, Missouri, and Indiana and, in a remarkable move, won all of Ohio's seats, to become the largest party in the House of Representatives. Illinois split theirs. Although Virginia stayed true to its main party, the Know Nothings' strong showing prompted Democrats to rethink their party's appeal.

The Democrats retaliated against this surprising result by escalating the slavery question. While the issue was never absent from local minds, the party made it their prime concern to revive their fortunes. Their newspapers attacked anyone who they deemed weak on protecting the institution. Their first victim was the *Wheeling Gazette*, a small Know Nothing newspaper. In the summer of 1855, the *Register* attacked it for Free Soil views, such as repealing the Fugitive Slave Act, emancipating slaves in the District of Columbia with compensation, and passing the Kansas-Nebraska Act. Hoping that its comments offended none of its readers, the *Register* accused the *Gazette* of treason to Virginia. No party in this state should advocate "the treasonable doctrines that the people of the different localities shall not frame their own laws, as is avowed in the declaration that there shall be no more slave territory," it stated. It was bad enough that the Know Nothings had been, it continued, "abolitionized in the North, but it proves to be infected with the same disease at the South, and in our own state, and section of the State." The Democrats encouraged people to leave that party, which "accepts such doctrines, and unite with those who have ever opposed them, in sweeping them away, that out own section of country may not rest under the imputation of being traitors to the Constitution, and

Fig. 2. John S. Carlile, ca. 1855 (Brady-Handy Collection, Library of Congress). Carlile as he appeared at the start of his time in the federal Senate. He first floated the idea of separate statehood in May 1861. After he carefully nurtured the notion of a new state untainted by secession but with slavery intact, his plan became the preferred means to resist secession. Contrary to previous histories, he never turned against the movement. Radicals turned it against him by supporting emancipation.

traitors to our interests." These strong comments appeared to have influenced the Clarksburg community, but not as Cooper hoped. A week later, the *Register* reported losing numerous subscribers. Cooper resisted and even mocked their threats. Despite the potential financial strains, he was "not . . . willing to sacrifice a vital principle of government to self-interest, as long as there were other means of producing an honorable livelihood for ourself and family, we incurred their displeasure and DEFIED their hostility. We imagine that there were never a more vindictive, unscrupulous and wicked combination against one poor individual that was formed in that order against us." Undeterred by the financial strain in an already difficult market, Cooper said he bought new type for the next volume of the paper, such was the dedication northwestern Democrats had for their party and for slavery.[11]

Another Democratic paper exceeded even these views. The *Star of the Kanawha Valley* attacked anyone whom they deemed to be unreliable on slavery. In 1855, they attacked the Know Nothings' candidate for lieutenant governor, J. M. H. Beale of Mason County. In a speech at Parkersburg, Beale said that slavery was evil and harmed society, but at the same time he "announced himself being a slaveholder, and not an abolitionist." In its attempt to give him an impartial hearing, the *Star* said that if he won the office, his victory will "be hailed by Northern Abolitionists as an antislavery triumph in Virginia."[12] The *Star* joined in the *Register*'s fight against the *Wheeling Gazette* as a Free Soil paper but added its rivalry with the still-Whiggish *Kanawha Republican* to the mix. It claimed that "the general tenor of the selections and editorials in the *Republican* have an awful squinting towards Freesoilism; and all we ask of the *Republican* is for it to define its position upon that subject as fully and as plainly as the 'Gazette' has."[13] Edited by Jonathan Rundle, the *Star* refused to compromise with anyone whom it considered to be weak or even moderate on slavery.

The Know Nothings tried in vain to defend themselves. Only one of their papers, the *Morgantown American Union*, has survived. Its editorials, nonetheless, indicate a strong support for slavery. In its inaugural issue in June 1855, the newspaper attacked Catholics and foreigners for stirring up the abolitionists. First, the power of the papacy threatened to outweigh the responsibilities for American citizens. "Against the political encroachments of Jesuitism, they are as determinedly opposed, knowing that wherever the Pope reigns, the ecclesiastical is superior to the civil power." Moreover, this power encouraged northern fanatics on slavery. "With mistaken notions of Liberty, and more erroneous ideas of their Constitutional prerogatives as citizens," the *American Union* stated, "they begin to dictate the abolition of Slavery, and in the ranks of mad-cap factionists, they join in a war upon the peculiar institutions of the

South and oppose the States in rights guaranteed by the Constitution." Taking away suffrage from foreigners and Catholics, therefore, made sense since abolition was a foreign idea, having, the editor claimed, "waxed strong and exacting by reason of trans-Atlantic sympathy and emigration, and it is no difficult matter to discover these well-defined elements." These appeals failed miserably in Monongalia County, where the Democrats outpolled the Know Nothings 1,316 (66.8 percent) to 653 (33.2 percent) in the governor's race in 1855. The voters in the Tenth Congressional District reelected Zedekiah Kidwell, a Democrat, to Congress. Their statements in later issues indicate why. The editors printed numerous columns defending themselves against accusations of bigotry and trying to distance themselves from the old parties. The latter was particularly serious because former Whigs made up their largest pool of potential supporters. The Know Nothings faced an uphill battle to keep enough former Whig voters in line against accusations of being soft on slavery.[14]

Northwestern Democrats used the 1856 presidential election to exact their revenge. They pilloried their opponents as troublemakers on every issue, especially slavery. The *Register* reported in April of that year that the Northern Panhandle ought to secede from Virginia and join Pennsylvania. "We hope that no objection will be made to their desire. Their interests and feelings are with Pennsylvania, and there is where they ought to belong," it wrote. With no love lost, the *Register* continued that if "Wheeling had been bought by the State twenty years ago, burnt and corn-planted on the ground, the Commonwealth would have made money by the operation." The newly arrived and allegedly antislavery Republican Party drew Democrats' special ire. When the *Register* discovered that a branch had opened in the Panhandle, it repeated this same idea: "We said some time ago that the 'panhandle' ought not to belong to Virginia." Other Democratic papers felt the same way. The appropriately titled *Fairmont True Virginian* attacked the *Wellsburg Herald* for apologizing for slavery. In a strongly worded proslavery editorial, it pilloried the Northern Panhandle paper for its sentiments: "How unlike your countrymen you must imagine slaveholders to be! We have no doubt that slavery is infinitely stronger than the tie that binds the several states of this Union together. The men of the South might sacrifice a good deal for the Union; but to suppose that they will give up property worth . . . hundreds of millions of dollars, is to suppose that they have no selfishness at all. Hence the efforts of the abolitionists and the encouragement which the *Herald* unintentionally gives them, all tend to a dissolution of our glorious Union." The *True Virginian* insisted that no apology was therefore necessary when slavery benefitted the country in many ways. The *Star of the Kanawha Valley* agreed. Calling the Know Nothings "the leading

On the Defensive, 1851–1860 / 49

humbug ever to deceive the people," the editor accused them of being a divisive force in national affairs. "They appealed to the lowest and basest feelings of our natures," as they "attempted to array all the various Protestant denominations against the Catholics," thereby "depriving one religious denomination of its political rights though the Constitution of our country grants the same rights and privileges to each and all." Responsible for this was "a set of office-seekers who were determined to break down the Democratic Party."[15]

This proslavery onslaught split the Know Nothings and defeated them in detail. The *Morgantown American Union* insisted that the American Party was safe on the subject. It blamed the Pierce administration for reopening the slavery issue with the Kansas-Nebraska Act. "The repeal of a time-honored compact and the annunciation of Squatter Sovereignty by the Nebraska-Kansas bid," the newspaper argued, has "ignited and fanned the flame of civil discord until rank disunion stalks abroad with menacing men." Moreover, the *American Union* claimed that the "recklessness of the Pierce dynasty has opened a chasm in which that possibility looms up in horrid ghastliness. We must say, further, that we do not believe, viewing the present condition under Pierce rule, that the Union would survive another four years of such administration as the last." The *Intelligencer* tried to take the middle ground between the Democrats and the Know Nothings by clinging to the Whigs. This year also saw the resurgence of the Old Line Whig Party in the northwest. In April, it printed the resolutions from the party's convention in Augusta County as proof that the party and its principles still existed. "The principles of the Whig party are *the* principles of the country," it proudly boasted. "No matter by what name our party may be designated by its opponents, our principles are living, Union-preserving principles, and when forgotten by the patriots of our country, may God have mercy upon our Union, for it will be tattered and torn." The *Intelligencer* sighed with relief when the delegates rejected a resolution to support former president Millard Fillmore and the Know Nothings in the election. The Old Line Whigs ultimately backed that ticket, much to the paper's deep regret. For the rest of the year, the *Intelligencer* continued following a middling line, condemning the North, abolitionists, and Republicans alike. It was not enough to overcome their opponents.[16]

As the election drew nearer, Democrats escalated their attacks. They expressed great concern for the fusion of Know Nothings with the Republicans in Pennsylvania that year. The *Register* met with disgust when it printed a report that local Harrison County men had cheered this development. "We imagined that there were no Fillmore men left in Virginia, with sympathies for the black flag of n—ism," it stated. The Know Nothings had, moreover, "put on the worst garb of fanatical disunion" and supported John C. Frémont "the standard bearer of the wildest, the maddest fanaticism to [President James] Buchanan, the champion of States rights, the Constitution and the laws." In the next issue, the *Register* went so far as to say the election was about one issue: "whether fanaticism or the Constitution is to reign supreme over the land." They confidently predicted that Buchanan would win, yet more eagerly sought that Virginia's voters send the Know Nothings a message to "indicate the estimation with which the sectionalists are held." The *Kanawha Valley Star* saw slavery and the Constitution as perfectly united in an appeal to the area's few Democrats. It invoked simple patriotism to both country and party. The latter had, it claimed, "never faltered for a moment, but battled with noble courage for those principles of the Constitution, which secures the same equality of privileges in the government."[17] Northwestern Democrats saw themselves as the only party committed to the status quo of slavery and the Union. Their attacks using both elements delegitimized their opponents and never gave them a chance to recover.

The Democrats' proslavery tactics paid off. Buchanan won a larger majority in the northwest than Pierce had four years before. In that election, the Democratic candidate received 15,181 (55.4 percent) votes from the region to his opponent's 12,245 (44.6 percent), a margin of 2,936 votes. Of the twenty-eight counties then in the region, eighteen went for the winner, while ten sided with the loser. In 1856, Buchanan received nearly doubled the margin as his predecessor, with 20,048 votes (59.7 percent) while Fillmore received 13,560 (40.3 percent), or a margin of 6,488 votes. Adding two counties (Pleasants and Upshur) to the region in the previous year mattered little. Of the thirty counties in the region in that election, twenty-five voted Democratic candidates, while only five favored the Know Nothings. Five counties switched allegiances, all toward the Democrats. Even Ohio County, a longtime Whig stronghold, swapped sides. The Republicans made their first showing in this election, receiving a mere 273 votes. All but 10 came from Northern Panhandle counties. The remainder came from the new Upshur County in the interior. Buchanan handily won the state with 86,959 votes (60.5 percent) to Fillmore's 56,821 (39.5 percent), again almost double the margin from 1852. The *Kanawha Valley Star* spoke for many Democrats in pronouncing victory. "It will be regarded as the day when the people of this confederacy decided that the Constitutional Rights of the slave-holding states shall be maintained and preserved inviolated," it argued, "and when the people of this Union decided by an overwhelming vote that the Constitution . . . recognized the institution of slavery and protected the rights flowing therefrom." Virginia's election results resembled most of its neighbors' presidential returns. Buchanan won in Illinois, Indiana, Pennsylvania, Missouri, Kentucky, and Delaware. Ohio went for Frémont, while the lingering Know Nothings won Maryland for Fillmore. Congress was a different matter. The Republicans replaced the nativists in the northern states but split Illinois, Indiana, and Pennsylvania. Ohio voted for the new party. Know Nothings won half of Maryland's seats but lost ground in Kentucky and Missouri. In the 1856 presidential election, therefore, northwestern Virginia showed unmistakable signs of remaining with its state.[18]

Although flush with victory, northwestern Democrats continued their attacks on dissenters into the new year of 1857. They had two objectives. The first was to remove John S. Carlile, whose election to Congress as a Know Nothing infuriated his many opponents. In April 1857, days after the presidential election ended, Democratic newspapers in the Eleventh Congressional District displayed a banner supporting Jenkins's candidacy. Carlile came under scrutiny for his land reform and revenue bill while in Congress. He proposed to sell Virginia's land holdings on the western frontier to pay for internal improvements, an old Whig idea. The *Intelligencer* praised him for the plan, but his critics condemned it as unconstitutional, believing only tariffs could provide revenue for the government. Citing the founders, a letter to the *Register* stated that the "Democratic policy has always been to keep the Tariff down to such a standard as will meet the expenses of government. . . . [To] favor this land distribution is nothing more than to favor a protective system. Mr. Carlile advances one of the most simple, foolish and palpably absurd propositions that can be conceived of." He faced stern opposition the entire way. A week later, he and Jenkins spoke in Upshur County. Carlile said that if he were reelected his land deal would bring Virginia out of its degraded state. His opponent "called upon him to know what he had done during the two years he had been in Congress that he should be re-elected, [and] asked if he had fulfilled his pledges to the people to put down the influence of foreigners and Catholics."[19] Knowing that each had proven proslavery views, the only way for Democrats to prevail over Carlile was to attack his record in office. It worked.

Fueled by proslavery resentment, the northwest removed the Know Nothing as its representative to Congress. Jenkins rode the Democratic wave to victory. He received 7,758 (53.8 percent) votes to Carlile's 6,653 (46.2 percent) votes, a threefold increase over the previous election, to win the Eleventh Congressional District. The same wave appears to have influenced the Tenth District too. Up there, Wheeling lawyer Sherrard Clemens pounded his Know Nothing opponent, a Mr. Dunnington (no first name is available), by a margin of 7,074 (71.5 percent) to 2,821 (28.5 percent) votes. This was also almost three times the difference in the previous election, when the Democrat won by 1,200 votes. Because the 1855 congressional returns by county are not available, it is difficult to fully evaluate the scope of the change. Yet even Whig stalwart Kanawha County felt the Democratic tide. In previous elections, the anti-Democratic candidate reliably received two-thirds of the votes. This time Carlile won the county but only 57 percent of the vote to 43 percent for Jenkins, ten points less than the county's norm for non-Democratic parties. The *Kanawha Valley Star* delighted in their victory. It suggested an epitaph for the Know Nothings:

Here in death, lying,

(As in life, it generally lied.)

Is the Great American Party,

Colossal in its premises;

The greatest benefit it has conferred on man

Is in dying without performing them.

It was an indulgent parent to its offspring

Who were of many kinds and colors,

And of widely differing faiths.

It fought the Catholic and foreigner

And the wild thirst for office;

And, finally in its benevolence,

Went for giving everything to everybody.

It did but little harm,

Chiefly for want of opportunity and power;

And with the purity and virtues always ascribed to the dead.

It went to a premature grave with them unexhibited.

The grief of its offspring is inconsolable,

Chiefly because it left them no offices or money

The worst thing it ever did

Was in not dying sooner!

Thoughtless Reader!

Learn in this veracious epitaph

How this great party died for its country's good,

Fortunate in having so true friend to weep

Over its ashes.

The American people are reconciled to their grief,

By the reflection that no country

Ever lost less by the death of a party

Than ours by this

The *Star* also held a mock funeral for their opponents outside of the office of the *Kanawha Republican*.[20] Northwestern Democrats saw this time as their shining moment. With their enemies prostrate, they could afford to be arrogant. But they still had work to do.

The region's conservative majority next targeted a new arrival in Eli Thayer. The Massachusetts-born businessman and politician embarked on what he called "an experiment in free labor" by founding a community called Ceredo. The group first arrived in Monongalia County but soon moved to more remote but more conservative Wayne County. In June, the *Intelligencer* praised their arrival as "the friendly invasion of Virginia." They promised to bring in fresh people and energy to the sparsely populated region. "A new style of cultivation, hitherto unthought of in old Monongalia, will be inaugurated, just as the German colonies have done in Texas and all the settlements in Western Pennsylvania," the newspaper boasted. It was a poor choice of words. The *Intelligencer's* critics pounced on the colony as an attempt to bring Kansas-style violence to Virginia. Over the next few months, the *Intelligencer* printed more favorable articles about Thayer and his activities. On August 5, it opined that "the people of that region of the country, as well as all over the Western division of our State, are beginning to take up to their true interests. This they can see only be reached by an influx of population—of the right kind of population—which does not consist of Captains and Colonels, but of bone and sinew laborers—men who have the heart and hands to go to work and rid out the wilds and open up the hills of our highly favored Western Virginia." These editorials infuriated an already aggressive sector of the population who viewed any deviation from their rule as an attack on the whole country.[21]

This positive spin incurred the wrath of the northwest's Democratic press. The *Kanawha Valley Star*, whose Charleston location placed it close to Wayne, expressed contempt for the settlement. "We are satisfied that Eli Thayer, his minions and confederates, now prowling about through our portion of the State," the *Star* stated, "are governed by mercenary motives in part, mostly by the hope of gradually building up an abolition party in the Commonwealth." Two months later, the *Star* said that Thayer's activities in Wayne and Cabell "have done much to cast a stigma on the fair name of those counties." Moreover, the newspaper condemned Thayer's presence as a threat to Virginia and every slaveholding state. "A man who comes into the State at the head of an organized society, the avowed purpose of which is to revolutionize public opinion; to introduce free-labor into the State," the *Star* argued, "and to oppose, indirectly, the cherished institutions of the State, and thereby injure the rights of slave-holders should, of course, be denounced by every Virginian."[22] The harsh sentiments of the

Fairmont True Virginian show how far Wheeling's rogue journal had sunk among its opponents, especially after Archibald W. Campbell—nephew of Reverend Alexander Campbell, founder of Bethany College in Brooke County—acquired the paper in 1856 and leaned it toward the Republicans. "We do not exchange with the *Wheeling Intelligencer*, and therefore cannot know much of its contents," its editor wrote, "but a friend of ours informs us that the german [meaning foreigner] with a white skin and a Black heart, who conducts that paper has been pouring out some of the vials of his Black Republicanism upon us." Elsewhere in this same issue, the paper condemned Thayer in equally harsh terms. Critical of support given to the colony in Parkersburg and Cincinnati papers, the editor regarded "the whole thing as a humbug, so far as any result affecting our institutions is concerned." The editor disliked the notion of northerners "squatting down upon our mountain lands." Moreover, he demanded that these newcomers mind their own business: "There are thousands and tens of thousands more of these Abolitionists who have so often traduced Virginia, who would nevertheless jump at an opportunity of getting any sort of a local habitation within her borders. We say, let the poor and oppressed come from Massachusetts as well as from Ireland to our noble old mother State, but them keep a civil tongue in their heads, and not slander the land that keeps them from starving."[23] The people of Wayne and Cabell counties felt the same way. In late September 1857, a meeting chaired by soon-to-be congressman Albert G. Jenkins passed resolutions opposing the project. The preamble accused Thayer of making "such representations of the enterprise as to induce a few persons to vote for such resolutions which were so worded that their phrazeology has been seized by the abolitionist press to represent that the sentiment of the people of this place was not antislavery." The other resolutions expressed devotion to Virginia and her institutions, especially slavery.[24] They worked. Thayer and most of his followers soon left the region altogether.

Within six months of defeating their last major opponent, northwestern Democrats received the first of many blows to their cause. National affairs turned decisively against their party starting the day after Buchanan took the presidential oath. The Supreme Court issued its infamous *Dred Scott* decision, which struck down the Compromise of 1850 and the Kansas-Nebraska Act. Northern opinion turned against the power of slavery—later known as the so-called Slave Power Conspiracy—and its Democratic supporters, whom they labeled "doughfaces," or northern men who supported slavery. In January 1858, after months of intense debate, President Buchanan approved of the Lecompton Constitution, which would have made Kansas a slave state. Democrats in Congress split on the matter, particularly when Senator Stephen A. Douglas of

Illinois—the architect of the above compromises—sided with the Republicans in opposition to it. Ultimately, Congress defeated the measure and delayed Kansas's entry into the Union until 1861. The northwest region of Virginia also felt its effects. Oddly, the surviving Democratic papers say nothing about the Lecompton affair. The always provocative *Intelligencer* did and attacked Governor Wise for supporting it. One editorial corrected the *Washington Star*, a Democratic paper, for saying the governor's actions represented the whole state. It was "unnecessarily precipitate and sweeping in its assertion, and mistaken, at least, by one half. We are sorry that the Western members of the Virginia delegation did give any grounds for such a belief—for we are very certain that it does neither themselves nor their respective constituencies any credit in the eyes of the world." To them, the governor was "a fire-eater, as a disunionist (in certain events)" and most important divided the state, having "become popular with one part of the people of the State and unpopular with another." Wise's actions on Lecompton "took all parties by surprise."[25]

Northwestern Democrats now faced attacks by the *Intelligencer* over the Kansas issue. Later that year, it reported that the *Wheeling Argus* told its readers that Congressman Sherrard Clemens had made a special deal with the former paper over his opposition to Lecompton. This was not true, and Clemens later supported the measure with his party. The *Argus* appears to have used such attacks on numerous occasions. Since none of its issues have survived, we have only its rival (and located next door in downtown Wheeling) the *Intelligencer* as a source. It could be as stubborn as the *Argus*, however. In March, it stated plainly that Democrats saw any dissenter as an abolitionist. The *Argus*, it maintained, acted in ways like France where Louis Napoleon suppressed newspapers at will. "The big Court Organ at the seat of Government, and the provincial Organs, like the *Argus*, set up an onslaught on these men [dissenters]—heaping on them such name as to take away their social caste and place them under the ban of dainty orthodox. Because a man opposes Lecompton, he is a 'negrophilist'—he is a 'wooly head'—a confrere of Fred. Douglas [sic], and all that sort of approbium [sic]," the *Intelligencer* opined. Though the evidence is slim here, northwestern Democrats united around the slavery issue to mollify divisions over Lecompton.[26] Yet no matter how hard they tried, the issue weakened their party for all to see, and they fought back using slavery. An 1858 column from the *Register* typified their anger toward the *Intelligencer*. It is worth quoting in whole:

> Any person who has a stomach sufficiently strong to read the frothy ebullitions that spume up daily and weekly from the columns of his journal

would frankly say, if questioned, the editor of the *Intelligencer* and that greasy, manumitted African, Fred Douglas [*sic*], were working together. We are sorry we were mistaken as to the origin of this wooly editor—never once supposing that he could be a Virginian but some venal scribbler who had been purchased out of Yankeeland, as is the manner of some to procure slaves in the South, for the use of his masters. And if he will come out into this "Hoop-pole region," as he terms one of the oldest and wealthiest counties in Western Virginia, we have our eye just now on a big, skinny n—, whom we will procure, at the expense of three shillings, current money, to imbue his lank digits in the ample folds of the editor's cravat, and give him such a general and thorough shaking up as will send terror to his jaundiced heart, paralysis to every bloodless limb, and scare him out of him every idea of being a n—-stealer again.[27]

This statement exemplifies the region's proslavery views at work. Cooper questioned everything about Campbell's origins and motives. Although mistaken about his birthplace—he was born in Ohio to Brooke County parents—and education at his uncle's college, the ironically New York–born Clarksburg journalist showed how his home base was truly Virginian. The notion of an enslaved person accepting money for his master to thrash Campbell out of his antislavery treason shines as a particularly harsh attack. Such an act would require the slave to protect his master's rights to hold him in bondage. These sentiments stand as proof that northwestern Virginia Democrats would never tolerate any questioning of the institution.

Yet the 1859 governor's election indicates that the Democrats lost ground in what should have been an easy victory. Again, slavery was the key issue here. Each side attacked the other for being weak on the subject. Democrats made their stances clear: slavery was legal, and they must oppose any attack upon it. Their candidate was John Letcher of Lexington. The Opposition, the name given to the coalition of former Know Nothings (the party collapsed after the 1857 election), Old Line Whigs, and others, attempted to form its own proslavery agenda. They selected an eastern slaveholder, William L. Goggin of Bedford County, as their candidate for governor, while a western slaveholder, Waitman T. Willey of Monongalia, stood for lieutenant governor. Letcher's signature on the Ruffner pamphlet from 1847 became the Opposition's key weapon against him. Even though he repudiated it just three years later, its legacy haunted him throughout the campaign. His supporters, according to his biographer, among the Democrats resisted having such a liability on the ticket. Letcher won their nomination, but the campaign proved to be a difficult one.

Northwestern Opposition papers attacked him over the Ruffner pamphlet. The party started its own journal, the *Clarksburg Weekly Campaign*, for this election. In April 1859, the newspaper said that they will "wager our heads that [he] will get the *antislavery* vote in Northern and Northwestern Virginia, bordering Pennsylvania and Ohio. Mark that, Eastern Virginians. We have no such feeling here, and it is nonsense, ridiculous nonsense, to try to conceal the fact of its hydra existence." Boney, Letcher's biographer, misinterpreted this statement to mean that the region was opposed to slavery. He probably believed, as many scholars still do, that the northwest was unreliable on the issue.[28]

The Democrat press retaliated against these attacks with vigor. Letcher did not visit the northwest during the election. One report from the Opposition *Wheeling Gazette* stated that he did not come due to a headache. Only a pair of Democratic papers from this time has survived, so a broader picture is not available. One was the *Parkersburg News*, which launched weak attacks on the Opposition. In May, it called them "obstinately consistent in bearing false witness against us." Their whole performance thus far consists of "a bare opposition, without even a difference of opinion, or an avowed theory of their own, as a pretext for the change." The *News* revealed, more than it realized, that the two parties were so closely aligned. This similarity in purpose led Letcher to jump in to save his party. To compensate for his absence and to motivate the faithful, he printed an open letter renouncing again the Ruffner pamphlet. He clearly intended it for his partisan audience. At the time, he claimed that he never regarded slavery as a moral evil. His status as a slaveholder "by purchase rather than inheritance" proved his sincerity. He continued by saying "such an opinion was held by a large number of the citizens of Virginia, on both sides of the Blue Ridge." In the last decade, the slavery question "has been much better understood, not only in Virginia, but throughout the South," where the question "has been discussed with an ability never before expended upon it." Having reconsidered his view, he "became entirely satisfied that not only that opinion, as to the social and political influences of the institution, was erroneous, but I acknowledged my error." Ruffner's pamphlet contained "many things so exceptional" that one man refused to help pay for its publication. The other newspaper, the *Kanawha Valley Star*, backed his view, saying that Mr. Letcher "is as safe a man as any Virginia statesman possibly can be."[29]

Letcher won the election, but the results indicated a cresting of Democratic support. The northwest gave him 16,744 (56.5 percent) votes to Goggin's 12,893 (43.5 percent). Compared to the 1856 presidential election, this represented a halving of the Democratic majority. In that ballot, they outpaced the Know Nothings by 6,488 votes. In 1859, the difference declined by 40 percent

58   /   Chapter 2

to 3,851. There was to be no such funeral in Charleston as had happened two years before. Even Ceredo, the only truly antislavery community in the northwest, voted for Goggin, the defender of southern rights. He received seventy votes to the twenty-nine given to Letcher. Historians agree that the Democrats won an empty victory. Charles Ambler went so far as to call it a defeat, but he erroneously said that "Democratic editors who spoke for the southern platform in western Virginia refused to concede that negro slavery had been an issue in the election and insisted that only southern rights and political theories in general had been involved." This is not true. The Democrats focused on slavery to the extent the limited evidence provides. They had to fight against the Ruffner pamphlet to keep the faithful in line and to withstand a strong proslavery onslaught by the Opposition. Henry Shanks was closer to the truth, arguing that the Ruffner pamphlet had a definite effect on the outcome. Wise's hostility to him lay behind the deterrence. Returns from congressional races in neighboring states indicate the rise of the Republicans in Ohio, Pennsylvania, and even Missouri. Indiana and Illinois balanced the two parties. The southern border states, on the other hand, rejected the Republicans in favor of an Opposition party in Kentucky and the Know Nothings in Maryland. Virginia itself elected twelve Democrats and one Opposition member to Congress, but he was not from the northwest. The region once again proved its reliability on slavery by choosing the same party as their state did.[30]

The first test of these views came just months later when John Brown and his followers raided the US arsenal at Harpers Ferry in Jefferson County. The abolitionist notorious for his actions in Kansas appears to have chosen the site more for containing weapons and its close proximity to sheltering mountains than for the area's alleged antislavery reputation. As Stephen Oates stated, the population in the neighboring four Virginia and two Maryland counties contained only five thousand enslaved males capable of bearing weapons. At most, he could "easily maintain himself in the Alleghenies" while his New England allies organized a political solution to slavery. Oates's numbers are correct, but Brown does not appear to have believed the area's whites would rally to them. Newspaper reports from northwestern papers are in fact scarce but point to a prompt and united response in favor of slavery and the Union. The *Intelligencer*, the first to report, urged calm on the day after the raid. With the telegraph carrying stories about a grudge against the railroad, government employees striking, and an attempted servile insurrection, panic would worsen things, it argued. Instead, the newspaper initially urged patience, stating that "time and its attending patient military and civil investigations are what are wanted, and until these are had and published, all speculation is but idle." At the bottom of this column, the editor issued an update indicating that an insurrection had in fact occurred. The next day, the *Intelligencer* had a firmer and more thorough opinion on the subject. Aiming for the middle ground, it condemned northern abolitionists and southern fire eaters with equal vigor. The North had to be taught a lesson in dealing with its fanatics, Campbell claimed, who attacked the Constitution and encouraged slave uprisings. A healthy revision will "teach the Northern people . . . to look upon their [abolitionist] principles in the proper light and will inspire in their minds more of a deep-seated hostility to their wicked and disorganizing ravings." The South, too, deserved a lecture. Sitting on top of four million slaves asked for trouble. "Our security," it wrote, "lies in advancing, not in retreating. We must look to the future of the two races. We must go back and read up the opinions of the fathers of the Republic as to the probable issue of slavery in this country." Recalling Jefferson's fear of another Haitian rebellion half a century earlier, the *Intelligencer* urged its readers to remember how "he dwelt so earnestly on his plan for a Central American colonization of the race. Something of this sort has got to be done." The *Intelligencer* responded to Harpers Ferry by defending slavery, but its critics saw in its pages what they feared the most: a chink in the armor of the slaveholding states.[31]

Democratic papers responded in the harshest terms. The *Kanawha Valley Star* expressed outrage and horror at the attack. "Never in the history of this government has anything occurred to equal the infamous plot attempted at Harpers Ferry. . . . An act of such outrage and infamy never was before perpetrated in this country!" A large meeting a month later in Charleston demanded a strong response to any abolitionist threat. Numerous militia groups formed there, primarily from the middling class of urban professionals whose livelihoods depended on the slave-labor-intensive salt companies, but they never left home. Wheeling sent its militia unit, the Virginia State Fencibles, to the scene, but they arrived after US Marines led by Colonel Robert E. Lee had suppressed the uprising. Although the Democratic *Daily Union* hailed the strong response of the city to the raid as proof of its being "uncontaminated by her Abolitionist neighbors," other Democrats took no notice of this. The *Parkersburg News* attacked the *Intelligencer*'s proslavery credentials, accusing it of allying with the Opposition *Richmond Whig* and of being soft on protecting slavery. Only the Democratic Party, the *News* stated, could "stand alone in its devotion to the Constitution and the Union, the only National party in existence. If this is established, if the Southern Opposition organization goes ever to the support of Abolition nominees, then the Democratic fold [is] the only place for National men in any quarter." Yet the *News* hoped that the *Whig* would back down. It opined that "it not only bear being classed as an ally of the

Wheeling Intelligencer or counted as the latest adherent to Black Republicanism in Virginia." Harpers Ferry further escalated the slavery debate in the northwest as across the rest of the state.[32]

Northwesterners, like all Americans, knew the importance of the 1860 presidential election. The one thing they feared most happened: the presence of a reportedly antislavery party in their midst. Ever since the Republicans started in 1854, the region's leaders of every party condemned them as abolitionists. A mere 273 northwesterners voted for them in the 1856 presidential election. The rededication of the *Intelligencer* and the *Wellsburg Herald* as Republican papers that summer shook the entire region. The party still, however, had shallow roots. In February 1860, the *Intelligencer* printed the proceedings of a Republican meeting in Hancock County. In truth, meetings and rallies had occurred in previous years, but no paper had until June 11 endorsed the party. On that day, the *Intelligencer* announced to the region, the state, and the country that it supported Abraham Lincoln of Illinois for president. The paper even sought to obtain the Republican National Convention for the city of Wheeling. In response to its critics, the paper defended its decision by printing articles by famous southerners on the negative effects of slavery. In April, it published an 1829 document titled "The Abolition of Slavery" that argued for the gradual elimination of the institution. Slavery, it predicted, impaired the white working man's ability to progress, impaired economic development, and hindered democracy by giving the master class a large degree of authority over whites and Blacks alike. Antagonized local Democrats viewed this as ill-disguised abolitionism and a sign of weakness on the northwest's part.[33]

The *Intelligencer* and the *Herald* provide the mistake that historians make about antebellum northwestern Virginia. The *Intelligencer* is the only surviving paper from this pivotal time. As a result, those researching the period, from Charles Henry Ambler to William A. Link, have relied on it too much as being representative of the entire area. This is wrong. When seen in the light of editorials and election returns from other parts of the northwest, it is clear that the *Intelligencer* represented a tiny and wildly unpopular minority party in a heavily proslavery and Democratic region, despite its self-proclamation to be the most widely read paper in western Virginia. This last part may still be true, but the election returns from 1860 demonstrate its dislike. Of the 36,615 votes cast, the Republicans received only 1,808 (4.9 percent) in the northwest. Almost all of those, 1,398 (77 percent), came from the four Panhandle counties (Hancock, Brooke, Ohio, and Marshall), which had a significant northern or foreign-born majority. The remaining 410 (0.1 percent) came from the rest of the region, mostly clinging to the Pennsylvania or Ohio borders. Their numbers, varying from 110 in Preston to one in Marion, were so small that they had no effect on the outcome. By comparison, neighboring Allegheny County, Maryland, had over 500 Republican votes, representing over 20 percent of that party's tally in that state. The Republicans did not win a single county in northwestern Virginia. Their best showing occurred when they placed second in Hancock County, atop the Northern Panhandle. They placed third in Ohio County, the *Intelligencer*'s home. The viva voce voting system made Republican voters, whoever they were, instantly unpopular among their neighbors. Overall, the 1860 election strongly resembled the governor's ballot the year before. The Democratic vote split into Breckinridge and Douglas wings, yet still prevailed. The former won 16,340 votes (44.6 percent), while the latter received 5,031 votes or 13.7 percent. Combined, they received 21,731 votes (58.4 percent). The Constitutional Union Party, the successor to the Opposition Party, received 13,436 votes (38.2 percent). Its candidate, John Bell of Tennessee, also won Virginia by a razor-thin margin of 322 votes (74,701 to Breckinridge's 74,379 votes). Despite that outcome, the region's whites showed their support for the status quo.[34]

The *Intelligencer* tried to rationalize why the Republicans failed in northwestern Virginia. Before the election, its editors offered two reasons why the region should vote for the party. Supporting Lincoln would "demonstrate the lack of sympathy between Virginia and the cotton States and dampen the ardor of these latter States in favor of disunion" and allow a different system" for the region that "will counteract and slaveholding oligarchy." The result irrefutably rejected both ideas. The notion that the region should side with the newly Republican states of Illinois, Indiana, and Pennsylvania, along with Ohio, had no place among white northwestern Virginians. The same spirit compelled Missouri to vote for Douglas, Delaware, and Maryland to support Breckinridge, and for Kentucky and the rest of Virginia to side with Bell. A better explanation comes from the narrow base of support. The party received almost all its votes in one area, the Northern Panhandle counties. This is consistent with the experiences of the other southern border areas where Republican support came from certain areas. The 1,346 Kentuckians who voted for Lincoln came from urban areas such as Louisville, as well as Campbell and Kenton counties south of Cincinnati. St. Louis and Baltimore centered the party's bases of support in Missouri and Maryland, while Delaware's northernmost pair of counties of New Castle and Kent received the bulk but still minority of Republican support. The rest of the border areas backed the conservative parties that defended slavery. If counted separately, the thirty-five counties placed in the middle of that area's voting patterns. They gave only 5 percent of their votes to Lincoln. Kentucky supported him less at 0.93 percent and but only 2.48 percent of Marylanders. Missourians sent but 10.2 percent of their ballots. Lincoln fared best in the smallest slave state, receiving 23.7 percent of Delaware's votes. He still placed third. On the other hand, more than half of Illinoisans, Indianans, Ohioans, and Pennsylvanians backed Lincoln. As in every election in the 1850s, northwestern Virginia stayed true to its state.[35]

In the 1850s, the region heeded Daniel Webster's advice long after he passed. Their political behavior in the pivotal decade discredits any notion of its impending separation from Virginia or affinity for its northern neighbors. In every election in the 1850s, white northwesterners supported parties that defended their state and the institution of slavery. Most of their votes went to one of them: the Democrats. The actions of their partisan press and their newly expanded voting base indicated considerable hostility to abolitionists and even to moderates. Their experiences fighting John S. Carlile, the Know Nothings, and Eli Thayer's Ceredo colony sharpened the blades with which the northwestern Democrats sought to cut out any dissent on slavery. Only the Kanawha Valley and its strong Whig tendencies deviated from this Democratic hegemony, yet even they showed the same vigor in defending slavery. All saved their harshest criticisms for the *Wheeling Daily Intelligencer*. Despite claiming to hold proslavery views, that newspaper never shook a reputation for weakness on the matter. Furthermore, the region's voters viewed its conversion to the Republican Party as an act of betrayal to the state of Virginia. Remarkably little secessionist opinion emerged in the region, at least in formal politics. The 1850s was not a time of calm for the region, as Ambler and Curry have claimed. Instead, northwestern Virginia spent that pivotal decade defending their home against several internal and external threats. Little wonder, then, that Virginia created Webster County in the northwest in 1860 to honor the man who urged them to stick together.

At the same time, a fatal flaw existed within these choices. Their rigid consistency in choosing proslavery parties led the region's whites to oppose any threat to the institution. Yet events after the 1860 election put those two elements against each other. The secession of the Lower South states in response to the Republican victory also tested the allegiances of the Upper South and border slave states. Disunionist opinion began to creep out even in the region, although various forms of Unionism grossly outweighed it. Secession proved to be the greatest threat to slavery seen so far. As the next chapter will show, northwestern Virginia faced a more severe test of its allegiances when events in 1861 forced them to choose between their state and slavery.

CHAPTER 3

Northwestern Virginia in the Secession Crisis, January–July 1861

On New Year's Day 1861, the white citizens of Parkersburg in Wood County met to discuss the now potent issue of secession. In the previous two weeks, South Carolina had declared itself independent of the United States in response to the election of Republican Abraham Lincoln in November. The six other Lower South states would shortly follow. Virginia, like the Upper South and border slaveholding states, debated their options. The Parkersburg meeting, headed by the county's notables such as judge John J. Jackson Jr. and state delegate Arthur I. Boreman, passed strong resolutions denouncing the idea. On the one hand, they condemned the non-slaveholding states for "violat[ing] the Constitutional rights of slaveholders" by failing to enforce fugitive slave laws. On the other, nothing could justify secession. The delegates "saw nothing in the election of Abraham Lincoln to the Presidency of the United States—as much as we may have desired the election of another—as affording any just or reasonable cause for the abandonment of . . . the best Government ever yet devised." These impassioned resolutions highlight the conservative attitudes of most white northwestern Virginians as they debated secession. Here, they acted not as an oppressed population itching for liberation as the Ambler-Curry thesis maintains. Instead, they responded like white citizens of a border slave state. Some may have desired disunion, others fervently rejected it, while most awaited developments. Virginia's secession, however, shattered any hopes for an orderly outcome. Within six months, the consequences proved worse than anyone could have predicted.[1]

This chapter deals with northwestern Virginia's experiences during the secession crisis of early 1861. Contrary to previous histories, statehood was not the inevitable outcome of the region's resistance to disunion. It was never a new idea. In past decades, the newspapers had printed snippets about people separating from Virginia, but the idea never amounted to more than an angry dream. In fact, when John S. Carlile suggested the idea at the First Wheeling Convention in May, many other delegates rejected it. They, like whites across the border states, preferred the safest, most conservative approach to resisting secession. The result of this phase was not statehood but instead the reorganization of the Virginia state government. This constituted not a halfway

63

stop toward statehood but a solid foundation on which Unionists could restore their government. They also shared with Missouri, Kentucky, Maryland, and Delaware the same reason for resisting secession. Many but not all whites in those states saw the federal Constitution as the best means to protect slavery. Yet President Lincoln and the US Army secured their allegiances to the Union by allowing them to restore self-government on their own terms and by protecting the institution of slavery. As this chapter shows, northwestern Virginia shared the same experiences except for lacking political independence. Each border state except Delaware experienced competing governments, battles large and small, vicious debates over secession rather than Union, and Blacks eager to achieve their freedom. Newspapers, convention minutes, and official documents make apparent the parallels between the northwest and the other border states. Still, the seed of West Virginia's quest for separate statehood had been implanted, if needing only careful nurturance. That would come later.

Secession shocked the Old Dominion's many regions. In general, most in the slave-rich Tidewater areas along the Atlantic Ocean backed the measure. The Piedmont and Shenandoah Valley districts preferred to wait and see what Lincoln would do, as did southwestern Virginia. The same was true for the northwest. In January 1861, the issue of leaving the Union now confronted the region's newspaper editors and voters alike. Already well rehearsed in defending their state against antislavery influences, white northwestern Virginians now had to handle a new threat: secessionists. The departure of the Lower South states moved some in the area in that direction. On January 12, a meeting in Wetzel County, a Northern Panhandle county as far removed from the Deep South or the Tidewater as one could get, blamed the "agitation of the slavery question" on "the denial by the North of the rights of the southern people in the territories of the U.S., the nullification of certain acts of Congress providing for the rendition of fugitive slaves, and the disposition of people of the Northern states to resist the execution of said law." At the same time, the rally still encouraged others to wait and see what Lincoln and the non-slaveholding states would do. The *Morgantown Star*, on the other hand, insisted that Virginia must first fix its internal issues. Its editor revived previously resolved inequities in the state constitution to resist "cowardly secession." He urged his readers to "exhaust every honorable means to procure equal laws and taxation for our section of the State within the State." If this was impossible, then "we shall not secede, but we shall demand a separation from Eastern Virginia."[2] Although disparate in their analyses of the issues of the day, few northwesterners advocated secession. Yet they also applied conditions to their Unionism.

The statewide debate on Virginia's future began in earnest on January 15.

Governor John Letcher heeded the legislature's call to convene a Constitutional Convention in early February. He ordered elections for delegates and a referendum on referring their decisions to the voters afterward. It was, his biographer stated, a compromise between the Unionist and secessionist camps to give each a chance to talk while delaying the decision for as long as possible.[3] In this, Virginia straddled the line between the other Upper South and border slaveholding states. Of the latter, only Missouri also called a convention to discuss disunion. Kentucky, Maryland, and Delaware rejected any such consultations. Among the Upper South states, white voters in North Carolina and Tennessee also disallowed official meetings. Arkansas approved one but elected a Unionist majority. In contrast, all seven of the Lower South states held conventions. Although negotiations occurred among the factions in each state, especially Georgia, their decisions supporting secession commanded big majorities. Louisiana's convention voted 82 percent to declare separation. The referendum in Texas, the only Lower South state to submit the issue to its voters, gave 77 percent in favor of departure.[4] Letcher's decision buoyed Virginia Unionist hopes against being forced into secession.

Debate in the northwest escalated in the wake of the announcement. The always controversial *Wheeling Daily Intelligencer* pitted the west against the east by, like the *Morgantown Star*, raising the remaining slave taxation issue from the 1850 constitution. If slaves were taxed at the same rate as other property, it argued, then "the State would raise just one clear million dollars in revenue than she now does, and the taxes on the poor whites who are the burthen for the State for the benefit of Eastern slave owners would be reduced from three quarters to one half." Moreover, the newspaper attacked the "suppositionous disunionists" by claiming that western Virginia had no common cause with the seceded states. "We are here on the banks of the Ohio, at the upper end of the Ohio valley, far north of the Southern boundaries of the State of Ohio, Indiana and Illinois, and they in the north, too, and they [are] free soil in their votes, too, because that is their interest. And not only this, but we are north of many of our Pennsylvania neighbors, and more than all we are north of Mason and Dixon's line, above which certainly no man can be Southern." While seemingly supportive of the Ambler-Curry "alienation" thesis commonly used to describe West Virginia's formation, those adherents have relied too much on the *Daily Intelligencer* as the main voice of the region. A critical review of other views of this event reveals how wrong it is.[5]

The conservative region dissented from the *Intelligencer*'s views. Many other papers and public meetings indicate a strong commitment to protecting Virginia and slavery. A meeting in Marion County reveals that some residents from there, Taylor, and Harrison counties blamed the non-slaveholding states. One resolution asserted that the "southern states have no reasonable grounds on which to base a hope that their rights will be respected, or that the Administration of Abraham Lincoln will be more conservative than the principles on which he was elected." Their ultimatum concluded that "when all constitutional efforts have been exhausted, it will be the duty and interest of Virginia to remain with the South." A meeting in Gilmer County echoed these views. Its attendees resolved that "a crisis has arrived in which it is neither safe nor honorable for our State and section to remain inactive spectators to the dangers by which they are surrounded." The Republican Party's course would, they believed, "end in the degradation and ruin of the [South]." Virginia must call a convention, while the North has "it in their power to reinstate the once friendly relations that existed between the two sections but just and reasonable that the initiative step for that purpose should be taken by the Northern states."[6] The *Kanawha Republican*, one of the region's most conservative papers, took a moderate stance. Its editor condemned secession as a "conspiracy against the Union [that] is now fully developed." After denouncing Senator James M. Mason as "a treasonable Disunionist," it stated to its friends that "the question now directly before them is Union or Disunion, their rights, peace, and prosperity in the Union, or civil war. It appears to us the prompt and patriotic action of the sovereign masses of the people, under God, can alone save the Union and the liberties of the Republic." Another letter from this same paper combined economic issues with the defense of slavery. The author, known as "A Tax Payer," wrote that joining the Confederacy violated the rights of free men. "Why sir," he asked, "there is not a negro sold, or hired on your streets, that is now allowed the privilege of choosing his master, and are we, at the insistence of a few hot heads, to be degraded below the level of a slave." It also meant higher taxes for all. Virginia now, he argued, cost every person $6.20 per year; the new regime would increase that amount to $9.00. "With such taxes as these, what is to become of us? With trade and commerce prostrated, every farm, horse, cow, pig, all the property of the citizens, would be brought to the auction block, to pay the taxes, and the whole would be swept away at one blow, and our whole people left completely bankrupt." He then appealed to everyone to vote for Unionist candidates and for reference to the people.[7] These expressions further contradict the notion of the northwest having more connections to Pennsylvania and Ohio. Instead, these white Virginians sided with their state and its institution of slavery against their enemies, for now anyway.

The convention election of February 4 reflected these diverse views. Voters in statewide elections picked their delegates to represent them in Richmond. As in 1829–1830 and 1850–1851, the northwest picked men whom they deemed to be reliable on slavery. Of thirty-two delegates, sixteen men (50 percent) owned a total of sixty-six slaves. Kanawha delegates owned the most. Spicer Patrick held the most with twenty-two, while his neighbor, George W. Summers, owned fourteen. James W. Hoge of neighboring Putnam County possessed six. Even those closer to the northern states had similar stakes in enslavement. William G. Brown of Preston County owned seven. Sherrard Clemens of Ohio County and Waitman T. Willey of Monongalia each held two slaves. John S. Carlile of Harrison owned one. Combined these slaveholding delegates had real estate wealth worth $10,400 and personal wealth amounting to $4,080. These amounts made them among the wealthier residents of the northwest. Yet they seem paltry when compared to their eastern counterparts in the convention. Four delegates, James C. Bruce of Halifax, William M. Ambler of Louisa, Wood Bouldin of Charlotte, and Jeremiah Morton of Greene County, each owned more slaves than all the northwestern delegates combined. Of the 135 conventioneers, 107 (80 percent) owned a total of 1,886 slaves, or an average of 14 each. The other delegates also possessed significantly more wealth than the northwestern men. Their median personal wealth was $14,000, and their personal wealth came to $15,346. Only in Virginia nativity did northwesterners (84 percent) slightly exceed the rest of the delegates (82 percent). As in the past, northwesterners also chose slaveowners to represent them in the convention. Although the northwest may have had less of a stake in the slave economy than most of Virginia, its nonetheless had one, and its white population chose to protect it.[8]

The diverse nature of the region's Unionism appears in the words of its convention delegates. As Daniel W. Crofts ably indicated, the anti-secession delegates divided into several camps, including fast ultimatumists who insisted on demanding Lincoln acquiesce to southern demands or else face secession; anti-coercionist or extended ultimatumists who sought compromises with the North until they became untenable; and unconditional Unionists who opposed secession at all costs. The northwesterners fell almost entirely into the latter camp.[9] Yet the record indicates that their representatives, far from being antislavery, expressed a strong devotion to the institution. They differed only in opposing secession as a threat to its integrity. On March 4, the day of Lincoln's inauguration in Washington, Waitman T. Willey of Monongalia made a forceful early argument that secession would ruin the state. The ability of masters to control their bondsmen and bondswomen concerned him most. If Virginia seceded, he asked, "what then?" The enslaved, he continued, would quickly discover that without the Constitution their "motives to flee across the line would be increased, because the Negro would know that whenever he crosses that line, he will be free. There will be no fugitive slave law for his recovery, and he will know it." Willey extolled the virtues of the federal government and asserted that Lincoln posed no danger to the South or to slavery. Secessionist demagoguery exaggerated the menace of personal liberty laws, which he said were rarely enforced. Indeed, far from showing how powerless Virginia was, Harpers Ferry demonstrated the state's strength. Willey then addressed the heart of the matter. "A dissolution of the Union will be the commencement of the abolition of slavery, first in Virginia, then in the Border States, and ultimately throughout the Union," he said. He followed by asking, "Will it not, sir, make a hostile border for Virginia, and enable slaves to escape more rapidly because more securely? Will it not, virtually, bring Canada to our doors?" Willey then appealed for state unity based on shared economic potential with slavery. Railroads, he argued, "are in a fair way of commanding a monopoly of the Southern trade and directing to the great natural outlet at Norfolk. There are in my own section of the State, North-western Virginia, mineral resources extensive enough to furnish the basis of an empire's greatness." He concluded by stating simply, "Let Virginia secede, and all these bright prospects are forever dashed to pieces." These are the words of a state patriot, not someone itching to from a new one.[10]

One northwesterner defended slavery more explicitly than Willey. John S. Carlile saw his home region as Virginian as any other part of the Commonwealth. On March 7, he called his constituents "a brave, and a gallant, and a law-abiding people." Moreover, he continued, they supported their state and slavery despite its limited presence in the region. "A more loyal people to the soil of their birth is nowhere to be found," he said, "a people devoted to the institution of slavery, not because of their pecuniary interest in it, but because it is an institution of the State, and they have been educated to believe in the sentiment . . . which I cordially endorse, that African slavery, as it is exists in the Southern states, is essential to American liberty." Like Willey, Carlile insisted that betraying the federal government meant disaster for the institution of slavery. As proof, he pointed to his personal status as a slaveholder, that occurred "not by inheritance, but by purchase." He also shared with Willey the view that secession invited abolition and economic ruin. The "extended frontier, with our defenseless seacoast, tell me the amount of money that would be required so to fortify the State, in the event of a revolution, as to afford the slightest protection not only to our slave property, but against those John Brown forays upon a larger scale?" He and Willey may have tailored their speeches to the convention, but this does not lessen their meaning. Each had a decade of experience successfully defending slavery and the South under their belts.[11]

George W. Summers of Kanawha took a more restrained view. After returning to his law practice following the 1851 governor's election, he reentered politics with force. He argued that Virginia had different issues at stake than the Deep South did. The status of western lands had little importance for the Old Dominion, he said on March 12. "What interest, compared to ours, has the Cotton states in the territorial question? Is there a man from South Carolina, Georgia, Louisiana, Mississippi or Alabama, who would leave the fertile fields of the South, to migrate with his negroes into Arizona or New Mexico?" he stated. Secession meant "the entire abandonment of all connection with and control over" the territorial question." The northwest had to protect the more than four hundred miles of border with free states. Summers declared that secession placed the entire state at risk. "We are to protect slave property in States south of us, but to lose our own. So far from secession rendering the institution of slavery more secure in Virginia, it will be the potent cause of insecurity," he implored the delegates.[12] Like Willey and Carlile, he concluded that secession meant ruin for slavery, their state, and the whole country.

Secessionists surprisingly accepted the northwest's stance on slavery if not its Unionism. On March 16, James Holcombe of Albemarle County demanded immediate departure to protect slavery from a Union poisoned by northern fanaticism. He urged the west and the northwest to consider their positions carefully. They would not be threatened by slave insurrections, but "the destruction of slave property would only affect you by the re-action of our ruin." Holcombe implored the "gentlemen of the West, to let us march, keeping together, through all the future, as our fathers have done in the past."[13] George Wythe Randolph of Richmond also saw the west as an asset. A grandson of Thomas Jefferson, he agreed that western Virginia had to be saved from the abolitionized North. Criticizing statements by Carlile and Willey, he lamented despite the region's mineral wealth "the population [is] restricted in the main to agriculture and to . . . agriculture not very productive" because "their labor is exposed to overwhelming competition of the North." Bringing them into the Confederacy would, he argued, allow them to "receive protection from northern industry, and they will be what they ought to be—the manufacturers and miners of a great nation." Though earlier critical of northwestern delegates, Randolph lectured to the convention that for all its faults, at least the region supported slavery. "Let not Western Virginia suppose that she has no interest in the slavery question, because she owns but few slaves. She has a vast interest in our system of labor," he said. Such views boosted northwesterners' morale by showing that they found allies in the opposing camp.[14]

These positive responses encouraged northwestern hopes to resolve a secondary issue on their minds. Heeding local advice, they sought to remove the ad valorem tax privileges on slave property in the 1851 constitution. Resolving this last remaining disparity may appear to sustain the Ambler-Curry thesis, but it is fairer to argue that northwesterners used it to delay secession. It almost worked. William G. Brown of Preston County, himself the enslaver of seven persons, first mentioned the issue on March 7. He said that redressing the tax issue was necessary to pay for the forthcoming war if Virginia left the Union. While he opposed war and secession, he declared that if "war must come, every dollar's worth I have shall be subject to taxation . . . to arm and clothe the true and brave men that we may send to the field." Surely, he believed, the east would wish the same for those defending their lives and property. Several days later, Waitman Willey cited his ownership of two slaves to move for a committee to investigate this matter. He asked the convention, "Why is it that because I am a slaveholder, I shall be exempt from the burdens of the Commonwealth, and my neighbor, equally worthy with me, though not a slaveholder, is to bear the burdens which I ought to bear?"[15] His motion failed, but it would reemerge later. He and his regional associates hoped that resolving the tax issue would unite Virginians in defense of the Union. It was ambitious but far from unrealistic.

Many eastern planters in the convention resisted any change at all. Equalizing the tax burden would, Miers Fisher of Northampton County said on March 18, weaken the state by continuing "to allow the stamp of inferiority for ever to be put upon us." Thomas Branch of Petersburg City called the idea poorly timed. He said that the "time [has] not yet arrived to agitate this question, but when the Convention shall have determined that the State shall leave the Union, then there should be a reorganization of the organic law upon the basis above stated." This stubbornness placed northwestern delegates on the defensive. William G. Brown maintained his home region's reliability on slavery, saying that their "peculiar property and every kind of property is much safer in the care and keeping of that people that have been denounced as Abolitionists here, than in the care and keeping of the mixed crowd that you see on your streets here shouting in a disorderly manner and at unusual hours." It is not clear whom he meant by the last statement, but it may have been an attempt to contrast the rowdiness of Richmond to the quiet stability of the northwest. If so, it was a questionable comparison. Benjamin Wilson of Harrison County similarly appealed for unity. He declared that "if we are to fight the battles of that interest, we contend that they should be subjected to the same rule of taxation as other property. We have no bargain to make, no measure to propose, but such as we believe will best promote the interest of Virginia." The eastern delegates must have rolled their eyes at these statements. A deadlock ensued.[16]

In the coming days, northwestern assertions of their reliability on slavery failed to resolve the matter. Between March 28 and April 2, Willey tried to break the impasse with a compromise. Beforehand, he discussed the timing of the whole affair by countering claims by Allen T. Caperton of Monroe that the taxation issue was calculated to increase dissensions with "a peace measure." He then turned the debate into one between non-slaveholding and slaveholding populations in the state, but with a twist. It was unfair, he said, for white working men and farmers to face full taxation while slaveholders did not, regardless of section. He demanded to know "whether the 43,000 non-slaveholding tax-payers in Eastern Virginia have not a right to be heard upon this floor as much as the non-slaveholding taxpayers West of the Blue Ridge?" He concluded by arguing that failing to address western concerns placed its wealth in the hands of others. Cutting the west's access to eastern ports exposed it to "Black Republican power by the diversion of capital from our state, concentrating it in the North, increasing Northern population and power, and increasing the ratio of representation against us, decade after decade," he argued, "while we stand here with this immense property untaxed, which if taxed, would be sufficient to obviate all these evils." Such sentiments intended to bridge the gap between the two sections, but failed.[17] By then secessionists and even some Unionists had grown wary of these attempts to win tax reform. Northwestern newspapers approved of the matter. The *Fairmont True Virginian* supported the proposed taxation changes. It opined that raising taxes now "is not to be entertained for a moment without feelings of indignation. Already as high as any people ought to bear, our taxes cannot be increased without subjecting us to great oppression." Only secession, it concluded, provided relief. The *Wheeling Daily Intelligencer* typically scoffed at the idea. It supported the first part of its idea about adjusting the taxes but called the secession part "a plan [which] ought to be patented, otherwise, it is possible Barnum may get hold of it, and exhibit it as a great curiosity alongside of the 'What is it?' " it reported. Given that the *True Virginian* represented the Democratic majority in the northwest, more people possibly adhered to its view than that of the controversial Republican *Intelligencer*. As much as they wanted to resolve the tax issue, even merging it with the defense of slavery, eastern Virginians saw it as a distraction.[18]

72 / Chapter 3

Fortunately for the Unionists, their diverse coalition withstood an important vote on secession. Together, they defeated a secession motion by a vote of eighty-eight to forty-five on April 4. Only three northwestern delegates, Leonard Hall of Wetzel, Franklin Turner of Jackson, and Samuel Woods of Barbour, supported it. This success gave Willey another chance to resolve the taxation issue. He moved again for a committee amid intense opposition. On April 10, Henry Wise, the former governor whose compromises made possible the state's 1851 constitution, retorted the northwesterners. He agreed with Caperton that it "was unjust to the people of Virginia, either East or West, to seize upon a moment like this . . . to divide us upon our own internal questions." Moreover, he continued, he wanted to see western resolve on slavery before he answered their concerns. "There are some men," he said, "from the East and from the West both, that I cannot rely upon any more to defend my rights upon the negro question; and I especially intend, before giving to these gentlemen additional power to tax slave property, to be well satisfied that they are willing to unite with me to defend the rights of slave property." Cyrus Hall of Pleasants and Ritchie counties also defended his region against Wise's attack. "Instead of keeping our people sound upon the slave interest of Virginia," he said, "you gentlemen of the East, will give the right of way for the extension of the underground railroad over Virginia soil. Instead of keeping the terminus of this Abolition improvement on the Western bank of the Ohio River, in a short time you will find its terminus in the valley of Virginia." He concluded, "If . . . we are going to have a fight with the North about this slave property of yours . . . I want that property to support us while we fight." William C. Wickham of Henrico County near Richmond, like Wise, denied that the east threatened western rights. Citing tax figures, he calculated that the proposal would triple the amount owned on slave property. In 1859, he said, the tax on slaves amounted to $326,487.60. The proposed increase would, if the average value of slaves was $500 apiece (a gross underestimate), rise to $1,000,000. He retorted to Hall that "the imposition of this tax on young negroes would be a more dangerous blow to the institution of slavery in the State of Virginia than any single act that could be done by the government." Still, the weight of the Unionist coalition, built by northwestern appeals to their reliability on slavery, approved Willey's motion by a large margin of sixty-three to twenty-six votes on the next day. This commanding majority appeared pledged to close the sole source of inequality of among Virginians. There was one problem. The date was April 11, 1861. On that night, South Carolinian secessionists rolled batteries of cannons into position along the Charleston waterfront. Had the convention resolved the tax issue, then northwestern Virginia could have taken different course. A unified state could have become a border state instead of just a portion of it. If the Ambler-Curry thesis were correct, every author on this topic would have cited this date as the decisive moment. None have.[19]

Events on the following day changed the course of American and Virginian history. The Palmetto State's cannonades upon Fort Sumter on the morning of April 12 began the Upper South's movement toward secession. When news arrived in Richmond later that day, few delegates sought to discuss piddling issues like taxation. Only allegiance to Virginia concerned them. The handful of remaining unconditional Unionists continued to fight. They first won a motion to send commissioners to determine Lincoln's actions. The meeting did not go well. The president refused to abandon federal forts and left open the possibility of military action to reclaim them. While they traveled to Washington for the meeting, Jubal Early of Franklin County told the convention that Virginia must remain loyal but vigilant. "This act," he said, "has done nothing to advance the cause of the Confederate States. In Virginia, the mass of the people will never be found sanctioning their cause." He, in an ironic statement given his later actions during the Civil War, continued that they must guard against allowing Confederate troops from marching across Virginia to attack Washington. His words sparked a confrontation with Thomas F. Goode of Mecklenburg County. A secessionist, Goode said that though the convention had been divided on the issue, the "great popular heart of Virginia is now throbbing with sympathy and unison with those gallant men who, upon Carolina's soil, are battling unto death for the common rights of the South." He singled out northwestern Virginians as potential traitors. Eastern Virginians "will neither be held in this government under a Republican administration by the powers at Washington, nor by the powers that, perchance, may lie West of the Allegheny mountains," he said. This indicated how lowly and how quickly the northwest had sunk in the eyes of other Virginians. Two days later, Lincoln fulfilled the convention's worst fears and called for seventy-five thousand troops from the loyal states to put down the rebellion. Only two slaveholding states—Delaware and Virginia—heeded the call, but the latter's contribution needs elaboration. The First Virginia Volunteer Infantry Regiment came from the Northern Panhandle counties without authorization from its state government, unlike the First Delaware. The convention shrugged off last-minute appeals by Unionists to vote on secession. The delegate who forwarded the motion was none other than William Ballard Preston, whose call for immediate and uncompensated emancipation after Nat Turner's rebellion in 1831 drew near-unanimous northwestern support at the time. A more extraordinary irony could scarcely be imagined.[20]

74 / Chapter 3

The northwestern delegation's response to Virginia's secession needs clarification. The final tally came to eighty-eight for approving the ordinance to fifty-five against it. Most of the dissenters represented the northwest, which I have defined as the thirty-five core counties. Of its thirty-two delegates, six voted for the measure, twenty-five against, and one—Benjamin Wilson of Harrison County—did not vote. Surprisingly, only one northwestern slaveholder of sixteen, Henry L. Gillespie of Fayette and Raleigh counties, supported the measure. Only two owners, Alpheus Haymond of Marion and George Berlin of Upshur, later changed their votes. More recent research by the Library of Virginia adds more information about this issue. If all fifty counties of the new state are included, the vote changes but not enough to alter the overall result. The number of supporters for secession increased from six to thirteen, opponents from twenty-five to thirty-two, and absentees from one to four. The Convention, moreover, expelled many northwestern members such as Carlile and Willey for abandoning the meeting in June. None ever returned. New men replaced them starting in November. One was William P. Cooper, the editor of *Cooper's Clarksburg Review*, who fled his home to represent Harrison County in Richmond. Almost all of them switched toward ratifying the secession ordinance. By then, of course, the northwest had embarked on its quest for independence. While the voters had yet to approve of the matter four weeks later, Virginia's shift in favor of secession put the northwesterners on edge.[21]

Feeling defeated, the region's dissenting delegates met in Sherrard Clemens's room at the Powhatan Hotel to discuss their course of action. Carlile was not among them, having returned home on April 19. None wanted to stop fighting against secession. For the past ten years, they had defended their state and the institution of slavery against its foes. In the convention, their appeals to protecting the practice came within inches of mending the state's divisions. If eastern Virginia had acquiesced then, a possibility if given enough time, then the northwest would have followed their state much as Georgians did following their Constitutional Convention in January.[22] Conversely, a united Virginia could have remained in the Union serving as the Kentucky of the east. However, the attack on Fort Sumter, Lincoln's call for troops, and the convention's support for secession dashed any such hopes. In 1900, James C. McGrew of Preston County wrote the only account of the meeting by a participant. He reported that the attendees agreed to return home immediately and "call public meetings, put on foot measures to resist secession, and ultimately bring about, if possible, what had been long talked about and desired—a division of the state." Since McGrew wrote four decades later, the report bears the mark of hindsight, particularly the last part. I can only infer from their later actions what they discussed. My best conclusion is that none would support secession, but neither could some bear to serve a federal government headed by Republicans. Clemens and Summers removed themselves from politics entirely after the meeting. Most went home to fight against ratification on May 23. As the delegates returned home, they faced a situation common to the border states. While the Upper South states left the Union, the quartet rejected secession, although their populations disputed the decision. Delaware's legislature voted to remain in the Union in January. Maryland saw in a single week its citizens attack Union soldiers transiting Baltimore, its legislature move from its capitol at Annapolis to Frederick over the issue, and an occupation by federal troops on its soil. Kentucky adopted neutrality from both sides. Missouri initially sought the same, but local Union militias seized power from Confederate sympathizers in St. Louis. Its governor and assembly fled its capital at Jefferson City. A Unionist convention in July formed a new government that kept the state in the Union. William Harris has pointed out that this formed the precedent for Lincoln to follow for Virginia's loyalists. This is difficult to sustain since the chaotic situations among the border states required him to improvise his responses. Which approach influenced another becomes hard to determine conclusively. Despite not yet being a state, northwestern Virginia fits nicely into this pattern.[23]

Resisting secession in the border states meant aligning the region with the hated Republican Party. As the Parkersburg meeting resolved in January, northwestern Virginians expressed great reservations about this northern-based party dedicated to restricting slavery to the western territories. At first, however, they need not have worried about what Lincoln would do about their situation. He was rather busy in April and May 1861. The looming rebellions of Tennessee, Arkansas, North Carolina, and the rest of Virginia, combined with mobilization in the North, occupied his time. Nowhere does northwestern Virginia appear on Lincoln's schedule for the entire month of April. Still, the mere accusation of cooperating with the new regime carried weight. Dallas Shaffer's study of the president and West Virginia and William Harris's study of his handling of southern Unionists both mention a meeting between Carlile and Lincoln that week, but their evidence fails them. Shaffer's citation of McGrew's narrative says nothing about any encounter. None of the pages in the Convention proceedings used by Harris refer to any such event. If anything, neither Carlile individually nor the group of northwestern Virginia Unionists even entered Washington at all on their return journey home except to change trains. Only one source from the period ever mentioned collaboration between northwestern Unionists and Lincoln, and it is unreliable. On May

1, Tom Surghnor, the now-secessionist editor of the *Barbour Jeffersonian*, citing "an unquestionable source," claimed that Carlile collaborated with Lincoln's cabinet after fleeing Richmond one step ahead of a treason charge. "We learn," he reported,

> that Carlile is in correspondence with Lincoln's Cabinet, and that he now has in his possession a letter from Cameron, Secretary of War, and a member of Lincoln's Cabinet, offering to send Black Republican troops into Northwestern Virginia for the purpose of subjugating the people, and separating this section of the State from the East. This information can be implicitly relied on, as it came from one of Carlile's supporters, who said that he saw the letter from the Secretary of War. The individual referred to here is truthful and reliable, and would not, under any circumstances, state what was not true.

On the contrary, none of this was true. Surghnor had clear partisan reasons to lie about Carlile's activities during this time. While the former Know Nothing congressman made few friends for his antics in the 1850s, he was no Republican. It is unlikely that he would have met the president without his fellow delegates if they did so at all. The first time Lincoln's government received insider information about the status of northwestern Virginia came from an April 25 letter from George W. Caldwell, the head of the area's Republicans. He outlined the plan for a meeting to organize local Unionists and asked what aid the federal government could provide. He asked Lincoln to "confer a favor upon thousands by favorably noticing it and responding even by a single line." A week later, John G. Nicolay, Lincoln's secretary, responded for the distracted president by that format. He asked for Caldwell to report back the proceedings of this meeting so that he could "receive and consult with such gentlemen as the Government may send to represent its views about the matter."[24] This inadequate line constitutes the only interest that Lincoln took about northwestern Virginia's situation in the wake of their state's secession. It was just as well given their ambivalence toward him. Still, as a good Republican, Caldwell likely fulfilled the request.

The region's Unionists scarcely needed encouragement from the president. Anti-secession agitation began within days of the convention's decision, to the point where Wheeling's mayor and chief of police issued a proclamation to calm the city's population.[25] Carlile fired his own first shot on April 22 in Clarksburg. More than a thousand people turned out on short notice. At his urging, the gathering discussed and approved of a resolution on how to respond to the secessionists. The governor and his officials, he proclaimed, already had violated the obligation made in February to await the voters' decision on May 23. Moreover, their actions left the northwest open to coercion. Exposed on the border with the northern states, Letcher's actions precluded "all hope of timely succor in the hour of danger from other portions of the State and demands that we should look to and provide for our own safety in the fearful emergency in which we now find ourselves placed by the action of our State authorities." At the same time, Carlile listed the many actions in which Letcher protected the eastern part of the state from federal intrusion while abandoning the west. Blocking port at Hampton Roads, seizing the federal customs houses and arsenals at Norfolk, Richmond, and Harpers Ferry, and insulting the flag meant that the secessionists "inaugurated a war without consulting those in whose name they profess to act." Thus, feeling their wishes betrayed at a time of extreme emergency, the meeting then moved to recommend "to the people in each and all of the countries comprising Northwestern Virginia to appoint delegates, not less than five in number, of their wisest, best, and discreetest men" to gather in Wheeling three weeks later "to consult and determine upon such action as the people of Northwestern Virginia should take in the present fearful emergency." A week later, he attended another rally in Fairmont. Its points indicate the more conservative type of Unionism in the area. The resolutions included maintaining allegiance to the federal government until released by Virginia in the forthcoming ballot and denouncing any "movement to tending to the division of our old commonwealth." Note how he did not call for separate statehood. Instead, he, like other border state Unionists, called for the maintenance of law and order.[26]

Secessionists used much stronger language in their activities. Even before Carlile's meeting, Guyandotte held a meeting supporting the convention's actions. After unfurling a Virginia flag on the banks of the Ohio River, its attendees resolved that secession was "the surest, if not the only remedy for the troubles which now environ and disturb her social and political systems." Days later, former governor Joseph Johnson countered Carlile with his own rally of the "Southern Rights Men of Harrison County." "War is upon us," bellowed the resolutions made by a meeting of a mere sixty men. "FREEMEN OF HARRISON! Will you stand by and permit this war to be waged without any interference or remonstrance? You are bound to assume a position," they asked. With the Union permanently dissolved, Johnson argued that there was no point in resisting. Doing so would "make such a start that others may be induced to follow, or at least wipe out the strain and stigma of being looked upon as coercionists and the minions of the bloody crew who are preparing to destroy our homes, and worse than all, the liberties of the Commonwealth."[27] On the same day, the Richmond convention approved the now departed Willey's changes to the ad valorem taxation plan. Before April 17, secessionist delegates opposed even mentioning this idea either for its potential for economic ruin or for its poor timing. Yet, just nine days later, the same men voted sixty-six to twenty-six to make these changes. Benjamin Wilson of Harrison, who abstained from voting on the secession ordinance, congratulated Morton and the others for their decision. Clarksburg, he added, was in turmoil. Citing the local paper, he said that Carlile's meeting sought to "throw off allegiance to Virginia. That proceeding was based upon the passage of the ordinance of secession and a refusal to pass the ordinance in relation to the tax question." He may have been mistaken, as the resolutions do not mention any such issue. Nonetheless, he went on about how Unionists had threatened secessionists and women having to arm themselves in response. "I hope, therefore," he said, "that the East will concede this act of justice and defeat the purposes of those who are seeking to make this question the basis of discord and division in the North-west."[28] Simultaneously, secessionists tried to mend the last barrier to full equality between Virginia's regions, while reminding northwesterners of their duties to their home state. They failed. Treason outweighed the tax issue.

Northwestern secessionists still faced considerable opposition. Governor Letcher received numerous letters that indicate the feelings of his loyalists after convention decided on the matter. The news was not always good. On April 18, C. D. Moss informed the governor that a Wheeling militia company had "offered their services to 'Old Abe' to aid in subjugating the Southern States." Amid the tumult of two local meetings, William P. Cooper, the former editor of *Cooper's Clarksburg Register*, asked Letcher for permission to raise troops. Such a company, he reassured the governor, would consist "of our mountaineers, who I believe, will be as good men for actual service as the world can provide." He did not say how he would accomplish this goal in such a divided town. He would soon flee to Richmond to serve in the Constitutional Convention. Jonathan Rundle told the readers of the *Kanawha Valley Star* on April 22 to prepare for war. "Now that the government exists no longer . . . it will be our duty, as well as our pleasure, to advance the interests of Virginia and the South alone." He flooded readers with false claims that Lincoln and the northern fanatics intended to incite a racial war. "Federal soldiers are flooding into Washington city by thousands; negroes are in the ranks with white men," he wrote, and with "civil war is commenced . . . it behooves every man who loves his species now calmly to consider how it can be stopped."[29] Such words, as I showed elsewhere, had a limited effect on the bulk of that county's white population. Other correspondents provided even more pessimistic assessments. On April

29, D. S. Morris, editor of the secessionist *Virginia Patriot* of Taylor County, remarked at how he had "lost, in consequence, of this change in my paper, several hundred of his subscribers" in several counties. On the same day, James M. H. Beale of Mason County, the Know Nothing candidate for lieutenant governor in 1855, pleaded for "a supply of arms. Give us arms. Give us arms."[30] Letcher had none to give. Instead, he further aggravated the situation by unilaterally allying Virginia with the Confederate government ahead of the referendum.[31]

Tensions escalated as the May 23 plebiscite approached. Newspapers waged wars of words on what the northwest would do. The *Intelligencer* made many provocative attacks. In a long, rambling column, it listed the west's alleged sufferings, little of which was true. "From time immemorial Western Virginia has been but the serf of the East, subjected to unjust taxation of unequal representation, caused which alone have heretofore been considered sufficient to justify separation in more instances than one," it wrote. Calling the convention "the culmination of the catastrophe everything that could be conceived," the *Intelligencer* asserted the violence inherent among the secessionists. The secrecy of their actions against the Union allowed Virginia to be taken over by Jefferson Davis. "Men of the Northwest, this is where Virginia stands today—this is how you stand—this has been your treatment, these indignities you have suffered," the paper called on its loyal readers. The *Kanawha Valley Star* responded with a brief and unsubtle message that reflected its support for secession. "Should the abolitionists of Ohio send an invading army into Western Virginia, not a soldier among them will ever return alive. The mountain boys would shoot them down like dogs," it declared. Still more men joined local guard units. The Kanawha Riflemen gathered men largely from slaveholding families from Charleston. Two more units, the Charleston Sharpshooters and the Coal River Rifles, joined them. Wheeling had both its Union Guard and a pro-secession militia, the Shriver Greys. In mid-May, local hostility drove the latter to leave Ohio County on the "last steamboat not required to undergo military inspection" according to its historian. After arriving in Parkersburg, they marched nearly three hundred miles to Charleston, and finally to Lewisburg in Greenbrier County in June. On May 10, the city saw the gathering of the First Virginia Volunteer Infantry Regiment, a three-month regiment formed in response to Lincoln's call for troops three weeks before.

Secessionists frequently complained to Letcher about their vulnerability from both outside and inside the region. On May 25, a letter writer from Nicholas County warned Letcher that western Virginia's "unprotected condition" required the governor to "have some troops along the Ohio River to keep [federal troops] out." On the same day, William D. Moore of Fayette County likewise warned Letcher that so many militias meant that he thought "it entirely unnecessary to enlist so many soldiers" but feared how many "openly avow hostile sentiments to our interests, and some few have acknowledged themselves ready to aid the armies of Lincoln."[32] The secessionist cause in the northwest operated at great disadvantages in the region. Separated from the east, which had problems of its own, and menaced by local Unionists, they had little chance of success of keeping the area under Richmond's rule.

The Wheeling Conventions offered Unionists an opportunity by which to prevail over the secessionists. The group that met from May 13 to 15 in Wheeling's federal customs house (now Independence Hall, as seen in figure 3), however, frustrated Carlile's idea for five delegates from each county. Their method of election was either poor or lacking. The 436 members represented only twenty-five northwestern counties. Five counties, Hancock, Marshall, Ohio, Monongalia, and Wood, contributed more than half of all delegates. Few came from the Kanawha Valley, and then by personal choice. More seriously, only nine of the northwestern delegates who served in the Richmond convention attended. Their collective backgrounds reflected its haphazard organization. Its members differed from the northwest's earlier leadership. Of the 436 attendees to the May convention, the 1860 census contained information on 296 men. Compared to those who attended the Richmond convention, those in Wheeling had a much lower median real estate wealth of $3,000 and a median personal wealth of $1,000. Only twenty-three members, a mere 7 percent, owned a combined fifty-six slaves. Of that number, only four had served in the Richmond Convention: Carlile, Willey, John J. Jackson Jr. of Wood County, and John S. Burdett of Taylor County. Waldo P. Goff of Harrison owned the largest number with seven slaves. Only 55 percent of the delegates were born in Virginia, as opposed to nearly all among the Richmond delegates. The bordering states of Pennsylvania (21 percent), Ohio (7 percent), and Maryland (4 percent) provided much of the rest. Foreign births, mostly Irish and German, accounted for 6 percent. The large representation from the Northern Panhandle counties accounts for this change. Landowning farmers made up the largest group at 34 percent, followed by merchants (12 percent), lawyers and attorneys (6 percent, including the hitherto little-known Francis H. Pierpont of Marion County), and landless farmers (5 percent). The remainder included artisans such as bricklayers, carpenters, and mill and factory workers, along with other professionals like lumber merchants and county court clerks. By comparison, my recent comparative study of military enlistments makes the First Wheeling Convention delegates out of step with the rest of the region. Northwesterners who joined the Confederate Army starting in mid-1861 tended to come from

Fig. 3. West Virginia Independence Hall, Wheeling, ca. 2010 (Library of Congress). In this building, white northwestern Virginia Unionists met to resist secession and to make their state both separate and free.

Virginia families with strong ties to slavery. Although the convention attracted men of substance whom the masses and Washington could respect and who not threaten slavery, it nonetheless appeared as more of a popular gathering than a legitimate legal body. It was better than nothing.[33]

Whatever its shortcomings, the convention provided the badly needed forum for discussing resistance to secession. They started off with well-intentioned but weak ideas about denouncing Virginia's pretended declarations. Willey concluded the first day's debate by agreeing with Carlile "that the time for compromises and talk had passed; that now nothing but decisive and prompt action could avert the impending dangers. This was the time to strike, and he knew a response to that declaration would come up from the entire valley of the Ohio to the Alleghenies." On the next day, James Wheat offered several well-considered but weak resolutions on negating the secession ordinance. One of them urged the voters to "vindicate their rights as Virginia freemen by voting against said ordinance of secession and all other measures of like character." Carlile went one step further that few had considered until now. On May 14, he moved that the convention authorize a new state out of the Tenth and Eleventh Congressional districts and Wayne County (whose location on the Kentucky border would cover the region's entire border on the Ohio River). In a bold statement, he resolved that the connection between these areas and the rest of the state "is hereby dissolved, and that the people of the said counties are in the full possession and exercise of all the rights of sovereignty which belong and appertain to a free and independent State in the United States, and subject to the Constitution thereof; and that the said committee be instructed to report a constitution and form of government for said State, to be called the State of New Virginia." Some cheered Carlile at the time, but his action shocked the convention. Previous hints about separation rarely moved past the editorial page, but Carlile brought it out into the open. This act was not as radical as it seems. In his view, removing the region from Virginia was a conservative move intended to restore law and order, not thwart it. It also preserved the status quo with regard to slavery. He said as much to the convention, asking them, "Can there be anything revolutionary in availing ourselves of the constitutional means provided in the organic law of the land, for the very purpose of protecting our interests?" Unless northwesterners acted by May 23, they "will have been transferred to the Southern Confederacy, and the Constitution of the United States . . . will no longer shield and support us." Some praised the act, but others criticized him. Willey, who like Carlile used slavery to unite Virginia in Richmond, uttered the strongest dissent. Separation constituted "treason against the State Government, the Government of the United States and against the Government of the C. S. A.," and he refused to support such an "insurrectionary or unconstitutional means of accomplishing an object which he thought could be accomplished according to law." Many criticized Willey for comparing their actions to rebellion. His words cooled but failed to cease the ardor sparked by Carlile's idea.[34]

The notion of separate statehood proved popular enough to pass the convention, albeit in a weakened format. On May 15, after much deliberation and compromise, the attendees concluded the convention by approving the "Report on State and Federal Relations" that combined Wheat's and Carlile's resolutions. Its fourteen resolutions included rejecting Virginia's secession ordinance, denouncing the links forged by Richmond and the Confederate government in late April, and encouraging voters to reject secession on May 23. Another resolution called for a second meeting to be held starting in June. The last ordered the formation of a central committee to draft a declaration to the region's population. The delegates then watered down Carlile's separation idea by declaring that they had the authority to "rightfully and successfully appeal to the proper authorities of Virginia, to permit us peacefully and lawfully to separate from the residue of the State and form ourselves into a government to give effect to the wishes, views and interests of our constituents." The desire for a peaceful and lawful separation was a fantasy, as Virginia had no intention of surrendering any of its territory, even if one region's white residents requested it. Still, Carlile's idea managed to make it into the public realm. The convention cheered its passage with only two audible dissents. One of them may have been Judge John Jay Jackson Jr., who, according to the minutes, said he wanted to go home to plant his corn. The document mentioned only appeals to law and order as reasons to resist secession. Nowhere does it cite inherent differences between the northwest and the rest of Virginia. This is perhaps understandable given the idea of a separate state had only started.[35]

On the other hand, the region's statements closely resemble those made in other border states made at this time. They all emphasized those states seeking to restore order amid the chaos of secession. On April 19, Governor Thomas Hicks of Maryland responded to the riots in Baltimore with a proclamation: it "is the imperative duty of every true son of Maryland to do all that he can to arrest the threatened evil." He called upon people to "abstain from all heated controversy upon the subject" and that it was his "intention . . . to preserve the people of Maryland from civil war." Likewise, on the next day, prominent Kentuckian James Guthrie headed a meeting in Louisville that explicitly linked the protection of slavery to his state's decision to remain neutral. While they recognized "her natural sympathies" lay with "those who have a common interest in the protection of Slavery," Kentucky "still acknowledges her loyalty and fealty to the United States." The resolutions rejected Lincoln's call for troops as well as those for the Confederacy and denounced secession as "a remedy for no evil, real or imaginary, but an aggravation and complication of existing difficulties." Senator Archibald Dixon then called on the gathering to rally to the flag and the Constitution. Except for the clause detailing a desire for separate statehood, West Virginia's report echoed the hopes of other border state Unionists for calm and the preservation of law and order. By these actions, the northwest had started to behave like the other border states.[36]

Their May 23 referendum supported both Unionists' and secessionists' claims to authority. In the thirty-five counties in northwestern Virginia, the voters rejected secession 28,604 (75.2 percent) to 9,445 (24.8 percent). Twenty-three of its counties voted in the negative, but ten more voted in the affirmative. No returns are available for Mason or Roane counties. If the additional thirteen counties of what later became West Virginia were included, the yes votes would more than double. According to Richard Orr Curry's research into the election returns, 34,677 (64.5 percent) voters rejected secession, while 19,121 (35.5 percent) in the full territory supported it. The statewide result backed secession by a vast margin. The most often cited figure is that 120,950 (85.6 percent) Virginians voted in favor, while 20,373 (14.4 percent) opposed it. This number does not include the northwestern counties. Still, two-thirds of the region's white population opposed secession, in many cases with varying degrees of allegiance. Brooke and Hancock counties went so far as to publish the names of local voters who supported secession in the *Wellsburg Herald*. Interestingly, party allegiance played no role in the matter. In the nineteen counties who voted for Breckinridge in 1860, fourteen opposed disunion. The four Douglas counties split evenly, while only two of the six Bell counties favored secession. Yet, in Kanawha County, the result indicates that few switched from Union to disunion. A comparison of polling data between the same precincts in the November 1860 presidential election, the February 4 convention delegates ballot, and the May 23 referendum indicates little change. Low slaveholding areas showed little enthusiasm for secession, while those with more slaves indicated more support for it despite being outvoted. James H. Cook's study of Harrison County, however, revealed the reverse. He found poll books that showed significant shifts toward secession that reduced the Unionist majority to a mere ten votes. Even so, each side saw the result as a sign of support and prepared to mobilize.[37]

While both sides organized soldiers, some of the convention leaders appealed to the Unionists' sense of duty. On May 25, Carlile, Pierpont, and seven others published "To the People of North-Western Virginia," a rushed clarion call for continued resistance to secession. The authors urged their fellow citizens to remain loyal to the Union. They called being an American citizen "a title more honored, respected, and revered than that of Potentate or King" that no man would "passively surrender it and submit it to be used by the conspirators engaged in this effort to enslave you." Secession was "bankruptcy, ruin, civil war, ending in a military despotism." Northwesterners ought not be "submissionists [or] craven cowards," but instead should act as "men who know our rights, and knowing, dare to maintain them." At the same time, the authors applied those former titles on those who "offered no resistance but have submitted to the filling up of armies and quartering of troops in their midst." To cap it off, they quoted Daniel Webster's comments about Western Virginia's unfair position in the now degraded parent state. As I showed in the previous chapter, he meant exactly the opposite, but that scarcely mattered to these authors.

This appeal shows how weak the Union cause was at this position. Having lost the referendum, the convention leaders feared being overwhelmed by shaken hearts who dreaded siding with the Lincoln administration. Hence, they reminded their neighbors of their duty to defend their country in northwestern Virginia. That said, like the earlier "Report on State and Federal Relations," they avoided any mention of who now occupied the White House and Congress by emphasizing their desire for law and order under the simple perfection of the federal Constitution. They need not have worried.[38]

Federal intervention quickly allayed Unionists' fears. On May 26, the US Army settled the matter as they marched into northwestern Virginia. Brig. Gen. George B. McClellan ordered his army of Ohio, Indiana, and Kentucky (who were mostly Ohioans) soldiers to occupy the region and to stabilize the situation. According to Curry, this plan began not in Washington but in Columbus, Ohio. Governor William Denison Jr. organized troops for McClellan's command for just such a purpose several weeks earlier. That said, the general informed his commanding officer, Lt. Gen. Winfield Scott, of his plans. The distracted president appears to have paid little attention to the region's affairs, but another decision of his made the western Virginia operation possible. His border state policy dictated that federal authorities respect their rights to self-government. He made no incursions into Delaware or Kentucky but was forced to intervene in chaotic Maryland and later Missouri. Lincoln's abeyance of Kentucky's declaration of neutrality on May 16 allowed Denison, McClellan, and General-in-Chief Winfield Scott to keep their western army available for action elsewhere. So contrary to Curry's argument that the trio acted independently, Lincoln guided their actions even if he did not specifically order them. Their decision to delay action until after the referendum saved the northwest for the Union. Three days later, these federal troops occupied the northern parts of the region around Wheeling, Morgantown, Parkersburg, and Clarksburg. On May 26, McClellan issued a reassuring proclamation to the people of the northwest. "VIRGINIANS," he began, "the General Government has long enough endured the machinations of a few factious rebels in your midst." He continued that rebels had failed to stop the citizenry from "expressing your loyalty at the polls," and now "seek to inaugurate a reign of terror, and thus force you to their schemes, and submit to the yoke of the traitorous conspiracy dignified by the name of Southern Confederacy." Many northwestern Unionists had used the same language when resisting secession, even when they placed conditions on accepting it. He later stated that the government stayed far from the region to prevent anyone from saying that it influenced the late election. Now completed, he said, "I have ordered troops to cross the river.

86 / Chapter 3

They come as your friends and brothers [and] as enemies only to the armed rebels who are preying upon you. Your homes, your families, and your property are safe under our protection. All your rights shall be religiously respected." It was like music to the ears of Unionist leaders.[39]

The best had yet to come. McClellan's declaration stated in the clearest language possible that neither he nor his men would interfere with slavery. Confederate claims that the federal presence "will be signalized by interference with your slaves, understand one thing clearly—not only will we abstain from all such interference, but we will, on the contrary, with an iron hand, crush any attempt at insurrection on their part." He then ordered his soldiers to defend the rights of Virginians. "I place under the safeguard of your honor the persons and property of the Virginians. I know that you will respect their feelings and all their rights," he commanded. In a single document, McClellan ensured the success of the Unionist cause in the northwest by giving the locals what they so dearly sought: a steady and firm hand and respect for all types of property. His specific mention of slavery solidified his status among local Unionists. There would be no revolution or change under his command. It is fortuitous that a conservative figure like McClellan took charge in northwestern Virginia. Across the state two days earlier, another Union general, Benjamin Butler, took the extraordinary step of allowing escaping slaves into his lines on the Virginia Capes instead of returning them to their masters. As a trained lawyer, Butler employed the legal term "contraband of war" to explain his actions to Washington. This action had widespread consequences for the entire Union war effort. Had he been in charge in Wheeling instead of Fortress Monroe, white northwesterners may have chosen to resist the Union instead of sided with it. Then there would have been no West Virginia.[40]

In late May and early June, Union troops secured the region's main points. The Baltimore and Ohio Railroad, a key route between Washington and the western states, became their first objective and their means of deployment. An element of McClellan's force commanded by Col. Benjamin F. Kelley of the First Virginia (Union) routed a Confederate garrison at Philippi in Barbour County on June 2 in what was the first land battle of the Civil War. McClellan then turned his attention to the Kanawha Valley. A few weeks before, its leaders, including George W. Summers and Benjamin H. Smith, traveled to Cincinnati to ask McClellan to leave them alone for the time being. His compliance, however, allowed secessionist militias to assert their authority over the region. Their control was far from complete. In late May, two men, Green Slack and Lewis Ruffner, left Charleston to attend the upcoming Second Wheeling Convention. Their departure provoked the local commander, Col. Christopher Tompkins of

Putnam County, to proclaim, "Men of Virginia! Men of Kanawha! To Arms! You cannot serve two masters. You have not the right to repudiate allegiance to your own State." His cautions and warnings against submission drew few to his cause. Tompkins soon found his position so untenable that he had to call upon Richmond for help. Governor Letcher, who like Denison had organized large numbers of troops since mid-April, sent four thousand soldiers led by his predecessor, Henry Wise, to the Kanawha Valley. Yet not even the presence of the man who enabled the 1851 constitution and hanged John Brown could prevent Kanawhans from welcoming US troops into the county in mid-June. On the retreat eastward, Wise described the situation to Letcher. The local militias "lost from three to five hundred by desertion. But one man deserted from the Legion." They were, moreover, "for nothing like warlike uses here." The whole Kanawha Valley, Wise concluded, was "wholly disaffected and traitorous." By the end of June, therefore, US troops had occupied the most important parts of northwestern Virginia for the Union war effort. With the Northern Panhandle, the Baltimore and Ohio Railroad, and the Great Kanawha River under their control, the Unionist cause held strong bases from which to defend the region against rebel incursions and the rising guerrilla threat. The population remained divided.[41]

The Second Wheeling Convention, held from June 11 to June 24 under Union Army protection, settled some of the political questions raised at the first. Its attendance fell more into line with Carlile's desires as expressed in the Clarksburg Resolution. The number and range of counties represented now included the Kanawha Valley, and even the city of Alexandria and Fairfax County around the federal capital. Its membership became more selective, due in part to actual elections held in some if not all counties. In all, the number of delegates decreased from 436 to 105. Even then, the convention sought additional legitimacy from "old and familiar leaders." On June 1, its Central Committee wrote to George W. Summers for his "lifetime devotion to these great principles of free government."[42] While he never responded to their request, Summers's activities since leaving the Richmond convention indicated his opposition to their mission. His participation in at least one secessionist meeting in Charleston indicated that he tried to straddle the line between allegiances.[43] His presence in Wheeling would have made little difference. The census had information on eighty of those in attendance. Half of its members served in the first convention. Not surprisingly, their respective delegations had similar economic characteristics. Their median real estate wealth amounted to $4,000, with $1,500 in personal wealth, slightly more than before. A total of ten men, one in eight, owned a combined fifty-one slaves. One delegate,

Lewis Ruffner of Kanawha County, possessed half of them. This time, more native-born Virginians attended, fifty-six, or 70 percent. Northern-born made up a further twenty, or one-quarter. Landowning farmers and lawyers made up half of the delegates, while merchants, physicians, and other professions made strong showings. These were the ideal kind of men whom Unionist leaders sought to back their plan: mostly southern, sufficiently wealthy, and sympathetic to slavery.

Rejecting secession required more than just the army's presence and reliable civilians. The convention moved first to form or "reorganize" the government of Virginia. On June 13, the delegates issued the "Declaration of the People of Virginia Represented in Convention at Wheeling." Sponsored by Carlile, it expanded on both the central committee's May 15 "Report on State and Federal Relations" and the May 25 appeal. It stated that the loyal people of Virginia sought for the "preservation of their dearest rights and liberties and their security in person and property, imperatively demand the reorganization of the government of the Commonwealth." The declaration also denounced "all acts of said Convention and Executive, tending to separate this Commonwealth from the United States, or to levy and carry war against them, are without authority and void." Finally, the convention vacated disloyal state officers, including congressmen, senators, sheriffs, and commissioners of revenue. The next day, the delegates formed the new government, which consisted of a governor, a lieutenant governor, and a cabinet of five advisers, the general assembly, and the State Senate. Wheeling served as their capital for the time being. The membership of each branch would come from the convention members. The declaration did not mention separate statehood at all. This is a sign not of abandonment or mitigation of the idea but rather of choosing the proper format. The document simply outlined the Reorganized Government's structure. Carlile said as much in these debates, and there is no reason to doubt his word. He felt that "a separation is worth nothing without the perpetuity of the Government to which we desire to attach ourselves, and that they must first address themselves to maintaining the Government." Adding the still controversial idea of statehood to the declaration could have undermined the whole enterprise.[44]

The convention then made another safe choice. Members unanimously chose Francis H. Pierpont to be the Union governor of Virginia. It is unclear why they picked him. Ambler, his only biographer, offered no answers. Pierpont, he believed, had no prior political experience and a reputation for opposing slavery based on a brief residence in Mississippi.[45] While he endorsed statehood, fighting the rebels came first. On June 17, his comments on the declaration passed the day before confirmed his status as a firm opponent of secession and a solid conservative on slavery. He condemned the rebellion as a long-standing conspiracy against the Constitution. "It must be obvious," he said, "that the crisis now upon us is not the result of any momentary revulsion that has come upon the country, or of any sudden outburst of feeling in any one section of the country; but that it is the result . . . of mature deliberation, concocted in treason, for the express purpose of breaking up constitutional liberty in this country." These statements exemplify the conservative nature of the northwest's Unionism at this point. They called the secessionists the true antislavery supporters for trying to disrupt the security of the federal Constitution.[46] On an auspicious day, June 20, 1861, the convention elected him to the governorship. His inaugural address did not mention slavery at all, but he frequently invoked "the law," "rights," and "principle" as virtues for those loyal to the Union. He declared, "We . . . are but recurring to the great fundamental principle of our fathers, that to the loyal people of a State belongs the law-making power of that State. The loyal people are entitled to the government and governmental authority of the State. And, fellow-citizens, it is the assumption of that authority upon which we are now about to enter."[47] From the outset, therefore, the new Reorganized Government sought to serve only Unionists. This constituted the only way to legitimize the administration given the heavy divisions within the region. They picked the right man to accomplish that goal.

The seceded government in Richmond never abandoned its claims over the northwest. On June 14, before Pierpont took office, his counterpart John Letcher issued his own proclamation to the people of the rebellious region. His strong choice of words indicated his desire to reassert his authority over them. Virginia, having exercised her right to secede, would now "assert her independence. She will maintain it at every hazard. She is sustained by the power of her sister Southern States, ready and willing to uphold her cause." At the same time, Letcher boasted that he could back up those words with action. He said that troops had been ordered to the northwest, based at Huttonsville in Randolph County, for the people's protection, but Letcher must have known about the defeat at Philippi two weeks before. Nonetheless he carried on with claims that "men of the Southern Confederate States glory in coming to your rescue." It is unknown how many heeded this call, but it matters not. McClellan's troops defeated the rebels at Rich Mountain in the same county on July 11. His success there led Lincoln to bring him to Washington to rebuild the Union Army after its defeat at Bull Run ten days later. His replacement, former Kanawha County resident William S. Rosecrans, faced more battles in

90   /   Chapter 3

the coming months. Northwesterners, Union or rebel, must have scoffed at Letcher's handsome but feeble boasts.[48]

President Lincoln, after months of contending with unprecedented unrest, finally chose to recognize northwestern Virginia's new status. In his special address to Congress on July 4, 1861, he detailed the extent of the unrest and his administration's countermeasures. It was a depressing list. States in rebellion, fallen forts, crippled finances, and infant armies all afflicted the country. Even the border states teetered on the brink. Lincoln's appeasement of white southern Unionists required him to accommodate erratic state governments stretching from the Atlantic Ocean to Kansas. By permitting Kentucky and Delaware to sort out their allegiances, they remained calm. Missouri and Maryland, on the other hand, required intervention and much conflict. Virginia's Unionists provided one of the few rays of hope. His government, he said, "has the less regret, as the loyal citizens have in due form claimed its protection. Those loyal citizens this Government is bound to recognize and protect, as being Virginia."[49] These words amounted to an acceptance of the statehood movement, but it came as part of his appeasement of the border states. He already had to deal with four states. Adding one more posed no problem if it meant keeping white citizens loyal.

Six months and two days earlier, the people of Parkersburg hoped that the new president would stand by the law despite their misgivings of his party. He confirmed their wishes with his judicious if limited handling of the situation. Their resistance to secession came not from any issues with eastern Virginia as believed by the Ambler-Curry thesis. In fact, their public statements indicate the same appeals to law and order as found in the other border states. Like them, white northwesterners rejected disunion as a radical threat to their entire society, including their control over the enslaved. Decades of proslavery agitation fueled their opposition, which manifested itself first in the Virginia Constitutional Convention. They served as the linchpin of the Unionist cause there. Indeed, they had built up sufficient credibility even among secessionists that they nearly repealed a lingering taxation issue. Virginia's secession and unauthorized actions in support of the rebellion drove the final wedge between the northwest and the remainder. The region's whites responded by holding conventions of their own to discuss and choose their modes of opposing secession. They concluded that reorganizing the Virginia state government best served that means. The idea of forming a separate state began in this time, but contrary to previous accounts, it elicited little enthusiasm from the first convention. Still, enough support put it on the list. None of these things would have happened without federal interference. Indeed, when US troops occupied the region, they promised to protect their institutions including slavery. The secessionists offered nothing but angry retaliation. As summer gave way to autumn, the once proud part of the Old Dominion now declared their independence from their parent state. The unthinkable now progressed toward a reality. As the next chapter will show, the new state still needed to create its constitution and contend with the ever-present war over slavery around them. Their troubles had only just started.

CHAPTER 4

The Conservative Phase of the West Virginia Statehood Movement, August 1861–February 1862

Having abandoned one home, northwestern Virginia Unionists now set about forming another. As soon as the Lincoln administration endorsed the Reorganized Government, its leaders began their quest to create a new state. With federal aid, they had the flexibility to create the new government in any way that they wished, such as offices, taxation, financing improvements, and the court system. All knew, however, that they must avoid one issue: slavery. The leading proponent of separate statehood, John S. Carlile, said as much in August 1861. In response to questions from Thomas Elder of Hancock County, he proposed that they must "say nothing about slavery. It is not necessary that we should." Previous Virginia constitutions never mentioned the subject, so the same should apply to West Virginia. He concluded that even "the most zealous anti-slavery partisan can see enough to convince him of the propriety of letting the question alone, its agitation, particularly now, can only tend to divide and distract us and perhaps defeat forever all hope of a new State."[1] With these words, he laid out the conservative plan for West Virginia, a mirror image of its parent: a slave state untainted by treason. The success of the statehood movement depended on this first phase. Northwestern Unionism stood on shaky ground. Many whites acquiesced to Virginia's secession rather than submit to the control of a northern-based and Republican-supporting federal government. Despite a strong Union military presence, the Confederates and guerrillas continually threatened the region's security. Keeping slavery off the table allowed the statehood movement to succeed.

Carlile's vision succeeded, but difficulties marred the process. Adherents to the Ambler-Curry thesis tend to speed through this phase of the statehood movement. The latter gave it more attention than most. In several chapters on the state's first constitutional debates, Curry found considerable opposition in the proceedings. Yet he continued Ambler's thematic approach where the author discussed topics in turn, with slavery being merely one of many. He thought it important enough to name one of his chapters "slavery clouds the issue." I believe that this description does not go far enough. The delegates dealt with topics as they developed, but only slavery threatened to bring more than inclement weather. I split the statehood movement into two phases, a conservative one that ran from August 1861 to February 1862, followed by the radical period that led until statehood in June 1863. This chapter deals with the first. Protected and encouraged by the federal government, the convention received a free hand to draft the new state's constitution. By analyzing its proceedings chronologically instead of thematically, I show how the mere mention of the word "slavery" could disrupt the statehood movement. Contrary to the hopes of Carlile and others, some antislavery elements emerged. Yet the prompt containment of the subject kept the proceedings moving ahead. After three months of debate, they produced a proslavery constitution whose existence belies any notion of the region being opposed to the institution.

The first months of hostilities brought the northernmost slave states under Union control. Maryland and Delaware calmed after the initial problems in April, May, and June but remained tense. Although defeated at Wilson's Creek in August, the federals still curbed the Confederate threat to Missouri. Guerrillas plagued the state for years to come. Kentucky saw the most dramatic change. Its governor and legislature declared their state neutral at the start of the conflict. They promised to side against any foe who first violated this pact. Lincoln's statement that he "would like to have God on his side but he must have Kentucky" may be apocryphal, but it nonetheless accurately sums up him his policy toward that state. Union forces trained in Illinois, Indiana, and Ohio while they awaited developments. The Confederacy, on the other hand, exercised no such restraint. On September 21, a rebel army led by former Episcopal bishop Leonidas Polk moved from its Tennessee base northward up the Mississippi River to occupy the town of Columbus, Kentucky. From this commanding position, Polk hoped to block the river with a chain to choke off Union shipping. Kentucky responded by siding with the Union and invited the federal army to drive out the invader. Donald Stoker has rightfully called Polk's actions a "cataclysmic strategic mistake nearly comparable to bombarding Fort Sumter." The Bluegrass state's conversion placed its men and resources into Union hands and exposed the Confederacy's western states to attack. Davis's government then recognized the secessionist legislatures of Missouri and Kentucky in November and December and added them to the Confederacy despite the actual situation in each area. He gained little from these empty declarations.[2]

Lincoln faced bigger problems but achieved more success. His war policies required him to maintain both support in the northern states but also the loyalties of the border states by preserving slavery. Any progress toward emancipation could upset this delicate balance. Yet, as James Oakes has pointed out, this resulted in a dual policy where Lincoln protected the institution in some areas but undermined it in others to appease his party's northern supporters. The latter led him to act against slavery in areas under federal control. In the fall of 1861 and the spring of 1862, he asked Congress to ban the institution from the western territories, ratify a treaty with Great Britain about suppressing the slave trade in the Atlantic, and approve a plan for compensated emancipation in the District of Columbia. He and the congressional Republicans achieved these goals in public and against the opposition of border state representatives. Even the Reorganized Government of Virginia's delegates rejected these measures. Its new senators, John S. Carlile and Waitman T. Willey, seen in figure 4 after having his photograph taken upon taking office, and representatives William G. Brown, Kieran V. Whaley, and Jacob Blair from the northwest, and Joseph Segar from the Eastern Shore, voted against these antislavery measures before Congress. Carlile alone opposed the First Confiscation Act in August 1861, with the House representatives not yet in place. In July 1862, Brown voted for the Second Confiscation Act, but both senators opposed it. Both Carlile and Willey opposed the compensated emancipation plan for the District of Columbia before the Senate on April 3. Blair and Brown rejected the House's bill eight days later, but the measure passed each body with large partisan majorities. Lincoln rapidly signed it into law on April 16. Likewise, in May, they each opposed the bill to forbid slavery in the western territories, the major Republican issue for the previous decade. Lincoln also protected slavery in the border states. On August 30, 1861, two days after Carlile responded to Elder's inquiry, the president rescinded Major General John C. Frémont's proclamation freeing the slaves of Missouri secessionists. As awkward as these policies appeared, they worked. Lincoln retained the allegiances of the border states while enacting antislavery programs demanded by his northern supporters. Thus far, the Confederacy proved to be a genuine threat to slavery in the border states.[3]

Northwestern Virginia stands as a particularly successful example of Lincoln's border policies. First, Union armies protected the region from enemy incursions if not the guerrilla menace. On August 20, Major General William Rosecrans, commander of the Department of the West, issued a glossy proclamation aimed at the loyal people of western Virginia. He praised "the vast majority of the people" for rejecting secession. He condemned the traitors' warnings that only the Confederacy could protect them from the "hordes of abolitionists [that] would overrun you, plunder your property, steal your slaves, abuse your wives and daughters, seize upon your lands, and hang all

Fig. 4. Waitman T. Willey, ca. 1860 (Brady-Handy Collection, Library of Congress). Willey started his career advocating for slavery. His famous amendment on gradual emancipation succeeded by exploiting the flights of the enslaved from northwestern Virginia. The change never freed a single slave but made statehood possible.

those who opposed them." He intended those words to reassure, like McClellan sought to do in May, the region's whites of the security of the situation and the maintenance of slavery. As Michael Woods has argued, the enslaved and Rosecrans's soldiers had different agendas. He cited numerous examples of

Union soldiers from Ohio and Pennsylvania aiding slaves as they escaped to freedom in their home states. They belied official federal policies to protect the institution in the border states. Woods errs in overstating white Unionists embracing emancipation. As this chapter and the next two will show, they retained strong proslavery views throughout the war and long afterward. Some would turn, but they earned the enmity of the majority in the process.[4]

Rosecrans's troops had much greater success in fighting Confederates. Occupying strong positions through the region, soldiers from Ohio, Pennsylvania, and Indiana and a few Virginia Unionists presented a formidable barrier to the rebels. As if the terrain was not enough, poor leadership and organization ruined Confederate efforts to recover the northwest. No fewer than four separate armies attempted to cross the mountains and eject their foes. William W. Loring, a one-armed Mexican War veteran from Florida, led the Army of the Northwest around Pocahontas County. The newly minted Henry W. Wise, the former governor who hanged John Brown over a year before, itched to lead his Wise Legion back into the Kanawha Valley. Another past governor, John B. Floyd, led the southernmost force in Wythe County. An actual northwestern Virginian led the fourth army, namely Clarksburg native Thomas J. Jackson. After recuperating from Bull Run, his small force combined with Loring's in Hampshire County. These forces totaled about ten thousand men. Faulty command arrangements, however, wasted their efforts. Wise and Floyd refused to cooperate with each other. Not even the guidance of the as-yet-little-known Robert E. Lee, appointed by Davis to coordinate their efforts, brought any success. At Carnifex Ferry on September 10, Rosecrans pounced on the hapless Floyd. Two days later, despite moving his troops in secret, Lee failed to capture the Union Fort Milroy on top of Cheat Mountain. He also lost his chief aide, John Augustus Washington, the grandnephew of the first president, in the battle. Davis sent Lee to South Carolina and Georgia afterward. Jackson's attempt to capture Romney in January 1862 also failed. The only successful Confederate effort in western Virginia came from Kanawha County native John N. Clarkson's cavalry raid on Guyandotte on the Ohio River. When local secessionists aided the attackers, Unionists retaliated and destroyed the town. Much like Sterling Price in Missouri and Polk in Kentucky, failure compounded failure in Confederate attempts to bring the slaveholding states under Richmond's control. Northwestern Unionists must have laughed at the misfortunes of their would-be "protectors" flopping around in the mountains easily brushed aside by loyal troops. With their government and slaves protected by the Union, at least in theory, northwestern Unionists proceeded with their plans to form a new state.[5]

During these military events, the Reorganized State government set about establishing its authority in the northwest, the Eastern Shore, and other areas under Union control. An ordeal developed over finding new Unionist officeholders. The June 13 declaration authorized Pierpont to vacate disloyal state- and county-level officers. This decision, however, required him to find replacements. Many prewar elites at first rejected the thought of submitting to the Lincoln-aligned regime. The president appointed federal offices in the region, including judges and prosecutors, with some of them. Pierpont faced difficulties when filling lower-level positions. His governor's papers contain many impassioned letters from northwestern Unionists about problems with their local administrators. A. F. Ritchie of Marion County blamed the refusal of two judges to take the oath on the lack of a solid policy. This "shifting, vacillating procedure," he and other Unionists claimed, caused "suffering" to public interest "from the want of properly qualified officers to execute the laws." Pierpont implemented such a policy shortly thereafter, but the problem remained. On July 8, he notified sheriffs in several counties that he deposed Judge George W. Thompson of Ohio County for refusing to take the oath. The governor's nephew, Frank P. Pierpont, a notary public in Ritchie County, received a report from several Unionists that the county's court clerks, sheriff, constable, and others had left for Richmond. Neighboring Taylor County reported that less than one-third of those approached to serve the new government refused the offer. The town of Kingwood in Preston County, furthermore, lost all its officers elected in 1860, causing the "interests of the town" to go "uncared for, its revenue uncollected, nor its levees laid." The sheer number of vacancies caused by these refusals led to widespread concerns for the new government's legitimacy throughout the region.[6]

The experience of Kanawha County reveals why many men chose to or refused to serve the Reorganized Government. The Pierpont Papers contain commissions from numerous counties, but Kanawha had both the largest numbers of warrants as well as letters from the actual participants. After many prewar elites refused to serve, one family group stepped forward to take local leadership. John Slack Sr. served as the sheriff in earlier years, with his son serving as his deputy. The former came under considerable attack during his tenure. In January 1860, many prominent Kanawhans signed a petition asking Richmond to remove Slack for mishandling tax revenue at a time when the salt business struggled.[7] Although he kept his job, the resentment at this treatment fueled his later decisions when many of the signatories supported secession. His brother Greenbury Slack, the new clerk of the county court, informed Pierpont about the troubles in finding new officeholders. "The Union men still hesitate," he began. "I told the presiding justice yesterday," he continued, "that we could not wait he must take a position one side or the other. He said that was decidedly in favor of the 'new government' but he could not take the oath at present and his course intimidates others. I intend to press the matter and if they still persist in refusing, I will so report and let their places be filled. There are, however, many of them whom I would very much regret to lose." The poor turnout for offices sustained Slack's warnings. Only five of the twenty-six men awarded offices had held power before. On top of the senior and junior Slacks mentioned above, they included David McComas (likely the judge mentioned in the letter), who kept his spot on the bench; John W. Field stayed on as commissioner of revenue, and Spicer Patrick became a justice of the peace. Their backgrounds indicate that the Slacks sought as many well-off and stable men as possible. In a county where one-third of the heads of households had no property at all, the Union officers came from its highest echelons. They had a median real estate wealth of $1,500 and personal property of $512. Their predecessors had comparable numbers of $1,963 and $512, respectively. Only slave ownership separated them. Fewer of the new officers owned slaves than before. In 1857, sixteen of twenty-four identifiable officeholders owned slaves, while thirteen of eighteen did three years later. Of the twenty-six who came forward in 1861, only eight held slaves. One, John E. Lewis, the county's second largest slaveholder, became a judge despite lacking previous experience. He did not last long. Contrary to Eric Foner's view that West Virginia came about in part by "an overthrow of the western region's own antebellum elite," the Reorganized Government instead tried to keep as many established figures in place as possible. They failed for one reason: doubts about its reliability on the slavery question. These Kanawha officeholders turned over because few believed it would protect against Republican policies. Future actions proved them right. The Slacks rose to power out of governmental desperation and necessity, not design.[8]

At the same time, its officeholders risked much for their collaboration. The initial choices quickly needed replacement. Clarkson's raid in October deliberately targeted polling stations and took two officers, Charles Leavens and Matthew P. Wyatt, as prisoners to Richmond. On December 30, John Slack reported to Pierpont that only five men from the original group of twenty-three remained in place. The process of selecting new officeholders sustained contemporary notions about how northwestern Virginians chose sides. Observers high and low connected the region's established classes with the tendency toward secessionist support. Colonel and future president Rutherford B. Hayes of the Twenty-Third Ohio Volunteer Infantry described the people who encountered in the region to his uncle. On August 17, 1861, while fighting guerrillas in Lewis County, he contrasted the two sides in the area. "The Secessionists in this region are the wealthy and educated, who do nothing openly, and the vagabonds, criminals, and ignorant barbarians of the country," he wrote. On the other hand, he sourced the Union men from "the middle classes—the law-and-order, well-behaved folks." He may have derived these observations from his unit's brief stay in Kanawha weeks earlier. Yet he was essentially correct. The Slacks represented the middle group of Unionists, while those reluctant to serve under them came from at least the "wealthy and the educated." The allegiances of the "vagabonds" and "ignorant barbarians" are more difficult to determine from Hayes's observations and the warrant evidence. In the absence of another major source of information, it may be forever unknowable where they stood.[9]

The separate but ever-present role of the federal government compounded the Unionists' problems. As mentioned above, Lincoln needed marshals, US attorneys, and district court justices to enforce federal laws in areas under his control. He selected local men for those offices without input from the state governments. Pierpont's was no exception. Once again, Kanawha County offers a rare glimpse into this process at work. Benjamin H. Smith, one of the county's leading figures and a prominent slaveholder, received an appointment as the US attorney for western Virginia. On paper, he was a good choice. He was an experienced lawyer who trained under Thomas Ewing of Ohio, the foster father of William T. Sherman. His son Isaac Noyes Smith, however, had sided with the Confederacy. Many other offspring of prewar elites had similar kinship ties to rebels. Lewis Ruffner, brother of the author of the famous antislavery tract of 1847, represented Kanawha in the Reorganized Government's assembly and the Constitutional Convention, but had sons and nephews in rebel service. The Slacks worried constantly about these divided allegiances. In a letter to Pierpont, John Slack doubted "whether there is a secessionist in the county who could not get up to a pretty strong position in his behalf and get it signed by many *quasi* Union men through mere motions of personal friendships or family considerations and thereby defeat the whole object in view." Greenbury Slack described the situation as a "set of 'Quasi' Union men here like B. H. Smith" who will "embargo any action that may be taken to affect the object we have in view especially when the liberty of a certain class of citizens and connections are involved." Despite these concerns, neither the Slacks nor Pierpont could correct the situation. Federal officers like Smith, Ruffner, and their counterparts in other counties lay beyond their authority.[10]

Federal policies toward secessionists further complicated the Unionist cause. The courts resumed operations in the summer of 1861. Congress passed the Act to Define and Contain Certain Conspiracies in July as part of Lincoln's policy to win back secessionists to their original loyalties. With Justice John J. Jackson Jr. presiding and Benjamin H. Smith acting as prosecuting attorney, hundreds of accused men appeared in the court, which moved between Wheeling, Clarksburg, and Charleston during the war. The first session in Charleston heard forty of those cases. The court released most defendants on a $500 bond, while more belligerent subjects paid between $1,000 and $5,000. None received a jail term, which allowed these accused rebels to roam free. Those who could not pay the bond or broke its terms faced imprisonment in the Wheeling Athenaeum or the Harrison or Kanawha jail and then ultimately at Camp Chase outside of Columbus, Ohio. A historian of the court described Jackson's approach to cases of disloyalty as "a most routine fashion" in which the judge "admonished the individual before the court and proceeded to the next case." Some Unionists supported leniency for friends. Jonathan Slack of Kanawha wrote to Pierpont in September asking for the release of his neighbor J. H. Goshorn, the first mayor of Charleston. "Notwithstanding he is a secessionist," he wrote, "he is the most liberal and tolerant towards his opponents as any other prominent man in this town." Ebenezer Patton of Harrison County lacked such supporters. Clarksburg residents appealed to Pierpont to remove this "notorious secessionist" who intended to "return and live among us." While Patton had taken the oath, the people were "very indignant that this mild policy should be pursued towards a man who is just put from his attempts to destroy the government." Federal policies contained a significant problem. The district court allowed many known secessionists, only some of whom had taken the oath of allegiance, to live freely within the region. Their status challenged the Reorganized Government's authority as well as encouraging a larger number of opponents to Lincoln and Pierpont's policies. This situation, a common one to the border states, would plague northwestern Virginia for many years.[11]

When the Second Wheeling Convention resumed on August 6, the weight of siding with the Republican-led federal government finally told. During the debate, the delegates set out the initial boundaries of the new state around thirty-nine counties with several more invited to join if they so desired. They also set a date for an election on the matter on October 24. Some spirited discussions developed. The delegates split into proponents of statehood and those who doubted its legality or timing. James G. West of Wetzel County, the committee chair, said that the time was now. The new state, he believed, posed no burdens to either the federal government or the new government of

Virginia. On August 15, A. F. Ritchie of Marion County disagreed. He produced a letter from the federal attorney general, Edward Bates, on the matter. He called the West Virginia plan "an original independent act of Revolution" at a time when the Union could not afford more controversies. He supported the west's resistance to secession but only to build a core of loyal men to "establish a *constitutional nucleus* around which all the shattered elements of the Commonwealth may meet and combine, and thus restore the old State in its original integrity." Separation now, Ritchie believed, would hinder efforts to suppress the rebellion by starting a debate on emancipation. "That the slavery question must come up in the formation or adoption of a Constitution," he said, "would not only create controversy in Congress, but bring about divided sentiment among our own people, which must result very disastrously." He simply asked for a delay on the matter to prevent damage to the Union cause in Virginia. Charles S. Lewis of Harrison County agreed with Ritchie. Opening the debate on statehood would allow "the emancipationist [to] raise his head in our midst; that there was danger of this being a free State or breaking up in confusion and he wanted to meet the question now and see whether this was the case or not." They predicted the future well. Far from being united on the matter, northwestern Virginia Unionists struggled with the impact of their new state project. Slavery divided them, just as it did the other border states.

John S. Carlile's careful negotiations saved the day. He rebutted his colleagues by urging the conservative promises of statehood. Separation would unlock their economic potential so much that "three years will not roll around until our population will be quadrupled, and there will be more people in the limits of the new State than there is in the whole State of Virginia today." Carlile saved his best for last. "Cut the knot now! Cut it now! Apply the knife!" he called to the convention. It was his finest moment. The delegates agreed. Two days later, the delegates voted fifty to twenty-eight. The result contains some surprising patterns. As James C. McGregor pointed out, no geographic basis existed for each side. Ohio and Harrison's delegations split their votes. Kanawha and Wayne's members supported the measure, but neighboring Putnam opposed it. Alexandria and Fairfax's representatives voted no. Instead, the tally indicates that many agreed with West, Carlile, and other conservatives that the new state offered the best option for all concerns, including safety on slavery. After convention president Arthur I. Boreman, who bizarrely voted no, wished them well, the voters would decide on the fate that Unionist leaders had set before them. Their vote turned what had been a vague notion even months before into a plan of action with considerable public support. In response, the federal army named its Wheeling base Camp Carlile after the new Unionist hero.[12]

The October 24 referendum on statehood revealed the strength of northwestern Unionism. Despite the risks to poll workers, the measure passed 18,408 (95.9 percent) in favor of forming a new state, with just 781 (4.1 percent) against. Only thirty-nine counties posted results, and even in those the numbers of potential voters fell far short of the prewar totals. Barbour, for example, had 311 supporters and just 7 opponents, but that represented a mere 18 percent of the prewar electorate. Braxton had only twenty-two vote from a pool of over one thousand. Those counties lay well within guerrilla country and beyond the protection of US soldiers, so it is remarkable that any votes occurred at all. Nearby Calhoun, Nicholas, and Webster did not post returns. Even more protected counties showed substantial cuts in the number of voters. High atop the Northern Panhandle far from the war, Hancock posted 263 to 67 from a pool of 884, or a loss of two-thirds. Harrison lost 57 percent of its voters in its 1,148 to 12 support for separation. Kanawha voted 1,039 to 1 for the new state, but that represented a loss of 60 percent. The *Wheeling Daily Intelligencer*, which is the only source available from this time, tried to spin the result as a major victory. It praised the turnout as a sign that Northwesterners "were not one whit less firm and inflexible towards the Eastern Virginia usurpers now that they were last spring." A vote against statehood would have "stimulated the secessionists to fresh life and vigor," but instead "we have disheartened them."[13] The military situation fed their fears. Although poorly led and outnumbered by Union forces, the Confederates never gave up on reconquering the region. Many northwesterners expected their imminent return. Their irregular forces specifically targeted the Reorganized Government's attempts to assert its authority. Even Union authorities complicated an already tense situation by allowing secessionists to roam free on bond. These factors would show themselves as northwestern Virginia Unionists formed their new state's constitution.

The state makers now tried to make good on the generals' and soldiers' achievements and sacrifices. On the day before Rosecrans sent his report, the Constitutional Convention began in Wheeling, meeting between November 26 and February 18, 1862. This gathering organized a wider range of counties than the previous meetings, including delegates from those on the southern fringes such as Greenbrier, Wyoming, Mercer, and McDowell counties. The convention's membership resembled the preceding Wheeling Conventions. As there, the delegates tended to come from the wealthier and middling classes, sustaining again Hayes's observations. The census contains information on forty-nine of the sixty-one attendees. Their median real estate wealth was $4,000, personal wealth $1,000. Neither figure represented a significant change from the Second Wheeling Convention, whose congregants had a median real estate wealth of $4,000 and $1,500 in personal wealth. The first had figures of $3,000 and $1,000, respectively. All but one, farmer Andrew Mann of Greenbrier, owned land. There were twelve farmers and thirteen lawyers. Only a handful served in the earlier conventions due to the requirement for elections for delegates in most but not all counties. Twelve attended the first, eight attended the second, and only two participated in both. Only six delegates owned slaves, as compared to ten in the Second Wheeling Convention. Combined they held a total of sixty-eight slaves; three Kanawhans, Benjamin H. Smith (representing Logan County), Lewis Ruffner, and James H. Brown, owned a combined fifty-nine. Significantly, native Virginians made up thirty-four (70 percent) of the delegates, with twelve from the northern states. In short, the men responsible for shaping the first West Virginia constitution shared common characteristics with other Unionists, including wealth, land ownership, and nativity. Although scarce among the delegates, slaveholding became a vital issue out of proportion to its numbers. Protected at least in part from the danger posed by Confederate troops and guerrillas, the northwesterners now needed to draft a constitution that suited their needs. Furious debate now began over what constituted those requirements.[14]

The convention succeeded for one reason. The delegates at the outset agreed to keep slavery off their agenda. Previous histories of the meetings, such as those by Ambler and Summers, Curry, and Stealey, read as if the topic posed no trouble for the convention. However, they viewed the minutes from an issue-oriented approach. They discussed the topics brought up by the delegates, such as the courts, the legislature, the powers of the governor, the controversial township system that replaced the established county courts, and the financing of internal improvements without regard for their timing. Reading the convention minutes this way obscures its priorities. Yet without editing and annotation like William Freehling and Craig Simpson's superb work on the Richmond Conventions, the minutes are challenging to read. Instead, I read the minutes chronologically to see how the delegates debated their work. The slavery issue appeared on only four occasions, but when it arose, the delegates acted quickly to stop any discussion and move forward. The *Intelligencer* tried to allay such fears before the convention began. Disregarding claims made by the conservative *Wheeling Press* that separation was an abolitionist move, the *Intelligencer* opined in mid-November that "in the division movement abolition has no existence." Moreover, it claimed that since the leaders consisted of slaveholders from interior counties rather than the Northern Panhandle,

104 / Chapter 4

slavery was secure. Those, it concluded, "who attempt to bring forward Mr. N— on all occasions . . . need not be surprised when to waken in the morning and find the two-edged animal cutting from the other direction." This view shows how deeply the region supported slavery. The *Intelligencer* tried to assure its readers that the statehood movement sought to protect the institution and not undermine it as its critics claimed, or so all hoped.[15]

The slavery issue emerged sooner than anyone feared. The first three days occupied purely procedural matters, but a delegate dropped the bombshell on the fourth. Robert Hagar of Boone stunned the meeting by raising the matter on November 30. As a local minister, he witnessed firsthand the connection between secession and slaveholding. While in exile in Gallipolis, Ohio, he wrote to Pierpont in July about how all the most influential people in Boone mobilized the lower-class people, namely the "judges, J.Ps, lawyers, sheriffs, court clerks, merchants . . . slaveholders and drunkards" outnumbered Union men like him. Now in the convention, he resolved to put a gradual emancipation clause in the new state constitution. "Negro slavery," he said, "is the origin and foundation of our national troubles." He described it as a plot to "overthrow our government," "incompatible with the Word of God," "detrimental to the interests of a free people," and "a wrong to the slaves themselves." Therefore, he moved that "the Convention inquire into the expediency of making the proposed new State a *free* state." His insistence on gradual abolition resembled the region's stances in the 1829–1830 convention but also indicates that he had not changed his views since that time. Still, his ideas struck where the delegates did not want to go. Loyal slaveholders wanted to keep the matter quiet, as the *Parkersburg Gazette* mentioned in response. The *Wheeling Daily Intelligencer*, reversing its position from before the convention, called ignoring slavery "simply preposterous. It is the great grievance to be remedied. Had it not been for that grievance we should not have been in revolution." The *Intelligencer* stated plainly what its readers in the region believed: "We have nothing to expect in the future except from the Free States."[16] The remainder disagreed.

The more conservative delegates immediately clamped down on Hagar's motion. Belying the *Intelligencer*'s claims, Daniel Lamb of Ohio County, a Pennsylvania-born Quaker but staunch conservative, suggested that the legislative committee delay discussing it. James H. Brown of Kanawha County, the owner of four slaves, took it one step further. He said that the legislative committee need not raise the issue at all. Only a state legislature should do so. Brown thought it was "manifest that in accordance with the Constitution of the United States that [the] question devolves on the legislature of the State and not on the Convention; that there is nothing now before this body properly on that subject." Lamb agreed to this idea, as did the other delegates. Brown made another motion to end the debate. His simple yet effective resolution stated "that it is unwise and impolitic to introduce the discussion of the slavery question into the deliberations of this Convention." Although the body held no vote on the matter, it appears that the other delegates unanimously agreed with him. His choice of words indicates a slam on Hagar. Seemingly synonymous, the words "unwise" and "impolitic" can also refer to a wide range of topics. Brown meant, however, to attack Hagar's intelligence, or the "unwise" part. He then put down his patriotism and citizenship with the term "impolitic." While the issue reemerged later in the convention, for the time being it would not "cloud" the proceedings, as Curry claimed. It may have saved the statehood process from collapsing as soon as it started.[17]

Once calmed, the delegates proceeded to discuss other issues. The conservative nature of the ensuing debate comes out in the minutes. While sometimes furious debate ensued in each, the delegates resolved many in due course. One of the first controversies involved adopting a new name for the state. The October 24 election asked the voters if they supported a new state to be named Kanawha, but their approval did not settle the idea. On December 3, the convention moved to change the name. The ensuing debate fell into two camps—those who sought to modify the name and those demanding more drastic change. Waitman Willey, taking time away from the federal Senate, said that he preferred "West Virginia" for it had long been in use. While he referred to Virginia as "the flesh-pots of Egypt" for its treason, he believed that the people of the northwest still owed some allegiance to the name. With flourish, Willey said, "Here are cherished memories connected with that old state in old times that will never be obliterated while memory holds her seat. Whatever may have been the course of Virginia towards us in recent times, even West Virginia owes a duty which she ought to have the magnanimity to acknowledge. On her soil our own goddess of liberty was born; and however much her devoted followers may have discarded her worship by the introduction of false gods, still I cling to the memories of the past, and I shall cherish that until memory is no more." The Ohio-born Gordon Battelle of Ohio County opposed such wistful sentiments. He preferred to keep the name Kanawha for more revolutionary reasons. "We are now forming a new State," he said, because "I for one would want a new name—a fresh name—a name which if it were not symbolical of especially new ideas would at least be somewhat indicative of our deliverance from very old ones." Willey's faction won in the end. Most delegates—thirty in all—chose the name "West Virginia," while only Battelle and eight others preferred "Kanawha." An additional five split among the names "Western Virginia," "Allegheny," and "Augusta."[18] Like with Hagar's slavery motion, ties to the Old Dominion remained strong among the delegates. The delegates sought to avoid too much controversy. The name they chose, of course, remains to this day.

The debate over voting methods provoked some spirited argument. Many sought to replace the existing oral or viva voce system with the secret ballot. Those with a northern background generally supported the idea. The Massachusetts-born Granville Parker of Cabell County said that viva voce worked only among equals. His experiences in his home state convinced him of the need for secret ballots. Employers in Lowell coerced their workers' voting decisions. He had seen intimidation by "open ballot, but never by viva voce—the espionage and dictation [were] carried to that extent that the agent or overseer would come and stand at the ballot box." The introduction of the secret ballot, or as he called it "every man's ballot" held in an envelope, solved the problem. Battelle echoed this idea. His constituents favored the idea for the freedom it granted. Viva voce, he said, gave "an undue power to men of wealth, influence and position—especially to party leaders—to unjustly control the exercise by others of the right of franchise. We may say this ought not to be so, that men ought to vote their real sentiments in the face of all intimidations; but that I judge does not alter the fact that they really do not." Native Virginians and southerners opposed this idea. Chapman Stuart of Doddridge County, who was born in Bath County, said that he had never seen secret ballots work elsewhere since the practice too was open to abuse. "One party will have their blue tickets," he said, while "the other white or red, or long and short; and I have never yet seen a gentleman cast a vote in our neighboring States that it was not distinctly known how he voted." He preferred the old way of "coming up and declaring how we vote" because it "inculcates principles of independence." James H. Brown of Kanawha likewise defended the proven system, which, he claimed, prevented corruption and encouraged equality among the classes. "On Virginia election days," he said,

the poor man feels his consequence, self-respect and equality with the highest and richest in the land, and when he votes it does him good to show it in the independent tone in which he proclaims aloud when called upon to cast his vote. The viva voce system tends to encourage a manly independence in the voter and leads him to prize the privilege of voting more highly—a most important consideration in an elective government.

The one system appeals to the voters as independent freemen, the other appeals to their fears and sense of inferiority. The one encourages a sense of equality and self-respect; the other suggests the want of both. The one is a Virginia system, long and dearly cherished by our people; and I cannot consent to part with it without a better reason than I have yet heard from the advocates of secret ballots.

Other Virginians pointed out flaws in this system. Robert Hagar moved everyone with his story about viva voce in Boone County's secession ballot. More there would have supported the Union, he said, but "it was declared previous to the election that any and all who should vote for the Union should be hung forthwith on the public square." Some Union men, he continued, tried to do so at the courthouse, but when they encountered "a drunken mob arrayed against them there, their hearts failed them." This situation tainted the vote due to "the power invested in the hands of a few there. They have monopolized the places—merchants, lawyers, prosecuting attorneys, and clerks." Despite this soaring language, most delegates backed the ballot box. The more conservative members knew that the outcome would not significantly change their view of the new state's politics.

The boundary issue also inspired intense discussion. On December 7, the convention resolved to bring into the new state seven counties beyond the original thirty-five, namely Pocahontas, Greenbrier, Monroe, Mercer, McDowell, Buchanan, and Wise. At the time, all had become battleground or guerrilla counties. Only Greenbrier sent a delegate to the statehood process. The latter two did not become part of the new state. Willey worried about the legality of bringing them in without their participation. "It cannot have my consent," he said, proposing instead "bringing them in and giving them an opportunity to vote upon the Constitution which we shall submit to them and then to ask the legislature, if they vote to come in—to give them at least an opportunity to include them within the limits of the new State." He further moved to reduce the number to just two, Pocahontas and Greenbrier. William G. Brown of Preston County (not yet sitting in Congress) argued that many of the counties included in the proposed state were "unsound upon the Union question." He cited census figures to show that the disloyal would outnumber the loyal. Brown concluded that if this occurred, someday "we may have the next executive officer of this State, sir, a secessionist. Ah, even the bandit guerilla [former Cabell County congressman Albert Gallatin] Jenkins may be made the governor of the new State of West Virginia by this operation, or some other man entertaining similar sentiments."[19] On December 10, the convention counted the enslaved when calculating the overall population of the new state. Opponents appealed to western unity to bring more counties into the new state, regardless of their wishes. Chapman J. Stuart, whom Curry called a major obstructionist in the Second Wheeling Convention and in the constitutional debates, appealed to western unity to rationalize his stance. Abandoning their fellow westerners exposed them to their mutual enemies. Leaving these counties out of the new state would, he said, "drive those people from you, and tie them up with the people of eastern Virginia with whose interests they are totally at variance. They will be trammeled, sir, and made 'hewers of wood and drawers of water' during the remainder of their governmental life." He proposed including more than a dozen additional counties from the Shenandoah Valley and southwestern Virginia in the new state, as he had done in the earlier meeting. In the end, the convention compromised, adding only nine more counties south of the Kanawha (Boone, Logan, Mercer, Wyoming, Raleigh, McDowell, Greenbrier, Monroe, and Pocahontas) and allowed for Pendleton, Hardy, Hampshire, Morgan, Berkeley, Jefferson, and Frederick to join the new state in the future. Only the last did not. The vote passed thirty-nine to seven, with Stuart voting in the affirmative.[20]

Slavery reappeared on December 14, but sufficient conservative opposition prevented any disruption. Battelle moved that the committee on general and fundamental provisions hear his motion to forbid slaves from entering the new state and that the legislature be empowered to "make such just and humane provisions as may be needful for the better regulation and security of the marriage and family relatives between slaves; for their proper instruction; and for the gradual and equitable removal of slavery from the State." He concluded with a statement ending slavery in the region after July 4 of a future year. These measures exemplify the same "gentle" form of antislavery politics as advocated by Henry Ruffner (who, coincidentally, died three days later in Charleston). Like Hagar, Battelle sought the most beneficial way for all to end the institution on terms that aided the enslaved by encouraging their marital and family structures, providing for their education in the future, and finally moving them elsewhere. Unlike Hagar, however, he made no political statement for none was needed. Nothing came from it. The convention ignored his statement by tabling the motion and, perhaps appropriately, next discussed the definition of treason in the new constitution. Thomas W. Harrison moved four days later to simply apply the Constitution of Virginia's version of that law to the new state. The delegates voted forty-one to two to support the measure to avoid more pointless distractions.[21]

The absence of the slavery issue allowed the convention to discuss many previously marginalized ideas. On December 2, a few days after Hagar's motion, Harman Sinsel of Taylor County and Granville Parker of Cabell County proposed plans for a public education system. They cited examples from Ohio and Pennsylvania for the new state to follow. Later that day, John Powell of Harrison County moved that the new state have laws restricting the sale of intoxicating liquors. The measure passed. On that same day, the delegates approved an anti-dueling provision, lifted from the Virginia constitution, for the new state. A plan to replace the powerful county courthouses and their cliques of lawyers with more democratic townships drew some ire. Every county would have between three and ten such subdivisions, each electing its own constables, supervisors, and justices. William Brown of Preston spoke for many conservatives when he called the idea "a Yankee institution," the likes of which will face "very serious prejudices to institutions coming from that quarter." The delegates debated the issue for several days. The New York–born Peter Van Winkle of Wood on January 18 lamented the size of each township. Chapman Stuart agreed that sparsely populated areas like his Doddridge County would impair voter turnout. More debate raged over the tenure of elected justices at two, three, or four years. On January 20, the delegates voted twenty-three to fourteen to make it four years. They exchanged more words about the powers of these township officers. In the end, the convention adopted this new structure into the new state constitution, but it would form a significant grievance in the future.[22]

The strength of the conservative nature of the convention again showed itself when slavery reemerged on January 27. Battelle had revised his earlier motion by abandoning the welfare of all slaves in favor of freeing the children of the enslaved in three years' time. The legislature would see to their "apprenticeship of such children during their minority, and for their subsequent colonization." The delegates, once again, did not respond to either one. James H. Brown's resolution on keeping slavery out of the convention had worked. Still, this third attempt to raise the issue caught national attention. The New York Post opined that it was folly to divide a slave state just to make another slave state. The Intelligencer sympathized and urged the population to remove slavery from the new state. "Every sensible and well-informed man in the Convention and out of it," it wrote on February 3, "knows that the destiny of Western Virginia is never to be with the South, nor with slavery." It asked the people to "tie sandbags and clogs around our early history . . . around the progress of the current generation." Battelle's resolutions sought to "assist nature, just as gentle medicine in careful hands arrests disease and gradually dispels it from the system." The delegates disagreed. They, again, paid

110 / Chapter 4

no attention to the resolution and carried on debating financing for internal improvements.[23]

Funding new roads, railroads, and canals drew the greatest attention. A north-south split emerged in the convention on the issue. Delegates from the Kanawha Valley desired them to improve ties between their section and the outside world. Those from better connected areas such as Harrison, Wood, Monongalia, and the Panhandle counties sought to avoid excessive debts. The latter won the initial motions. The final one, on February 3, failed by a margin of twenty-five votes against Kanawha's ideas to twenty-three in favor, much to the valley delegates' frustration. Some claimed that this lack of support could have ended the statehood movement. Chapman Stuart called it "the most fatal stab that has yet been given to the prospects of the new state." Henry Dering of Monongalia County worked out a compromise that suited both sides. The convention accepted without debate motions that kept a Virginia law allowing the state to subscribe to stock plans and corporations for improvements as Kanawhans desired but required that any investments "shall be paid for at the time of subscription" or from taxes "levied for the ensuing year, sufficient to pay for the subscription in full" as the others sought. As other scholars have argued, the compromise allowed the convention to overcome a major hurdle with relative ease. Yet it would not have been possible if slavery plagued the hall. This peace did not last long.[24]

Deeply upset at his earlier snub, Battelle carried on his antislavery campaign. The conservative elements in the convention prevented him from delivering a longer speech, which fortunately has survived. Equally fortuitous for the statehood movement, he did not have the chance to use it. Battelle's speech constituted the most important northwestern Virginia antislavery tract to appear since Henry Ruffner's in 1847—and equally ironic given that his brother Lewis represented Kanawha County in the convention. In his speech Battelle urged the end of slavery as "a matter of principle and a matter of expediency." At the heart of its appeal, however, lay an attack on slavery intended to counter the same approach of its supporters. He lamented the attachment of statehood leaders like Carlile and Willey to slavery when they could have abandoned it in previous years. They, he said, defended a system that they "admitted by themselves to be injurious to the State—have, because great folly existed somewhere else, not only permitted but carefully encouraged that system to strengthen with its own growth, until it has well-nigh plunged a whole commonwealth from seaboard to river, in irretrievable ruin!" He was wrong about these men knowing slavery harmed northwestern Virginia, as the population unflinchingly supported the institution before the war. Otherwise, he correctly laid the basis for the war and Virginia's divided status on slavery. As a product of law, he continued, the convention had every right to discuss slavery, which would poison the new state if not removed. The leaders' intransigence, moreover, invited outside interference from Congress or northern states on the issue. Battelle painted a rosy picture of West Virginia's slaveless future. It is worth quoting in whole: "I take it for granted that we all desire, in behalf of the new State which we are seeking to inaugurate, that it shall at once, and with no tardy pace, enter upon that high and honorable career of prosperity that has been so long and so iniquitously denied us as a people; that our virgin land shall be tilled; that our immense mineral wealth shall be disemboweled, that school houses and churches shall crown our hill tops, and that the whole land shall smile with fruitful fields and happy homes." This wistful statement stinks of overselling. Most white northwestern Virginians believed that their region already looked like this, if maybe in need of enhancement as in the public education debate mentioned above. Yet his speech carried weight in public even if he never presented it to the convention.[25]

Back in the hall, Battelle resumed his campaign to the Assembly. He moved on February 12 for a gradual emancipation plan for the region's slaves. It simply began that "no slave shall be brought, or free person of color come, into this State for permanent residence after this Constitution goes into operation." This clause added free Blacks to his earlier resolution, but otherwise it to sought to maintain the racial status quo. Battelle changed the wording of the more controversial second clause from its earlier iteration. It laid out a staggered plan for freeing the region's slaves: "All children born of slave mothers after the year eighteen hundred and seventy, shall be free—the males at the age of twenty-eight, and the females at the age of eighteen years; and the children of such females shall be free at birth." He delayed the start date from 1865 to 1870 and staggered the freedom ages between male and female slaves to ensure the softest possible blow to the master class. He also removed the colonization plan. Finally, Battelle attached a provision for a ballot on the emancipation question for separate consideration by the voters and called for a committee to ensure its fulfillment. Despite this softening, convention leaders such as Ephraim B. Hall of Marion, Chapman Stuart, John M. Powell of Harrison, and Peter Van Winkle of Wood sought a vote to table (to reject) these motions to settle the matter once and for all. The result shocked everyone. The delegates voted twenty-four to twenty-three to table the measure without further debate.

The source of this support is difficult to ascertain. Until this point, only Hagar's motion of November 30 elicited any response at all from conservatives, namely Brown of Kanawha's "unwise and impolitic" rule. They gagged Battelle's two previous resolutions on December 14 and January 27. Yet the February 12 resolution was the first to invite a vote on the slavery issue, and the delegates barely rejected the measure. The evidence used by other historians supports only why conservatives would oppose it, not why free state backers would support it. One clue from the former comes from a letter a week beforehand from Henry Dering to Senator Waitman Willey. Battelle told him that Congress would reject the statehood bill without some action on slavery, a presumptuous argument given federal policy on the matter at the time. Dering feared that "Batell [sic] and his little party will bring up the subject and altho [sic] they will not be able to carry his proposition, yet it will produce disturbance, not only in the convention, but elsewhere both in our own state, and abroad in other struggling states and in y[ou]r body [Congress]." He was barely wrong, as the narrow vote shows. Yet this statement does not explain why so many previously adverse delegates would support the motion. The roll call, furthermore, does not suggest any clear answer. Conservatives like Brown and Ruffner of Kanawha—both slaveholders—and Sinsel, Stuart, Van Winkle, and Hall of Marion voted yea. Nays included Battelle, Hagar, Powell of Harrison, and Brown of Preston (another slaveholder). A geographic analysis likewise reveals no firm patterns. Delegates from the same county split their votes. The Northern Panhandle and Kanawha Valley had as many opponents as supporters. The numbers exclude, however, the fifteen delegates, amounting to a quarter of the whole convention, who cast no vote. Even a pair more in attendance could have changed the outcome. In the absence of other sources, it is unlikely that historians will come up with a satisfactory answer.[26]

Regardless of its origins, the close vote forced the convention to seek a compromise. Previous histories of the convention have tended to read the debates thematically to emphasize the issues that emerged along the way. This method makes slavery but one of many concerns, even if seen as important. Reading the minutes chronologically, the motive behind the compromise becomes clearer. The delegates knew the extent of proslavery views throughout northwestern Virginia. They understood that the statehood project hinged on maintaining the racial status quo. The convention could afford to give ground on some radical ideas on townships and funding internal improvements, but never on slavery. In this sense, the fate of the new state hung in the balance. On February 13, after what must have been a restless night, Joseph S. Pomeroy of Hancock suggested that a committee made up of equal members of both factions investigate and report on what he called "the vexed question" of slavery. Yet he limited the motion solely to Battelle's first provision on barring free or enslaved Africans from the new state, and not the more divisive second part on gradual emancipation. This would at least maintain the status quo. Benjamin Smith, who represented Logan, supported both voting immediately and referring the matter to a committee if the convention so desired. The upset Battelle asked that the absent delegates (specifically Chapman Stuart) return before any vote occurred, which promised to delay the ballot until later that day. This allowed the members time for further discussion, which they tried to reject. John Dille of Preston declared his support for a compromise on the first provision, knowing its prospects for acceptance. He was "willing to say that if this Convention can be reconciled upon that first proposition, and that proposition can be inserted in the Constitution with the cordial approbation of the friends of the proposition and those who may be averse to the whole proposition, that I think we ought to accept it." Compromise would allow the new state to go forward, he continued. It was essential to "concede to the feelings and prejudices of our people and to the feelings and prejudices of those to whom we must look if we expect admission as a state into the Union." At the same time, he opposed the second clause. These sentiments reduced the distance between supporters and opponents. Pomeroy sympathized but continued with his committee resolution. James H. Brown of Kanawha (a supporter) and Elbert Caldwell of Marshall (a dissenter) asked him to relent so the convention could resolve the issue quickly. James Hervey of Brooke, a dissenter, also backed an immediate vote despite his belief that a free state was inevitable. By this point, any opposition to compromise ceased.[27]

Even then, the vote surprised the delegates. Dille, backed by President John Hall of Mason, asked Pomeroy to revoke his motion. Battelle tried again to stall for time to allow Stuart to return, citing his promise to his counterpart. Granville Parker (a dissenter) of Cabell also backed the measure. At this point, supporter Stuart arrived and immediately prepared to vote. Battelle made one last defense of the committee idea to delay any vote, but quickly relented. The convention, at last, voted forty-eight to one to incorporate the Black exclusion clause into the constitution. The lone holdout was William Brumfield of Wayne, who rejected entreaties to make the vote unanimous. He had previously supported the dismemberment ordinance in August. Why he acted this way is unclear. Perhaps the measure was too radical for him. If Battelle or Hagar had been the sole opponent, this would be a much simpler story. Instead, they voted for it. Hiram Haymond of Marion then moved to close the slavery issue once and for all. He asked the delegates, and Battelle in particular, to never mention slavery again. The latter sought and received a personal guarantee preventing any action against him. Predictably, the *Wheeling Daily Intelligencer* lamented the result. It accused the free state advocates of surrendering to their opponents. Dille and Brown of Kanawha outgeneraled them by advocating a compromise and then cutting off their line of retreat, namely finding an alternative motion. It said the deal had no meaning since the war prevented anyone from bringing slaves into the new state. "We answer no," it opined, "for there is no man in the State who could suppose such a thing." This exaggerated the support for a free state in the region. Proslavery men like Brown, it concluded, "knew that this was the cheapest bargain ever he made in his life" when he supported Dille's motion. The delegates reached the compromise out of a duty to form a new state along the same lines as the old one, namely with slavery intact. They prevented debate by agreeing to the more suitable of Battelle's motions. It promised, at least, to maintain the status quo on the issue. It was simply put the best option available to the state makers.[28]

The compromise succeeded in its main aim of removing the major obstacle to passing the constitution. Formalities occupied the last two days of the convention, capped by a forty-nine-to-zero vote on February 18 to send it to the voters. The delegates must have sighed with relief that the ordeal had finally ended.[29] Critics appeared from the frustrated advocates of a free state. The *Intelligencer*, their main vehicle and sadly the only newspaper that covers this period, printed numerous letters from around the region complaining about the new constitution. Its own editorial applauded the document as a big improvement over its eastern-controlled predecessors, but the paper lamented the surrender to the slave interest. "West Virginia as a slave state has no hope in the world," it opined. "She must be free before ever she can be anything. Unless she is, her history will be that of little Delaware or Maryland, instead of her thrifty neighbors on either side of us." A writer from Marshall County argued that more would support the constitution if it included Battelle's clauses. He called the document "good enough . . . for a free State in all other respects, save for the gradual emancipation clause, marred blotted, stained and contaminated with the odor of a slave code." Henry of Hancock also deplored the stench of slavery in the constitution, calling it "merely a subterfuge to make the public believe that some sacrifice has been made in order to meet the free state men." Each of these authors mentioned the need to satisfy Congress, which they suspected contained enough antislavery men who could reject the new state bill. "G. W. Z." of Ritchie County said as much in early March. "We cannot get into the Union this time," he declared, because Congress would see the proslavery constitution "as a joint out of the middle of the backbone, and will hurl it back again and again, until we as a free people, shall have the privilege of coming to the polls and there say what we will have—a free or a slave state." In this, they proved prescient but also premature. Some critics of the constitution spoke about the flawed township system, the political districting, and the troublesome judiciary, as the *Clarksburg Telegraph* remarked in early March. It made no mention of slavery. It is a pity that more conservative sources have not survived to balance this analysis. The radical ones have misled historians ever since.[30]

In his annual message to Congress in December 1861, President Lincoln said what should have been common knowledge to posterity. He praised the border states for siding with his administration. "Noble little Delaware led the way," he said, then continued to Maryland, which "was made to seem against the Union" for attacking troops and burning bridges at the outset of the rebellion. Now, they had firmly sided with him. Maryland, Kentucky, and Missouri, "neither of which would promise a single soldier at first," Lincoln boasted, "have now an aggregate of not less than 40,000 in the field for the Union." He saved the best for last. He praised western Virginia Unionists for remaining loyal to the federal government. "After a somewhat bloody struggle of months, winter closes on the Union people of western Virginia, leaving them masters of their own country," he wrote. This simple sentence accurately described the situation at the time. Between April and December 1861, he allowed each to sort out their internal affairs and their allegiances to the federal government. In northwestern Virginia's case, the US Army fended off rebel efforts to reclaim the area. He did not see the region as unique to the war as later historians have done. In support of this policy, he also encouraged their quest for statehood. By calling them "masters of their own country," Lincoln granted them, along with the other four, the freedom to choose their fate.[31]

The conservative phase of the West Virginia statehood movement depended on this policy. Between November 1861 and February 1862, delegates turned the idea of separation into a workable constitution. They successfully drafted a document that provided for a court system, elected offices, taxation for internal improvements, a new name for the state, and a controversial township system to replace the old elite-controlled county courts. They refused to discuss slavery, knowing well as John S. Carlile did that it could disrupt the entire effort. Individuals like Robert Hagar and Gordon Battelle received the convention's derision when they raised the issue four times. The delegates tabled the matter without a vote on three occasions. On the fourth, the result shocked everyone. From where this support came will remain a mystery, but it was strong enough to force a compromise. Although it was close, the conservative idea of a new state untainted by treason but with slavery became a reality. Without this phase, the statehood movement would have collapsed. Carlile's statue, instead of Pierpont's, would stand today outside Independence Hall in Wheeling if what happened next had not occurred.

Events had already begun to change. When Lincoln gave this address, he also hid a major secret. One week earlier, on December 6, 1861, he met privately with George Fisher, Delaware's sole congressman. He floated to him a plan for gradual and compensated emancipation for the border states. Lincoln believed that the state with the smallest enslaved population in the area would respond most positively to this idea. In turn, Fisher took the idea to the governor and State Assembly. They famously turned him down cold. Only Delaware's State Senate voted five to four to approve the plan. Feeling defeated, Lincoln had to change tactics. As the new year dawned with the rebellion gaining strength, he needed a larger effort to turn the tide. So, still in secret, he expanded the plan to all the border states. This scheme required publicity, but he waited for several months before announcing it. He knew that it would cause even greater controversy than it did in Delaware. Yet it would have a profound impact on West Virginians.

CHAPTER 5

The Radical Phase of the West Virginia Statehood Movement, March 1862–June 1863

On May 3, 1862, a patrol from the Twenty-Third Ohio Volunteers encountered two white men and their enslaved persons near Princeton in Mercer County. Moses Ward and William C. Blaine left Charleston in December, dragging their bondspeople with them over the mountains. Early the next morning, the regiment's commander, Colonel Rutherford B. Hayes, commented to his superior about their allegiances. "They hesitated about taking the oath to support Governor Peirpont's [*sic*] government. They will take the oath to the United States," he wrote. He called their stance "simply mean[ing] secession" and asked that "these wealthy scoundrels ought to be treated with the same severity as other rebels." Many military officers fighting in northwestern Virginia like him had sought a harder line against their enemies from the start of the war. They soon received their wishes. Two months before, President Lincoln announced a plan for compensated emancipation and colonization for the enslaved in the border states. The quartet's rejection of this idea is well known, but historians have neglected the responses of northwestern Virginia. Contrary to previous accounts and their attempts to avoid the subject, northwesterners became one of the plan's strongest supporters. This chapter deals with this transformation. Ward and Blaine knew that the war would turn against slavery and left Union-controlled territory early to protect their enslaved property. Their conservative Unionist family and friends soon wished that they had. The second or radical phase of the West Virginia statehood movement had begun.[1]

This chapter contains a new interpretation of how West Virginia became a state. The Ambler-Curry thesis maintains that Congress compelled the region to accept emancipation as a condition for statehood. The only dissenters, James Oakes and Elizabeth Varon, have argued that the region obeyed the Lincoln administration's need to create a free state in a previously slaveholding area. Neither view is true. On the contrary, both sides fail to see how the statehood movement changed during the war. Whereas in the first or conservative phase West Virginians opposed even mentioning slavery, in the second or radical

117

phase new leadership abandoned that approach. I argue in this chapter that radicals who rose to command the movement in early 1862 encouraged the federal government to free their slaves. Using previously neglected evidence, a new view emerges of this process. The conditions caused by the war split the statehood movement and placed new people in charge who supported gradual emancipation. The friction that caused the division came from Unionists seeing their conservative counterparts place their connections to secessionist family and friends ahead of their political allegiances. The experience of Kanawha County best shows this trend. These changing attitudes influenced the northwestern Virginia leaders in Congress. Instead of being forced to emancipate, all but one of its representatives specifically requested that the Lincoln administration compel the new state to become free. The famous Willey Amendment to the statehood bill came not from external forces but from within the state itself. The enslaved played an important role in that process. The president, his cabinet, and the Republicans agreed. The concurrence of radical Unionists and the enslaved supporting the Lincoln administration's border state emancipation policy brought West Virginia into statehood in June 1863. My approach challenges existing accounts about this subject. Little in them will hold up afterward.[2]

Less than three weeks after the Constitutional Convention submitted its product to the voters, Abraham Lincoln changed the entire game with his border state emancipation plan. On March 6, the president asked—this time publicly—Missouri, Kentucky, Maryland, Delaware, Tennessee's Union government, and the Reorganized Government of Virginia to free their enslaved persons with a pledge for their colonization and compensation for owners. Their reactions to his plan included both opposition and support. On March 11, the House of Representatives voted ninety-seven to thirty-six to endorse the president's plan. Three weeks later, the Senate followed suit thirty-two to ten. Almost all the border state delegates opposed the measure, as many historians have pointed out. They tend to forget, however, that only one of those dissenters, John S. Carlile, represented Virginia. The others, namely Senator Waitman T. Willey and Congressmen Jacob B. Blair, William G. Brown, and Kellian V. Whaley, said aye. Joseph Segar of the Eastern Shore did not participate in these ballots. These votes may seem bizarre given their previous opposition to Lincoln's successes in ending slavery in the western territories, on the high seas, and in the District of Columbia. Yet they make sense when none of those bills touched upon a particular state. Like residents in other border areas, the northwest Virginians opposed federal imposition on the states of any emancipation measure, a key criticism leveled by conservatives.

They could, on the other hand, support it if they agreed to it. As I will show in this chapter, they did. Regardless of the bill, for any northwestern Virginian to vote against slavery constituted a major deviation from the norm. This change exerted a powerful influence on the forthcoming referendum on the new state's constitution.[3]

Instead of facing one choice on the April 3rd ballot, northwestern Virginia Unionists now had two. The official measure asked them to approve of the proposed constitution with its Black exclusion law. Many counties, however, held an unofficial poll on gradual emancipation. Gordon Battelle of Ohio County suggested it in his unpresented but published speech set for late January. The lack of legal authorization from the Constitutional Convention or the Reorganized Government did not deter its supporters. On March 10, Brooke County radicals began to organize their polls. The *Intelligencer* suggested that the "same be done in every county of the New State, so that all the delegates may be equally instructed." Doing so would mean that "there is no estimating the amount of good that may result from it" in the legislature or Congress.[4] A meeting in Upshur County on March 17 followed their example, as did an April 1 rally in Tyler County. The *Middlebourne Plain Dealer* reported that a Tyler County meeting attended by "a respectable number of the citizens" agreed to ask the voters whether they supported or opposed the gradual emancipation of slavery. On the day of the election, the *Intelligencer* reported that "books for this purpose have been prepared and will be found at all the polls in the city," meaning Wheeling. Voting on this measure meant, the paper concluded, that "there can be no such thing as a sincere and ardent new State man, who is not also a free State man."[5] Curry called this ballot "the turning point" of the statehood movement. This argument understates what changed. The second ballot came about not from any inherent antislavery beliefs from the region or even the Northern Panhandle. Instead, Lincoln's border state emancipation plan provided the turning point for West Virginia. Its white people responded in kind.

The preparations had mixed but still astonishing results. Only fourteen counties held both ballots, along with a poll taken from the Third (West) Virginia Infantry then fighting guerrillas at home. Almost all of them took place along the Ohio and Pennsylvania borders. Even then, the numbers indicate great motivation to back the measure. The constitution passed with a margin of 18,862 to 514. The gradual emancipation ballot succeeded with 6,052 to 618 votes. Wherever both choices occurred, the newly radicalized electorate supported emancipation. In Cabell County, for example, 271 backed the constitution while 4 opposed; at the same time, 244 supported the second ballot and 26 rejected it. Upshur County ran 601 for the constitution and 311 for emancipation. Monongalia, respectively, had a wide difference of 1,148 and 649. Wetzel ran at the low end with 491 to 96 for each measure. Tucker County, beset by guerrillas, still managed to turn out 69 votes for the constitution and 55 for emancipation. Those few must have faced trouble afterward. Despite its preparations, Tyler County did not record a vote for emancipation, but 696 supported the constitution. Guyandotte in Wayne County had an interesting experience. Of the 201 voters, only 23 were civilians. The rest were soldiers from other counties. A remarkable 177 of them supported emancipation, including all but two of the civilians. At the same time, John Laidley, the Commonwealth attorney in Kanawha, arrived to condemn the proceedings to the public and voted "a very emphatic No." He, accompanied by James H. Brown, also of Kanawha, and John Hall of Wood, the president of the Constitutional Convention, "held court" in Wayne to "exert their influence to prevent any expression of the people on the Gradual Emancipation clause."[6] As a result of this conservative intervention, the county (as opposed to the town) did not report any votes on the latter measure. Although these results indicate wide variations in support, this observation misses the vital point. It is remarkable that these counties held the vote at all. The radicals shocked the normally conservative region by generating enough political strength to organize a rival ballot on an unpopular topic under wartime conditions and yet received considerable support.

The election result showed the widening gulf among Unionists. Conservatives found themselves caught between their political allegiances and their family connections. As Laidley's "court" showed, they tended to act with impunity in front of their partitioned communities. As early as February, Harrison County experienced these fractures. A meeting held that month resolved to take issue with "the recreant politicians and secession tricksters who had taken possession of the uppermost seats in the councils of our county." In particular, the rally condemned John J. Davis and John C. Vance for having been "detrimental to the best interests of the loyal people of Harrison County" and asked them to resign. These "neutral-ground-compromise men" like them, the resolutions continued, represented an "element more dangerous and destructive to putting down the rebellion, than the open and avowed secession soldier in the ranks of his army." In April, a Harrison correspondent informed the *Intelligencer* that they had some "prominent secessionists here, and some who have had a great influence over a certain class of people." Willis Patton and Dr. Austin, he claimed, armed secessionists but fled to the rebel army for protection. Despite being "too cowardly to fight for the cause they so manfully defended while there was no danger," these men returned home a few months later. Patton's local friends, the author stated, "went to work and bailed him out" after the court charged him with treason. Inexplicably, he afterward worked as a lawyer for accused secessionists. In each case, the actions of high-placed Union men toward their rebellious family and friends drew the condemnation of loyal citizens.[7]

Kanawha County provides the best record of how the Unionist cause factionalized. The Slack family then in charge of the county dispatched numerous letters to Governor Pierpont about the behavior of more conservative Unionists over a dispute over office holding. Other counties may have had similar experiences, but the Pierpont Papers contain only those from Kanawha. In September 1861, a flood seriously damaged its salt refineries and the towns along the river. The disruption to that vital artery threatened to unsettle the local economy as much as the guerrillas did. Benjamin H. Smith, the US Attorney and a prominent local figure, wrote to Pierpont in March 1862 about clearing "[a] dredge boat that was worked off; it is thought may still be reclaimed as it lodged a few miles below town" and resume river traffic and its vital toll revenue.[8] He asked William J. Rand, his brother-in-law, to lead these efforts. He in turn hired the services of toll collector Elisha Williams, a known secessionist, to perform the work. When word of his employment became known, the Slacks and other county leaders took issue with the appointment. In May, Green Slack wrote to Pierpont about the matter, coyly spiting their first names in the process.

> Our mutual friend "Benny" [Benjamin H. Smith] after being foiled in his efforts last winter to get a good place for his "sympathizing" brother in law in the capacity of collector of tolls (including the use of money which was an important item in broken down aristocracy)—has succeeded in "fixing the papers" so as to get "Billy" [William J. Rand] into the place of general superintendent of roads and rivers and treasurer and has already given a "good job" to a secession spy [Williams]. This was done in the absence of Mr. Ruffner and myself, or I am free to say (without egotism) that it would not have been done.[9]

While open to the charge of nepotism, Smith could defend his actions on the grounds that few loyal white Kanawhans or enslaved persons were available to do the work. A lack of alternatives, not disloyalty, therefore, probably prompted his actions. Slack, with considerable egotism, spoke for another group who refused to accept a known secessionist working for the same government that he had initially sought to overthrow. This event started what became the Civil War in Kanawha County among conservative and uncondi-tional Unionists.

In June, the radicals began a countywide effort to remedy the situation in their favor. The Slacks founded the Union Club of Charleston to protest Smith's actions. It published its constitution and resolutions in the *Kanawha Republican* and later the *Intelligencer* for all to read. Its third article left no doubt about its views on secessionists and their allies. "The objects of this club are to defend ourselves against secret sworn enemies in our midst who seek to crush and destroy our Union loving, and law-abiding citizens and to build up the doomed cause of rebellion, by insinuating themselves into offices and employing rebels as officers or laborers under them to the exclusion of loyal men, or otherwise aiding or abetting rebellion, particularly obstructing the course of justice," it read. The club directed this policy not only against seces-sionists but also toward conservatives who bent the rules. Another resolution welcomed "all loyal men—men who prove themselves as such—back to our midst, but perjured traitors we will treat as such."[10] By this, they meant Smith and Rand. They contended that the pair had acted improperly by employing a known secessionist in the county government and were therefore unfit to hold office. Rand's appointment "meets our unqualified disapprobation. He has given no evidence whatever, of either support for, or sympathy, with either the Government of the United States or the restored Government of Virginia, since the passage of the Ordinance of Secession, but on the contrary has openly associated and sympathized with the enemies of both since that." The Union Club then asked Rand, but not Smith, to resign.

Smith's response to these attacks shows the conservative mindset at work. In a July letter to Pierpont, he reveals both a different view of the Rand affair and a criticism of his fellow Unionists. Smith informed the governor that the Union Club had its facts wrong. Rand was not a secessionist, he argued, although it was common knowledge that his son Noyes served in the Twenty-Second Virginia. At worst, Rand employed a friend to recover the boat when no other options existed. Smith referred to the Union Club as a mob trying to disrupt loyal men for its own ends and against his own. After attending one of their meetings, Smith denounced their actions as extremist. To Pierpont, he described the meeting as "only calculated to raise a quarrel among Union men, to divide and weaken us. This is no time for such folly. But we suspect that selfishness is at the bottom of the proceeding. I regard the present proceeding as a lawless attempt to control the free and prudent action of the Board in the performance of their duty."[11] As one of the county's leading figures and a prominent public official, Smith took the club's accusations of disloyalty as criticism of his own loyalties. He determined to carry on as before unfettered by this factionalism.

Undeterred, the Union Club likewise carried on its activities. In August, it gathered signatures to ask the governor to take direct action against Smith, Rand, and Williams. In the petition, the club gathered the "unanimous vote of hundreds of our people, assembled together . . . respectfully requested Mr. Rand to resign, which request was formally, and in respectful language presented to Mr. Rand by the Executive Committee of the Union Club of Kanawha Court House." Although Rand said he would resign, "Mr. Smith would not allow him to do so."[12] They also claimed that Smith had manipulated the improvements board for his own ends. He operated it without informing two of its five members of its decisions and used the remaining three to support his agenda, namely the appointment of Rand and Williams. The petition gathered several hundred names, although it is unclear how many came from Kanawha County. Thousands of refugees had fled there from the guerrilla-infested interior counties. The Union Club could easily have solicited their signatures. The petition indicates how the radicals refused to compromise with the rebels and their associates in the broad Unionist coalition. The petition made it clear that only the truly faithful could govern. It declared that "the day of demagogues are past with us: for it is self-evident that it requires efficient and heavy blows, well directed, and well laid on, in order to save our Government, our freedom and our rights in a Free Government, vouchsafed to us by the Living God."[13] The unconditional Unionists turned on anyone they considered to be too close to the enemy. If other parts of northwestern Virginia had similar experiences with factionalized Unionists as Kanawha did, then the region's political relations radicalized to the point where basic institutions, including slavery, faced severe risk.

This escalating split between northwestern Virginia Unionists also occurred in the halls of Congress around the same time. The Reorganized Government had a front-row seat in these proceedings. Historians tend to exclude that body from these deliberations, but in fact they participated in all of them. The positive votes for the region's delegation had help from within beyond what happened in Kanawha and other counties. In May 1862, Granville Parker of Cabell County sensed that the statehood movement needed help to overcome conservative intransigence. He composed and circulated around Washington a pamphlet calling for Congress to accept their statehood in exchange for supporting the "Nation's Proposal" on gradual emancipation. Titled "An Appeal of the People of West Virginia to Congress," Parker, writing as the "Loyal People of West Virginia," laid out the perceived grievances that existed within the Old Dominion over the previous forty years, such as taxation, representation, suffrage, and internal improvements. Yet he specifically targeted local figures who he claimed were "wolves in sheep's clothing" for thwarting the statehood movement from within by their proslavery views. Congress, they argued, had to act fast to secure West Virginia from these internal and external foes, especially since General McClellan—whom that region's loyalists held in high esteem for his actions a year earlier—seemingly had the rebellion at his mercy with his Peninsular Campaign. The best way to do this, he concluded, was to embrace the gradual emancipation measures then under discussion. This nearly forgotten document, which has been cited only twice before, indicates two purposes. First, it shows that intractable conservative elements in the Northwest continued to control the region's affairs and the statehood movement. The radicals, like the Slacks, therefore needed outside assistance to overthrow them on the one issue they clung to most dearly, slavery. Second, the pamphlet hinted to Lincoln and some members of Congress that they had an ally in the border states who would support their controversial and thus far unsuccessful plans for emancipation. This document, which appears as Appendix A, changes everything that we know about how West Virginia abolished slavery.[14]

Their timing was no accident. Earlier that month, on May 6, the Reorganized Government in Wheeling gave its approval to separating the northwest into a new state, thereby fulfilling the constitutional obligation. The bill allowed for the merger of forty-four counties with a provision for three more—Berkeley, Jefferson, and Frederick—to join in the future. On May 29, Willey submitted the bill to the Senate. His speech, however, could have come from the pages of the *Intelligencer* and *Wellsburg Herald*. He outlined the radical vision for the new state and its importance to the Union. First, he stated that the people of northwestern Virginia acted constitutionally by rejecting the parent state's secession. Richmond took them for granted when Letcher chose to side with the Confederacy in May 1861. Their resistance, embodied by the Wheeling Conventions, was therefore legal and necessary. Willey cited the desertion of local officeholders as the prime requirement for those meetings. Those former potentates abandoned their posts and left the remainder without effective government. "We were without the means for enforcing the laws for redress of civil grievances or for punishments of crimes and misdemeanors. We were without legal protection of life, liberty, and property," Willey told the senators. He then asked them, "What were we to do? What could or ought we have done?" His answer told his Republican colleagues what they wanted to hear and what the country needed: a loyal government in the border South made up of citizens willing to embrace their policies.

His next words outlined the value West Virginia presented to Lincoln's border state emancipation plan. First, its geography pointed the region toward loyal states like Ohio, Pennsylvania, and Maryland. The nation would also benefit from its industry, economy, and access to plentiful resources that Virginia neglected to exploit. Thus positioned, slavery appeared meaningless to its white residents. Despite having vigorously defended the practice in the past, Willey cited the free labor ideology familiar to readers of the *Intelligencer* and *Herald* readers and decried by everyone else. Slavery, he said, had "never flourished there. It never can. The inexorable laws of climate forbid it." Steady declines in the numbers of bondspeople in the region supported this view. He claimed that in 1860 roughly 12,700 slaves resided in northwestern Virginia, but that number now amounted to not more than "nine or ten thousand." Their flights to freedom conveniently solved the problem for whites. Deeply moved, famed Massachusetts Senator Charles Sumner asked Willey to direct this memorial to the Committee on Territories. With this speech, he identified the radical agenda for West Virginia statehood. The region's white population, with some Black help, threw off their shackles, picked up the reins of government, and chose what many believed at the time to be the winning side. The problem still lay in asking those same northwesterner men to support a Republican administration which almost none of them had previously supported and working for the end of slavery, one of the key institutions of the southern states.[15]

Conservatives fought back immediately. Trouble began when the Senate assigned the bill to the management of John S. Carlile. In his report on June 23, he tried to sabotage the bill by adding fifteen more counties from southwestern Virginia and the Shenandoah Valley to the new state and requiring a new convention to meet with freshly elected Unionist delegates from them. He also added a gradual emancipation clause that freed slaves born after July 4, 1863, but retaining the rest. He intended this odd mix of contrasting policies to thwart the statehood movement. Carlile knew full well that neither conservatives nor radicals, in the region or in Congress, would accept it. The former could never support emancipation, nor would the latter accept the inclusion of new counties who would in turn never approve of any antislavery measure. Sumner, emboldened by Caldwell's pamphlet, said as much in his response to Carlile's bill. He opposed the inclusion of another slave state and two more proslavery senators under any circumstances and moved to amend that clause to end the institution upon the granting of statehood.[16] The Senate also rejected the change after much spirited debate on June 26. Events on July 1 saved the bill from inevitable disaster. Supporters of West Virginia statehood argued that they could not deny the measure that its radical faction earnestly sought. John P. Hale of New Hampshire said that he would be a hypocrite if he voted against anyone supporting the president's border state emancipation plan. He said that he would hail the admission "of a slave State into the Union with a clause in her constitution for gradual emancipation and abolition . . . with more satisfaction and gratification than I would a free State outright." Benjamin Wade of Ohio likewise argued that West Virginia offered the federal government an opportunity to see a slaveholding state voluntarily end the practice. He asked the senators to consider "if you find another slave community that will voluntarily come to Congress and pray you to permit them to come in with a constitution that shall finally wipe out slavery in a few years?" The pamphlet combined with Willey's earlier statements had their intended effect on that august body. Carlile's obstruction failed to attract support from any quarter. Only more pressing business that day and on July 7 prevented the Senate from voting on the statehood bill at that time.[17]

The next debate day decided the fate of both the West Virginia statehood movement and the fate of slavery in the border states. On July 14, the Senate resumed its debate of the former bill. Lyman Trumbull of Illinois sought more time for the debate, but Wade of Ohio insisted on rushing it to a vote. The West Virginians, he said, were entitled to a decision on this matter. With a vote of twenty-five to eleven, the body proceeded with the abbreviated discussion. They first rejected Sumner's immediate emancipation amendment eleven votes to twenty-five. Willey of Virginia then put forth his own modification. It called for the new state to free the children of the enslaved upon accession and declared that no loyal citizen "shall be excluded from the enjoyment of any of the privileges and immunities to which such [a] citizen is entitled," by which he meant slave ownership. It also sought a state convention to ratify these provisions and submit them to popular referendum. Once approved, the president would confirm the issue, but Congress would be excluded from the process. Willey's idea tried to steer a middle course between pro- and antislavery influences. It freed only the youngest enslaved people, but also sought to prevent radical Republicans in Washington from stopping even that limited process. It was by any measure unworkable, yet it still showed that someone in the border states supported the president's plans. Wade and James Lane of Kansas worked with Willey to modify to make the bill more practical. The result still bears his name: "The children of slaves born within the limits of this State after the fourth day of July, eighteen hundred and sixty-three, shall be free; and all slaves within the said State who shall, at the time aforesaid, be under the age of ten years, shall be free when they arrive at the age of twenty-one years; and all slaves over ten and under twenty-one years, shall be free when they arrive at the age of twenty-five years; and no slave shall be permitted to come into the State for permanent residence therein."

I must analyze his proposal in full. The first part, which freed slave children born after July 4, 1863, came directly from Carlile's initial bill from a few weeks before. Willey added the next two categories to spread out the effects of emancipation. They were, however, essentially meaningless. As mentioned above, he admitted that the only slaves remaining in the region consisted of the very young and the very old. The enslaved within those age ranges had largely escaped to neighboring free states. The remainder, mostly the parents of young slaves, were so few to no longer pose a serious concern for the white majority. The last phrase about forbidding slaves from permanent residence resembles the Constitutional Convention's exclusion law, although it allowed at least in law free Blacks. That too was a moot point since very few from that group lived in northwestern Virginia before the war. The Willey Amendment was not a completely empty gesture. While it barely touched the remnants of slavery in the region, it had a big impact on the statehood movement. It satiated the Republicans' need for a border state to enact their emancipation policy, while empowering the West Virginia radicals' battle against their conservative opponents. Carlile tried to scuttle the idea during that debate with more lengthy blather, but Wade would have none of it. More important business ceased debate on the issue.[18]

Later that day, the border state delegation to Congress, including a pair of Tennesseans, visited Lincoln over his plans for them. The encounter had mixed effects. In a report about the president's proposal, most of the attendees opposed him. While they had no problem voting for troops and taxes to support the war effort, they drew the line at emancipation. The speed at which Congress voted for his plans for the enslaved in the District of Columbia and in the western territories denied them the ability to fully consult with their constituents. This rapidity made them fear that federal authority would override the constitutional ability of states to abolish slavery. They also balked at the cost, which they doubted the federal government could raise. Their biggest criticism came in the strategic implications of emancipation. It would, they claimed, "not have strengthened the arm of his government or weakened that of the enemy" for these loyal states would never have deserted to the enemy. Lincoln should continue his soft policy to assure rebellious persons that the Union would protect their rights and property. Carlile voted with this group of twenty representatives and senators, which has received the historians' attention. Less well known was the minority report that appeared the next day, which appears as Appendix B. The several dissenters indicated significant divisions within the border states. They represented a faction who believed it was irresponsible to resist the growing pressure to deal with the rebellion and its cause in slavery. Victory, they claimed, depended on antislavery men in the southern states. "The Government," they said, "cannot maintain this great struggle if the support and influence of the men who entertain these opinions be withdrawn. Neither can the Government hope for early success if the support of that element called 'conservative' be withdrawn." Men like them were willing to ask the white population in the border states "calmly, deliberately, and fairly to consider your recommendations." A total of seven delegates signed this document, including one each from Delaware (Fisher), Missouri (John W. Noell), Kentucky (Samuel L. Casey), and Tennessee (Andrew J. Clements) and three from the Reorganized Government of Virginia (Brown, Blair, and Senator Willey). Horace Maynard of Tennessee and John B. Henderson of Missouri submitted separate but similarly oriented dissents in the coming days. Lincoln and the congressional Republicans must have seen a grand opportunity as they read these two responses. Their hopes for southern Unionists to support their policies had come at least partially true. Even better, one group stood out from the rest: West Virginia. On top of that, neither their statehood bill nor the Willey Amendment sought compensation.[19]

Given this context, Senate Republicans had good reasons to pass the West Virginia Statehood Bill. On an anxious July 15, they tried to speed through the act. Carlile and other conservatives debated the bill as much as possible. They even tried to delay the bill until Congress's December session, but without success. Stressed out by the affair, Wade then called for a vote. The tally was almost entirely partisan. The twenty-three supporters included twenty-one Republicans, one northern Democrat (Henry M. Rice of Minnesota), and one border state Unionist (Willey). The seventeen dissenters represented both parties, including seven Democrats (including Lazarus Powell of Kentucky), six Republicans (one being a disgruntled Sumner), one Know Nothing (Anthony Kennedy of Maryland), and three border state Unionists (Garrett Davis of Kentucky, Robert Wilson of Missouri, and Carlile of Virginia). The latter's choice made him a pariah in the region then and ever since. This constituted almost the entire body of the Senate at the time. The absent James Pearce of Maryland would have voted against it, but an illness that felled him later that year prevented him from attending. Likewise, John B. Henderson of Missouri probably would have supported it given his stance in favor of Lincoln's emancipation policy. Even if they had voted, the outcome would not have changed.

With the Senate's approval, the statehood bill now went to the House. It, however, would not meet again until December. Much would happen in that time.[20]

Carlile's negative vote had massive consequences for him across the northwest. The radical press attacked him mercilessly. The *Intelligencer* carried multiple stories in the following days that condemned his betrayal of the cause. "Civis" asked its readers, "Can such duplicity and treachery on the part of a representative pass unnoticed by the people?" The *Wellsburg Herald*, another radical paper, denounced Carlile's disrespectful behavior toward the president at the meeting with the border state delegation. If the voters had their say, it opined, "his language could not have been blunter than would be the vote of condemnation that would be recorded against him." "New State" called for friends of the movement to "call meetings all over the proposed new State and speak out" to let Congress know that "Carlile is misrepresenting the feelings and sentiments of the people of the new State." A meeting in Taylor County consisting of seventy-five "best and most influential citizens" attacked Carlile for "voting with secessionists and secession sympathizers" by opposing the statehood bill. The conservative *Ritchie County Press* went so far as to reject their previous support for him. "We have ever been the friend of Mr. C.," it opined, "but this act of baseness and ingratitude has placed him among ingrates, beyond the hope of a resurrection, and brings down upon him the eternal execrations of nineteen-twentieths of his constituency." These selections should suffice to prove what the ascendant radicals and others thought of his actions.[21]

Carlile spoke for an increasingly besieged group. Despite the efforts of Curry to rescue them, conservative voices were rare. Much of their criticisms focused on their mistaken belief that Congress forced them to accept emancipation as a condition of statehood. Peter G. Van Winkle wrote to Willey in June that he opposed emancipation in the Constitutional Convention to avoid having it "supposed that slavery caused, except as one item as many, our desire for separation." If Congress dictated it, then it would "produce the deprecated effects." Carlile's own newspaper, the *Clarksburg National Telegraph*, lamented this dictation a few days later. "What right has Congress to impose such terms upon the people of any State. Let Congress either refuse it or grant it. We are opposed to Congressional dictation on the subject. Let the people determine the question for *themselves* in *their* own way." Neither of these sources wanted to admit the obvious about their region's affairs: the radicals were taking over and sought, and obtained, congressional assistance to prevail over their foes. Carlile admitted as much in a speech that he gave in Indianapolis on July 30. "Never did I feel the slightest alarm for the ultimate triumph of my country," he began, "until during the last session of Congress, when I saw a controlling working majority carrying out the policy of such men as [abolitionist] Wendell Phillips—then and on then, I felt there was danger." He expressed great faith in the loyal population in suppressing the rebellion, but he "fear[ed] the spirit that controls the dominant party in Congress." Its latest decision on emancipation now aimed at "the overthrow of the established rights of the States, which, in their view, no longer exist." It was therefore up to the loyal people to elect men to save the country from the Republicans. Carlile failed to realize, as many northwestern conservatives did, how much the war had changed the region's affairs. Emancipation no longer deterred an increasing number of whites who now saw slavery as the cause of the nation's distresses. Indeed, they wanted Congress to decide the matter. No conservative could fathom such a change. Carlile did not abandon the statehood movement; it abandoned him.[22]

Statehood would have to wait in the summer of 1862. The war intervened after the Confederates turned the tables on a larger Union force besieging Richmond. Upon arriving in March, the massive federal army led by McClellan seemed poised to capture the rebel capital and finally end the insurgency. In May, however, an aggressive Robert E. Lee defied military logic by attacking his larger opponent along the Virginia Capes in early June, known to history as the Seven Days Battles. He won, despite losing most of the battles and one-third of his soldiers in the process. Hurled back to the James River, McClellan withdrew his forces back to Washington by water. Lee rested his troops for a time before pursing his foe northward. Lincoln placed Major General John Pope in charge of a new force, the Army of Virginia, to protect Washington. Needing troops, the new commander brought regiments from across the northeastern states as well as from northwestern Virginia. Although plagued by guerrillas, many Union units from the region moved by water and rail from as far away as the Kanawha Valley to the outskirts of Washington. As they left, the troops repaid Carlile's actions by relabeling the camp outside of Wheeling after the statehood movement's new hero, Willey. When Pope failed to stop the Second Battle of Bull Run in late August, Lee's seemingly unstoppable rebels stood just miles from Washington. Instead of attacking the well-defended capital city, his army headed northward again into Maryland. The two forces clashed once again along Antietam Creek on September 17. That titanic battle became one of the bloodiest days in American history. Although it resulted in a strategic victory for the Union, Lee's army escaped to northern Virginia. At the same time, a similar event occurred in the western theater around Perryville, Kentucky. Both Confederate armies hoped to win over border state whites unhappy with Lincoln's emancipation overtures to their cause. Each overestimated the extent of support in Maryland and Kentucky, and their depleted and frustrated armies returned to their bases.[23]

Relieved Union morale imparted important effects on the course of the war. Lincoln, after a long debate that began during the Peninsula Campaign, used the occasion to issue his Emancipation Proclamation, which converted his war aims to freeing enslaved persons in rebel areas and recruiting Black men into the army and navy. His act exempted areas under federal control including the four border states, Tennessee, occupied parts of Louisiana, and portions of eastern and northern Virginia, but also in his words "the forty-eight counties designated as West Virginia." These simple words stem from the support given by the fledgling state's representatives for his emancipation plans had their intended effect on the Republican-led White House. Afterward, they could do little wrong in his eyes.[24] Governor Pierpont furthered his standing with the president when he stood alone among the border states when he endorsed the Emancipation Proclamation at the Altoona Conference in Pennsylvania. Called by Pierpont and several other Union governors, the meeting allowed Lincoln to gauge support from across his domain. Several executives declined to attend, including Kentucky, Missouri, and Delaware. Pierpont's approval of the Proclamation, reinforced Lincoln's confidence in the region's quest for statehood.[25]

While the two main armies clashed along the Potomac, another Confederate force tried the same strategy in northwestern Virginia. In September and October, William W. Loring resumed his efforts to reclaim the Kanawha Valley. He succeeded where Lee, Floyd, Wise, and Jackson had failed a year earlier. Brushing aside the few remaining Union troops in the area, the Confederates captured Charleston on September 12. For the men of the Twenty-Second Virginia, the occupation served as both a homecoming as well as an attempt to reestablish the old regime. William Clark Reynolds, a clerk from Kanawha Salines, recorded his reactions in his diary. On September 11, he reported, "Reached the Kanawha Valley!" Two days later, he wrote, "Reached my home after an absence of fourteen months. Our army continued to drive the enemy before it. [We] had a considerable skirmish at Charleston." Reynolds, like his comrades, was most eager to see his family. On September 14, he reported that he "went to Malden and saw my relations and friends." Reynolds still had military duties to fulfill. After seeing his family, he reported for guard duty in Charleston. He said that he "stood sentinel for six hours over the vault of the Bank of Virginia burnt by the Yankees."[26] Other soldiers used their time in Kanawha to fulfill other obligations. The regimental history reported that Richard Q. Laidley and Noyes Rand married their wives and sent

132 / Chapter 5

them eastward to Greenbrier County.[27] For Kanawha's Confederates, the occupation was a return. For the Slacks and their allies, it was a time of reckoning.

As in Maryland and Kentucky, the Confederates overestimated the appeal of their cause in the Kanawha Valley. Recruitment, one of their top priorities, fell flat. At first, Loring boasted that he could enlist as many as five thousand soldiers from the area.[28] He soon discovered that few potential recruits remained there. Many residents, not just Unionists, fled west toward the Ohio River with the Union Army rather than face Confederate conscription and/or reprisals. Those who remained proved reluctant to join up. Recruiting duty tore William Reynolds from his family in the Salines. He recorded in his diary that on September 17, "Maj. Gen. Loring gave me authority to raise a company of cavalry." Two days later, he reported meager results. He said that he "went over to Chap Reynolds's and he and I went up to the mouth of Field's Creek trying to raise recruits for my company. Was not very successful everybody having already volunteered."[29] The regimental history of the Twenty-Second Virginia also reported few enlistments, and those who did sign up quickly changed their minds. It reported that the regiment "alone gained approximately 75 men, although a few deserted during the retreat from Charleston."[30] Loring also used a newspaper to win popular support from the area. Titled the *Guerilla*, it is the only surviving Confederate source from northwestern Virginia during the war. Its two issues reveal the desperation of their attempts to win support. They first called on local businesses to use Confederate currency. Inflation had ruined the appeal before it began. "A great many merchants have re-opened their stores to the public. Others, however, still keep themselves and their goods shut up in the dark, because they have some scruples about taking Confederate money," the newspaper reported. Loring and his officers knew that they could not force the merchants to take their currency, so they used their newspaper to kindly encourage compliance. The *Guerilla* hoped that "they will soon come to their senses and show that they appreciate their deliverance from the Northern vandals, by immediately opening their stores and offering their goods at the same rate they sold to the Yankees. And it is well here to add; that it is a great wrong and outrage, and it speaks poorly for anyone to take advantage of his fellow being in-adversity."[31] Loring's chief of staff, Henry Fitzhugh, a prewar Charleston banker, issued a general order to the population regarding the value of Confederate currency. "The money issued by the Confederate Government is secure, and is receivable in payment of public dues, and convertible into eight per cent bonds. Citizens owe it to the country to receive it in trade; and it will therefore be regarded as good in payment for supplies purchased by the army. Persons engaged in trade are invited to resume their business and open their stores," Fitzhugh proclaimed to what he hoped was his people.[32] There is no sign that these financial appeals worked.

Frustrated with the lack of response, Loring then resorted to using the slavery issue to win support. Conveniently for him, Lincoln announced the Emancipation Proclamation during the occupation. Using the *Guerilla*, the Confederates called the order to free slaves in areas in rebellion a desperate move. "Lincoln seems to be getting to the last stages of infamy and despair," it reported, leaving him "baffled and defeated at every point, he is now writhing under the punishment he promised us." The latest Cincinnati papers, it continued, reported that "on the first of January 1863, [he will] cause to be emancipated all slaves, or persons of African descent, who shall then be in the employ of any person residing in any State still in rebellion against the United States."[33] The newspaper added that Lincoln's acts further isolated him from the Union cause. Shifting its war aims from restoring the Union as it was into a crusade against slavery would alienate Unionists who still supported the institution. "Poor Abe," the *Guerilla* stated, "like a drowning man, has for the last month been grasping at every little straw, but all has been of no avail, and he is now in the last struggles of death, with not the least hope to cheer him in his last moments."[34] Because the proclamation threatened to undermine slavery, the basis for southern society, Loring anticipated a warmer response. Despite the Kanawha Valley being the largest slave-owning area in northwestern Virginia, the menace of emancipation did not translate into more Confederate support. At the end of October, Loring's army withdrew having achieved little except securing a few thousand bushels of salt.[35] Upon his return to the Shenandoah Valley, the Confederate War Department replaced him with John Echols. Loring spent the rest of the war in the western theater, particularly around Vicksburg. The departure of his army allowed for the resumption of Union government under the Slacks.

The occupation confirmed the radicals' worst fears about the loyalties of their neighbors. While exiled in Point Pleasant in Mason County, Green Slack wrote a candid letter to Pierpont about the situation. The occupiers left the county "entirely robbed and stripped of everything that is cutable." Many families suffered as a result. The prewar elites who grew rich off the salt business provided the basis for the area's secessionists, noting "there is not a salt maker in the Kanawha Valley who has ever before been accused of entertaining very strong Union sentiments except Lewis Ruffner and Fred Walker." Even conservative Unionists came under suspicion. Slack deplored the way that these elites deferred to Confederate officials. He wrote, "These men are very eloquent and lavish in their praise of the higher officers of the Confederacy, for their gentlemanly bearing and honorable deportment towards citizens and even Union men."[36] When the occupation revealed what Confederate tyranny had to offer, Slack reflected the frustration that radicals felt for those who could openly support the Confederacy when it was clear they had nothing to offer. Slack particularly resented the continued conservative tolerance of Confederates in the county. Benjamin H. Smith managed to obtain permission for his son Isaac to return from Confederate service and resume his normal life without taking the oath of allegiance. A possibly exaggerated column in the *Fairmont National* of August 1, 1863, stated that Smith "with a profusion of tears and most piteous appeals prevailed on the [Grand] Jury not to find an indictment against his own son for treason."[37] True or not, they granted his wish. Isaac's name does not appear in any of the US district court record books. Slack, the county sheriff, saw this as an attack on the rightful authority and on himself. In an October letter to Pierpont, he stated that he understood "that Ike Smith (the idol of old Benny's heart) after refusing a great many offers of protection if he would come home and be loyal has after acting as Commissary Clerk for the army during its occupation of Charleston, graciously concluded to stay and resume his place at the bar providing he can do so without taking oath to the 'Pierpont and Green Slack Government' (pardon me for associating those names, it's only a quotation.)" No radical Unionist could see this situation as "gracious." Secessionists, particularly women, remained a constant source of irritation to local Unionists. "The great question now before us," Slack wrote, "is what to do with the rebels in our midst. Many of the rascals have gone and left their rebel wives to communicate information and insult Union men claiming the protection which common gallantry awards to their sex. How are we to deal with them?"[38] He concluded that the time had come for radicals to demonstrate that they were the proper authority in the county.

Pierpont did not have an answer to this query. Conservatives continued to place personal connections above their political allegiances. Isaac Noyes Smith and John P. Hale, both officers in the Twenty-Second Virginia, resigned their commissions and attempted to resume their lives in their home county as if nothing had happened. A physician turned salt maker, Hale had paid for his unit's cannons out of his own pocket at the start of the war. Benjamin H. Smith, Isaac's father, and Lewis Ruffner nonetheless asked Pierpont to pardon the pair. They argued that neither man posed a threat to the Union government or the population. "They never took the oath of allegiance to the Southern Confederacy, having persistently refused to do so. During their detention within their jurisdiction, they steadily and entirely rejected all overtures of business or office urged upon them. These gentlemen of high standing and nice sense of honor are most valuable members of society whom the community here we may say unanimously desire to remain among us undisturbed," the authors argued.[39] Ruffner's participation here is especially interesting. His impeccable Unionist credentials and dedication to the new state should have placed him at odds with secessionists. Yet, in this case, he placed his connections to Hale above all that. The two had been business partners in Ruffner, Hale and Company, which John Stealey calls "a central sales agency" formed by many of Kanawha's salt manufacturers in 1856 to deal with the declining market.[40] Business apparently took precedent over politics. Slack already knew of Benjamin H. Smith's attitudes, but Ruffner's actions must have frustrated his attempts to assert Union control over the county.

Local Unionists thus demanded even tighter security in the valley. Green Slack, now back in Charleston, wrote to Pierpont in December 1862 that unconditional Unionists preferred the Eighth Virginia, made up of locally recruited soldiers, to fulfill this role. "There is intense feeling among the citizens," Slack wrote, "at the bare moment of the fact of the removal of the Regt. Several of our citizens began to talk about 'packing up' to leave. For it is a fact well understood here that our Union citizens feel a greater security under the protection of the 8th than under 3 times the number of other troops." Moreover, they were better equipped than another unit to enforce federal and state rule. "The secessionists and secession sympathizers," he wrote, "have a greater terror at the presence of that regiment than they have at the presence of any other set of men."[41] Slack neglected to mention that his son Hedgeman commanded the unit, which would have added to his authority. About two weeks later, the *Wheeling Daily Intelligencer* printed a letter from "Kanawha Valley" echoing the same ideas. The author, who was possibly Green Slack himself, said that the soldiers in the Eighth were "well skilled in the use of the rifle and fully acquainted not only with all the roads and bypaths of that mountainous country, but also with the proclivities and antecedents of all the inhabitants, knowing their friends from their foes, whatever might have been their professions of loyalty."[42] The latter skills would have been ideal for the Slacks. The occupation exposed the strong ties between the men of the Twenty-Second Virginia and conservative Unionists. Returning the Eighth Virginia to the Valley, therefore, would bolster their cause by keeping those loyal in charge and the secessionists and their supporters at bay. It is entirely likely that other areas experienced similar tensions between radicals and conservatives, but their sources either did not survive or remain undiscovered.

The House of Representatives took up the Senate's bill when Congress resumed sitting on December 9. The ensuing debates were both short in duration

136 / Chapter 5

and narrow in scope. Conservative members repeatedly focused on the constitutionality of the Reorganized Government of Virginia's authorization to divide their state. Republican Martin Conway of Kansas wished that the House had made western Virginia into a territory so that an enabling act could turn it into a state. His home underwent that process only two years before, albeit after much controversy between its dueling Lecompton and Topeka constitutions. William G. Brown of Virginia responded with the radical view. The bill, he argued, was both constitutional and expedient by virtue of its enforcing federal and state laws since 1861. The statehood bill was, furthermore, inspired by the 1796 act by which Virginia allowed Kentucky to separate. He also cited his presence in the House as proof of legitimacy. As for expediency, he said that northwestern Virginia had a larger population than Kansas and more territory than any New England state. It also placed more troops in the field than required by War Department quotas. Numerous petitions, finally, proved that its people wanted statehood as soon as possible. These strenuous arguments enervated the radical cause. Schuyler Colfax of Indiana then chimed in with a statement that should forever end any constitutional criticisms of West Virginia's statehood process. The federal executive and legislative branches proved the legality of Virginia's Union administration by accepting its senators in July 1861; presidential recognition, payments to the treasury, supplying troops to the army, and its later notice of congressional apportionment that brought four representatives (Brown, Blair, Whaley, and Joseph Segar of the Eastern Shore counties) into the House all demonstrated the state's validity. He forgot to include that the judicial branch also recognized Union authority due to the functioning of federal district courts in the region. Yet the conservatives refused to relent. Conway carried on by saying that Kansas was a territory that sought statehood, while northwestern Virginia's desire to bud from its parent without its constitutionally required consent. The venerable John J. Crittenden of Kentucky echoed this sentiment. He stood on the constitutional requirements for the process. Just because the Letcher government in Richmond was illegal, he argued, did not make the Pierpont administration in Wheeling legal. Against this attack came rebuts from the radicals including other southern Unionists. Horace Maynard, one of the two congressmen from Union-occupied Tennessee, had no problems with the legal concerns. This was, he said, no time to mince words with traitors.[43]

A two-hour debate on December 10 sealed the matter. John W. Noell of Missouri agreed with the bill, arguing that Congress had a duty to protect the republican form of government. The Reorganized Government of Virginia did precisely that when it rejected secession. Supporting them meant subverting the rebellion and protecting, not undermining, the constitution. At this point, Joseph Segar of the Eastern Shore finally spoke for other Virginia Unionists on the matter. He had no sympathy for the rebels, but he accused the statehood bill of being "retributive justice" against his constituents. Like other opponents, he claimed that the Reorganized Government lacked popular support, but added the slavery issue that his counterparts tried to avoid. "The people made a pro-slavery constitution, but Congress has virtually made for them an anti-slavery one," he said. This act was "a flagrant departure from the great doctrine that the States may of right manage their domestic affairs." He, like other conservatives, could not accept that the radicals had taken over Virginia and Congress alike. His words had no impact on the coming vote. At two o'clock that day, the House of Representatives voted ninety-six to fifty-five in favor of the West Virginia Statehood Bill. The breakdown indicated that, as in the Senate, partisanship decided the matter. Supporters included eighty-two Republicans, six Democrats, one Unionist (Sheffield of Rhode Island), one border state Democrat (Noell of Missouri), and six border state Unionists. The latter group included three of Virginia's four congressmen (Brown, Blair, and Whaley) as well as Andrew Clements and Maynard of Tennessee and Samuel Casey of Kentucky. The opposition came from twenty-nine Democrats and twelve border state representatives (including Segar); thirteen Republicans sided with them. Benjamin Thomas, a Unionist from Massachusetts, also opposed the bill.[44]

Responses to the news in northwestern Virginia showed how far apart slavery had separated radicals and conservatives over the statehood process. The radical press loved Congress's action as vindication for their cause. Not even word of the defeat at Fredericksburg dampened the news. "Glory to God in the Highest," bellowed the *Intelligencer* on December 11, "at last we are rewarded for all our labors and have reached that happy haven where our works do follow after." It then called for meetings in Wheeling. Other communities also celebrated the event. Despite being Carlile's hometown, Clarksburg held one two days later. Fireworks, speeches, and a parade marked the event outside of the courthouse. "Are we, the people of West Virginia, not now a free people?" asked a reporter to the *Intelligencer*. "Thank God, the tie, which has bound us to that rebellious Trans-Allegheny part of the state is severed—yes, severed forever," they concluded. Likewise, Marion County cheered the approach of statehood as a victory over the conservatives. "I.M." reported that opponents cited "abolition, abolition, and Congressional dictation" as their main criticism of the separation movement. Supporters would have to confront people like this when the convention reassembled to vote on approving the Willey Amendment.

138 / Chapter 5

They had to remain strong in order to resist calls of "Abolitionist! Abolitionist!" "You honest Virginia, you are the haggard villain, the blue light ghost! I hope in God that the time is at hand when all such traitors in West Virginia will get their rights. N—dom is not my king nor master."[45] Conservative voices are noticeably absent from the written record, but it is clear from these radical statements that the congressional act dealt them a bitter blow.

Despite these positive sentiments, supporters feared that the Statehood Bill faced another serious obstacle. As required by the Constitution, Congress sent the act to the White House for Lincoln's signature within ten days on December 15. Illinois senator Orville Browning (who voted against it) took the bill to his friend and fellow Republican. He reported to his diary that the president "was distressed at its passage and asked me how long he could retain it before approving or vetoing. I told him ten days. He wished he had more. I replied I would give him a few days more." Despite the questionable legality of this delay, no one asked about the extension. Browning's observation about the president's mental state is also debatable. Surely, he had much on his mind with the defeat at Fredericksburg occurring four days earlier. His famous statement "if there is a worse place than Hell, I am in it" comes from this date. On the other hand, Lincoln had been monitoring the congressional debates on the bill. He knew well that two issues, namely its constitutionality and its expediency, dominated those discussions when he referred the matter to his cabinet for their opinions on December 23. By doing so, he asked them two opposite questions that guaranteed careful deliberation on legal, strategic, and political factors. This long delay prompted much concern among the West Virginia delegates. Pierpont visited the president personally and sent a letter and two telegrams to him about the bill. Willey, Brown, and Blair, along with Archibald W. Campbell, editor of the *Intelligencer*, J. W. Paxton, one of Pierpont's advisors, and E. M. Norton, the US marshal for Western Virginia, also lobbied the president and the cabinet. Blair recalled years later that he, Willey, and Brown saw Chase, Seward, and Montgomery Blair, the postmaster general, about the bill, but not Stanton, Bates, or Welles. A frustrated Pierpont dictated a final telegram to the president. "I am in great hope you will sign the bill to make West Virginia a new State. The loyal troops from Virginia have their hearts set on it; the loyal people in the bounds of the new State have their hearts set on it; and if the bill fails, God only knows the result. I fear general demoralization and I must not be held accountable," signed Pierpont. Historians often read this message as an act of desperation, but the governor crafted it to carefully emphasize the value of West Virginia to Lincoln as head of the Union war effort. He used the term "loyal" twice to clarify the value of the new state's military contribution and political assets to Lincoln. As if the former was not strong enough, Pierpont used the latter to underscore the popular support for the border state emancipation policy. Lincoln could not have missed such an obvious sign.[46]

Nor did he. This bill was exactly what he had hoped for since March 6. Since that time, the other border states had turned down his compensated emancipation plans cold. The Emancipation Proclamation hardened that opposition. Missouri's convention tabled the idea by a wide margin in October. A December attempt also failed when both radicals and conservatives opposed the gradual measures. Kentucky's legislature denounced the plan because it "would excite the people of the disaffected States to still greater exertion to overthrow the Government." Delaware elected more conservative figures in its last election that prevented any discussion of the matter. Maryland opposed any debate at all before the proclamation in September, when some cracks began to emerge among the state's hitherto unified Unionists. In Lincoln's mind, only West Virginia among the border states supported his plans. Being an astute politician, he saw and exploited the opportunity.[47]

On the last day of 1862, Lincoln made his decision on the West Virginia Statehood Bill. The president met with Willey, Blair, and Brown on that wintry day. He told them about the opinions of the cabinet members. They were split evenly on the act. Bates, Welles, and Blair opposed the bill for its lack of constitutionality. Bates, the attorney general, called the Reorganized Government's provisional nature a violation of the letter and the spirit of the Constitution and the law in general and thus outweighed any expediency. His counterparts repeated that view. Seward, Chase, and Stanton supported the bill. Chase repeated Speaker Colfax's sentiments in the House earlier that month by citing the federal government's support for Pierpont's administration as proof of its constitutionality. Seward and Stanton agreed on the same terms. Notably, only two of these opinions mentioned the word "slavery." Stanton cited it once in his brief statement when he wrote that the act by which "the Geographical boundary heretofore existing between the free and slave states will be broken . . . surpasses all objections which have occurred to me on the question of expediency." Blair used the term twice but to contrast the free west from the slave east. He opposed the bill because it contradicted the upcoming Emancipation Proclamation. The "re-establishment of Federal power in Eastern Virginia extinguishes Slavery there," he wrote, "and thus removes the great cause of oppression upon the West." These contrasting opinions left Lincoln to cast the deciding vote. His opinion, which he read before the West Virginia delegates, was in Jacob Blair's later words "the clearest, most pointed, and conclusive of all that was read to us. Above all it was the most *satisfactory* to us." Lincoln dismissed those who refused to support for the Reorganized Government, whether secessionist or Unionist, as irrelevant to the matter. He asked, "Can the government stand, if it indulges Constitutional constructions by which men in open rebellion against it, are to be accounted, man for man, the equals of those who maintain their loyalty to it? Are they to be accounted even better citizens, and more worthy of consideration, than those who merely neglect to vote? If so, their treason against the Constitution, enhances their constitutional value! Without braving these absurd conclusions, we cannot deny that the body which consents to the admission of West Virginia, is the Legislature of Virginia." Furthermore, he concluded that the precedent of dividing a state in wartime was "no precedent for times of peace." West Virginia may have separated, but he argued that it was "difference enough between secession against the Constitution, and secession in favor of the Constitution." The legalistic views of the conservatives held no sway with the president.[48]

Lincoln then answered the expediency question with great brevity. He cited the northwestern Virginians' support for his war policies. The Union "can scarcely dispense with the aid of West Virginia in this struggle," he began, "much less can we afford to have her against us, in Congress and in the field." These last words indicate that Lincoln knew of the region's votes in March, April, and July. The region had been, he wrote, "true to the Union under very severe trials. We have so acted as to justify their hopes; and we cannot fully retain their confidence, and co-operation, if we seem to break faith with them. In fact, they could not do so much for us if they would." He owed it to them, therefore, to reciprocate their desires. Lincoln's next sentence provides perfect proof that he linked the border state emancipation policy with his decision to approve of West Virginia statehood. "Again," he wrote, "the admission of the new State turns that much slave soil to free; and thus, is a certain, and irrevocable encroachment upon the cause of the rebellion." He concluded that "the admission of West Virginia into the Union is expedient." For the third time in the fledgling state's history, a federal official sang words that West Virginians wanted to hear. Their fears dissipated when the president, seen in figure 5 a year later, signed three little words to the bottom of the document: "Approved, Abraham Lincoln."[49] Although much remained to be done, the West Virginians had won the biggest battle for statehood.

The news of the presidential signature evoked cheers from the radicals. The *Wheeling Daily Intelligencer* gave its wholehearted support. "Never," it proclaimed, "were a people more delighted with a New Years' gift, for never did a people have such a one before." The president's actions "doubly endeared himself to the people of West Virginia by this act of his, which frees the bonds

Fig. 5. Abraham Lincoln, ca. 1862 (Library of Congress). Upon becoming president, Lincoln first paid little attention to northwestern Virginia. Yet he respected its drive for statehood as part of his need to retain as many white southern Unionists as possible. When radicals took over its government and supported his plan for border state emancipation, he happily signed the statehood bill.

of their ancient oppressors; and brings to them at last the realization of their long agone dreams and deferred hopes of two generations." Likewise, the wives of three of West Virginia's leaders praised Lincoln for signing the bill. Mrs. Francis H. Pierpont, Mrs. Samuel Crane (state auditor), and Mrs. Lucian A. Hagans (secretary of state) thanked him for having "us from contempt and disgrace. The wildest enthusiasm prevails. The people are running to & fro, each one anxious to bear the Glad Tidings of this great Joy. A Happy New Year to you Mr. President. May not another hair turn grey. May your cares be less, and may you live to receive the benedictions of our children's children." The Confederates attacked it immediately. Letcher told the General Assembly in Richmond that he would never surrender the region for any reason and demanded its return. Northwestern conservative views on the matter are unclear. No copy of the *Clarksburg National Telegraph* has survived to give us Carlile or his editor R. S. Northcott's immediate opinions, but they must have raged at seeing their movement surrender to the radical Republicans.[50]

Conservatives awaited the forthcoming Constitutional Convention to thwart or at least modify the gradual emancipation requirement in the statehood bill. With the convention set for early February, they had six weeks in which to mobilize their supporters and faced an uphill battle. The radicals had dug in deep. Appeals to racial fears, a common conservative tactic, fell on deaf ears. One editorial in the *Intelligencer* claimed that gradual emancipation would have no appreciable effect on the number of free Blacks in West Virginia. The departure of many of the region's bondspeople nullified the effects of freeing them. "The truth is that the proclamation of freedom will be the exodus of the negro from among us. A few will remain with their old masters, a few will linger around our own towns and cities as waiters and porters in hotels and steamboats, but the great bulk of emancipated slaves will scatter abroad and seek positions in other States where their services may be required," the editorial opined. The slaves, therefore, would solve the white radicals' problem for them.[51] Another editorial two weeks later demanded that the convention strictly comply with the gradual emancipation clause. "It therefore behooves all friends of the new State to be awake and on the alert to see that the *right* men are elected and returned, and that all the Delegates, both new and old, are *instructed* to carry out the wishes of their loyal constituent," pleaded its author.[52] The italicized words indicate the strength of radical conviction in driving forth their agenda. A year earlier, even the mention of emancipation shook the region. Now, few dared to say otherwise.

Conservatives mobilized all the same as the convention neared in early February. An anti-statehood meeting took place in Wheeling on February 4. A radical Mr. Ross and a conservative Mr. Richardson competed for the seat of Battelle, who had died the previous summer. The latter attacked his opponent as an abolitionist and supporter of Republican tyranny. He concluded his hour-long speech by calling upon the voters of the "great importance of their at once asserting their manhood" by resisting Ross and his cohorts. Sherrard Clemens, the former Democratic congressman, still bearing wounds from his duel with O. Jennings Wise six years earlier, emerged from seclusion to speak to the crowd. The record of the meeting that appeared in the *Intelligencer* contains only descriptions but not his actual words. It claimed that his "almost savage ferocity of his denunciations" against the restored government and the new state amazed the audience. He questioned the constitutionality of each and attacked Pierpont, Willey, Wade, Sumner, and other officials for their actions in support of such measures. At the same time, he "exalted the patriotic Carlile to the skies." Finally, the report states that Clemens "announced himself as a Butternut," a term usually ascribed to Confederates but now in common use against conservative Unionists. That this meeting occurred is not in dispute. The statements made during it, however, may not be accurate.[53] A month later, Clemens wrote to Pierpont regretting some of the things he said. He denounced as "falsehoods" any claims of his disloyalty. On the contrary, his views on the "revolutionary and unconstitutional" controversy surrounding the statehood movement resembled those of many Republicans in Washington, including Bates, Seward, and Congressman Stevens. "Do not allow yourself to believe I have faltered in my devotion to the Union," he urged the governor. "Every Union man ought to stand in favor of the constitutional right, law, order, and the fundamental principles of government without which our liberty is the song in the cage of the bird," he concluded.[54] Despite his personal misgivings, Clemens's sentiments did not lead to a conservative victory, but it was close. Ross, the radical, won by a mere two hundred votes. Although defeated, the opposition to emancipation and statehood remained strong.

Nonetheless, radicals constituted a majority in the convention when it reconvened on February 12, a year after it had last met. In many ways, this session was a mirror image of the last. Willey himself started with a long speech about his proposed amendment. After asserting that the Reorganized Government was perfectly legal, he stated that his bill served the public good. Since it freed few slaves down the road, no whites would lose out while most stood to benefit. "Shall it be said we shall not remove the obstruction of a few hundred thousand dollars' worth of slaves out of the great highway of our State to wealth, prosperity and power," he said. Willey continued along a line that he would not have said in years past. "Certainly," he stated, "it cannot be the value of the property or interests affected by the act of admission, which constitutes the objection of the opponents to this measure. It must be the value attached to slavery as an institution and a desire to see it perpetuated and diffused all through our western counties, as it is in the eastern section of the state, which prompts this opposition to a division of the state." His view coincided with those of the radical delegates.[55] For conservatives, however, the Willey Amendment still went too far. Some tried to disrupt the proceedings with demands for compensation and set up a committee of five to investigate the matter. James H. Brown of Kanawha interrupted the convention by demanding compensation for loyal masters. The federal Constitution's Sixth Amendment, he argued, required the government to repay owners of property taken for public purposes. The committee agreed that precedents and law allowed for compensation. They recommended passage of the Willey Amendment with a plan for compensation to loyal masters after statehood. Brown, described by Granville Davisson Hall, the convention's secretary in 1902, as "the special champion of the slaveholding interests," dissented and moved that Congress set aside two million dollars to pay owners to give up their slaves immediately. The label could have applied to others. Shortly thereafter, James S. Wheat of Morgan County moved that any compensation come from the sale of rebel property, including the enslaved. In his heavily divided area, all the masters sided with the Confederacy. "I have never seen a slaveholder that is loyal. I know, sir, that if this compensation is to be paid to loyal men, you will not lose a dollar. Let us tell them we will donate it. Whenever we appropriate for public uses, I am willing to pay," Wheat said. In response, he moved to amend the proposal to pay the compensation from the sale of rebel property, including slaves, rather than by raising taxes on the loyal. The next day, the old obstructionist, Chapman Stuart, countered the motion. He, like a few others, was a loyal slaveholder. He explained to Wheat about the risks he ran in his position. "I want to show you one . . . and if you don't believe he is loyal, come along with him and he will show you what sacrifices you have to make to be loyal." He said that he "would not be standing on this floor today had it not been for the fear I had of the agitation of this present subject now before us."[56] Conservatives like him would not give up without a fight.

Their opposition complicated but did not delay the passage of the Willey Amendment. After five days of bickering, the delegates voted down both Brown's proposition and Wheat's proposal by a narrow margin of twenty-eight to twenty-six. This alone shows how strongly conservatives opposed emancipation even at this late stage in the statehood process. Each motion failed for different reasons. The convention's majority would never accept the first for it was unworkable in practice. As Stuart's outbursts stated, all slaveholders felt threatened. The second called for the unpopular idea of both immediate and compensated emancipation. They went with the original plan. In a polar reversal of the earlier constitutional debates, the delegates voted fifty-four to zero with two abstentions to approve the Willey Amendment unchanged. The convention closed on February 20 after approving a referendum on its actions a month hence.[57]

The more hardcore conservatives carried on the fight in other ways. Their conservative newspaper, the *Clarksburg National Telegraph*, ceased publication when Northcott left its editorship to command the Twelfth West Virginia Infantry. He later spent nine months in the notorious Libby Prison in Richmond.[58] The surviving newspapers can attest to their opinions. The *Intelligencer* carried many stories about opposition to the new state. A meeting held in Ohio County on March 9 condemned the new constitution as abolitionist in nature and degrading to white labor. One speaker, Robert Sweeney, said that the influx of free Blacks meant more competition for jobs. White men who "now receive $1.50 per day would then only get 75 cents." The meeting resolved that it was the "duty of the Democratic Party, and of all who are opposed to abolitionism, to rally to the polls and vote against the amendments," which were "injurious to our best interests." A proposed conservative convention in Parkersburg failed to take place. Not only did few supporters appear, but the Wood County sheriff refused to open the courthouse to, of all people, Judge Jackson, a stubborn opponent of the amendment. He probably returned to his corn afterward. The voters, meanwhile, approved the new constitution by 28,321 votes in favor to 572 against. One-quarter of the votes came from soldiers, almost all of them supportive of the measure, including those from as far away as the Fourth West Virginia Infantry then encamped near Vicksburg, Mississippi. Even Richard Orr Curry, a perceptive observer of the statehood movement, called it a "solid endorsement by northwestern Unionists." Not even the destructive Jones-Imboden raid across the northwest in April and May had the power to change many minds. The stage was now set to make northwestern Virginia into a state of its own.[59]

As early as May 1862, Chester Hubbard of Wheeling summed up the process that made West Virginia a state one year before it happened. He wrote to his friend Willey how the term "abolitionist" has lost "all its terrors to me." Now, he supported both "a new state and a free state." If not, he concluded that "the Butternut will hand us over to the tender mercies of Eastern Virginia for all coming time."[60] No clearer statement exists to support how radicalized the movement became. A combination of the war's impact on the home front in northwestern Virginia and changes in the Lincoln administration's emancipation policies split the Unionist faction in two. The conservatives, who had previously been in control, lost ground to the radicals. They had only themselves to blame. Many counties experienced what Kanawha did when its established figures placed their kinship ties to Confederates and secessionists ahead of their loyalty to the Union. In response, radicals jumped ahead by devoting themselves unconditionally to the federal government. While hardly abolitionists, they became enthusiastic supporters of Lincoln's border state emancipation policy. All but one of the Reorganized Government's federal representatives backed the president's plan when few others would. Little wonder then that Hubbard's views proved so popular and powerful in the formation of West Virginia.

As Colonel Hayes's captive slaveholders discovered, events changed fast for northwestern Virginians between March 1862 and June 1863. At the beginning of the period, West Virginia appeared ready to enter the Union as a slave state. Yet, a year later, it ranked first among the border states to abolish the institution. The radical takeover of the statehood movement explains this transformation. Previous historical interpretations that centered the region's limited connections to slavery have tended to see those ties as timeless. This is wrong. It took a two-stage process to turn white West Virginians against slavery. The conservative phase contained the issue. If it had continued into 1862, it is unlikely that their proslavery constitution would have passed a Republican-led Congress. It took the following radical phase to achieve that important goal. It grew out of many whites seeing the war affect the region in deeply personal ways. Guerrillas attacked the sanctity of their homes. Conservative Unionists tainted the integrity of their government by placing kinship ties to secessionists ahead of their allegiances. These experiences radicalized Unionists to support stronger measures against the rebellion, including straying loyal citizens. Kanawha County showed this trend clearly, and others may have followed it as well. The role of the enslaved themselves was also crucial. By escaping to free territory, they made whites' approach to emancipation much easier. Instead of seeing this as a unique experience of West Virginia, history ought to see it as the first of the border states to end slavery on their own. Maryland and Missouri followed suit in 1863 and 1864, respectively, while neither Kentucky nor Delaware rejected it outright. Now that Lincoln's signature certified the Willey Amendment to the West Virginia Statehood Bill on April 20, the Thirty-Fifth State would enter the Union formally as the fifth border state two months later. The legacies of the radicals' support for emancipation would plague it for years afterward.

CHAPTER 6

West Virginia under Radical Rule, June 1863–December 1869

The clouds cleared just in time for the West Virginia statehood inauguration celebrations on June 20, 1863. Thousands of people turned out in Wheeling for the noontime parade. Hosted by Chester Hubbard, the ceremony began with a prayer from the Reverend J. T. McClure. After invoking God's guidance, two governors spoke to the gathering. Francis Pierpont, the chief of the Reorganized Government of Virginia, expressed his desire "to see West Virginia free from all the shackles that shackle man" and that she "grow to be the proudest State in all the glorious galaxy of States that form the nation." He then introduced Arthur I. Boreman, the first governor of the new state, to speak. His inaugural address laid the radical agenda for his administration. First, it set out the reasons for the occasion. He recounted the many eastern abuses of the west, including "unfairness and inequality of legislation," their "unjust majority in the legislature," and taxation for the "construction of railroads and canals in the East" while having "refused to make any of the modern improvements" to connect to the west. Hence, the west had "the proud satisfaction of proclaiming to those around us that we are a separate State in the Union." His words echoed those of Waitman Willey explaining his antislavery amendment, the editorials of the *Wheeling Daily Intelligencer*, Caldwell's pamphlet, and every history of this event since published. No doubt that Major Theodore Lang of the Sixth West Virginia Cavalry and future *Intelligencer* editor Granville Davisson Hall recalled Boreman's words in their books three decades later.

The governor then set out his plans for the new state. The security situation demanded, he believed, strict and severe measures to suppress the rebellion. He asked "the indulgence of a generous constituency" to accommodate his need to suppress their common enemies. He reminded the crowd that the enemy has "applied the torch to public and private property, murdered our friends, . . . and robbed and plundered our people." One need only see the "gaunt hunger [that] stares many families of helpless women and children in the face." The crowds needed little reminding of that as they applauded. To end the rebellion, Boreman asked his people to obey his policies. "Shall we coincide with those who carp and cavil at everything that is done by the administration in Washington," he began. He then pointed out the need to obey the suspension of habeas corpus, to not object to the destruction of slavery, and to keep the war going until victory. "We want no peace," he continued, "except on the terms that those in rebellion will lay down their arms and submit to the regularly constituted authorities of the Government of the United States. Then, and not till then, will the people of West Virginia agree to peace."[1] Ominously, he did not mention what his administration would do about the formerly enslaved. These dire words dictated the new state for the next nine years.

Boreman's statements indicate the deep divisions caused by emancipation in the new state during its first years. Over twelve months earlier, radicals disregarded the region's proslavery views to overcome their conservative opposition both at home and in Congress. President Lincoln rewarded their efforts with his signature on the statehood bill, but the rifts among Unionists widened further for the remaining two years of the war and for the four succeeding years. West Virginia experienced this time as did two of its sister border states. While Kentucky and Delaware remained in conservative hands, radicals gained control in Missouri and Maryland by promising stern war measures against the rebels. Each in this trio endured bitter debates over proscriptions against returning Confederates to prevent them from mingling with conservatives and the future status of the formerly enslaved. Previous works on West Virginia's experience do not agree on what to call the period after statehood. Some call the period *reconstruction*, the common term for the postwar years in which the victorious Union tried to establish new governments in the defeated Confederacy to preserve peace and enforce emancipation. Others refer to the period as unique to West Virginia's experiences. John Stealey labels the era *counterrevolution* due to the internal responses by conservatives and former Confederates against the radical regime.[2] This chapter offers the more appropriate term *redemption*, meaning to redeem a person or place from sin. As in the other border states, white West Virginia radicals saw their opponents as degraded traitors who would undermine the war's sacrifices if they attained power. The latter, conversely, saw their opponents as abolitionist fanatics who openly collaborated with the Black Republicans to end slavery and deprived them of their rights as white men. Conflict defined West Virginia's first years. Neither side would back down. Despite the furious attacks of more numerous conservative opponents, the radicals retained their strength until undermined by external, not internal, factors. Their rebellion continued long after the rebels surrendered at Appomattox.

Statehood brought no closure to West Virginia's internal security problems. If anything, it exacerbated them. The guerrilla war continued unabated

Fig. 6. Arthur I. Boreman, ca. 1860 (Brady-Handy Collection, Library of Congress). As West Virginia's first governor, Boreman spent his two terms fending off incessant attacks by conservative Unionists and former rebels. He succeeded due to effective enforcement of proscription laws. Radical rule faltered only after the Fifteenth Amendment split the Republicans into regular and "let-up" factions.

throughout the state. Bands raided at will soldiers and civilians alike, only to disappear into the hollers and hills. No number of troops could eliminate the guerrilla problem. In its second act ever, the state legislature authorized

150 / Chapter 6

Boreman, who like Carlile and Willey also had his picture taken upon taking office (figure 6), to take measures for self-defense. On June 23, he called for federal assistance. Neither measure accomplished much. In September, citizens in Gilmer County, the heart of guerrilla country, pleaded with the governor for help. "All of the leading and most active officers of the County have been compelled to leave their homes and have for months been refugees," the petition began. It then appealed to Boreman's patriotism by pointing out that "unless we have troops stationed here it will be impossible to organize the county into Townships and participate in the fall elections." There was little he or anyone could do given the area's remoteness. The state militia lacked weapons. Many of its troops served outside of its boundaries, such as the Seventh West Virginia Infantry with the Army of the Potomac, and the Fourth Infantry at Vicksburg. Most of the army under General William Averell at Droop Mountain in November 1863 came from Ohio and Pennsylvania. The Union victory that day in Pocahontas County, called "West Virginia's Gettysburg" by one scholar, did not in fact end the Confederate menace to the new state. Instead, the guerrillas plagued it for years to come.[3]

A bigger issue came with returning Confederates. Even before the war ended, many rebels abandoned the fight in response to calls from home. They posed a potential security threat to the new state. Federal policies, as shown in chapter 4, allowed former rebels facing treason charges to post bail and remain at large among family and friends. The case of Isaac Noyes Smith and John P. Hale showed their neighbors in Kanawha County how closely kinship ties with conservative Unionists affected the allegiances of both. As more returned in 1863, the problem threatened to become more acute for state authorities. Former rebels could with relative ease influence the political behavior of their Unionist kin to question federal and state war policies. Radicals feared this would affect the first elections in the fall. On October 9, the *Intelligencer* wrote that loyal men should never vote for a man "who has opposed the new State, the Emancipation Proclamation, the Confiscation Act, the arming of negroes to kill rebels, or any measure calculated to render treason odious, impoverish traitors, and put down the rebellion." The editors later described slavery as ruinous to the country: "Freedom has . . . always pursued a defensive policy. Slavery has always been aggressive." Its harmful effects on the federal government had to stop. "We have tried the one," the *Intelligencer* proclaimed, "and our present condition is the result. The other is the only way now open to peace and permanent tranquility." The conservative *Morgantown Monitor*, edited by William P. Willey, the senator's son, responded by defending the credentials of Congressman William G. Brown. It asked its readers if it was "not conservatism" if Brown favored "a vigorous prosecution of the war under the Constitution . . . a hearty support of the Administration in all its constitutional measures for the suppression of the rebellion . . . a restoration of the Union as it was and the Constitution as it is." He was also "opposed to all the radical intriguing and scheming for the abolition of slavery."[4] Brown won reelection, while conservative Peter G. Van Winkle beat radical *Intelligencer* editor Archibald Campbell for the legislature's vote for the Senate. While the radicals retained control of the state government, conservative gains caused them much concern.

Boreman responded by increasing the penalties for disloyalty to the new state. An original oath came just days after the new legislature first sat, itself borrowed from the Reorganized Government's version of June 1861. The new one required that all officeholders swear allegiance to the United States and to West Virginia. This soon proved inadequate. In November 1863, the legislature passed an even more stringent oath that demanded much of state officers. First, it demanded that the candidate "have never voluntarily borne arms against the United States." This was simple enough, but the rest of the oath was confusingly worded to disqualify as many as possible. Candidates also had to declare that they had never "given no aid or comfort to persons engaged in armed resistance" against the federal and state governments. This included "countenancing, counselling, or encouraging them in the same." These three words implied a wide range of activities. Harboring a former rebel, as Smith and Hale's friends and family did, fell under this provision. Nor could a candidate swear that they had ever sought or held an office in the Confederacy. This provision would impact the eastern and southern counties that later came under Boreman's control as the war slowly turned in the Union's favor. Officials there faced expulsion for having served the Confederate and Virginia state governments during the war, having never seen a Union soldier for most of it. It also jeopardized conservative Unionists in other counties who had secessionist friends and family.[5]

The oath had a mixed effect on the new state. The federal district court headed by John J. Jackson continued to carry over hundreds of treason charges between sessions. Only twelve took the new oath in the court's combined sessions in Wheeling, Clarksburg, and Charleston in April 1864, and all had to post bond. Even fewer faced the full force of the law. The court seized the property of two Kanawha County Confederates, George S. Patton and John N. Clarkson, both then serving far away in the rebel army. The fates of the slaves, with Clarkson owning seventy-one and Patton only one in 1860, are unknown. These represented but two cases out of hundreds before the federal court in

West Virginia. Had more been prosecuted like this, the history of the state could have been quite different. Its old antebellum ruling class would have been financially ruined. Yet it remained intact.[6] Many there continued to see the new state as illegal and temporary, fully expecting the war to end in a negotiated settlement that would return the area to Virginia. The radical *Wellsburg Herald* reported that those of "the butternut persuasion in this locality" thus regarded the oath "with the greatest antipathy and abhorrence." It was "an infringement of their rights" and "unconstitutional." The *Herald* exposed their hypocrisy: "It is quite a noticeable feature that their constitutional rights are, in their estimation, synonymous with the liberty which they enjoy of embarrassing the government in its efforts to put down the rebellion."[7]

Boreman also enacted the first measures to purge slavery from the new state. Shortly after passing the new oath, the legislature modified the Virginia slave code to the needs of the Willey Amendment to the state constitution. One law required owners to provide for slave minors. Another forbade masters from bringing in new slaves to the state, even if they had been in northwestern Virginia prior to its independence. If they did, the new law freed them after six months. A third law forbade masters from taking their slaves out of the state to deprive them of their legal right to emancipation. Finally, the act forbade the sale of slaves to pay claims or taxes. These provisions passed the House of Delegates amid heavy debate. The Senate, on the other hand, tabled motions to free families of enslaved men who volunteered for military service and to pay three hundred dollars per slave in compensation to loyal masters. The senators, however, passed new rewards for capturing fugitive slaves, established procedures for the delivery of runaways, repealed the offense of speaking or writing against the institution, and allowed for the education of the formerly enslaved. This bill passed, surprisingly, unanimously and without debate in October 1863. The radical agenda had, in less than two months, undermined the institution of slavery that had once united all white Virginians together. The enslaved played a major role in this process. Those who could depart for Ohio and Pennsylvania over the previous two years considerably eased the state government's job. Conservatives, on the other hand, still balked at the notion of emancipation. They especially resented the willingness of radicals to support and even encourage the federal government to make West Virginia a free state.[8]

Implementing the township system further fueled conservative resentment of the new state. The Constitutional Convention approved of this substantial change from the long-established county court system. Many lawyers made their fortunes and reputations in those forums. The new arrangement divided up counties into townships governed by popularly elected supervisors and boards. Boreman praised the new system in his first governor's address in January 1864. Despite some delays in implementing the new system, he praised the "manifest great industry and intelligence, and an honor purpose on the part of the Legislature to give the friends of the system proposed by the Constitution the benefit of a fair trial of it before the people." This was far too generous. The township system posed a serious threat to the old regime. Prewar elites could not control them as they had the old county courthouses. This meant, however, finding loyal citizens dedicated to keeping the administration safe and secure from any perceived threats. To see men who dared to end slavery above them was too much for the conservative Unionists and their Confederate kin. After the events of 1863 they needed to rebuild themselves into a new party dedicated to restoring the antebellum status quo.[9]

The war itself gave ammunition to both conservatives and radicals in the border states. After Ulysses S. Grant triumphed over the Confederates in east Tennessee, Lincoln elevated him to the nation's highest military command. Now in charge of every Union soldier and sailor, he began a broad campaign that he and others hoped would crush the rebellion once and for all. Each army would act in what he called "concentration in time," each simultaneously engaging opponents from Virginia to Louisiana. He personally accompanied three armies in the former, while Sherman directed the western army toward Atlanta. A fifth army led by Nathaniel Banks worked its way up the Red River in Louisiana. By June, stubborn Confederate resistance stymied them all. One band of resistance, led by Major General David Hunter, invaded the Shenandoah Valley from West Virginia but accomplished little but the end of his career. The optimism of the spring now gave way to concern. Border state radicals called for sterner measures to press on to victory, but conservatives also gained ground with the war weariness. Maryland Unionists rose sufficiently to hold a convention and a referendum on immediate emancipation. It passed by a narrow margin to become the second border state to free its slaves after West Virginia. Missouri's radical faction likewise overcame their conservative opponents in late 1864, as did Tennessee's. Kentucky and Delaware, however, rejected any such moves. Like with any race, the competition was not far behind. West Virginia's conservatives rebuilt their strength using racialized attacks on emancipationists. One of those was the *Wheeling Daily Register*, edited by Lewis Baker, it became the leading conservative journal in the state. His editorship started after Hunter jailed him for criticizing his leadership. A year later, after the war ended, Baker cited his imprisonment as his motivation for opposing the radicals.[10]

154   /   Chapter 6

The federal election of November 1864 provides a solid example of the two sides clashing. Radical fears for their place appeared months beforehand. Race and emancipation formed the core of their concerns. Radicals started a new newspaper, the *Morgantown Weekly Post*, to remind readers that Lincoln was not in favor of racial equality. Editor Henry M. Morgan urged fellow Unionists to avoid feeling "alienated in their sympathy toward the Government because of the policy of the President in enlisting negroes to fight against the rebels." The *Post* cited a letter from Lincoln to an Illinois judge saying how Black enlistment was only a war measure. The *Intelligencer* warned voters that if the Democrats won, they would return West Virginia to the old state. Worse yet, "we will come under the rule of those who are now our enemies in the field and will put upon us not only all the old inequalities of which we so long complained, but, in addition, our proportion of the ruinous taxes which have been enacted since." The new *West Virginia Journal* began in October to promote the radical cause in the Kanawha Valley. Its editors proclaimed that "politically we are unconditionally for the Union" and supported the president "in all measures necessary to a vigorous prosecution of the war against the rebellion." For local affairs, it promised to "advocate only such men for office as we believe to be thoroughly Union." In the same issue, the editors urged voters to "suffer no false logic or chicanery" when choosing candidates: "This is a real struggle going on in this country. The question to be decided is whether the people— the masses—shall rule, or be ruled by certain individuals or families who indirectly claim that prerogative." The election for the state House of Delegates of a known conservative Unionist prompted a major response from the paper. Spicer Patrick, a long-serving physician, salt maker, and slaveowner, won, the *Journal* claimed, with the help of "every rebel sympathizer in the County [who] voted his ticket. This is something for a 'good Union man' to be proud of." These editorials pointed to the future that radical Unionists desired: separate statehood, northern-style economic development, victory over the rebels, and no racial equality.[11]

The 1864 presidential election validated those desires. Lincoln and east Tennessee's Andrew Johnson won, but the results indicated continuing sensitivity in the border areas. Lincoln won every state except Kentucky and Delaware, as well as McClellan's home state of New Jersey. West Virginia voted for the president by a two-to-one margin, 23,152 votes to 10,483 for McClellan. On closer inspection, the statewide results show more conservative support there as well. In the Northern Panhandle, the margins tended to be narrow. Ohio County, the fount of northwestern Virginia Unionism, gave Lincoln only 2,138 votes to McClellan's 2,008. Broken down further, the Democrat won

Table 5. Wheeling, West Virginia, Election Returns by Ward, 1864 Presidential Election

Ward	Lincoln		McClellan	
	Votes	Percentage	Votes	Percentage
Washington	202	39.7	306	60.3
Madison	194	48.6	205	51.4
Clay	256	56.6	196	43.4
Union	348	60.1	231	39.9
Center	198	46.2	230	53.7
Webster	246	61.3	155	38.7
Ritchie	295	55.9	232	44.1
Richland	112	41.1	160	58.8
Liberty	137	54.1	116	45.9
Triadelphia	160	47.4	177	52.6
	2,148	51.7	2,008	48.3

Source: *Wheeling Daily Intelligencer*, November 9–10, 1864. The original Wheeling ward returns contained mathematical errors, which I corrected.

five of Wheeling's ten wards, as table 5 indicates. This is a remarkable indication of conservative Union strength. In 1860 the city had only one hundred slaves, eleven of whom had fled, and significant numbers of Irish and German migrants who had little support for slavery. Yet they voted Democratic in big numbers despite the war.

The statewide result is less reliable due to the lopsided voting tallies. Broken down into four parts of the state, the returns reveal how conservative strength was highest in the Northern Panhandle and central counties like Harrison. McClellan won only Wetzel County, but the others gave him respectable support. The Kanawha Valley and Eastern Panhandle areas voted strongly for Lincoln, though guerrilla activity and Unionist intimidation influenced those elections. Many counties submitted no returns at all. Had those areas been more secure, it is possible that the Democratic vote would have been higher. Otis K. Rice and Stephen W. Brown noticed a drop of five thousand votes from the Willey Amendment referendum eighteen months before. They argue that the difference in the two election results represented the "many Unionists who reluctantly supported a necessary condition for statehood [but also who] wanted no part of Lincoln's war measures."[12] While that would not have changed the national outcome, it would have given a closer result, akin to returns in the Northern Panhandle.

The press responses to the election results unsurprisingly indicated little respect between the two sides. The *Intelligencer* showed no sympathy for the Democrats' strength despite the outcome. "All those who voted for McClellan made a great mistake," the editors stated on November 15, "but it is not necessary to suppose, nor do we suppose that all made it willfully. The leaders high in the councils of the Democrats are men who are traitors to their country and allies to Jeff. Davis." It reserved harsh criticism for Wetzel County. It doubted the county's allegiances to the Union, calling it a "South Carolina at heart" for voting Democratic. "Her recent vote does her great injustice," the *Intelligencer* concluded. Even if we account for the newspaper's partisan biases, these indicate strong displeasure for the result. The *Morgantown Weekly Post* echoed these sentiments. While Lincoln's platform aimed at victory over the rebellion and the end to its root cause in slavery, McClellan's stances were merely "intended to catch the votes of the ultra-Peace men." Democratic "friends and supporters wore two faces, and at no time did they make a square, stand-up fight on a well-defined issue. They angled for votes with any and all kinds of bait, and votes cast for McClellan mean anything or nothing, as his supporters may chance to believe." The *Telegraph* hailed the election returns but lamented the actions of what it labelled "the Wheeling clique." It claimed that soldiers and citizens had been treated with "utter disregard" in how nominees were chosen. The editor of the *West Virginia Journal*, still grinning with joy from Lincoln's overwhelming victory in the valley, condemned its cross-town rival, the *Kanawha Republican*, of disloyalty. It described the editors as seeing the world with "but one eye on us . . . and that is the secesh eye. It is terribly indignant at us 'mud-sills' because we don't obey its dictates and eulogize its warm sympathies for prominent secessionists and traitors." The *Republican*'s editor, Enos W. Newton, "vouches for [returning rebels] in every conceivable shape, form, and manner asked of him."[13]

West Virginia, despite its internal divisions, next voted for the most revolutionary Union war measure of all: the passage of the Thirteenth Amendment to the Constitution, which abolished slavery nationwide. Lincoln used his election triumph in November to press forward with this controversial bill before Congress. West Virginia supported him, along with many other border state radicals, every step of the way. On April 8, 1864, senators Willey and Peter G. Van Winkle supported the amendment. John S. Carlile, who continued representing Virginia, was absent. During the House's first attempt at passage in

December, William G. Brown did not vote, but the state's other two congressmen—Kellian V. Whaley and Jacob B. Blair—cast ayes. On January 31, 1865, when the House of Representatives revisited the issue, all three voted for the amendment. It is noteworthy at how closely these tallies compare to the other border states and their respective regimes. Each senator from radical Missouri and Maryland voted for it, while those from conservative Kentucky and Delaware opposed it. Conversely, they split their votes in the House. Four of Kentucky's seven congressmen voted for it, along with Delaware's lone representative. On the other hand, seven of Missouri's eight and four of Maryland's five congressmen also supported the amendment. Four years before, white northwesterners separated from Virginia to protect the institution from the anarchy of secession. In January 1865, its wartime leaders now happily signed slavery away.[14]

The radicals in the state legislature had, in fact, acted before Congress did on ratifying the Thirteenth Amendment. The House heard the bill first on January 26, presented by James H. Ferguson of Cabell County. This is significant. Before the war, lawyer and planter Albert Gallatin Jenkins ruled that county. He was killed in combat in May 1864. Ferguson's move to end slavery seven months later showed how far West Virginia politics had changed during the war. A few days beforehand, the *Intelligencer* urged such an action to show the other border states how to approach emancipation. It then asked the state legislature to follow Missouri, Tennessee, and Maryland in passing the amendment. Each of those had embarked on abolishing slavery in the previous months, albeit due to radicals controlling their governments. The *Intelligencer* condemned Delaware for its stubborn opposition to emancipation. While everyone else was ending the institution, "little Delaware . . . hugs the old institution of slavery as though the safety of the State depended on the perpetuity of that effete system."[15] Radicals elsewhere in the once slave-rich Kanawha Valley had also turned against the practice. The *West Virginia Journal* condemned the institution for forcing people to immigrate to the far west. "The very name of slavery," it stated on January 27, "is a prompter to those fleeing from oppression, and they do not stop to enquire whether the reality yet exists here, but plod on the far west where every foot of soil is free." The *Register*, the leading conservative newspaper, lambasted the radicals for their attitude. Every Republican knew, the paper claimed on January 31, that "by how slight a tenure they hold their political power. They are fully aware that the day is not far distant when the people of West Virginia will take part in the direction of affairs of state." This was a weak threat, and they knew it.

The state legislature's debates on ratification met with heavy divisions.

158 / Chapter 6

On January 31, the House of Delegates began after its second reading. Daniel Lamb of Ohio County proposed to amend the state constitution because he claimed it lacked the legal authority to abolish slavery. Others called his idea a delaying tactic. Ferguson stated that he had once been a supporter of slaveholders' rights but now embraced emancipation. The legislature had the authority to act without amendment, he asserted, and he "wanted to strike the shackles off the slaves and make them what God intended them to be—free men, and he wanted to do it as speedily as possible." Lamb's motion failed. On February 1, the House of Delegates passed it after a short debate. Spicer Patrick, now the speaker, owned twenty-two slaves in 1860, which made him the largest slaveowner in the legislature. He voted in favor of the amendment. He said that "his own servants—all who were efficient—went off in '62, leaving only two old and infirm slaves. One of these became infatuated with freedom not long since." The House passed it twenty-nine votes to seventeen. The Senate took up the matter two days later. Daniel Haymond of Ritchie County, who at the age of seventy-seven was the oldest member of either house, moved to add compensation to the bill. James Burley of Marshall County suggested three hundred dollars, but the senators rejected both measures. With no further debate, the bill passed with a vote of seventeen to one, Haymond being the lone dissenter. John H. Atkinson of Hancock County declared, "Slavery is dead at last." To this, Daniel Peck of Ohio County lamented, "Yes, and the smoke of its torment ascendeth up forever and ever!" This statement, which comes from Revelations 14:11, serves as a fitting epitaph for slavery in the latest free state. Ratification of the Thirteenth Amendment came shortly thereafter, and Governor Boreman signed the bill on February 3.[16] Seeing so much support for enslavement at this late date says much about how the institution dug its claws into the now former northwestern Virginia. The process also resembled Missouri's and Maryland's passages of the act, where passing similar bills required radical control of the legislature. The conservative assemblies in Kentucky and Delaware rejected even hearing them. They kept doing so for decades afterward.

Sensing that conservatives would merge with former Confederates, Boreman then sought to limit their political rights. In his annual message in January 1865, he condemned the former as "the disloyal in our midst who have remained at home [to] feed and harbor these marauders and murderers," while the latter prepared "to do their devilish work." He called upon the legislature to impose stiffer penalties than before on anyone suspected of disobedience. The radicals complied. In February, the House of Delegates began debating a new oath for voters. Authored by Daniel Lamb, the bill confined citizens to their townships and their supervisors to prevent mobility. Aretas B. Fleming of Harrison, a future state governor, then added a provision by which an applicant's qualifications could be challenged by another person. James H. Ferguson of Cabell then moved to include a list of disqualifications. An officer could demand that a voter prove that they were not guilty of any of those offenses. It carried on the November 1863 oath with some minor modifications. Anyone seeking to vote must swear that they not having held or attempted to hold an office of authority or provided voluntary support to any government "hostile or inimical to the United States, the Reorganized Government of Virginia, or the State of West Virginia." It omitted the notorious clause about "countenancing, counselling, or encouraging them in the same" from the earlier oath, but the other provisions proved to be far harsher. After a committee reconciled these competing bills, the House of Delegates approved it thirty-three to nine. The Senate concurred days later, and Boreman signed the bill on February 25. Days later, a similar oath passed forbidding former rebels from filing lawsuits to recover lost property. Being unable to vote, teach, practice law, or sue indicated where radicals placed former rebels at one step above the previously enslaved. The *Intelligencer* and other radical papers supported this idea. Conservatives thought it was, in the words of the *Register*, an "impolicy" and would add to the "difficulty in organizing some of the border counties and the supremacy of the law." They were remarkably prescient.[17]

Within two months, the great Civil War ended in a Union victory. While Sherman marched northward through the Carolinas, Grant's armies in Virginia launched a major offensive in late March to overwhelm the Confederate defenses around Petersburg and in the Shenandoah Valley. Rebel leader Jefferson Davis fled Richmond along with Lee's troops in early April. Lincoln himself visited the newly captured capital, the long-desired goal of Union arms, on April 4. While whites shunned him, the formerly enslaved greeted him like a biblical figure. Federal armies finally cornered Lee's forces around Appomattox Court House four days later. In an emotional moment, the rebels surrendered to Grant the next morning. No fewer than eight West Virginia Union regiments and many Confederate units observed the ceremony. More rebel armies surrendered over the next few months, with the raider CSS *Shenandoah* finally capitulating in November. The West Virginia state presses split on the matter. The *Intelligencer* denounced conservative views of Lee being "such a model Christian" for whom it "would be heathenous to fil to recognize him as a first-class subject for national admiration." The ringleaders of the rebellion "richly deserve death." The *Register*, on the next day, took the moral high ground and attacked its rival for such talk. It called on its readers to support the president's policies toward the former rebels. The *Intelligencer*'s "claims of humanity and the higher duties of manhood forbid the exercise of cruelty and the gratification of a spirit of revenge," it wrote on April 13. All may have sighed with relief and hoped for an orderly transition from war to peace. It was not to be.

Neither would get their chance. Two days later, a border state Confederate supporter named John Wilkes Booth assassinated Lincoln at Ford's Theater. "Murder most foul," declared the *Intelligencer*, which added black bars to its pages that day. It mournfully continued that they "have no words to express the thrill of horror which ran through this community last Saturday morning, on the receipt of the news announcing the murder of the President." The editors declared, "We think of Abraham Lincoln as of Moses, that man of God who led Israel nearly into the Promised Land." The *Register* equivocated on the martyred president. "While our opinions of his political course are unchanged," it began by maintaining its ground, "our bitterness of feeling is all gone, our prejudices all uprooted, and, with deep sincerity, we mourn his loss." On May 20, the *Morgantown Weekly Post* hailed the late president's "generous nature that never distinguished the human character." The *Clarksburg Weekly National Telegraph* praised his successor, Andrew Johnson. The newspaper wrote that while the loyal people "have lost in the untimely death of Mr. Lincoln a good, wise, and beloved ruler . . . one truly worthy has succeeded him, and one who will carry out the wise policy of his beloved and lamented predecessor."[18] With the war now beginning to end, West Virginia's radical rulers now faced their greatest challenges: a large influx of former Confederates whose allegiances to the new state they doubted, significant numbers of conservative Unionists whose opposition was already well known, a federal government in turmoil as it began reconstructing the nation, and a small but important presence of African Americans now in their midst.

The end of the war in the summer of 1865 tested the new state like no event since its creation. Confederates now returned to their home counties and families. Milton Geofsky claimed that these men acted "in good faith and without desire for revenge, Confederate soldiers laid down their arms and returned in peace to build anew and start again as useful citizens." This is wrong. They intended to thwart the government of the state created in their absence and restore traditional elites to their antebellum status. The former editor of the *Kanawha Valley Star*, Jonathan Rundle, declared upon his return from Confederate service, "If you [Union men] will treat us right and not insult us, we will keep quiet; but if you don't, these hills will be filled with sharpshooters." Rundle's sanguine comment confirmed the radicals' biggest fears of continued resistance. Governor Boreman informed his brother that returning rebels could expect family to welcome them back coolly in a May 1865 letter about family friend Kenner B. Stephenson, then returning from rebel service: "Poor fellow he should have taken my advice at the beginning, but he would not. On his mother's account (who in my opinion has never been a rebel) I will have to aid him to get back. But he will not be able to stay. The people will treat him coolly. So much so that he will not feel at home. Indeed, the people say that none of those renegade rebels shall return. I have not much sympathy for them. I was always fond of Kenner however & hope he will do better for the future." Conservative Unionists warned their Confederate friends about the risks. Those who sought a quiet return home could not be guaranteed safe transit. R. J. McCandlish of Lewis County warned his neighbor Jonathan M. Bennett, a former Confederate auditor, about the challenges returnees faced: "I hardly know what to say in relation to your coming here at this time. Many have returned who I should think would be more obnoxious than yourself and are remaining unmolested. So that I hardly think there would be any objection to your return merely to settle up your business—although it might be more prudent to delay it for a while." The army itself had to address this potential for conflict between these former friends turned enemies. In July, the First Separate Brigade based in Charleston laid down a general order directing its soldiers to treat returning Confederates as if they had no rank, nor could they express any sympathy for their cause. "No punishment is too severe to inflict upon a man even partially restored to citizenship after having committed treason," the order read. The troops received orders to monitor "these subdued people" and promptly report any transgressions. The war for West Virginia continued long after Appomattox.[19]

Undeterred, former Confederates expressed their determination to restore their rule by politics. In mid-1865, they managed to place three of their number to county and state offices. Greenbrier County elected former major Henry W. Matthews, another future governor, to the House of Delegates. Putnam County sent doctor J. J. Thompson to the Senate. Greenbrier County placed Samuel Price, the former secessionist lieutenant governor of Virginia, to a judgeship. These constituted only the three most famous former rebels to assume West Virginia office in 1865 alone. The first two refused to take the oath and were denied their seats. Boreman personally refused to commission Price to prevent a "high and important office to one who has so recently been engaged in efforts to destroy and to overthrow the government of the United States." He and the legislature acted properly, but in the process, they antagonized further a wide range of opinion in many parts of the state.[20]

A pair of legal cases further radicalized Boreman's government toward greater action. William A. Quarrier of Kanawha, a former Confederate officer, applied for reinstatement to the bar. With the help of Benjamin H. Smith and George W. Summers, both able lawyers and of impeccable Unionist credentials, he handwrote a seventy-seven-page affidavit explaining why he should return to his profession. With their legal advice, Quarrier argued that he had never been disloyal to West Virginia. He owed his allegiance to Virginia and obeyed its decision to secede. Yet when the Reorganized Government assumed the Commonwealth's place in the Union, it maintained its legality. When Pierpont vacated state offices in 1861, he did not include attorneys. Moreover, he had taken the oath to the federal government and to West Virginia and ought to have his rights restored. As such, the new state had nothing on him. Quarrier, Smith, and Summers included as much of their legal knowledge as possible in this document, including Jefferson's Virginia and Kentucky Resolutions of 1798 and, rather strangely, speeches by John C. Calhoun. None impressed the circuit court judge, Daniel Polsley. Despite calling his motion "elaborately and ably argued by two of the oldest and most learned counsel of the State," he concluded that Quarrier had vacated his place at the bar due to his failure to swear allegiance to the Reorganized Government and his rebellion against the United States, and only attorneys who took the oath of November 1863 could practice law in West Virginia. The *Intelligencer* hailed the decision for it "vindicates the great principles that underlie our system, as it is a correct decision of the important questions of law involved." It was only fair, it continued, since men like Quarrier who supported the "causeless and wicked attempt to overthrow our laws" must not be allowed to return to "the bosom of the communities they sought to ruin, demand, with unblushing effrontery, immediate restoration to the responsible official and highly honorable positions which they abandoned in the interests and treason."[21] The similarly oriented *Parkersburg Weekly Times* agreed, arguing that "there is no allegiance due to a state as a separate allegiance" and that the judge "rendered a just decision." The *Register* condemned the decision by lamenting how the "rebel farmer, mechanic, physician, and preacher can return to their professions, why can the lawyer not do the same?" These were devastating attacks on Quarrier's sense of duty and to the cause of former Confederates seeking to practice law. They would not be insulted like that again.

A second case posed a greater threat to the Boreman's administration. Charles James Faulkner, one of northwestern Virginia's leading figures in the 1829–1830 constitutional debates and briefly the US minister to France, supported secession in 1861. After serving on Stonewall Jackson's staff during the war, he returned home to Berkeley County expecting to resume his law practice. Lawsuits from wartime Unionists created considerable demand for his skills from other former Confederates, especially since the suitor's oath deprived them of that vital right. Yet, like Quarrier, he refused to take the oath of allegiance to West Virginia despite receiving a federal pardon. In January 1866, as soon as he could, he took his case to the State Court of Appeals on the basis that the oath applied only to state officials like teachers and legislators, not to lawyers. He condemned the oath as ex post facto and therefore unconstitutional, referring to it as "not an oath of allegiance, nor of fidelity, not to purge the person taking it of any present or subsisting disloyalty." Unlike Quarrier's legal argumentations, Faulkner's case prevailed on this simple technicality. The court agreed and allowed him to take the oath. He quickly became one of the state's leading attorneys. Boreman and other radicals took immediate notice of this dangerous precedent. The relative ease of Faulkner's victory could embolden other rebels to become lawyers. In turn, this could undermine their proscriptions on voting, teaching, suing, and possibly even returning West Virginia to Virginia. The legislature moved quickly to remedy the situation. In an extraordinary twist of fate, Faulkner successfully defended the legality of the new state's creation before the Supreme Court after Virginia sued to reclaim Jefferson and Berkeley counties in 1866 and decided in 1871. The latter case legitimized West Virginia's formation under federal law.[22]

The radicals took the strongest measure possible to prevent former Confederates from entering public life. In February 1866, they used their majorities in the House of Delegates and the Senate to turn the wartime oaths into an unappealable constitutional amendment, which created a registration system that required all voters to be properly identified prior to casting their ballot. Electoral officials possessed the power to inquire into the past allegiances of potential voters. If satisfied, they could vote after taking the oath to the United States and to West Virginia. The amendment exempted only honorably discharged Union veterans and minors. On top of these steep requirements, the radicals added a further complication. Any other person could challenge the allegiances of a voter, and it was up to the accused to prove their innocence. Combined with the impact of the township system, which localized authority to a select few, this threatened to disqualify large numbers of voters. In every county, the wartime allegiances of many were public knowledge. Conservative Unionists became especially entrapped in this process. The legislature passed another law that immunized officials from lawsuits, knowing full well that disenfranchised former Confederates could not sue. This deprived conservatives of their last means of redress for their kinsmen and allies. Daniel Lamb, one of the authors of the state constitution, wrote to Gideon D. Camden, a former Confederate who once faced a treason charge, calling for unity between their groups: "We have inaugurated a vigorous campaign against the Radicals. Consult some of your leading men & give us whatever aid you can. However, we may differ on certain points, yet in many we concur. We want a real peace—so do you. We want to put an end to prosecution and proscription & so do you; and we are going to do it. If we can find no better way, we propose, like Gen. Grant, to wear out the adversary 'by mere attrition.'" Other conservatives echoed his call to arms. The *Register* opined days later that the radicals need not fear retaliation. Its faction simply desired "only fair play and are willing to concede to our opponents, notwithstanding their past misdeed, all that we claim for ourselves." The more conservative *Lewisburg Times* went even further. Its editor denounced the proscriptions as unconstitutional and fraudulent, but also deeply offensive to the people. "We ask of any honest man of good sense," its editor wrote on May 12, "whether he would not regard himself as insulted by being regarded as no better than any man who, though solemnly sworn upon the word of Almighty God, in support of the Constitution" and yet defends measures "designed to rob his fellow citizens of most sacred rights." The *Intelligencer*, now edited by Granville Davisson Hall, responded to these simplistic appeals with similar strident language. It claimed that conservatives stood for "repudiating the national debt, for repudiating the State of West Virginia, for assuming the debt of the confederacy and the rebel debt of Virginia, and in general for extolling and glorifying treason, and bringing everything honorable and loyal into disrepute."[23] The two camps, radical Republicans and conservative Confederates, thus stood far apart on the forthcoming referendum.

Attriting the enemy, as General Grant found out during the war, took time and resources. In the May 1866 referendum, conservative voters had the first but not the second. The voters approved of the amendment by a margin of 22,224 (59.2 percent) in favor and 15,302 (40.8 percent) opposed. This tally, as the *Intelligencer* lamented the next day, "although large, falls very considerably behind the registration, and will not equal the poll at the Presidential election of 1864." Still, the results were deceptively close. Despite so many voters disqualified by choice or law, the conservative vote was still strong. Wood approved it 1,375 to 924, along with Harrison's 1,256 to 985. Hancock approved it narrowly 384 to 289. Conversely, Ohio rejected it 1,910 to 1,610. Southern and border counties represented the suppression of votes at least in parts. Greenbrier voted 216 to 189 to reject. Pocahontas, Morgan, Monroe, Wyoming, and Mercer supported the amendment despite being thick with disenfranchised former rebels. Several counties reported no results, but they would not have affected the outcome. Despite the controversy, the measure became part of the state constitution. The registration bill from February had its intended effect. It removed as many as twenty thousand men from state citizenship. Those afflicted had few avenues of recourse. The courts could not help them. Election supervisors in many counties, the *Register* reported, "had not examined the law and were not familiar with its provisions and were guided, in many cases, solely by their own will." Since radicals occupied those positions, conservatives needed to better organize for the next election. They would name their own inspector and members of township boards who would "afford as much greater advantages in future contests than we have ever yet enjoyed." Their only hope of success and defending their claims to citizenship involved overthrowing the radical regime in the legislature.[24]

The next state election set for October 1866 provided such an opportunity. For this campaign, the conservatives used every trick available to them to appeal to their voting base. They named themselves the White Man's Party, a clear indication of the conservatives' desired constituency. At its convention in Parkersburg, the party passed a simple platform of only three planks: to follow the national Democratic Party agenda, to maintain the integrity of the state of West Virginia, and to remove "the many unconstitutional, unwise, and oppressive measures" used by the radical administration, which "merit the unqualified disapprobation of everyone who honestly desires the welfare of West Virginia, and the maintenance of free principles and good government therein."[25] They expected the combination of simple patriotism and overt racism to prevail over their foes. Kanawha County lawyer Benjamin H. Smith, mentioned earlier, stood as their candidate for governor. He was as solid a figure as the Democrats could find, since he served as US attorney for West Virginia during the war, but he had a son disenfranchised due to his Confederate service. Many white conservatives could relate to his situation. The Republicans renominated Boreman. Each party campaigned across the state in the weeks before the October ballot. The newspapers taunted their opponents. The *Register* called Boreman "the dictator of West Virginia," and congressman Chester Hubbard "the overseer of the Negro-Poor" on October 5. Later that month, the *Intelligencer* printed a list of Smith's votes in the 1861–1862 Constitutional Convention. They included votes opposing prohibiting alcohol, for raising taxes and going into debt, for maintaining viva voce voting, against the School Fund, and against emancipation.[26] Racial barbs occupied much of the campaign. The *Register* claimed that the radicals would use numerous unconstitutional measures to implement Black suffrage if reelected. The *Intelligencer* called out its rival editor who "still shoots at inferior game" since President Johnson also supported the same issue as part of his Reconstruction plan.[27] This was an exaggeration given the east Tennessee former Democrat's troubles with the Republicans in Congress at the time, but it still stung their opponents' pride. The Conservatives' appeals to race failed to budge the radical grip on power. Boreman was reelected with 23,455 (58 percent) votes to Smith's 16,983 (42 percent). When compared to the amendment referendum held six months earlier, both sides gained votes at the same rate.

Flush with success, the Boreman government entered 1867 with greater confidence than before. In his annual address, the governor hailed the achievements of the previous year. The state improved its financial status, built an insane asylum, and settled the state capital question. The school question was, he regretted, in a mixed condition. Several unruly counties along the Kentucky and Virginia borders had failed to conform to expectations due to "the calamities of the war and the lingering spirit of disaffection as well as the absence of a knowledge of the workings and benefits of the system." The latter comment attacked their sense of civility. The same issues plagued the basic administration of those areas to the point where an unauthorized government operated in Lewisburg in Greenbrier County. Many of those in charge there were "men of superior intelligence, some of them learned in the law, and are therefore the more culpable." The unrest reached the point where, Boreman continued, he sought federal troops in Monroe County. Finally, he said it was necessary to reinforce the proscription law to prevent illegal voting and grant more authority to state attorneys. The legislature enacted those measures in February 1867, along with Boreman's direct instructions to county registry boards to vigorously enforce the oath. Most important, he endorsed the state legislature to pass the new Fourteenth Amendment to the federal Constitution. He claimed that the new act would not change the hitherto ban on African American suffrage. "No state is required to confer or refuse it, but each is left to decide the question for itself," he wrote. As such, the radicals hoped to continue to skirt the race issue like they did during the previous election. With these enhancements, they confidently believed that their power was secure.[28]

The radicals' ability to evade the race issue contributed to their victory. Despite conservative attacks on their opponents as advocates of Black suffrage, the 1866 election returns indicate they failed to stir the voters. The reason stems from the offloading of racial matters onto the federal government and the African American people themselves. Even the *Intelligencer*, which had agitated so strongly for emancipation, took a curt, patronizing approach to Blacks. On April 2, 1867, it called upon them to "show that you are not the lazy, dishonest, and incapable class that you have so long been represented to be. Show that you are willing to work and anxious to improve and elevate themselves. Discourage all loafing in your houses. When you get work stick to it. Save all you can and educate yourselves and children as fast as possible. So, will you come to be respected in due season." Its editor used this walloping comment to essentially absolve West Virginia's radical whites from responsibility for the Blacks' condition. Furthermore, the state allowed the Bureau of Refugees, Freedmen, and Abandoned Lands, better known as the Freedmen's Bureau, to handle Black affairs. This agency of the War Department set up offices across the former Confederacy and some of the border states to implement Reconstruction policies. These included negotiating labor contracts, marriages, banking, and, most of all, education. While the state organized schools for whites, the Freedmen's Bureau did the same for Blacks, although only in Jefferson, Berkeley, Kanawha, and Harrison counties. Each founded a university in 1867, with West Virginia University starting in Morgantown for whites, and Storer College for Blacks opening in Harpers Ferry. Still, neither administration offered much success to the state's white and Black students. The 1867 superintendent's report outlined numerous shortcomings in the school system. More populous counties had fewer problems than smaller ones. Schools suffered from the absence, not just shortages, of books and papers, poor facilities, low salaries, and inefficient administrators, and "a general apathy to intellectual culture" came from people who lacked any education and sought to undermine if not resist their efforts. In sharp contrast, a school for Black children that opened in Wheeling that year reported considerable success. Led by "a teacher of their own color and behavior and the scholarship of the students are worthy of imitation," the report lamented. The closure of the Freedmen's Bureau in 1868 left the few Black schools in the care of the state government, where they languished due to neglect like white schools had.[29]

Furthermore, this comfort allowed Boreman's government to pass the Fourteenth Amendment to the federal Constitution with relative ease. On January 16, the day after his governor's address, the House of Delegates voted forty-three to eleven to approve the change. The Senate likewise endorsed it on the next day eighteen to four. By these actions, West Virginia ranked among the first among the states, and first of the border states, to ratify the controversial amendment. Only Missouri followed suit days later. The conservative states each rejected the measure in 1867 but approved it in the twentieth century. Delaware did so in 1901; Maryland, whose radicals had been overthrown months earlier, waited until 1959. Kentucky delayed ratification until 1976. Once implemented in June 1868, the new acts granted citizenship, civil rights, and equal protection of the law to all persons born or naturalized in the United States. This included African Americans. The acts also set new voting rights that reduced the voting base if a state prevented any group except former rebels from suffrage, forbade former rebels from sitting in Congress, and removed any claims on the national debt for Confederate actions. This broad package drew little criticism at the time from either faction's press. A year later, however, the *Register* condemned its implementation for threatening white civil rights and Black suffrage through the back door. Loyalty oaths remained in force despite citizenship guarantees. Black voters held more rights than disenfranchised whites. Meanwhile, alleged Confederate sympathizers like Greenbrier judge Nathaniel Harrison remained in office. Finally, by allowing Congress the power to enforce these laws, the *Register* claimed that "it shall have the power to impose negro suffrage upon every State in the Union."[30] This spiteful analysis had little effect on West Virginia's affairs. White radical voters could, therefore, cast their ballots knowing that their party would not change the state's racial hierarchy. This is correct, but the implements of change loomed on the horizon.

A pair of events in 1867 offered hope for aggrieved conservatives. First, as mentioned above, Maryland's radicals lost power in late 1866. Without the war to unite them, the Republicans splintered into pro- and anti-proscription factions. The former, deprived of Henry Winter Davis's leadership upon his death in December 1865, lost ground to its rivals. Led by Montgomery Blair and Reverdy Johnson, the antis demanded the repeal of barriers to voting. The sight of many family and friends being deprived of citizenship compelled their actions. The issue divided the state's Unconditional Unionist convention that May. In the elections that fall, the conservatives won by a narrow margin. After rejecting the Fourteenth Amendment in March, they held a Constitutional Convention in April 1867 that overthrew the radical regime. Proscriptions topped their discard pile. Despite seeking federal intervention, the Maryland radicals lost the ensuing referendum by a commanding margin of 47,152 (67.1 percent) to 23,036 (32.9 percent). An instructive comparison exists here. While Maryland's radicals split due to internal causes, namely weak leadership, West Virginia's possessed internal unity and good leaders and remained intact. Their ability to remain in power continued.

Maryland's collapse gave West Virginia only one remaining ally in Missouri. An event in resolved that state, however, further threatened the radicals' grip on power. On January 14, 1867, the US Supreme Court ruled in two related cases, namely *Cummings v. Missouri* and *Ex Parte Garland*. Catholic priest John A. Cummins refused to take the oath of allegiance to Missouri but failed to overturn it in the state courts. Augustus Garland had been a Confederate senator from Arkansas but received a postwar pardon.

Congressional proscriptions forbade him from practicing in the federal judiciary. The Supreme Court struck down both bans as unconstitutional bills of attainder. Their ruling allowed former rebels to preach and to practice law in the federal courts but left alone state courts and voting procedures. Radical rule remained intact, but Maryland's redemption and the precedent-setting decisions gave glimmers of hope to West Virginia's conservatives.[31]

Although secured by oaths and proscriptions, Boreman's increasingly radical government encouraged both resistance and discouragement among whites. A previously unthinkable act occurred in April. The famed former slave Frederick Douglass addressed a crowd in Wheeling on the subject of "Sources of Danger of the Republic." Starting in St. Louis, he toured the country around this time to urge the granting of suffrage to Blacks and to women, as well as the impeachment of President Andrew Johnson. Such an appearance would have been impossible before radical rule and still aroused debate during it. The *Intelligencer* approved of Douglass's speech. On the following day, Granville Davisson Hall, its editor, attacked the *Register* for ignoring the event. "If the lecture had been a failure, or if it had been thinly attended, we should have heard from the organ," it opined. "The idea of presenting the people with both sides of a question is something that never occurs to them," Hall continued his barbs. The *Buckhannon Advocate* echoed this sentiment, praising Douglass's appearance as a triumph. "Surely times are changing," it opined, "when a man of his color is so well received and countenanced by a large and intelligent audience in West Virginia. It presumes that six years ago, many who listened and were pleased would have scouted the idea." Back then, other speeches by Horace Greeley, Cassius M. Clay, and Thomas Hart Benton received less attention, while "a Republican meeting was broken up by a mob," it concluded.[32] The *Register* said nothing about Douglass's presence. Baker claimed that he was moving his facilities at the time. Whether this was true or not, he missed an opportunity to comment on this important challenge to the state's racial structure. His conservative readers would have devoured his comments on a Black man lecturing whites on their politics and radicals cheering him. Nonetheless, they undoubtedly heard about the event from other sources, which enervated them to act.

The October 1867 state election returns indicate a substantial shift in white opinion. Boreman won reelection, while the radicals gained two senate seats and lost none in the House of Delegates. The actual numbers of voters, however, declined significantly. In the previous year, the radicals won with a commanding margin of 6,674. It had declined by almost two-thirds to 2,254. A third of that drop came in Ohio County where the Boreman tally halved from 2,081 to 1,091; the Conservative vote there also dropped from 2,224 to 1,797. Other counties showed similar but less dramatic reductions. Some even increased. Exhaustion best describes the election result. The constant battling between radicals and conservatives wore out the average West Virginia man's desire for politics. The former carried on the wartime bickering as if the surrender at Appomattox had not happened. The *Intelligencer* called on the "Union people" to fulfil their "duty of every man who believes that as between the part of the country during the war and the party of Vallandingham & Co." Conservatives, on the other hand, denounced as useless such wartime rhetoric. The *Register* asked its supporters to "derive their motives for action from some other source than a 'Union' which none but radicals threaten, or a 'rebellion' which even radicals know to be dead." The arrogant *Greenbrier Independent* called on radicals to switch sides and defend the white race. "Will you come out from among those who are for putting down white men, and putting up with negroes," editor Benjamin Harlow opined in October. More issues like the failures in building railroads, settling on a location for the new state capital, and establishing new counties such as Grant, Mineral, Lincoln, and eventually Summers also weighed on the voters' minds. The state would make little progress so long as its factions refused to cooperate.[33]

The new year of 1868 showed how far apart the two sides were. Boreman's annual address could not hide the slowness of his administration. Armed insurrection declined from the previous year to only Wayne and Logan counties, mainly due to "Captain" Bill Smith's agitation. Randolph, Tucker, and Barbour saw much resistance opposed to the election registration laws. The situation there compelled the governor to request federal troops to restore order since he feared the local response of turning families and friends against each other. "None of the militia was armed, and I wished to avoid, if possible, for the purpose of arming and use of neighbors," he wrote. This added to the US soldiers still stationed in Monroe County for the same purpose. He praised the small surplus in the state budget, which is no small feat given the unrest and demands of paying for the school system, the state hospital, the new university at Morgantown, and other burdens. Despite some poor administration, Boreman hailed progress made in the education program. Only twenty-nine counties had reported on their status in the previous year, but 363 schools had thus far been built to bring the state total up to one thousand in three years. While some of the facilities were "very ordinary structures," he praised them for "displaying the good taste and liberality of the neighborhoods." The governor concluded that it was necessary to support the federal government's Reconstruction policy, as symbolized by the passage of the Fourteenth

Amendment. Restoring order to the rebellious states was, he said, "making successful and certain progress in the right direction." These views did not inspire much confidence. The *Register*, Boreman's biggest critic, called parts of his address "unimportant for any purpose, save to waste ink and to weary the reader." Their statement reflects as much their frustration with being unable to dislodge the radical governor in the last elections as from any flaws in the annual report. West Virginia made glacial progress in its endeavors, but even this was remarkable given the obstacles it faced.[34]

The radicals' grip on power began to erode with some critical errors in 1868. Some of them bordered on the petty, such as J. F. Caldwell exercising virtually dictatorial powers over Greenbrier County. He removed so many ex-rebels from the voting list that he earned the title of "Old Scratch." According to an older source, Caldwell struck all but seven from the Lewisburg voting list: himself, his son, two Irishmen, and three African Americans.[35] The choice of immigrants and Blacks seems dubious, but it still points toward the racialized feelings of native-born conservative white men fearing corrupt officials, immigrants, and Blacks ruling the county when they could not vote. In March, the state impeached and removed Judge William Hindman for refusing to enforce the lawyer's test oath. He claimed that *Ex Parte Garland* rendered such measures unconstitutional. The legislature disagreed, declaring it applied only to federal and not to state courts. The act drew intense newspaper discussion. The *Register* condemned the action as "the brute force of a Radical majority, in obedience to supposed party necessity . . . to gratify the insane clamors of 'loyalty.'" Baker tried to take the center ground by pointing out that Hindman was a Boreman appointee. Hall of the *Intelligencer* simplistically argued that the legislature "simply discharged an imperative duty when they removed him from office."[36] Both assessed the situation soundly, but the conservative deserves the edge here. For a radical judge to break ranks as Hindman did indicates emerging cracks in that faction's control over the state. The *Intelligencer's* legally sound but politically soft response failed to repair the situation. Conservatives smelled blood and organized to exploit their opponents' weaknesses.

Events at the federal level revealed further cracks in the radical administration. Starting in February, President Andrew Johnson faced impeachment charges for disobeying numerous acts of Congress. All three West Virginia representatives, Chester Hubbard, Bethuel Kitchen, and Daniel Polsley, voted in favor of the articles. The Senate tried Johnson on the eleven counts in a long, intense public hearing in March and April. Eventually, the senators whittled down the list to a mere three charges, each pertaining to alleged violations of the Tenure of Office Act, a radical tripwire designed to give them an excuse to impeach the president for disobeying their control over Reconstruction policy. On May 4, the Senate voted thirty-five to nineteen on each charge, one vote short of the two-thirds needed for conviction. West Virginia's Peter G. Van Winkle ranked among the eight Republicans who opposed the charges and led to their rejection. Willey voted to convict. Missouri's delegation also split, with John B. Henderson, one of the dissenters from Lincoln's border state emancipation plan from July 1862, choosing nay, and Charles Drake siding in the affirmative. Maryland, Delaware, and Kentucky's conservative senators all voted to acquit. In his written opinion, Van Winkle cited evidentiary flaws such as the president composing a letter removing Secretary of War Edwin Stanton from his position but not sending it. Historian Michael Les Benedict called this opinion "almost a perverseness" since he arrived at these conclusions by using a "far more restrained interpretation of the law" that "appeared to be almost a parody of the legal dissertations prepared so painstakingly by his peers."[37] The *Intelligencer*, appalled at Van Winkle's decision, could not have agreed more. "West Virginia's Betrayer" read its headline on May 18. The people are now "covered in shame and filled with indignation at his treachery." The *Register*, flush with joy, praised the Republican dissenters as heroes. They transformed radical "models of goodness and greatness into perjured scoundrels" and with it brought "tumbling down the whole structure of Radicalism and in removing the last vestige of it from sight." As with the Hindman case, the conservative press identified another vulnerability in their opponent's façade. They prepared for the upcoming fall state and presidential elections with vigor.

The two races held in October and November 1868 indicate that West Virginians started to tire of the prolonged fighting. Boreman decided to step down as governor and replace the disgraced Van Winkle in the federal senate. William E. Stevenson, also of Parkersburg in Wood County, replaced him. With service in the State Senate and as its president, he was a dedicated radical. The Democrats ran businessman Johnson N. Camden. Despite opposing secession in 1861, he left his Harrison County home with his family and two slaves for Richmond during the war. Camden served as part of the Virginia delegation to the Confederate provisional congress in Montgomery and ended the war at Appomattox. West Virginia should have proscribed him for this, but inexplicably did not. At the federal level, former general in chief Ulysses S. Grant ran for president as a Republican on the platform of "let us have peace." Former New York governor Horatio Seymour stood as a Democrat. The *Intelligencer* tied the federal and state elections together as a continued fight for the Union. In a column in late August that could have been written four years earlier, Hall implored radical readers to vote properly. "As West Virginia votes in October," he wrote, "so will she undoubtedly vote in November, and if in October she emulates the example and covets the condition of Kentucky, and casts herself into the arms of her enemies and destroyers, be sure she will give her voice in November for a renewal of that rebellion which has cost her people so many woes." The *Register* replied to this argument with one of its own. "Our record in this State has shown a series of defeats from each of which we have risen with new strength and unabated zeal," opined Baker on October 15. After losing by twelve thousand votes in 1864, he continued, conservatives have rebounded to "have to-day a majority of the registered votes of the State. If we choose, we can redeem her from Radical hands at the coming election." Harlow of the *Greenbrier Independent* urged his supporters to "vote the white man's ticket." If victorious, he continued, then "Radicalism will be overthrown, and the country will be redeemed."[38]

The results almost vindicated their faith. Since West Virginia held the two ballots within weeks of each other, the results show that the gap between the two sides narrowed but had not yet closed. Stevenson won the governorship 26,844 (54.7 percent) to Camden's 22,218 (45.3 percent). These results show extraordinary jumps in votes if not percentages since the 1866 ballot when Boreman beat Smith 23,455 (58.0 percent) to 16,983 (42 percent). The conservative Democratic Party may have fallen short of victory, but they had rebounded. The proscriptions, though still legal, were not having their intended effect. The federal election, on the other hand, showed a wider gap between the two sides. Grant won the state 29,224 (58.9) to Seymour's 20,372 (41.1 percent). The Republican vote gained about 10 percent over the Democratic tally. With Grant still the great war hero, his personal reputation and platform convinced sufficient marginal voters to support him in West Virginia as well as in other states to win the election. The conservative vote, nonetheless, made some inroads into radical rule, but the latter continued to hold firm.[39]

As the calendar advanced into 1869, the tide turned against the state's radical administration. The party remained united, if with fewer votes due to the Supreme Court cases undermining proscriptions and from the passage of the Fourteenth Amendment granting citizenship to Blacks. Yet they split after an important act occurred at the federal level. Boreman's last message as governor offered a positive assessment of the state. He cited a handful of incidents of unrest in Marion and Cabell counties, which he quelled with federal troops. The finances showed a small deficit, but the free schools, asylum, penitentiary, and universities all progressed according to plan, or so he claimed. These were small victories. When he departed for the Senate, Boreman left a state in disarray. His attempts to restrain the conservative vote had crumbled. His successor inherited a terrible situation that worsened early in his administration. In February 1869, Congress sent the Fifteenth Amendment to the Constitution to the states. Granting voting rights to all persons regardless "of race, color,.or previous condition of servitude," it promised to be the most radical of the three Reconstruction-era amendments. Unlike with the Thirteenth and Fourteenth Amendments, however, resistance marred West Virginia's ratification process. Even Republicans cracked at the idea of Black voting. One of the state's congressmen, Daniel Polsley, turned against the amendment, an ominous contrast to the unanimity the state gave to the previous measures. Many newspapers opposed it, such as the radical *Point Pleasant Register* on the one hand, and the conservative *Wheeling Daily Register* on the other. Its editor, Lewis Baker, opined on March 2 that what he called the "Negro Amendment" would never obtain approval of three-quarters of the states. "The tide is against and not with the universal suffrage movement," he wrote that day. Not even the "inferior class of men . . . now in power" would pursue the "false metaphysical idea, the equality of the races" that would bring into our Congress "the ignorance and barbarism of the negro population." The votes in the State Assembly reflected the rising opposition. On that same day, the House voted twenty-two to nineteen to approve. The Senate also narrowly endorsed it ten to six. This made West Virginia the second state after its wartime cousin Nevada to ratify the amendment, and the first by far among the border states. Missouri ratified it almost a year later, in January 1870. Tennessee, Delaware, Kentucky, and Maryland approved the measure only in the twentieth century. Yet in each case, even the radical *Intelligencer* admitted that many Republicans disliked the bill. Granville Davisson Hall wrote that day that they "allowed themselves during the campaign to be frightened into denying that they were willing to extend suffrage to the negro, and in some cases went so far as to give pledges against it. Now they see the folly and weakness of letting the enemy dictate their position and drive them into a corner. They realize the necessity of voting for this amendment and yet cannot do so without personal inconsistency and some bad faith." A year later, the *Greenbrier Independent* coldly opined that ratifying the amendment was the act "of a West Virginia hog and horse thieving Legislature." The weight of West Virginia's slaveholding past began to catch up with its radical state makers.[40]

Under this pressure, the Republican Party fractured in twain. On one side stood the radicals, who remained dedicated to the proscriptions. Their new rivals were the "let-ups," who sought to remove the regulations to restore peace. The latter received two unexpected sources of support. In May, the *Intelligencer*, once unrelenting in its opposition to degraded rebels and their conservative allies, asked its readers to support change. Yet Hall argued from what he thought were positions of strength. Disenfranchisement, once necessary for "self-protection" and to "maintain the republican form of government," was no longer unnecessary. "The power of the south is thoroughly broken, her negroes voting, the people who made the rebellion cured of any wish ever to renew it," he continued. Even Tennessee and Missouri, who had their own let-ups, now turned against them for these reasons. Remaining radicals called for unity against let-ups because it would strengthen the Democrats. They forgot that "there is nothing to make the Republican organization throughout the country stronger than it has been." With Grant in power, the party feared nothing. An anonymous writer to the *Parkersburg Times* called "Aurelius," later identified as Boreman, encouraged the radicals to reject such talk. Obeying Hall's ideas would "place it [West Virginia] at the disposal of its would-be destroyers." The *Intelligencer* editor defended his stance by publishing a letter he received from famed *New York Tribune* editor, Horace Greeley, in November. As part of his new policy of Universal Amnesty for Universal Suffrage, he favored ending proscriptions because radical defeat was inevitable. The margins for Republican victories in West Virginia and other states narrowed with each election despite barriers to voting. Moreover, Greeley said that the sons of rebels, who did not face proscriptions, will replace their fathers at the ballot box but with the same views. "How much longer," he asked, "do you think that iceberg under a July sun will be safely habitable?" It was a pertinent question. In the next day's *Register*, Baker reprinted the column with the acidic comment "we will not attempt to disguise the pleasure with which we note the assumption of this position by our contemporary." He called on Democrats to rally for one final effort to remove the hated proscriptions. A unified party could combine with "nearly, if not quite, one-half of the Republican party would cooperate" to abolish the disabilities. Once eliminated, communities would revive with men who "feel that they share the privileges of Government whose responsibilities they help to bear, they become contented, active, and useful citizens, uniting with their neighbors." The splits among Republicans provided the turning point in West Virginia's period under radical rule. Like in Missouri, the state's radicals collapsed due to external factors caused by the Fifteenth Amendment.[41]

The notion of Black voting further widened the divides in the governing party. For the first six years of the state's existence, the radicals avoided the race issue by off-loading it onto the federal government and the Freedmen's Bureau and by keeping Blacks out of office. In May 1867, the election of a Black man as inspector of elections in Fairmont, Marion County, drew much newspaper attention. The *Register* condemned the *Intelligencer* for this act, while the latter shifted the blame to the conservatives. "Instead of the Radicals having elected the Negro," Hall wrote on May 28, "it is his conservative, democratic, rebel sympathizing friends who did the job." He cited Democrats electing a Black man in Boston and another in Tennessee. This was thin evidence, but it shows how the radicals also played the race card. Two years later, however, the situation had changed. On May 13, 1869, Hall endorsed granting suffrage to African Americans. In response to the *Mason County Journal*'s opposition to the Fifteenth Amendment for granting voting rights to ex-Confederates as well as Blacks, he wrote that "in the esteem of the Republican people the balance is in favor of the negro, for he has committed no crime against the civil structure of society, while the ex-rebel has." Moreover, for Democrats to support granting suffrage "to white rebels while denying it to Black Republicans, then there is no common ground on this question between you and the liberal wing of the Republican party." The *Register* saw this and exploited it to the maximum. Hitherto, Baker wrote on June 16, "the Republicans of West Virginia were as much opposed to negro suffrage as the Democrats." Dishonesty aside, the numbers of disenfranchised former Confederates outnumbered Blacks by twenty thousand to a mere two thousand. If Republicans changed their policy, Baker concluded, "it involves neither principle nor honor" and no "shirking of duty on the part of the Democratic masses." This was a fair assessment. The radicals depended on keeping the racial status quo. Their failure cost them at the polls that fall.[42]

The 1869 state elections placed the incumbent regime onto its last legs. The let-up faction turned out in strength. A September meeting in Wood County chaired by Jacob Diss Debar, the creator of the state emblem, called for an end to proscriptions. Another gathering in Wayne asked for the same. Boreman organized the *Parkersburg State Journal* specifically to press the radical cause in the election. In its inaugural issue, he appealed to the citizenry's better angels. "You ought to know that it takes time to heal the bitterness engendered by strife," Boreman wrote. He ended with a pathetically weak conclusion: "If the Republican party can be preserved as a unit and you can preserve yourselves from indiscretion, you will have a working majority of Republicans in the Legislature, who will take up this question calmly and dispassionately and deal with it as it should be dealt with. *We know this to be a fact.*" Few in the state shared these wistful sentiments. Even those in the Kanawha Valley backed the removal, resolving that they "no longer wish to keep a large body of our fellow-citizens perpetually disfranchised and thereby perpetually disaffected." In a remarkable admission, Governor Stevenson apologized for the harm caused by the proscriptions. The result of the election indicated massive splits in the Republican Party. The House of Delegates now had thirty-two Republicans and twenty-four Democrats, but eleven of the former were let-ups. The Senate, on the other hand, had eighteen Republicans and only four Democrats. It is unknown how many were let-ups. The prospect of the formerly enslaved voting placed the radicals' once mighty grip on power into an untenable position. Their voters no longer responded to degrading the patriotism of conservatives and former Confederates while casting themselves as loyal and virtuous. Conservatives, on the other hand, may have fallen short of an outright victory, but they also demonstrated greater vitality by asserting white racial unity. They entered the new decade ready to strike the final blow for against the wartime administration.[43]

Like Maryland and Missouri, West Virginia endured a tense period of radical rule during and after the Civil War. The similarities demonstrate the pernicious impact of slavery on the new state. Each saw the wartime rise to power of a party committed to enacting federal war aims, but especially emancipation. After defeating the rebellion, all three required proscriptions against former Confederates to prevent them from undermining those policies. Governor Boreman said as much in his inaugural address in June 1863. West Virginia had no place for opponents of federal policies and particularly emancipation. His administration went to great lengths to keep conservative Unionists down and former rebels out of power. He succeeded thanks to effective enforcement at the township level; proscriptions nullified the latter's political power. The radicals further cemented their rule by avoiding the race issue. By offloading Black education on to the Freedmen's Bureau and mitigating the impact of the Fourteenth Amendment, West Virginia's rulers managed to avoid charges of favoring Blacks. Accusations like that, which were untrue, cost Maryland's radical regime power in 1866. The passage of the Fifteenth Amendment, however, split the ruling radicals and allowed the conservative Democrats to gain control of the legislature in 1870. A nearly identical process occurred in Missouri at almost the same time. Kentucky and Delaware remained under conservative rule during this period. These comparisons more than justify placing West Virginia into the category as a border state.

Redemption best describes the process of abandoning radical rule in those states. "Reconstruction" and "counterrevolution" fail to grasp the intense feelings each side felt toward the reins of power. The first cannot apply to West Virginia in any case since federal plans never applied to it, nor did the federal government need to intervene except at the state's specific request. Counterrevolution is a better term, but it implies that a revolution occurred in the first place. The radicals tried to implement improvements during their tenure, but they spent most of their nine years in power fighting for their existence. Besieged by Confederates for the first two and their angry veterans and their conservative Unionist allies for the next seven, Boreman, Stevenson, and their party achieved precious little beyond emancipation. If they had managed to build new railroads, open more mines and factories, and better implement their much-heralded free school system, they could have withstood their opponents. Having achieved little beyond freeing the enslaved, therefore, no revolution occurred. The conservatives and former Confederates, moreover, rallied around a hyperpoliticized belief in their right to citizenship and mission to purge West Virginia of the radicals who collaborated with the federal government and the radical abolitionists. This was not counterrevolution, for theirs was not a revolt. It was a quest to redeem this part of the border South from the sin of ending slavery.

EPILOGUE

West Virginia's Redemption, 1870–1872

The new governor opened the new decade on a somber note. Reading like a funeral dirge, William E. Stevenson's first annual message marked the surrender of radical control over West Virginia. In it, he announced the end to proscriptions against former Confederates. The "prompt and decisive measures" brought by the war's requirements to suppress the rebels "were not . . . intended to be perpetual, but only to remain in force until all danger to the public peace was past," he began. The situation had by now changed, and "good order now prevails; and the laws are respected and obeyed." As such, he urged legislators to abandon all disabilities against voting in the state, as well as those against lawyers, teachers, and suitors. This statement belied claims by the preceding governor, and is likely dishonest, but it tells of the resigned nature of the radical cause for the last two years of its formal existence. Between January 1870 and the passage of the new state constitution in April 1872, a coalition of conservative Unionists and former Confederates took power in West Virginia. This situation was not counterrevolution since no revolution occurred, as Randall Gooden and John Stealey have argued. Instead, in this time, the new administration purged the new state of its radical rulers for committing the heinous sin of supporting the abolition of slavery. West Virginia's experience was not unique but one shared by Missouri, the last remaining border state under radical rule. Its phase also ended that year. Both collapsed due to their internal contradictions on race and slavery as well as the external power of their conservative opponents.[1]

The new legislature, which was already divided between radicals, liberal Republicans or let-ups, and Democrats, further split as soon as it started in January. It started soundly with near-unanimous motions to remove proscriptions within the first two weeks. This placidity changed within days when a delegate from Pendleton County moved to amend the state constitution. William Henry Harrison Flick, a Union veteran and let-up, resolved to remove one word from Section III, Article One of the 1863 constitution. The original clause permitted that "the white male citizens of the State shall be entitled to vote at all elections held within the election districts in which they respectively reside" excepting only minors, the insane, the destitute, or anyone "who is under conviction of treason, felony, or bribery in an election" so long as "such disability continues." Flick simply sought to omit the word "white" from that sentence to restore a measure of peace to the state. Instead, both sides read deeper implications into it. Radicals understood it to grant political rights to former traitors, while conservatives believed it granted votes to Blacks and hence the introduction of racial equality. Even worse, the state constitution required that proposed amendments must pass in the next session before being presented to the voters. The vote reflected this animosity. The House of Delegates chose thirty-eight to eighteen to back the amendment, while the Senate passed it eighteen to four. Radicals made up most of the dissenters, but one was Francis H. Pierpont during his single term in the West Virginia legislature. This act drove deeper wedges into the already fractured legislature.[2]

Federal actions bought the radicals some time. On March 30, 1870, the Fifteenth Amendment became part of the US Constitution. Two months later, an enabling act gave the federal courts in West Virginia the authority to decide the legality of proscriptions, citing the Supremacy Clause. Justice John J. Jackson of Parkersburg acted quickly. A conservative Unionist who served in the Wheeling Conventions but set accused traitors free on bail during the war and led the opposition to the Willey Amendment in 1863 now had abilities denied him during and after the war. He appointed federal officers to investigate proscriptions in many counties, such as former Union Major Carlos A. Sperry in Greenbrier. In August, Sperry ordered the arrest of infamous J. F. Caldwell of the local Board of Registration, for denying Dr. J. L. Nelson's loyalty oath. This caused a flurry of exchanges between the US attorney, Nathan Goff (a once-captured Union officer), and his federal counterpart Amos Akerman, himself a former Confederate. Before those officials could decide the right approach, Jackson's court tried to take its own action. He aimed to make a federal jury indict registrars for violating the Fifteenth Amendment rights of former Confederates. Despite giving them strict and neutral instructions, the jurors refused to do so and released the officials. Another case in Mineral County heard by judge Hugh Lennox Bond resulted in the conviction of John McElwee for denying W. S. Alkire his rightful ballot. Stevenson stood up to end the matter with a September circular to the state judiciary. Calling Jackson's actions "a concerted and mischievous plot to subvert the plainest provisions of our State law," he ordered his attorney general to hold firm on enforcing proscriptions. Their responses prevented conservatives from using federal law against the new state. If they had, it would have been ironic given the radicals' support for Lincoln's border state emancipation plan, which led to the formation of the state itself. This messy affair ended in a Democratic defeat at the time, but the elections in two months' time became their final victory over the radicals.[3]

The 1870 state ballot offered the voters a choice between two terrible options. The Democrats had now become the dominant party. Having arisen with the abolition of proscriptions, they solicited former rebels and anyone unhappy with the Republicans into their ranks. Race enhanced their appeal. At their June convention in Charleston, soon to be the state capital, they rejected the Flick Amendment as a plot to introduce Black suffrage. Its platform condemned the federal government for its Reconstruction policies and interference into state affairs and opposed racially integrated schools. It called the latter "a radical policy of mingling the races in those institutions and destroying the education system for the benefit of Blacks." The party ran for governor John Jeremiah Jacob of Hampshire County, who had spent the war in Missouri. This made him an ideal candidate for Democrats in need of someone free of wartime allegiances. On the other hand, the Republicans suffered from internal divisions and unpopular platform. Their convention in Parkersburg was the first in state history to allow Black delegates, whose presence undermined its already shaky appeal. Its nine-plank platform made them appear not just conservative but obsolete and desperate for any votes. First appealing to the Union and the Declaration of Independence, the agenda called for support of the Fifteenth Amendment. It then endorsed the Flick Amendment to further the "spirit of magnanimity and forgiveness" of the age. Dissenters called it a disaster that proposed, in the words of Cyrus Newlin of besieged Monroe County, to put degraded traitors into positions of power by elevating "that class of late rebels upon the same footing precisely as the men who, to satisfy and insatiate ambition, had led these people astray, and had contributed their utmost to plunge the country into war, and who, since the close of the war, had never lost an opportunity of stirring up opposition to law and make it impossible, in the section where he lived, to enforce civil law without the aid of the military." His words had little effect on the election. Nor did an exchange of letters between former rebel David Goff of Randolph County and Harrison County Unionist Luther Haymond over bank transactions. Both showed that little narrowing had occurred between the two sides. When Haymond praised proscriptions as necessary "to show their disapprobation to those who had so needlessly plunged this country into Civil war," Goff scoffed. The South started the war and "there the error and the Sin is to be found," he replied while surrendering nothing. His side won the election and with it restored to power many former rebels. The result reversed the previous ballot with handsome margins. Democrats won a commanding forty of the House's fifty-six seats. In the Senate, they received only ten of its twenty-two seats, but the support of a handful of liberal Republicans gave them a working majority. With both houses of the state legislature out of their control for the first time since statehood, radical rule over West Virginia had effectively ended. At almost the same time, Missouri underwent the same process of collapse. Its let-up faction undermined their unity and gave conservative Democrats the advantage.[4]

The new regime began in January 1871 on a mission to scour West Virginia of its radical foundations. Reviving their motto from five years earlier of "White Men Must Rule," Democrats moved quickly to overthrow the remaining proscriptions. The Flick Amendment came up soon as required by law for approval by referendum. It was not without controversy. Soon, however, a debate began over going even further by creating a new constitution. The idea came from, interestingly, Spencer Dayton, a let-up Republican of Barbour County. He called it "the next legitimate step in the revolution that will not go back" in a letter to former Confederate Jonathan Bennett of Lewis County in October 1870. The recipient agreed, so that the convention could "wipe out all the officers who hold their places by fraud and force." Conservative editors agreed on the matter but disagreed on the Flick Amendment. Lewis Baker of the *Register* supported the convention but opposed the latter as a back-door to Black voting. William P. Cooper, once editor of the powerful *Cooper's Clarksburg Register* before the war, another former Confederate, and now heading the *Parkersburg Gazette*, suggested putting both before the voters. Granville Davisson Hall of the *Intelligencer*, predictably, opposed the convention. In January and February, the legislature, now in its new home in Charleston, approved of both but staggered their times. The House voted thirty-eight to seventeen to send the Flick Amendment to the voters in late April. Five days later, the bodies passed the convention bill by similar if strict party margins for its own referendum in August. The relative ease by which the conservative-dominated legislature passed both measures gratified their need for white men to take over the state. In only three months, they began purging West Virginia of what they deemed to be radical abolitionist rule. By doing so, they sought to deny their opponents access to its power, a shocking turn of events if ever one existed.[5]

The results of the two referendums surprised few observers. In April, the Flick Amendment received a wide margin of support. Although Logan and McDowell counties sent no returns, the measure passed 23,516 (78.8 percent) to 6,323 (21.2 percent). This amounted to one-third of the tally in the previous governor's election. Many counties posted numbers reminiscent of the lopsided ballots made during the war. Braxton had 524 supporters and 3 against; Wayne's tally was 608 to 1. Only Doddridge, Grant, Hardy, Harrison, and Marshall voted against it. Strangely, Ohio County's numbers showed a massive decline. With 434 for and 368 opposed, these were substantially lower than the more than 2,000 on each side in previous ballots. The *Intelligencer* blamed this on "an utter absence of interest" with those voting doing so "we presume, as a matter of abstract duty." These are weak excuses given the heavy turnouts in previous elections. The real issue was the double threat posed by Black voting and removing the proscriptions against former rebels. The convention referendum bears this out. The voting in August nearly doubled over the Flick Amendment ballot in April if still representing only half of the total electorate. In all, 30,220 (53.1 percent) supported holding a new Constitutional Convention, while 26,638 (46.9 percent) opposed it. Each number nearly equaled the previous turnout. It was also much closer due to the broader range of issues at stake. Adopting a new constitution involved legal matters, infrastructure, taxation, structure of the legislature, and the like. The result showed that many wished to cling to the 1863 constitution if modified to allow Blacks and former rebels to participate at least. The supporters were soon disappointed. Conservatives intent on complete overhaul had no wish to retain remnants of the radical regime. They wanted to clean the slate.[6]

In a freezing winter of January 1872, seventy-eight delegates met in Charleston on a mission of salvation. The conservative nature of the event dominated the whole affair. Many stayed in a hotel built by John P. Hale. He, and others, did so to spite the radical regime then in charge. John Stealey has researched every aspect of the convention in his recent massive book, so I need only to emphasize a few issues pertinent to my work. The demographics of the seventy-six delegates reveal a resumption of the antebellum elites. A mere one dozen of the delegates were Republicans, whom their opponents called disparagingly "the twelve apostles." Of those, just Waitman T. Willey had served in the Wheeling Conventions. The rest came from the state's suppressed conservatives. Confederate veterans numbered twenty-one, as opposed to only five Unionists. Many had prior political experience in the Virginia legislature or as lawyers and clerks. Most ominously, twenty-four previous slaveholders attended the event, but all except a pair who moved to West Virginia after the war knew about slavery. The Wheeling Conventions and the first Constitutional Convention saw few if any from the master class participate in forming the new state. The radical embrace of emancipation proved too great for most. Stealey's research also reveals that many employed Black or Mulatto servants in what he ominously called "some institutional continuity in many delegates' dependence on domestic labor in the home."[7] While the rest of the state looked on, the convention consisted of men determined to remove every element of the previous regime.

The delegates went to work on January 16, 1872. Former congressman, rebel officer, and member of the 1850 Constitutional Convention Charles Faulkner of Berkeley County led the conservative majority. Their first acts included removing all obstacles to suffrage. While the previous legislature formally abolished test oaths and registration, the new constitution ensured that the state could never revive them. The former fell sixty-four to two, a certain sign of how strongly conservatives opposed such measures. Some sought to return to viva voce voting, but the secret ballot won in the end. The delegates left the status of Blacks unclear despite much debate over including the limiting word "white" in qualifications for office holding in the final document. They resolved to hold a separate ballot at the same time as ratification to let the voters decide. Despite radical fears for their main, if not only, accomplishment, conservatives also maintained the free school system. They did, however, impose segregation, which would plague West Virginia's educational system until the 1960s.

Other changes restored elements of the political system of the antebellum period. The new governorship would have no veto power, a response to its use during Boreman's administration, and little influence with the legislature. Members of the new House of Delegates served two-year terms while senators sat for four. They abolished the hated township system in favor of a restoration of the county court system of antebellum times. Finally, the conservatives sought amnesty for their Confederate allies and families. The delegates compromised by granting political rights but maintaining civil penalties for wartime actions. The convention wrapped up its business on a precipitous date that many lamented: April 9, the anniversary of the rebel surrender at Appomattox Court House. A popular referendum approved of the new constitution in August. With the highest turnout since 1860, West Virginians gave their new document a mixed endorsement. A total of 42,344 (52.9 percent) supported it, while 37,777 (47.1 percent) opposed it. The large turnout and yet close result indicate a resurgence of radical opposition to the new constitution, which abandoned the war's achievements. At the same time, it legitimized that West Virginia would survive as a separate state. The separate ballot on allowing African Americans to hold office resembled the gradual emancipation measure held a decade earlier. Almost every county reported in, but only Fayette, Hampshire, Jefferson, and Marion mentioned any dissenting votes. With this act, white conservative West Virginians had finally purged the radical regime that formed the state in 1863. West Virginia still lives under its redemption constitution born from the region's antebellum elites retaliating against the radicals' wartime embrace of emancipation.[8]

Conclusion

This book has shown how every history about West Virginia's formation is wrong. The reason is simple. The Ambler-Curry thesis, which has controlled the study of the subject for decades, neglected the major issues facing white and Black Americans in the Civil War era: slavery and emancipation. The notion of northwestern Virginia separating out of irreconcilable social, economic, and cultural differences, which led to its dismemberment in the Civil War, is historically untenable. It is based on flimsy research and weak reasoning. Later historians of the state have merely repeated the thesis with little or no investigation of its reliability. This lapse continues to influence the broader literature. Some of the finest historians of the Civil War are guilty of perpetuating this flaw, but it is not their fault. Nor are the students of the narrower field of the border states guilty for either reiterating the same story or excluding West Virginia from their analyses. These acts are forgivable. Since the main texts on the subject have barely changed in over a century, historians have committed no crime in taking the creation of the Thirty-Fifth State for granted.

My work offers a new interpretation of this event. I have argued that *the region experienced the Civil War in the same ways as the border states of Missouri, Kentucky, Maryland, and Delaware.* Like that quartet, white West Virginians resisted secession in 1861 for the same reason. They all shared the view that disunion threatened slavery. Contrary to the Ambler-Curry thesis, northwestern Virginia had a long connection to slaves and slaveholders. Comfort with enslavement best describes white relationships both to the enslaved in their midst, with the other parts of Virginia, and to the broader nation. Contrary notions stem from the region's support for gradual emancipation in the 1829–1830 state constitutional debates. Their stance, which almost succeeded with support from across the state, led eastern elites to view northwesterners as unreliable on slavery and continued to restrict their suffrage rights. As I argued in the first chapter, despite some grizzled resentments, this did not lead to a permanent split among Virginia's regions. Northwestern whites viewed such disabilities as an affront to their patriotism, but they remained faithful to their state. A new generation of leaders consisting of men who owned slaves broke the impasse in the following decade when they used proslavery appeals to attain the pivotal constitution of 1850–1851. The northwest's whites then used their new political powers to defend the institution against internal and external foes. None of the other reasons cited for causing the state's internal differences, such as Scots-Irish culture, allegations of neglect of internal improvements, and commonalities with neighboring non-slaveholding states, stand up to scrutiny. As shown in chapter 2, they responded powerfully to any hint of antislavery threat to their homes. Whether it was a radical newspaper, a Kansas-style free labor colony, the Know Nothing Party, or John Brown himself, white northwestern Virginians acted in defense of their homes, their state, and their racial privileges. Far from fragmenting as 1861 began as the previous view maintains, the Old Dominion had by that year united like never in its past.

West Virginia's path to statehood developed from the conditions wrought by the war. The secession of the seven Lower South states prompted intense debates in the four Upper South and four border slave states. Caught in the middle, the northwest formed a significant Unionist faction in Virginia's deliberations. In chapter 3, I showed how the region's delegates used the same proslavery tactics to prevent secession during those precious weeks. When the war began in April 1861, the distraught northwest saw its parent submit to the Confederacy. The area did not stand idle in those winds. Like their four border neighbors, the region rejected secession despite having misgivings about the Republican-led federal government. Their decisions stemmed from their need to restore order, and no other factor as previously believed. Among the border states, only Kentucky had fewer Republicans than did northwestern Virginia. Its path, instead, came from the common hope that President Lincoln would fulfill his promise to protect slavery where it existed. He did that and more. He allowed the loyal slave states except Maryland to sort out their allegiances without his interference. Union armies entered the region only after the May 23 referendum, not before. The same approach kept Missouri and Kentucky in the Union cause. Statehood, however, was not the inevitable outcome of this resistance. Instead, the white population maintained a conservative approach that resulted in the Reorganized Government of Virginia. With Lincoln's support and the federal army's protection, white northwestern Virginians successfully resisted secession.

Remaining loyal to the Union carried its own risks. Lincoln's patience turned out to have limits. As chapter 4 argued, he maintained his tolerance of slavery during the fall and winter of 1861 and 1862. This allowed the first or conservative phase of the statehood movement to proceed. The Constitutional Convention created the new state's early legal basis, but only by keeping slavery off the agenda. A sudden near-miss late in the proceedings compelled the delegates to enact a compromise Black exclusion law. While they thought they had averted a crisis, changes at the federal level almost upended the enterprise. In March 1862, Lincoln introduced a plan for the border states to free their enslaved persons. The other states famously resisted this idea, but as chapter 5 pointed out, West Virginia supported his plan. Its Unionists split into radical and conservative factions over emancipation, completely belying the small numbers of enslaved persons in their midst. The former gained control over the latter by backing the gradual abolition of slavery in the new state. An overjoyed Lincoln signed the West Virginia Statehood Bill to thank the one border area to support his otherwise unpopular policy. The radicals paid a heavy price in the following nine years of their rule. As chapter 6 argued, Maryland and Missouri retained their wartime radical administrations, while Kentucky and Delaware stayed under conservative rule. The latter hounded the radicals during the state's first decade for supporting emancipation. Conservatives and former rebels fought furious campaigns to purge the new state of their opponents. Like their border state cousins, the radicals retained power using proscriptions. They fell in 1870 only after federal, not state, actions undermined their coalition. They achieved that goal in their constitution two years later. For those who say that West Virginia was not a border state, I respond simply that it was not a border state *yet*, but it became one because of the conditions brought to that area by secession, civil war, and emancipation.

My argument also consigns to history the notion of slavery being unimportant to West Virginia. Its white population viewed the institution as an essential part of their region's social structure. Slavery was the glue that had held Virginia together since colonial times. Virtually all whites, whether from the east or the west, supported the institution as part of their heritage. Far from being opposed to slaveholders, the western population elected them to political office throughout the antebellum period. The only antislavery views come from narrow and unrepresentative sources. Indeed, supporting slavery made possible the 1850 constitution. When that document abolished property qualifications and equalized the white population, they unified around protecting slavery in their region, within Virginia, and even in the southern states. Whites supported the practice despite, not because of, the actual limited numbers of enslaved persons. If anything, the relative paucity of slaves made whites more comfortable and conservative with the institution. Their defenses of slavery in the 1850s laid the groundwork for opposing secession in 1861. While that act fractured the region, white Unionists first saw the Reorganized Government and then statehood as defenses of the institution. This approach allowed the first state constitution to pass. When radicals took over and openly supported and encouraged emancipation, the Unionist coalition fragmented badly. Conservatives viewed any such measure as an attack on their society, but they faced well-organized and -defended proscriptions that prevented them from retaliating. Conservative Unionists could not bear the formation of West Virginia without slavery. The credibility of the Ambler-Curry thesis thus erodes forever when compared to the driving force of slavery and emancipation behind the state's formation, and not notions of long-standing grievances.

This study has broad implications for historians of the state and of the Civil War. First, West Virginians should reinterpret their origins. Instead of being a marginalized part of the Old Dominion, they ought to view themselves as their ancestors did: the northwest was a complete part of Virginia until its attempt at secession in 1861. It bore the same legacies as its parent, especially slavery. Their resistance came from whites rejecting disunion as a form of abolition and not inherent differences. My approach renders those views obsolete. Second, Civil War historians should see West Virginia as a key part of the border area. It may have become a state later than the others, but that must not prevent it from rising to their level in the literature. The similarities between them with the war and emancipation should prompt serious rethinking of the membership of that important area. These reasons explain why history should see West Virginia as *the fifth border state.*

APPENDIX A

An Appeal of the People of West Virginia to Congress, Suggesting for the Consideration of Members Material Facts; Accepting the "Nation's Proposal" for the Gradual Abolishment of Slavery, and Asking That Body to Give Its Consent to the Erection and Admission of the New State into the Union at Its Present Session [May 22, 1862]

Soon after publishing my last letter, I drew up the following Appeal; and after submitting it to some friends, I went to Ironton, Ohio, and had a large number printed in document form, and immediately enclosed a copy to each member of Congress, the President, and each member of his Cabinet, and the learning Republican journals of the country. I ventured to subscribe it in the manner that appears.

Gentlemen: A Constitution conforming to our wishes in all respects but one, the informal spontaneous, and nearly unanimous express of such Counties throughout the proposed State (being about twenty) as had an opportunity to speak upon the matter, which our Delegates in convention *unwarrantably* suppressed, with the almost unanimous consent of the Legislature of the mother State, have been laid before your honorable body for its consent agreeably to the 3d Section, Article 4th, of the Federal Constitution. The action by the Legislature of the mother State, has, in our judgment, placed the people of the proposed State in *direct communication* with your body, to negotiate for its consent to the erection and admission of West Virginia into the Union, upon such terms as shall be agreed upon by your body and ourselves, subject only to the fundamental compacts contained in the 8th Section of the 8th Article of the new Constitution; touching the public debt, and the 1st Section of the 9th Article of the same, touching titles to the land—and without further resort to that body. Our Convention still exists, and can be re-convened whenever necessary to carry into effect the terms that may be agreed upon.

It is proper for us to say, as mitigating in some measure the wrong done us by the Convention, in withholding the matter from our decision, that the Delegates thereof were elected and the Convention, as it supposed, had completed its labors and adjourned, (though subject to be reconvened), before there had been any definite or authentic expression of the views of the Nation, or our people, upon the subject.

OUR CLAIM ON CONGRESS FOR PROMPT ACTION AT ITS PRESENT SESSION

When we ask Congress to change the oldest State in the Union, so as to make two States instead of one, and four Senators instead of two, we expect to make out a case, the justice, equity and propriety of which shall satisfy all loyal and fair minded men, that we *merit* what we ask, and which shall readily evoke the exercise by Congress of a power purely discretionary.

It is now about forty years since the *expediency* of dividing the State was first discussed, some contending that the Blue Ridge, and others the Alleghany Mountains, ought to constitute the boundary. The Seaboard and Piedmont Districts, in order to make sure of the Valley, extended internal improvements of all descriptions into that section, uniting the people commercially and socially with Richmond; and after Baltimore had extended a branch of its road to Winchester, our Legislature denied future charters. The growing of slaves for the Southern markets, served also to attach and assimilate the Valley to the East, and to alienate it from the West. In proportion as the East has been lavish to the Valley, it has been sparing to the West; and of the forty-four millions of State debt, created prior to January 1st, 1861, and expended in internal improvements, only one and a half millions have been expended West of the Alleghanies. And when Baltimore proposed to extend branches of its road throughout our territory, at its own expense, the Legislature refused to grant charters for the purpose—being neither willing to improve our country themselves, nor permit any one else to do it.

Of the half million slaves in the State in 1860, only about ten thousand were owned West of the Alleghanies The Valley and the East have co-operated to enact and constitute a system of taxation more unequal and unjust to the West than anything of the kind before known. By it, no slave, though worth

$2,000 in the market, can be valued over $300 for the purpose of taxation; and no slave under the age of twelve years, though worth $600 to $800, can be taxed at all. *In this way two hundred million dollars worth of slave property*, owned almost exclusively in the Valley and the East, has never been taxed at all, while every other species of property has been taxed to its full value. And almost every species of income, even to the earnings of day-laborers, which go daily to support their families, are either taxed, or are liable to be taxes; and also nearly every branch of business, except the growing, working, and selling of negroes, by requiring licenses to be taken and paid for at enormous prices. The poor man, who buys a piece of wild land, with a view to clear up and make him a home, has to pay $1.00 tax to the State before his deed can be recorded—this being in addition to the recording fee; and so with all forms of legal process, whether relating to the living, or the settlement of estates of the dead. All this starting injustice and oppression exists now throughout the State. *Everything pays tribute to the slave power.*

Besides, the East early adopted a system of "land law" which has for eighty years, and does to-day, treat the lands West of the Alleghanies as *"waste and unappropriated," and has continued to sell them and grant patents of any portions to anybody who will pay, until the whole country has become shingled over, and some five or six patents deep. Two, three, and frequently more have paid taxes on the same land, at the same time.* The result has been to increase the revenue drawn from the West, to keep the titles to land unsettled—plenty of work for lawyers, and a defrauded and impoverished people. The Legislature has repeatedly exonerated lands in the Valley and in the East of taxes justly assessed; whilst, by the same act, it enforced the payment of the like tax against lands of the West by ordering their sale. There is one statute of limitation relating to lands East, and another relating to the lands West, of the Alleghany Mountains.

These are some of the wrongs which the people of the Valley and the East—they having a large majority in both branches of the Legislature, increased in the Senate by a mixed or property basis—have practiced on the people West of the mountains. And is it any wonder, that when a year ago, these oppressors—the measure of whose iniquity had become full—plunged into treason and rebellion against the Government of their choice which had bestowed every blessing, without one single wrong that could be specified, that the loyal and true, though long oppressed and abused people of the same West, should have rallied around the nation's flag, and at the same time have embraced the first opportunity ever offered for making their escape from such bondage? As we are human, we could not have done otherwise; and still we had a terrible enemy to battle with in our very midst. The minions and tools of the slave oligarchy in the East were thick among us. JENKINS, WISE & Co. were gathering their forces and a terrible doom was denounced on all who should hesitate to take up arms and defend the State ("after a majority had voted her out," as they contended, "against ruthless invaders.") Many of our counsellors and guides in matters of constitutional rights and duties, had either openly joined the enemy, or stood silent in trembling suspense. The plan so timely proposed by General MCCLELLAN to give effectual protection to our loyal people was thwarted by the treason or the weakness of former leaders.

It was at this trying crisis that some bold men, from among the people, struck for re-organizing the State Government, and that accomplished, then for a new State, and eternal deliverance from our worse than Egyptian oppressors in the East. Light broke through the thick darkness, and we awoke as if from a dream.

About this time the Stars and Stripes were unfurled by the sons of Ohio, Indiana and Kentucky, upon the "sacred soil," and our young men and middle aged gathered around the Nation's standard. The spell of years that moment was broken, and our people began to stand up in the majesty and strength of conscious manhood. We have continued to rally, leaving our wives and children, aged dependents and property, to the mercy of the guerrilla and bandit, until our people to-day are as largely represented in the loyal arm as the other portions of the country, where no such sacrifices had to be made.

The effect of the loyalty of West Virginia thus thrown into the scale at a moment when the fate of our country trembled in the balance, when the mere accidental use of an ex. instead of an abdicated, Governor's name to a telegram, could, under the Providence of God, have saved from destruction a Government like ours, no man can calculate. But whatever may have been its weight and effect, we feel that the Federal Government has fully paid us by its liberal and timely aid. We only claim to have done our duty faithfully in this great crisis. Meantime, our people have pressed forward the New State project with equal vigor. We felt that the Almighty has opened the way for our deliverance, and we were resolved to improve it. The minions of the power of the East were everywhere busy among us. They *affected* to be friendly leaders and guides still. They at first openly opposed the measure, but finding the people were resolved they changed tactics, and *pretended* to favor it. But, with a view to retain the leadership of the measure and wreck the whole project upon a *failure*, as they confidently expected, to *harmonize* the views of our people, which were supposed to be *pro-Slavery*, with the views of the Republican Congress on the subject of Slavery, and receive their reward, when the should return to Richmond with West Virginia, foiled in her purpose, and still in chains.

Some of the "wolves in sheep's clothing," managed to get themselves chosen Delegates to the Convention to frame the Constitution, and it was through their influence and misrepresentation that the question of gradual emancipation was not permitted to go through to these decision of the people, and through their influence the clause is now wanted in the instrument. And the same persons used every effort to prevent the spontaneous and informal vote, which, in spite of them, was given in favor of emancipation. They are too well known now to be able to deceive the people again. They boldly contended that it was the wish of the Federal Government that the Convention should be silent and ignore the question of slavery; and, if it were otherwise, it would be unsafe to refer the question of emancipation to the people at this time; that they would get mad with excitement and tear things to pieces! Fortunately, neither of these assertion or predictions have proven true. The "Nation's proposal" we now have, and the people, have of their own accord, and in defiance of the commands and warnings of these men, given their votes without "undue excitement, and without having torn anything to pieces."

THE NECESSITY OF IMMEDIATE ACTION BY CONGRESS

If Congress shall defer its action upon the subject until the next session, there is imminent danger that the accession of new members from the Counties of the Valley and the East, that will be elected and sent into the Legislature as soon as the rebellion shall be crushed in that section, and the East and Valley secure thereby a majority of both branches of the Legislature adverse to separation, and as the Legislature will be convened in extra session before Congress shall meet again, such legislature will repeal the act already passed, giving consent and the consent of that body cannot be obtained afterwards. There is no doubt such will be the disposition and action of the Legislature as soon as it gets power.

There were members from the Valley and East of the Blue Ridge, in the Legislature at its recent session, and although they personally acknowledged the merits and just claims of West Virginia, yet, out of regard to the known sentiment of their constituents, they felt themselves constrained to vote against it. This is actual demonstration, if any be needed, that the loyal portion of the people East of the Alleghanies will never consent to let Western Virginia go. They will say that they love us too well to think of a separation, and that our co-operation is indispensable to enable them to hold in check the great number of unregenerate traitors that shall continue among them. But it is quite uncertain whether the loyal people of the whole State combined will be able, for some time at least, to out-vote the disloyal potion (unless the latter shall be disenfranchised) and so subject the whole State to loyal rule; whereas, taking the cis-Alleghany people, separate by themselves, and there can be no doubt as to their power to control the disloyal. The disloyal portion of the Valley and East will desire to hold on if they can control, oppress and torture us; otherwise, they will be for letting us go.

CERTAIN OBJECTIONS ANSWERED

First. That Congress ought not to regard the consent of the present Legislature which has been given, as satisfying the requirement of the 3d Section, 4th Article, of the Federal Constitution, because all the Counties of the mother State, though invited, were not in fact represented. Such objectors would therefore have us simply decline the way of escape, now providentially opened, from unparalleled oppression, and wait until our oppressors shall have regained their former power, "bound us hand and foot," and remanded us to our former bondage. Whatever loyal West Virginians might have done a year ago, they are now prepared to strike down the unholy oppressor whenever and wherever opportunity may offer.

We deem it unnecessary to say anything in support of the *legal competency* of the present Legislature to give the required consent to the separation. LETCHER and his co-conspirator through their reason, committed against both the State and Federal Government, abdicated; and the powers of the State, incapable of annihilation, returned to the people. The disloyal portion could not take advantage of their forfeiture for they were confederate with LETCHER, *participes criminis*, equally guilty, and to allow it would be to allow a party to "take advantage of his own wrong." The loyal people alone had the right to take advantage of the forfeiture, and re-produce and re-organize the Government. Full notice was given to all loyal people throughout the State, and all who would and could be, were represented in the Convention which convened in Wheeling, the 11th of June 1861, and re-organized the Government, and caused to be elected and convened at Wheeling, the present Legislature. If all loyal people were not represented, it was their own fault or misfortune, and on account of either, it would have been wrong to have permitted the whole machinery of Government to remain suspended, especially as there exists no power to compel an election and return of Delegates. If a County or Senatorial District, neglect or refuse to elect and return Senators or Delegates, there is no power to compel, and those elected and returned, must ex necessitate rei, constitute the legal body, and its acts bind all.

But it is unnecessary to elaborate this point, as ever branch the Federal Government has now for nearly a year been recognized its legitimacy in various forms, and by the most solemn and deliberate acts. It is, therefore, too late to take exception, even if any valid ground had existed, which we deny.

The Legislature and the Governor during vacation, have granted Writs of Election, whenever applied for by the people in any County or District of the State, and elections have been held, and Delegates and Senators returned, and admitted into their respective branches, without hinderance from any quarter. Northampton, Accomac, Fairfax, Loudon, Berkeley, Hampshire and Hardy, were all represented at the late session.

Others who admit the strict *legality* of the consent given by the Legislature, object that it is morally wrong—wrong in the forum of conscience, to effect a division of the State, until every section shall be represented in the Legislature. This objection we have already answered, and need only add that no loyal mind will hesitate to say where such objectors' sympathies lie.

Others object that it is unjust and unfair in the loyal people of West Virginia, to separate themselves from the loyal people in the Valley and in the East, at this time of their trouble. We would ask who, and where, are those loyal people of the Valley and the East? Where have they been during the fearful struggle of life or death, to our glorious Government? Have they rallied around the old flag in this their country's peril? Have they become voluntary exiles from home, family, and all that is dear, rather than submit to and affiliate with fiendish traitors? Have they abandoned all to the mercy of marauders and bandits as West Virginians have done, to battle for their country? If they have, we have not heard of it. But are they not rather, with some bright exceptions, avaricious and no souled loyalists—these "submit to the powers that be" patriots, whether that power be JEFF. DAVIS, or any other, no matter, if only their persons and property are kept safe? In the bold, open, but deluded rebel, there is something to admire; but in the "submit to the powers that be" loyalist, in these times, there is nothing.

But the most important inquiry which all loyal Western Virginians have to make in this respect, is this: have not these now professed friends and loyalists, of the Valley and the East, done as much, and been as ready as any others during the past forty years to impose and continue the unjust oppression to the West? Have they ever lifted a voice or a finger towards alleviating our unjust burdens? What possible claim then can they have on us now to remain and help them to reconcile their Confederates in our oppression, until they can again unite to remand us to our former vassalage? Will any sane loyal man hold up his head and say we owe them anything but retaliation—were we unchristian enough to acknowledge and pay such a debt, which we trust none of us are disposed to do? On the score of true merit the balance is already largely in our favor. And is there any member of Congress who will desire to retain us to help reconcile among themselves, our common oppressors east of the Alleghanies for the last forty years, so they may again jointly resume and exercise that prerogative, rather, than help us escape? If there is we should like to see him hold up his head also, and assert it. But there are none. Such thoughts can only exist in minds unhinged by the mania of secession, or other like malady. Nevertheless we wish it understood that to help true and live loyal men anywhere, none will make greater sacrifices than loyal West Virginians.

But others object that we should not ask for separation at present, because Congress and the re-organized Government of Virginia will require our aid to help reclaim and restore the rebellious East. If it is thought by these Governments, or either of them that loyal West Virginians can serve the cause better, connected than separated, in this respect, and after the re-organized Government shall remove to Richmond, where we understand it hopes soon to go, we will consent to do so most cheerfully, and shall respectfully ask Congress to adopt the following course of action, which will enable us to give that aid without endangering our final deliverance by the establishment of the new State. It is this: For Congress to pass an act at its present session, giving its consent to the division and admission of West Virginia, *to take effect when the qualified voters thereof shall accept the "Nation's Proposal,"* made by Congress, pursuant to the recommendation of the President, on the 6th of March last, in relation to the gradual emancipation of, and compensation for the few slaves of loyal men now remaining among us, not exceeding 2,000 in number. Our Convention, or the Commissioners appointed thereby, can arrange with your body the details to be embodied in your act, and our people will accept, and ratify the same, by a vote of at least twenty to one, at any time thereafter, when the President shall notify the Commissioners aforesaid, that our services in that respect are no longer required. The Commissioners, or Convention, will then submit the provisions to the qualified voters, who are sure to ratify the same with the unanimity before state, and the separation will thereupon become consummated. The action on the part of your body at its *present* session, (making itself a party thereto,) will place the matter for a certainty, beyond the reach of the *repealing power* of *unfriendly* State Legislatures, if such shall have the power, and add to the new Constitution a provision which nearly all the people earnestly desire, but which our Convention omitted, and denied us an opportunity to insert, for causes already stated. The *competency* of Congress to give such *conditional* consent is clear on general principles, and has been sanctioned repeatedly by Congress. Missouri was admitted March 2d, 1821, *on condition* that its Legislature should thereafter consent to the "compromise measures" proposed by Congress. Its Legislature having thereafter consented, and compiled with the condition annexed, its formation became complete and perfect, August 28th, 1821, upon announcement of the fact by proclamation, as the act of Congress provided, and without further action by Congress. Volume 3d, page 797, Statutes at Large. So did Michigan, Ib, Volume 5th, page 49. So did Wisconsin, Ib, Volume 9th, page 233. So did Iowa, Ib, Volume 9th, page 177, and so with Kansas. In these cases it is true that the States were formed out of Federal Territory. But it is very clear, that after the Legislature of the mother State gives its consent to the division, fixes the boundaries, and prescribes such other fundamental provisions as she judges the best interest of the whole State requires, the segregating people must stand subject only to such limitations, in substantially the same relation to Congress as the residents of Federal Territory. The former must be as free to negotiate with Congress for its consent, and to make and receipt propositions, as the latter are. In the case of Missouri, the condition annexed by Congress, had relation to the slave institution in that State.

In most of the other cases cited, the conditions annexed by Congress related to boundaries. There can be no question therefore, as the entire right to propriety of Congress, annexing the condition proposed, to its consent, and however much dictation, and improper interference, the minions of the slave power may affect to see in it, nineteen-twentieths of our loyal people earnestly desire the provision, and desire Congress to do for them *as a favor*, what their unfaithful delegates failed to do in the Convention. We beg the members of your honorable body not to suffer your minds to be abused by a class of men among us who are, or have been enemies to the new State in disguise. They have spared and will spare no pains to defeat it. Some are members of the Convention and perhaps the commission appointed by that Convention, and others of the Legislature. 'Tis the outside pressure of an earnest and determined constituency, whom they have deceived and now attempt to betray, that makes them assume their present guise. Their highest aspiration is to defeat the whole project, and deliver over West Virginia, with tightened chains and a broken spirit, to her former oppressors.

Compare West Virginia *as she is*, with what *she might have been*, if she had been set free from the oppression and thraldom of an accursed slave oligarchy and its minions. Her salubrious climate, fertile soil and fine streams, attracted the attention of Washington and his co-patriots. Soon after the Revolution, they patented and attempted a settlement of a large portion of her land. Their great influence and combined efforts were directed in that end. The great free West was then, and for a long time afterwards, an unbroken wilderness; and still the tide of emigration and capital has flowed from the East to the West, veering around our repulsive border as the mighty river bends its course around the repellent features of the projecting rock, until it has filled up the vast valley with States Imperial, reached the base of the Rocky Mountains, and sent back its refluent wave; nay, it has o'er-leaped that stern barrier, peopled the land of gold, and is fast filing up the whole Pacific slope. And where is West Virginia? Comparatively a wilderness still! Look on either side of our beautiful Ohio. On the one hand is a thrifty, happy and loyal people. Their hills are covered with green pastures, and waving grain, are worth $15 to $30 per acre; and on the other side, we find similar hills, but they are still, in a great measure, covered with primeval forests, and worth from 50 cts. to $1 per acre; and a large portion of her people, roaming bands of marauding guerrillas, mad with treason, and "seeking whom they may devour." Your own minds can run out the contrast and assign the cause.

We have just read the proclamation of our good and sagacious Chief Magistrate, restating the "standing proposal" of the Federal Government and using the following significant language:

> It now stands as an authentic, definite and solemn proposal of the Nation, to the States and people most immediately interested in the subject matter. To the people of these States I now earnestly appeal—I do not argue. I do beseech you to make the argument for yourselves. You cannot, if you would, be blind to the signs of the times. I beg of you a calm and honest consideration of them, ranging, if it may be, far above partisan and personal politics.

All this the people of West Virginia have calmly and deliberately done, and desire to be the first to accept and carry the same into practical operation, as we have been the first to reclaim and re-organize a loyal State Government; and we entreat your honorable body to help us in the manner before indicated or in any other your superior wisdom may suggest. And we entreat you not to let our enemies, in whatever form or guide they may appear, misrepresent us. We know our present position is awkward and embarrassing, and hence we stand in greater need of your aid. You know the causes that have placed us in this predicament. Our sentiment and that of the Nation are now fully known on the subject. In these times of great and sudden changes, startling facts and stern realities, the known character of your body leads us to hope that no matter of the mere *form* or *technicality* will be permitted to stand between us and the great object which both of the negotiating parties are so desirous to attain. Nor will you let the fallacious, though specious, argument it may be, of our enemies, that the whole State is soon to be reclaimed to loyalty, accept the "National proposal," and a millenial harmony is to exist between the East and the West, and that the "lion and the lamb," the oppressor and the oppressed, are to lie down in love together. Let us not be deceived; but remember that the same physical, commercial and geographical necessities, the same political, moral and social antagonism, will still exist as they always have between the sections East and West of the Alleghanies; and the line of their separation is, and will remain, as marked and permanent as the Alleghanies themselves, absolutely necessitating, now and always, separate peoples.

Confiding in the justice of your honorable body we have frankly disclosed our present condition with our hopes, fears and desires, and what seems to us to be our just merits, and "appealing from FESTUS unto CÆSAR," we commit our Destiny into your hands. If disenthralled and permitted to set up for herself, West Virginia will at once "spring forth into newness of life, with JOY and FREEDOM in her wings"—to bless and be blessed; but if remanded to her worse than former bondage and chains, the young and loyal West, bound indissolubly to the disloyal and now *self immolated* East, the living Hindoo widow bound to the corpse of her deceased husband, she will become lost to your country, and no pen can adequately depict the anguish and utter despair that will settle with crushing weight upon the hearts of her loyal people. But we *know* that some *timely action* of your body will save us from such a fate.

THE LOYAL PEOPLE OF WEST VIRGINIA.

May 22, 1862.

Reprinted from Granville Parker, *The Formation of the State of West Virginia and Other Incidents of the Late Civil War* (Wellsburg, WV: Glass & Sons, 1875), 123–134.

APPENDIX B

Report of the Minority to Lincoln's Border State Emancipation Plan, July 15, 1862

Reply of the Minority:
Washington, July 15, 1862

Mr. President: The undersigned, members of Congress from the border states, in response to your address of Saturday last, beg leave to say that they attended a meeting on the same day the address was delivered, for the purpose of considering the same. The meeting appointed a committee to report a response to your address. That report was made on yesterday, and the action of the majority indicated clearly that the response, or one in substance the same, would be adopted and presented to you.

Inasmuch as we cannot, consistently with our own sense of duty to the country, under the existing perils which surround us, concur in that response, we feel it to be due to you and to ourselves to make to you a brief and candid answer over our own signatures.

We believe that the whole power of the Government, upheld and sustained by all the influences and means of all loyal men in all sections, and of all parties, is essentially necessary to put down the rebellion and preserve the Union and the Constitution. We understand your appeal to us to have been made for the purpose of securing this result. A very large portion of the people in the northern States believe that slavery is the "lever-power of the rebellion." It matters not whether this belief be well founded or not. The belief does exist, and we have to deal with things as they are, and not as we would have them be. In consequence of the existence of this belief, we understand that an immense pressure is brought to bear for the purpose of striking down this institution through the exercise of military authority. The Government cannot maintain this great struggle if the support and influence of the men who entertain these opinions be withdrawn. Neither can the government hope for early success if the support of that element called "conservative" be withdrawn.

Such being the condition of things, the President appeals to the border State men to step forward and prove their patriotism by making the first sacrifice. No doubt, like appeals have been made to extreme men in the North to meet us half way, in order that the whole moral. Political, pecuniary, and physical force of the nation be firmly and earnestly united in one grand effort to save the Union and the Constitution.

Believing that such were the motives that prompted your address, and such the results to which it looked, we cannot reconcile it to our sense of duty, in this trying hour, to respond in a spirit of fault-finding or querulousness over the things that are past. We are not disposed to seek for the cause of present misfortunes in the errors and wrongs of others who now propose to unite with us in a common purpose. But, on the other hand, we meet your address in the spirit in which it was made, and, as loyal Americans, declare to you and the world that there is no sacrifice that we are not ready to make to save the Government and institutions of our fathers.

That we, few of us though there may be, will permit no man, from the North or the South, to go further than we in the accomplishment of the great work before us. That, in order to carry out these views, we will, so far as may be in our power, ask the people of the border States calmly, deliberately, and fairly to consider your recommendations. We are the more emboldened to assume this position from the fact, now become history, that the leaders of the southern rebellion have offered to abolish slavery among them as a condition to foreign intervention in favor of their independence as a nation.

If they can give up slavery to destroy the Union, we can surely ask our people to consider the question of emancipation to save the Union.

With great respect, your obedient servants

John W. Noell,
Samuel L. Casey,
George P. Fisher,
A. J. Clemens,
William G. Brown,
Jacob B. Blair,
W. T. Willey.

Reprinted from Edward McPherson, *The Political History of the United States during the Great Rebellion*, 2nd ed. (Washington, DC: Philip and Solomons, 1865), 217–218.

Notes

INTRODUCTION

1. Theodore F. Lang, *Loyal West Virginia from 1861 to 1865* (Baltimore: Deutsch, 1895), 3–4, 9, 133–141; Granville Davisson Hall, *The Rending of Virginia: A History* (1902; repr., Knoxville: University of Tennessee Press, 2000), 31.

2. Eric Foner, *Reconstruction: America's Unfinished Revolution, 1863–1877* (1988; updated ed., New York: Harper Perennial, 2014), 37–40; James M. McPherson, *Battle Cry of Freedom: The Civil War Era* (New York: Ballantine, 1988), 297–304, 297–298; William A. Link, *Roots of Secession: Slavery and Politics in Antebellum Virginia* (Chapel Hill: University of North Carolina Press, 2003), 8–9; Allen C. Guelzo, *Fateful Lightning: A New History of the Civil War and Reconstruction* (New York: Oxford University Press, 2012), 367; James Oakes, *Freedom National: The Destruction of Slavery in the United States, 1861–1865* (New York: Norton, 2013), 293–299, quotes on 293 and 294; Elizabeth Varon, *Armies of Deliverance: A New History of the Civil War* (New York: Oxford University Press, 2019), 199 and 301; and Aaron Astor, "The Border War," in *The Cambridge History of the American Civil War*, vol. 1, *Military Affairs*, ed. Aaron Sheehan-Dean (New York: Cambridge University Press, 2019), 471–494, paragraphs on 480 and 489.

3. Charles Henry Ambler, *Sectionalism in Virginia from 1776 to 1861* (Chicago: University of Chicago Press, 1910), 13; James Clyde McGregor, *The Disruption of Virginia* (New York: Macmillan, 1922), vii; George Ellis Moore, "Slavery as a Factor in the Formation of West Virginia," *West Virginia History* 18, no. 1 (October 1956): 5–89.

4. Richard Orr Curry, *A House Divided: Statehood Politics and the Copperhead Movement in West Virginia* (Pittsburgh: University of Pittsburgh Press, 1964), 2–3; John Alexander Williams, "The New Dominion and the Old: Antebellum and Statehood Politics as the Background of West Virginia's 'Bourbon Democracy,'" *West Virginia History* 33, no. 4 (July 1972): 317–407 and his *West Virginia: A History*, 2nd ed. (Morgantown: West Virginia University Press, 2001); Link, *Roots of Secession*; Mark A. Snell, *West Virginia and the Civil War: Mountaineers Are Always Free* (Charleston, SC: History Press, 2011); Eric J. Wittenberg, Edmund A. Sargus Jr., and Penny L. Barrick, *Seceding from Secession: The Civil War, Politics, and the Creation of West Virginia* (Eldorado Hills, CA: Savas Beatie, 2020). See also Joseph H. Riggs, "A Study of the Rhetorical Events in the West Virginia Statehood Movement," *West Virginia History* 17, no. 3 (April 1956): 191–251; Richard Orr Curry, "Ideology and Perception: Democratic and Republican Attitudes on Civil War Politics and the Statehood Movement in West Virginia," *West Virginia History* 44, no. 2 (1983): 135–155; and C. Stuart McGehee, "The Tarnished Thirty-Fifth Star," in *Virginia at War, 1861*, ed. William C. Davis and James I. Robertson Jr. (Lexington: University Press of Kentucky, 2005).

5. Booker Talliferro Washington, *Up from Slavery* (Garden City, NY: Doubleday, 1901); Wilma A. Dunaway, "Slavery and Emancipation in the Mountain South: Evidence,

204 / Notes to Pages 5–6

Sources, and Methods" (Virginia Tech University Libraries, n.d.), https://scholar
.lib.vt.edu/faculty_archives/mountain_slavery/slave.htm#To%20access; "History
of Slavery in West Virginia," Wikipedia, https://en.wikipedia.org/wiki/History_of
_slavery_in_West_Virginia.

6. John E. Stealey, *Antebellum Kanawha Salt Business and Western Markets* (Lexington: University Press of Kentucky, 1994); see also his "Slavery in the Kanawha Salt Industry," in *Appalachians and Race: The Mountain South from Slavery to Segregation,* ed. John C. Inscoe (Lexington: University Press of Kentucky, 2001), 50–73; Wilma Dunaway, *Slavery in the American Mountain South* (New York: Cambridge University Press, 2003); John W. Shaffer, *Clash of Loyalties: A Border County in the Civil War* (Morgantown: West Virginia University Press, 2003); Kenneth Fones-Wolf, " 'Traitors in Wheeling': Secessionism in an Appalachian Unionist City," *Appalachian Journal* 13, nos. 1 and 2 (Spring/Fall 2007): 75–95; Scott A. MacKenzie, "The Slaveholder's War: The Secession Crisis in Kanawha County, Western Virginia, 1860–1861," *West Virginia History* New Series 4, no. 1 (Spring 2010): 33–57, "Forming a Middle Class: The Civil War in Kanawha County, West(ern) Virginia, 1861–1865," *West Virginia History* New Series 9, no. 1 (Spring 2015): 23–45, and "Voting with Their Arms: Civil War Military Enlistments and the Formation of West Virginia, 1861–1865," *Ohio Valley History* 17, no. 2 (Summer 2017): 25–45; Michael E. Woods, "Mountaineers Are Becoming Free: Emancipation and Statehood in West Virginia," *West Virginia History* New Series 9, no. 2 (Spring 2015): 37–71. Mark Guerci's unpublished thesis also deserves mentioning: "It Took a War: The End of Slavery in West Virginia" (bachelor's thesis, College of William and Mary, 2011).

7. Charles Henry Ambler, "Disfranchisement in West Virginia, Part 1," *Yale Review* 14, no. 1 (May 1905): 38–59; Charles Henry Ambler, "Disfranchisement in West Virginia, Part 2," *Yale Review* 14, no. 2 (August 1905): 155–180; Milton Geofsky, "Reconstruction in West Virginia, Pt 1," *West Virginia History* 6, no. 4 (July 1945): 295–360; Milton Geofsky, "Reconstruction in West Virginia, Pt 2," *West Virginia History* 7, no. 1 (October 1945): 5–39; Richard Orr Curry, "Crisis Politics in West Virginia, 1861–1870," in *Radicalism, Racism, and Party Realignment: The Border States during Reconstruction,* ed. Richard Orr Curry (Baltimore: Johns Hopkins University Press, 1969), 80–104; Gordon McKinney, *Southern Mountain Republicans, 1865–1900* (Knoxville: University of Tennessee Press, 1978); Stephen D. Engle, "Mountaineer Reconstruction: Blacks in the Political Reconstruction of West Virginia," *Journal of Negro History* 78, no. 3 (Summer 1993): 137–165; Randall S. Gooden, "The Completion of a Revolution: West Virginia from Statehood through Reconstruction" (PhD diss., West Virginia University, 1995), and Adam Zucconi, "Bound Together: Slavery and Democracy in Antebellum Northwestern Virginia, 1815–1865" (PhD diss., West Virginia University, 2016). See also Randall Gooden's " 'Neither War nor Peace': West Virginia's Reconstruction Experience," and Kenneth Fones-Wolf, "A House Redivided: From Sectionalism to Political Economy in West Virginia," in *Reconstructing Appalachia: The Civil War's Aftermath,* ed. Andrew L. Slap (Lexington: University Press of Kentucky, 2010), 211–236 and 237–268; John E. Stealey III, *West Virginia's Civil War–Era Constitution: Loyal Revolution, Confederate Counter-Revolution, and the Constitution of 1872* (Kent, OH: Kent State University Press, 2013), 1, 5, 13, and 24.

8. Edward S. Smith, *The Borderland in the Civil War* (New York: Macmillan, 1927); Barbara Jeanne Fields, *Slavery and Freedom on the Middle Ground: Maryland during the Nineteenth Century* (New Haven, CT: Yale University Press, 1985); Patience Essah, *A House Divided: Slavery and Emancipation in Delaware, 1638–1865* (Charlottesville: University of Virginia Press, 1996); Aaron Astor, *Rebels on the Border: Civil War, Emancipation, and the Reconstruction of Kentucky and Missouri* (Baton Rouge: Louisiana State University Press, 2006); William C. Harris, *Lincoln and the Border States: Preserving the Union* (Manhattan: University Press of Kansas, 2011); Stanley Harrold, *Border War: Fighting over Slavery before the Civil War* (Chapel Hill: University of North Carolina Press, 2010); Christopher Phillips, *The Rivers Ran Backward: The Civil War and the Remaking of the American Middle Border* (New York: Oxford University Press, 2016); Matthew E. Stanley, *The Loyal West: Civil War and Reunion in Middle America* (Urbana: University of Illinois Press, 2017); Robert M. Sandow, *Deserter Country: Civil War Opposition in the Pennsylvania Appalachians* (New York: Fordham University Press, 2009); David G. Smith, *On the Edge of Freedom: The Fugitive Slave Issue in South Central Pennsylvania, 1820–1870* (New York: Fordham University Press, 2013); Stephen I. Rochenbach, *War upon Our Border: Two Ohio Valley Communities Navigate the Civil War* (Charlottesville: University of Virginia Press, 2016); Matthew Salafia, *Slavery's Borderland: Freedom and Bondage along the Ohio River* (Philadelphia: University of Pennsylvania Press, 2013); Bridget Ford, *Bonds of Union: Religion, Race, and Politics in a Civil War Borderland* (Chapel Hill: University of North Carolina Press: 2013); Allison Dorothy Fredette, *Marriage on the Border: Love, Mutuality, and Divorce in the Upper South during the Civil War* (Lexington: University Press of Kentucky, 2020). See also Allison Fredette, "A View from the Border: West Virginia Republicans and Women's Rights in the Age of Emancipation," *West Virginia History* New Series 3, no. 1 (Spring 2009): 57–80 and Christopher Phillips, *The Civil War in the Border South* (Santa Barbara, CA: Prager, 2013).

9. Gary W. Gallagher, "Contending for the Border States," in *The Great Courses: The American Civil War*, iTunes audiobook (Chantilly, VA: Teaching Company, 2000); and Gary W. Gallagher and Joan Waugh, *The American War: A History of the Civil War Era* (State College, PA: Spielvogel Books, 2015), 27.

CHAPTER 1: NORTHWESTERN VIRGINIA'S PATH TOWARD RECONCILIATION, 1829–1851

1. "Letter Address to a Member of the House of Delegates, signed by A Mountaineer [John G. Jackson], *The Richmond Examiner*, Jan. 15, 1803," in *West Virginia: Documents in the History of a Rural Industrial State*, ed. Ronald L. Lewis and John C. Hennen Jr. (Dubuque, IA: Kendall/Hunt, 1991), 71–73; see also Stephen W. Brown, *Voice of the New West: John G. Jackson, His Life and Times* (Mercer, GA: Mercer University Press, 1985).

2. Charles Henry Ambler, *Sectionalism in Virginia from 1776 to 1861* (Chicago: University of Chicago Press, 1910), 13, James Clyde McGregor, *The Disruption of Virginia* (New York: Macmillan, 1922), 1, 7–9; Richard Orr Curry, *A House Divided: Statehood Politics and the Copperhead Movement in West Virginia* (Pittsburgh: University of Pittsburgh Press, 1964), 24; Eric J. Wittenberg, Edmund A. Sargus Jr., and Penny L. Barrick, *Seceding from Secession: The Civil War, Politics, and*

the *Creation of West Virginia* (Eldorado Hills, CA: Savas Beatie, 2020), 8. They wrongly cite Curry, *House Divided*, 119 as the source. See also Kenneth Fones-Wolf, "Caught between Revolutions: Wheeling Germans in the Civil War Era," in *Transnational West Virginia: Ethnic Communities and Economic Change, 1840–1940*, ed. Kenneth Fones-Wolf and Ronald L. Lewis (Morgantown: West Virginia University Press, 2002), 18–50. Also of value are Grady McWhiney and Forrest MacDonald, *Cracker Culture: Celtic Ways in the Old South* (Tuscaloosa: University of Alabama Press, 1989), Grady McWhiney, *Attack and Die: Civil War Military Tactics and the Southern Heritage* (Tuscaloosa: University of Alabama Press, 1984), 141–192, and David Hackett Fischer, *Albion's Seed: Four English Folkways in America* (New York: Oxford University Press, 1991), 605–782.

3. McGregor, *Disruption of Virginia*, 1; Curry, *House Divided*, 23; L. Diane Barnes, "Urban Rivalry in the Upper Ohio Valley: Wheeling and Pittsburgh in the Nineteenth Century," *Pennsylvania Magazine of History and Biography* 123 (July 1999): 201–226. See also Richard C. Wade, *The Urban Frontier: Pioneer Life in Early Pittsburgh, Cincinnati, Lexington, Louisville and St. Louis* (Chicago: University of Chicago Press, 1959) and Kim Grunewald, *River of Enterprise: The Commercial Origins of Regional Identity in the Ohio Valley, 1790–1850* (Bloomington: Indiana University Press, 2002).

4. John E. Stealey, *The Antebellum Kanawha Salt Business and Western Markets* (Lexington: University Press of Kentucky, 1994), 156. For a description of enslaved Kanawha laborers loading barrels of salt onto boats, see Wilma Dunaway, *Slavery in the American Mountain South* (New York: Cambridge University Press, 2003), 95.

5. Gerald W. Sutphin, "River Transportation," in *West Virginia Encyclopedia*, http://www.wvencyclopedia.org/articles/93; Wallace Venable, "West Fork River," in *West Virginia Encyclopedia*, http://www.wvencyclopedia.org/articles/1002; William H. Gillespie, "The Monongahela River," in *West Virginia Encyclopedia*, http://www.wvencyclopedia.org/articles/2018.

6. Billy Joe Peyton, "To Make the Crooked Ways Straight and the Rough Ways Smooth: Federal Government's Role in Laying Out and Building the Cumberland Road" (PhD diss., West Virginia University, 1999). See also his "Turnpikes," in *West Virginia Encyclopedia*, http://www.wvencyclopedia.org/articles/797.

7. George Rogers Taylor, *The Transportation Revolution, 1815–1860* (New York: Holt, Reinhart, and Winston, 1964), 55; see also Sean Patrick Adams, *Old Dominion, Industrial Commonwealth: Coal, Politics and Economy in Antebellum America* (Baltimore: Johns Hopkins University Press, 2004).

8. Wayland Fuller Dunaway, *History of the James River and Kanawha Company* (New York: Columbia University Press, 1922).

9. Kenneth W. Noe, *Southwestern Virginia's Railroad* (Urbana: University of Illinois Press, 1994); James D. Dilts, *The Great Road: The Building of the Baltimore and Ohio, the Nation's First Railroad, 1828–1853* (Stanford, CA: Stanford University Press, 1996); and Albert Fishlow, *American Railroads and the Transformation of the Ante-bellum Economy* (Cambridge, MA: Harvard University Press, 1965).

10. Stanley Harrold, *Border War: Fighting over Slavery before the Civil War* (Chapel Hill: University of North Carolina Press, 2010), 44, 48, 60 (twice), 88; *Parkersburg Gazette and Western Virginia Courier*, April 20, 1850. For a recent treatment of slave escapes from northwestern Virginia, see William J. Switala, *Underground Railroad in Delaware, Maryland, and West Virginia* (Mechanicsburg, PA: Stackpole Books, 2004).

Notes to Pages 15–22 / 207

11. "Memorial of the Staunton Convention to the Legislature of the State of Virginia, August 1816," in Lewis and Hennen, *West Virginia: Documents*, 73–74.

12. Charles Henry Ambler and Festus Summers, *West Virginia: The Mountain State*, 2nd ed. (Englewood Cliffs, NJ: Prentice Hall, 1958), 133–135.

13. *Proceedings and Debates of the Virginia State Convention of 1829–30* (Richmond: Samuel Shepherd and Company for Ritchie and Cook, 1830), 74–76, 86–88; Otis Rice and Stephen W. Brown, *West Virginia: A History*, 2nd ed. (Lexington: University Press of Kentucky, 1993), 91.

14. *Clarksburg Enquirer*, April 19, 1830; *Wheeling Gazette*, April 6, 1830; *Wheeling Compiler*, March 10, 1830; the last two came from Ambler, *Sectionalism in Virginia*, 170–171, 174.

15. Allison G. Freehling, *Drift towards Dissolution: The Virginia Slavery Debate of 1831–1832* (Baton Rouge: Louisiana State University Press, 1982), 157–159.

16. Thomas R. Dew, *Review of the Debate in the Virginia Legislature of 1831 and 1832* (Richmond: T. W. White, 1832) and Benjamin Watkins Leigh, *A Letter of Appomattox to the People of Virginia Exhibiting a Connected View of the Recent Proceedings in the House of Delegates on the Subject of the Abolition of Slavery and a Succinct Account of the Doctrines Broached by the Friends of Abolition in Debate, and the Mischievous Tendency of Those Proceedings and Doctrines* (Richmond: Thomas W. White, 1832).

17. US Department of the Interior, Census Office, Manuscript Census Schedules, Harrison, Kanawha and Ohio counties, Virginia, Schedules 1 (Free Population) and 2 (Slave Population) for the Seventh (1850) and Eighth (1860) Census (hereafter cited as Census Sample). Northwestern Virginia in 1850 consisted of the following counties: Barbour, Braxton, Brooke, Cabell, Doddridge, Fayette, Gilmer, Hancock, Harrison, Jackson, Kanawha, Lewis, Marion, Marshall, Mason, Monongalia, Nicholas, Ohio, Preston, Putnam, Randolph, Ritchie, Taylor, Tyler, Wayne, Wetzel, Wirt, and Wood. Pleasants, Upshur, Calhoun, Roane, Tucker, Clay, and Webster formed between 1850 and 1860. The others include Boone, Logan, Wyoming, McDowell, Mercer, Raleigh, Monroe, Greenbrier, Pocahontas, Pendleton, Hardy, Hampshire, Morgan, Berkeley, and Jefferson. Grant, Mineral, Lincoln, Summers, and Mingo joined after the Civil War.

18. Stealey, *Antebellum Kanawha Salt Business*, 156.

19. Curry, *House Divided*, 23.

20. Jonathan Dean Wells, *Origins of the Southern Middle Class, 1800–1861* (Chapel Hill: University of North Carolina Press, 2003); Jennifer R. Green, *Military Education and the Emerging Middle Class of the Old South* (New York: Cambridge University Press, 2008); Frank J. Byrne, *Becoming Bourgeois: Merchant Culture in the South 1820–1865* (Lexington: University Press of Kentucky, 2006); L. Diane Barnes, *Artisan Workers of the Upper South: Petersburg, Virginia, 1820–1865* (Baton Rouge: Louisiana State University Press, 2008); and Michele Gillespie, *Free Labor in an Unfree World: White Artisans in Slaveholding Georgia, 1789–1860* (Athens: University of Georgia Press, 2000). See also Jonathan Dean Wells and Jennifer R. Green, eds., *The Southern Middle Class in the Long Nineteenth Century*, ed. (Baton Rouge: Louisiana State University Press, 2011).

21. Historical Census Browser, University of Virginia, Geospatial and Statistical Data Center, http://mapserver.lib.virginia.edu/collections/stats/histcensus/index.html (site discontinued); John E. Stealey III, *West Virginia's Civil War–Era Constitution:*

Loyal Revolution, Confederate Counter-Revolution, and the Constitution of 1872 (Kent, OH: Kent State University Press, 2013), 113.

22. John C. Inscoe, *Mountain Masters: Slavery and the Sectional Crisis in Western North Carolina* (Knoxville: University of Tennessee Press, 1996); Noe, *Southwest Virginia's Railroad*; and Census Sample. For more on the Appalachian image, see Henry Shapiro, *Appalachia on Our Mind: The Southern Mountains and Mountaineers in the American Consciousness, 1870–1920* (Chapel Hill: University of North Carolina Press, 1986) and Allen W. Batteau, *The Invention of Appalachia* (Tucson: University of Arizona Press, 1990).

23. Wells, *Origins of the Southern Middle Class*; Green, *Military Education and the Emerging Southern Middle Class*, esp. 34–35 for her definition of the middling class; Byrne, *Becoming Bourgeois*; John A. Williams, "The New Dominion and the Old: Antebellum and Statehood Politics as the Background of West Virginia's 'Bourbon Democracy,' " *West Virginia History* 33, no. 4 (July 1972): 334–337.

24. The figures for Ohio County, and later in Harrison and Kanawha, come from the Census Sample.

25. *Wheeling Daily Intelligencer*, January 25, 1861.

26. Barnes, *Artisan Workers of the Upper South*; Gillespie, *Free Labor in an Unfree World*.

27. See Matthew Mason, "Paddy vs. Paddy: Labor Unrest and Provincial Identities along the Baltimore and Ohio Railroad, 1849–1851," in Fones-Wolf and Lewis, *Transnational West Virginia*, 3–17.

28. James Oakes, *Freedom National: The Destruction of Slavery in the United States, 1861–1865* (New York: Norton, 2013), 293–294; see also Daniel Sunshine, "West Virginia's Attempt to Split Up Virginia Betrays the History of Both States," *Washington Post*, January 29, 2020, https://www.washingtonpost.com/outlook /2020/01/29/west-virginias-attempt-split-virginia-up-betrays-history-both -states/.

29. The lists of officers come from J. H. Newton, G. G. Nichols, and A. G. Sprankle, *History of the Panhandle Being Recollections of Ohio, Brooke, Marshall and Hancock, West Virginia* (Wheeling, WV: J. A. Caldwell, 1879), 185–186.

30. The lists of officeholders come from Henry Haymond, *History of Harrison County, West Virginia, from the Early Days of Northwestern Virginia to the Present* (Morgantown, WV: Acme, 1910), 230–232.

31. The lists of officeholders come from William S. Laidley, *History of Charleston and Kanawha County, West Virginia, and Representative Citizens* (Chicago: Richmond-Arnold, 1911), 151–158.

32. William G. Shade, *Democratizing the Old Dominion: Virginia and the Second Party System, 1824–1861* (Charlottesville: University of Virginia Press, 1997), 159–160.

33. Donald W. Gunter, "George William Summers (1807–1868)," Union or Secession: Virginians Decide, an Online Exhibit at the Library of Virginia, https://edu.lva .virginia.gov/online_classroom/union_or_secession/people/george_summers (site discontinued). A biography of this figure is sorely needed. Until then, there is only A. Clinton Loy's "George W. Summers and His Relation to the Formation of the State of West Virginia" (master's thesis, West Virginia University, 1937), and Amacetta Laidley Summers, *My Dearest Husband: The Letters of Amacetta Laidley Summers to George W. Summers, 1842–1843*, ed. Patricia Clark Bulla (Charleston: University of West Virginia, College of Graduate Studies Foundation, 1989).

34. Sadly, no biography, not even a master's thesis, exists of Carlile. Until one appears,

Jonathan Berkey's entry on the Library of Virginia's website must suffice. See Berkey, "Carlile, John S. (1817–1878)," in *Encyclopedia Virginia*, Virginia Humanities, https://encyclopediavirginia.org/entries/carlile-john-s-1817–1878/. Clemens also lacks a biography; his entry in the Congressional Biographical Dictionary is the only source on his life. See US Congress, "Sherrard Clemens," in *Congressional Biographical Dictionary*, http://bioguide.congress.gov/scripts /biodisplay.pl?index=C000502.

35. Willey has only one biography, Charles Henry Ambler, *Waitman Thomas Willey, Orator, Churchman, Humanitarian* (Huntington, WV: Standard Print and Publishing, 1954), but it is dated and shows its author's long-held beliefs about West Virginia's history. A useful supplement comes from Allison Fredette's entry in the *Encyclopedia Virginia*. Fredette, "A. Waitman T. Willey (1811–1900)," in *Encyclopedia Virginia*, http://www.EncyclopediaVirginia.org/Willey_Waitman_T_1811-1900.

36. Pierpont has a major biography, Charles Henry Ambler, *Francis M. Pierpont: Union War Governor of Virginia and Father of West Virginia* (Chapel Hill: University of North Carolina Press, 1937). Boreman has only a dissertation that should have been published. See Isaiah Alfonso Woodward, "Arthur Ingraham Boreman: A Biography" (PhD diss., West Virginia University, 1970); James Oakes, *The Ruling Race: A History of American Slaveholding* (New York: Norton, 1982), 57–65, 144–147.

37. Henry Ruffner, *Address to the People of West Virginia; Showing That Slavery Is Injurious to the Public Welfare, and That It May Be Gradually Abolished, without Detriment to the Rights and Interests of Slaveholders. By a Slaveholder of West Virginia* (Lexington, VA: R.C. Noel, 1847). Future West Virginia governor William E. Stevenson was indicted for distributing Helper's book; see Granville Davisson Hall, *The Rending of Virginia: A History* (1902; repr., Knoxville: University of Tennessee Press, 2000), 72.

38. "Document: The Inequality of Representation in the General Assembly of Virginia: A Memorial to the Legislature of the Commonwealth of Virginia, Adopted at Full Meeting of the Citizens of Kanawha, [9 August 1841]," *West Virginia History* 25, no. 4 (July 1964): 284–285 and 294.

39. Ritchie County borders Pleasants County, named in 1851 for Virginia governor James A. Pleasants (1822–1825). In a bizarre coincidence, Ritchie's son Thomas Jr. killed Pleasants's son John Hampden Pleasants in a duel in 1846. See also Charles Henry Ambler, *Thomas Ritchie: A Study in Virginia Politics* (Richmond: Bell Book & Stationery, 1913).

40. Census Sample, 1850 and 1860; Shade, *Democratizing the Old Dominion*, 269–271; Kenneth R. Bailey, *Alleged Evil Genius: The Life and Times of Judge James H. Ferguson* (Charleston, WV: Quarrier Press, 2006), 15–18; *Kanawha Republican*, unknown date, reprinted in *Parkersburg Gazette and Western Virginia Courier*, September 21, 1850.

41. *Register of the Debates and Proceedings of the Virginia Reform Convention*, comp. William G. Bishop (Richmond: Robert H. Gallagher, 1851), 8, 16, and 19 (hereafter cited as *Virginia Reform Convention*).

42. *Virginia Reform Convention*, 116–117, 127, 200.

43. *Virginia Reform Convention*, 282, 293.

44. *Virginia Reform Convention*, 316–318.

45. *Virginia Reform Convention*, 333, 336, 337; *Parkersburg Gazette and Western Virginia Courier*, May 3, 1851.

210 / Notes to Pages 37–47

46. *Virginia Reform Convention*, 338; Craig M. Simpson, *A Good Southerner: The Life of Henry A. Wise of Virginia* (Chapel Hill: University of North Carolina Press, 1985), 78–87; Curry, *House Divided*, 22–23; Rice and Brown, *West Virginia*, 98. Only the statewide tally has survived, preventing a more detailed analysis of who supported and opposed the constitution of 1851.

47. If Pleasants County's vote had not been rejected, the difference could have been narrower, but as it was a Democratic stronghold it is unlikely to have changed the result. Michael J. Dubin, *United States Gubernatorial Elections, 1776–1860: The Official Results by State and County* (Jefferson, NC: McFarland, 2003), 283–287.

48. *Cooper's Clarksburg Telegraph*, May 12, 1852.

CHAPTER 2: NORTHWESTERN VIRGINIA ON THE DEFENSIVE, 1851–1860

1. Daniel Webster, *Mr. Webster's Address at the Laying of the Corner Stone of the Addition to the Capitol, July 4, 1851* (Washington, DC: Gideon, 1851), 15–16. Two examples of sources using Webster's statement include "To the People of Northwestern Virginia," *Kingwood Chronicle*, May 25, 1861, and James Clyde McGregor, *The Disruption of Virginia* (New York: Macmillan, 1922), 68–69.

2. Michael J. Dubin, *United States Congressional Elections, 1788–1997: The Official Results of the Elections of the 1st through 105th Congresses* (Jefferson, NC: McFarland, 1998), 275; and *United States Presidential Elections, 1788–1860: The Official Results by County and State* (Jefferson, NC: McFarland & Co., 2002), 115.

3. *Cooper's Clarksburg Register*, November 12, 1851. Cooper also stated here how difficult it was for papers to prosper in the northwest.

4. *Wheeling Daily Intelligencer*, August 24, 1852, and September 6, 1852. See also John Lewis Kiplinger, "The Press in the Making of West Virginia," *West Virginia History* 6, no. 2 (January 1945): 127–176.

5. *Wheeling Daily Intelligencer*, November 9, 1852, and November 10, 1852.

6. *Parkersburg Gazette and Courier*, July 30, 1853; *Wheeling Daily Intelligencer*, February 28, 1854.

7. *Cooper's Clarksburg Register*, April 11, 1855.

8. *Cooper's Clarksburg Register*, April 23, 1854; August 23, 1854; August 30, 1854; September 13, 1854.

9. *Wheeling Daily Intelligencer*, February 3, April 19, and June 22, 1855. The Know-Nothing Platform of 1855 is found in the June 30, 1855, edition of the *Morgantown American Union*. John David Bladek argued in " 'Virginia Is Middle Ground': The Know-Nothing Party and the Virginia Gubernatorial Election of 1855," *Virginia Magazine of History and Biography* 106, no. 1 (1998): 119–128, that this middling stance was common among Virginia's Know-Nothing papers. Ultimately, it undermined their ability to become permanent.

10. Dubin, *United States Congressional Elections, 1788–1997*, 275; Tyler Anbinder, *Nativism and Slavery: The Northern Know Nothings and the Politics of the 1850s* (New York: Oxford University Press, 1992), 164–165; *Cooper's Clarksburg Register*, June 13, 1855.

11. *Cooper's Clarksburg Register*, July 25, 1855, and August 1, 1855.

12. *Star of the Kanawha Valley*, April 4, 1855.

13. *Star of the Kanawha Valley*, August 8, 1855.

Notes to Pages 48–59 / 211

14. *Morgantown American Union*, June 30, 1855; Dubin, *United States Congressional Elections, 1788–1997*, 275; Bladek, " 'Virginia Is Middle Ground.' "

15. *Cooper's Clarksburg Register*, April 25, 1856, and August 22, 1856; *Fairmont True Virginian*, April 19, 1856; *Star of the Kanawha Valley*, May 16, 1856.

16. *Morgantown American Union*, June 7, 1856; *Wheeling Daily Intelligencer*, April 3, 1856, and May 22, 1856.

17. *Cooper's Clarksburg Register*, October 24, 1856, and October 31, 1856; *Kanawha Valley Star*, October 23, 1856.

18. Dubin, *United States Presidential Elections, 1788–1860*, 135; *Kanawha Valley Star*, November 11, 1856.

19. *Wheeling Daily Intelligencer*, April 10, 1857, and April 17, 1857.

20. Dubin, *United States Congressional Elections, 1788–1997*, 275; *Kanawha Valley Star*, June 2, 1857.

21. *Wheeling Daily Intelligencer*, August 2, 1857, and August 5, 1857.

22. *Kanawha Valley Star*, June 30, 1857, and September 1, 1857.

23. *Fairmont True Virginian*, September 7, 1857.

24. *Cooper's Clarksburg Register*, September 25, 1857.

25. *Wheeling Daily Intelligencer*, January 28, 1858.

26. *Wheeling Daily Intelligencer*, February 18, 1858, and March 10, 1858. Clemens appears to have taken criticisms seriously. In mid-1858, he fought and lost a duel with O. Jennings Wise, the editor of the southern rights' journal the *Richmond Enquirer* and son of the governor. His serious injuries essentially ended his political career, depriving northwestern Democrats of one of their most able figures. A healthy Clemens could have had a profound influence, for or against, on the West Virginia statehood movement. Craig M. Simpson, *A Good Southerner: The Life of Henry A. Wise of Virginia* (Chapel Hill: University of North Carolina Press, 1985), 178–179.

27. *Cooper's Clarksburg Register*, July 16, 1858.

28. *Clarksburg Weekly Campaign*, April 18, 1859; F. N. Boney, *John Letcher of Virginia: The Story of Virginia's Civil War Governor* (Tuscaloosa: University of Alabama Press, 1966), 75–90. See also William S. Hitchcock, "The Limits of Southern Unionism: Virginia Conservatives and the Gubernatorial Election of 1859," *Journal of Southern History* 47, no. 1 (February 1981): 57–72.

29. *Wheeling Gazette*, April 21, 1859; *Kanawha Valley Star*, July 13, 1859; *Parkersburg News*, May 5, 1859. Goggin did not visit the northwest either, but according to Henry T. Shanks, Willey deemphasized slavery in favor of internal improvements. He based this on a single letter in the Willey papers in the West Virginia and Regional History Collection. The newspapers at the time clearly disagreed and made a big effort to attack Letcher as weak on slavery. Henry T. Shanks, *Secession Movement in Virginia, 1847–1861* (New York: Garrett and Massie, 1934), 59.

30. Michael J. Dubin, *United States Gubernatorial Elections, 1776–1860: The Official Results by State and County* (Jefferson, NC: McFarland, 2003), 283–287; *Wheeling Daily Intelligencer*, June 14, 1859; Charles Henry Ambler, *Sectionalism in Virginia from 1776 to 1861* (Chicago: University of Chicago Press, 1910), 325; Shanks, *Secession Movement in Virginia*, 61.

31. Stephen B. Oates, *To Purge This Land with Blood: A Biography of John Brown*, 2nd ed. (Amherst: University of Massachusetts Press, 1984), 212 and 274; *Wheeling Daily Intelligencer*, October 20, 1859.

212 / Notes to Pages 60–67

32. *Wheeling Daily Intelligencer*, October 24, 1859, December 16, 1859, November 30, 1859, and January 11, 1860; *Parkersburg News*, October 20, 1859 (the page itself reads October 13, but this is most likely an error). See also Scott A. MacKenzie, "The Slaveholder's War: The Secession Crisis in Kanawha County, Western Virginia, 1860–1861," *West Virginia History* New Series 4, no. 1 (Spring 2010): 33–59.

33. *Wheeling Daily Intelligencer*, June 11, 1860, and April 20, 1860. On the microfilm, someone scribbled "First Republican Meeting in W. Va" on the second page. See also Richard G. Lowe, *Republicans and Reconstruction in Virginia, 1856–1870* (Charlottesville: University of Virginia Press, 1991).

34. Ambler, *Sectionalism in Virginia*; William A. Link, *Roots of Secession: Slavery and Politics in Antebellum Virginia* (Chapel Hill: University of North Carolina Press, 2003); Dubin, *United States Presidential Elections, 1788–1860*, 159, 170, 184–186.

35. Shanks, *Secession Movement in Virginia*, 61; *Wheeling Daily Intelligencer*, November 3, 1860. See also Dubin, *United States Presidential Elections, 1788–1860*, 159–185; and Frank H. Towers, *The Urban South and the Coming of the Civil War* (Charlottesville: University of Virginia Press, 2004).

CHAPTER 3: NORTHWESTERN VIRGINIA IN THE SECESSION CRISIS, JANUARY–JULY 1861

1. *Wheeling Daily Intelligencer*, January 3, 1861. By the time this story appeared, via a Cincinnati newspaper, three more states had declared their separation: Mississippi, Florida, and Alabama. Three more, namely Georgia, Louisiana, and Texas, did the same later that month.

2. Quoted in the *Wheeling Daily Intelligencer*, January 8 and 14, 1861.

3. F. N. Boney, *John Letcher of Virginia: The Story of Virginia's Civil War Governor* (Tuscaloosa: University of Alabama Press, 1966), 104–105; William A. Link, *Roots of Secession: Slavery and Politics in Antebellum Virginia* (Chapel Hill: University of North Carolina Press, 2003), 9–10; see also his "This Bastard New Virginia: Slavery, West Virginia Exceptionalism, and the Secession Crisis," *West Virginia History* New Series 3, no. 1 (Spring 2009): 37–56.

4. See William R. Freehling, *The Road to Disunion*, vol. 2, *Secessionists Triumphant* (New York: Oxford University Press, 2007), 490–496. For more on the conventions in other states, see William C. Harris, *Lincoln and the Border States: Preserving the Union* (Manhattan: University Press of Kansas, 2011), 26; Patience Essah, *A House Divided: Slavery and Emancipation in Delaware, 1638–1865* (Charlottesville: University of Virginia Press, 1996), 161–162; Daniel W. Crofts, *Reluctant Confederates: Upper South Unionists in the Secession Crisis* (Chapel Hill: University of North Carolina Press, 1989); James W. Woods, *Rebellion and Realignment: Arkansas's Road to Secession* (Fayetteville: University of Arkansas Press, 1987), Michael P. Johnson, *Towards a Patriarchal Republic: The Secession of Georgia* (Baton Rouge: Louisiana State University Press, 1977).

5. *Wheeling Daily Intelligencer*, January 16, 17, and 21, 1861.

6. *Wheeling Daily Intelligencer*, January 19, 1861; *Fairmont True Virginian*, January 26, 1861; *Parkersburg News*, January 26, 1861.

7. *Wheeling Daily Intelligencer*, January 21, 1861.

8. Data about the backgrounds of the delegates throughout this chapter come from two sources. The first is the list of delegates found in George H. Reese, ed.,

Notes to Pages 67–76 / 213

Proceedings of the Virginia State Convention of 1861, Volume 1, February 13—May 1 (Richmond: Virginia State Library, 1965), 783–787; and the 1860 Free and Slave Census schedules for every Virginia county, all found at Ancestry.com.

9. Crofts, *Reluctant Confederates*, 104–106.
10. William W. Freehling and Craig M. Simpson, eds., *Showdown in Virginia: The 1861 Convention and the Fate of the Union* (Charlottesville: University of Virginia Press, 2010), 16–21 (hereafter cited as *Showdown in Virginia*).
11. *Showdown in Virginia*, 22–30.
12. *Showdown in Virginia*, 43–48.
13. *Showdown in Virginia*, 61–74.
14. *Showdown in Virginia*, 49–61.
15. *Showdown in Virginia*, 134–136.
16. *Showdown in Virginia*, 138–139.
17. *Showdown in Virginia*, 145–147.
18. *Fairmont True Virginian*, March 30, 1861; *Wheeling Daily Intelligencer*, April 1, 1861.
19. *Showdown in Virginia*, 148–150.
20. *Showdown in Virginia*, 160–164. For Lincoln's response to the Virginia delegation, see "Reply to a Committee from the Virginia Convention, April 13, 1861," in Lincoln Papers, Library of Congress, Washington, DC. For the First Virginia Union Infantry Regiment, see "The First West Virginia Infantry," *West Virginia History* 55 (1996): 41–94; and Mark E. Bell, " 'In the Hearts of Their Countrymen as True Heroes': A Socio-economic, Political, and Military Portrait of the 1st Virginia (U.S.) Infantry, 1861" (master's thesis, Shippensburg University, 2000).
21. Library of Virginia, "How Virginia Convention Delegates Voted on Secession, April 4 and April 17, 1861, and Whether They Signed a Copy of the Ordinance of Secession," *Virginia Memory*, https://www.virginiamemory.com/docs/votes_on_secession.pdf.
22. See Johnson, *Towards a Patriarchal Republic*.
23. For Carlile's actions, see James Clyde McGregor, *The Disruption of Virginia* (New York: Macmillan, 1922), 183. For the McGrew narrative, see Granville Davisson Hall, *The Rending of Virginia: A History* (1902; repr., Knoxville: University of Tennessee Press, 2000), 516–535; Harris, *Lincoln and the Border States*, 138.
24. Dallas Shaffer, "Mr. Lincoln and West Virginia" (PhD diss., West Virginia University, 1965), 16, cites James Morton Callahan, *History of West Virginia Old and New* (Chicago: American Historical Society, 1923), 1:340–342, but it repeats the McGrew account mentioned above. Nowhere does it say that any of the northwestern Virginia delegates visited Lincoln. William C. Harris, *With Charity for All: Lincoln and the Restoration of the Union* (Lexington: University Press of Kentucky, 1997), 21–23, credits George H. Reese, ed., *Proceedings of the Virginia State Convention of 1861, February 1 to May 1, 1861* (Richmond: Virginia State Library, 1965), 1:468, 474, and 477, and 3:168–169, but only the latter even mentions Carlile, and nothing about him meeting Lincoln. For the *Barbour Jeffersonian* quote, see *Richmond Daily Dispatch*, May 11, 1861. For the Caldwell letter, see John G. Nicolay to George W. Caldwell, May 1, 1861, in *Papers of Abraham Lincoln: Series 1. General Correspondence. 1833 to 1916*, Library of Congress, Manuscript/Mixed Material, https://www.loc.gov/item/mal0970300/. See also Dallas S. Shaffer, "Lincoln and the 'Vast Question' of West Virginia," *West Virginia History* 32, no. 2 (January 1971): 86–100.

214 / Notes to Pages 76–82

25. "Mayor's Proclamation, April 19, 1861," in *The Thirty-Fifth State: A Documentary History of West Virginia*, ed. Elizabeth Cometti and Festus P. Summers (Morgantown: West Virginia University Library, 1966), 293–294 (hereafter cited as *Thirty-Fifth State Documents*).

26. "Clarksburg Convention, April 22, 1861," in *West Virginia: Documents in the History of a Rural Industrial State*, ed. Ronald L. Lewis and John C. Hennen Jr. (Dubuque, IA: Kendall/Hunt, 1991), 89–90. Carlile's statement that Richmond acted illegally "by seizing ships" may refer to the capture of the Gosport dockyard at Norfolk, but he does not refer to it by name in the Clarksburg Resolutions; *Wheeling Daily Union*, May 3, 1861.

27. *Kanawha Valley Star*, April 30, 1861; "The Southern Rights Convention, April 26, 1861," *Thirty-Fifth State Documents*, 297–298.

28. *Showdown in Virginia*, 204–206.

29. *Kanawha Valley Star*, April 22, 1861; see also Scott A. MacKenzie, "The Slaveholder's War: The Secession Crisis in Kanawha County, Western Virginia, 1860–1861," *West Virginia History* New Series 4, no. 1 (Spring 2010): 33–59.

30. C. D. Moss to Letcher, April 18, 1861; W. P. Cooper to Letcher, April 23, 1861; James M. H. Beale to Letcher, April 29, 1861; and D. S. Morris to Letcher, April 29, 1861; Virginia Governor (1860–1864: Letcher), Executive Papers of Governor John Letcher, 1859–1863, Accession 36787, State Government Records Collection, Library of Virginia, Richmond (hereafter cited as Letcher Papers, LVA).

31. "Governor John Letcher's Proclamation, April 24, 1861, Richmond, VA," in *The Rebellion Record: A Diary of American Events, with Documents, Narratives, Illustrative Incidents, Poetry, Etc.*, ed. Frank Moore (New York: Putnam, 1861), 1:146.

32. *Wheeling Daily Intelligencer*, April 27, 1861, and April 30, 1861; *Kanawha Valley Star*, April 30, 1861; "The First West Virginia Infantry," *West Virginia History* 55 (1996): 41–94; Lowell Reidenbaugh, *27th Virginia Infantry* (Lynchburg: H. E. Howard, 1993), 5–6; MacKenzie, "Slaveholder's War"; "A Virginian" to Letcher, May 25, 1861, and William D. Moore to Letcher, May 25, 1861, both in Letcher Papers, LVA.

33. US Department of the Interior, Census Office, Manuscript Census Schedules, Harrison, Kanawha and Ohio counties, Virginia, Schedules 1 (Free Population) and 2 (Slave Population) for the Seventh (1850) and Eighth (1860) Census. For the list of delegates, see Virgil A. Lewis, *How West Virginia Was Made: The Proceedings of the First Convention of the People of Northwestern Virginia at Wheeling, May 13, 14, and 15, 1861, and the Journal of the Second Convention of the People of Northwestern Virginia at Wheeling, Which Assembled, June 11, 1861, and Continued in Session until June 25; Adjourned until August 6th, 1861; Reassembled on That Date, and Continued in Session until August 21st, When It Adjourned Sine Die* (Charleston, WV: News-Mail Company Public Printers, 1909), 55–57; and Scott A. MacKenzie, "Voting with Their Arms: Civil War Military Enlistments and the Formation of West Virginia, 1861–1865," *Ohio Valley History* 17, no. 2 (Summer 2017): 25–45.

34. Lewis, *How West Virginia Was Made*, 57. Before the convention, Willey confided to Chester D. Hubbard of Ohio County his preferences for a conservative transition to statehood. "I am constitutionally and educationally a man of law and order," he wrote. Continuing, he wished to "first, exhaust every legal and constitutional means of securing a division of the state (always supposing the ordinance of secession passes) and resorting to the *ultima ratio* [lit. "final thought," but better

Notes to Pages 83–89 / 215

translated as "last option," meaning statehood] only when these have failed." While this is a great letter, it duplicates what he said in the convention. See "Waitman T. Willey to Chester Hubbard, May 6, 1861," in Lewis and Hennen, *West Virginia: Documents*, 90–92.

35. Lewis, *How West Virginia Was Made*, 58. Granville Davisson Hall, the convention's reporter, said in 1902 that Jackson had not planted any corn for many years. See his *Rending of Virginia*, xxxix.

36. Moore, *Rebellion Record*, 1:72–77.

37. Otis Rice and Stephen W. Brown, *West Virginia: A History*, 2nd ed. (Lexington: University Press of Kentucky, 1993), 120; Freehling, *Road to Disunion*, 526; *Wellsburg Herald*, May 31, 1861. For voting records, see Richard Orr Curry, *A House Divided: Statehood Politics and the Copperhead Movement in West Virginia* (Pittsburgh: University of Pittsburgh Press, 1964), 143–147; MacKenzie, "The Slaveholders' War," 44; and James H. Cook, "The Secession Crisis in Harrison County, West Virginia" (master's thesis, West Virginia University, 1993).

38. "To the People of North-Western Virginia, May 25, 1861," *Kingwood Chronicle*, May 25, 1861, reprinted in Lewis and Hennen, *West Virginia: Documents*, 94–96.

39. Curry, *House Divided*, 59–65; "George B. McClellan, Proclamation to the People of Virginia, and His Address to the Soldiers of the Expedition," in Lewis and Hennen, *West Virginia: Documents*, 113–114.

40. James Oakes, *Freedom National: The Destruction of Slavery in the United States, 1861–1865* (New York: Norton, 2013), 93–103. In his 1887 memoirs, McClellan bragged about writing these documents at his dining room table in Cincinnati without the aid of his wife and other guests. Indeed, he claimed that he acted alone in Western Virginia and never received any input from Washington, even after informing them about his actions there. This likely stems from the general's hatred for President Lincoln. Ethan Rafuse does a fine job arguing for the commanding general's pivotal role in saving the region for the Union. *McClellan's Own Story: The War for the Union, the Soldiers Who Fought It, the Civilians Who Directed It, and His Relations to It and to Them* (New York: Charles Webster, 1887), 49–55; Ethan S. Rafuse, *McClellan's War: The Failure of Moderation in the Struggle for the Union* (Bloomington: Indiana University Press, 2005), 96–117.

41. Terry Lowry, *The Battle of Scary Creek: Military Operations in the Kanawha Valley, April–July 1861*, rev. ed. (Charleston, WV: Quarrier Press, 1998), 49; Clayton R. Newell, *Lee vs. McClellan: The First Campaign* (Washington, DC: Regnery Press, 2010); Craig M. Simpson, *The Good Southerner: The Life of Henry A. Wise of Virginia* (Chapel Hill: University of North Carolina Press, 1985), 252–261; MacKenzie, "Slaveholder's War"; see also Mark A. Snell, *West Virginia and the Civil War: Mountaineers Are Always Free* (Charleston, SC: History Press, 2011).

42. Office of the Central Committee, Wheeling to the Hon. George W. Summers, June 1, 1861, Francis M. Pierpont Executive Papers, 1861–1865, box 1, folder 2, Library of Virginia (hereafter cited as Pierpont Papers, LVA).

43. *Kanawha Valley Star*, May 7, 1861.

44. Lewis, *How West Virginia Was Made*, 125–126.

45. Charles H. Ambler, *Francis H. Pierpont: Union War Governor of Virginia and Father of West Virginia* (Chapel Hill: University of North Carolina Press, 1937), 25–28 (his experiences with slavery) and 98 (his selection as governor).

46. Lewis, *How West Virginia Was Made*, 159.

216 / Notes to Pages 89–97

47. "Francis H. Pierpont's Inaugural Address, June 20, 1861," *Thirty-Fifth State Documents*, 325–327.

48. "Governor John Letcher's Proclamation to the People of Northwestern Virginia, June 14, 1861," in *Thirty-Fifth State Documents*, 316–318; Jack Zinn, *The Battle of Rich Mountain* (Parsons, WV: McClain, 1971).

49. Abraham Lincoln, "Message to Congress in Special Session, July 4, 1861," in *Collected Works of Abraham Lincoln*, ed. Roy P. Basler (New Brunswick, NJ: Rutgers University Press, 1953), 4:418–441. The specific quote is on 428.

CHAPTER 4: THE CONSERVATIVE PHASE OF THE WEST VIRGINIA STATEHOOD MOVEMENT, AUGUST 1861–FEBRUARY 1862

1. Quoted in *Wheeling Daily Intelligencer*, August 28, 1861.

2. Donald Stoker, *The Grand Design: Strategy and the U.S. Civil War* (New York: Oxford University Press, 2012), 51.

3. James Oakes, *Freedom National: The Destruction of Slavery in the United States, 1861–1865* (New York: Norton, 2013), 141–191, 263–264; for the First Confiscation Act, see US Congress, *Congressional Globe*, 37th Cong., 1st Sess., 431 (House) and 434 (Senate) (hereafter, *Cong. Globe*.); for the Second Confiscation Act, see *Cong. Globe*, 37th Cong., 2nd Sess., 3267–3268 (House) and 3274–3276 (Senate); for the others, see Edward McPherson, *The Political History of the United States during the Great Rebellion*, 2nd ed. (Washington, DC: Philip and Solomons, 1865), 209–213.

4. US War Department, *The War of the Rebellion: A Compilation of Official Records of the Union and Confederate Armies* (Washington, DC: Government Printing Office, 1880), series 1, 5:576–577; Michael Woods, "Mountaineers Becoming Free: Emancipation and Statehood in West Virginia," *West Virginia History* 9, no. 2 (Fall 2015): 37–71.

5. Emory M. Thomas, *Robert E. Lee: A Biography* (New York: Norton, 1997); Terry Lowry, *September Blood: The Battle of Carnifex Ferry* (Charleston, WV: Pictorial Histories, 1985); Clayton R. Newell, *Lee vs. McClellan: The First Campaign* (Washington, DC: Regnery Press, 2010), 229; W. Hunter Lesser, *Rebels at the Gate: Lee and McClellan on the Front Line of a Nation Divided* (Naperville, IL: Sourcebooks, 2004), 193–212; Mark A. Snell, *West Virginia and the Civil War: Mountaineers Are Always Free* (Charleston, SC: History Press, 2011); Joe Geiger, Jr. "The Tragic Fate of Guyandotte," *West Virginia History* 54 (1995): 28–41; James I. Robertson, *Stonewall Jackson: The Man, the Soldier, the Legend* (New York: Macmillan, 1997), 294–320; Thomas M. Rankin, *Stonewall Jackson's Romney Campaign: Jan. 1–February 20, 1862* (Lynchburg, VA: H. E. Howard, 1994); Richard A. Sauers, *The Devastating Hand of War: Romney, West Virginia during the Civil War* (Glen Ferris, WV: Gauley Mountain Press, 2000); David G. Martin, *Jackson's Valley Campaign: November 1861–June 1862* (New York: Da Capo Press, 2003); and Jack Zinn, *R. E. Lee's Cheat Mountain Campaign* (Parsons, WV: McClain, 1974).

6. A. F. Ritchie to Pierpont, July 1, 1861, reel 5827, images 337–338; Pierpont to A. F. Ritchie, July 25, 1861, reel 5827, images 178–195; Pierpont to Sheriffs, July 8, 1861, reel 5827, image 599; Frank P. Pierpont to Pierpont, July 25, 1861, reel 5828, images 385–386; Joseph Hen to Pierpont, June 11, 1861, reel 5829, images 420–426; John J. Brown to Pierpont, August 26, 1861, reel 5830, images 330–331,

Francis M. Pierpont Executive Papers, 1861–1865, box 1, folder 2, Library of Virginia (hereafter cited as Pierpont Papers, LVA).

7. Virginia General Assembly, Legislative Petitions of the General Assembly, Kanawha County, box 131, folder 11, January 12, 1860, State Government Records Collection, Library of Virginia, Richmond.

8. Green Slack to Pierpont, August 27, 1861, box 2, folder 1, Pierpont Papers, LVA. The warrants for new officeholders in July–August–September 1861 are in box 2, folders 2–4, Pierpont Papers, LVA; Eric Foner, *Reconstruction: America's Unfinished Revolution, 1863–1877* (1988; updated ed., New York: Harper Perennial, 2014), 38.

9. Scott A. MacKenzie, "Forming a Middle Class: The Civil War in Kanawha County, West(ern) Virginia, 1861–1865," *West Virginia History* New Series 9, no. 1 (Spring 2015): 23–45, 32–33; John Slack to Pierpont, December 30, 1861, reel 5833, image 12, Pierpont Papers, LVA; *Diary and Letters of Rutherford Birchard Hayes: Nineteenth President of the United States*, ed. Charles Richard Williams (Columbus: Ohio State Archaeological and Historical Society, 1922), 2:68. See also John Alexander Williams, *West Virginia: A History*, 2nd ed. (Morgantown: West Virginia University Press, 2001). Private Jesse Tyler Sturm of the Fourteenth West Virginia Infantry made a similar comment in his postwar memoirs. In his home area of Marion and Harrison counties, he described the sentiment "was pretty divided between friends of the union and those for secession, those in official authority belonging to the latter class." While this is a great source, I do not use it here. His unit did not form until August 1862, and he did not record his memories until the early 1900s. Hayes, on the other hand, wrote from firsthand experiences. See *"From a Whirlpool of Death . . . to Victory: Civil War Remembrances of Jesse Tyler Sturm, 14th West Virginia Infantry*, ed. Mary E. Johnson (Charleston: West Virginia Division of Culture and History, 2002), 1.

   Northwestern Virginia continued to have representatives in the Confederate Congress and secessionist state assembly throughout the war. While they appear to have been elected by soldiers and refugees, their choices were not purely symbolic. To cite one example, Charles W. Newlon, the delegate for Monongalia, Preston, and Taylor counties in Richmond, lived in that area before the war but fled to Rockbridge County in 1861. See *Genealogical and Personal History of the Upper Monongahela Valley, West Virginia*, ed. Bernard L. Butcher (New York: Clearfield Company, 1912; repr., Baltimore: Genealogical Publishing, 1978), 610–611. See also Kenneth C. Martis, *The Historical Atlas of the Congresses of the Confederate States of America, 1861–1865* (New York: Simon & Schuster, 1997), 134–138; and *The General Assembly of Virginia: A Bicentennial Register of Members*, ed. Cynthia M. Leonard (Richmond: General Assembly of Virginia by the Virginia State Library, 1978), 474–488.

10. MacKenzie, "Forming a Middle Class."

11. US District Court for the Charleston Division of the Southern District of West Virginia, Law Court Record Book, US District Court for the Clarksburg Division of the Northern District of West Virginia, Law Court Record Book, and US District Court for the Wheeling Division of the Northern District of West Virginia, Law Court Record Book, Record Group 21: Records of District Courts of the United States, 1685–1991, National Archives and Records Administration Mid-Atlantic Region, Philadelphia; Jacob C. Baas Jr., "John Jay Jackson Jr.: His Early Life and Public Career, 1824–1870" (PhD diss., West Virginia University, 1975), 116;

Jonathan Slack to Pierpont, September 8, 1861, reel 5830, images 579–580; Alexander C. Moore to Pierpont, October 11, 1861, reel 5832, images 13–14, Pierpont Papers, LVA.

12. For Ritchie and Lewis, Virgil A. Lewis, *How West Virginia Was Made: The Proceedings of the First Convention of the People of Northwestern Virginia at Wheeling, May 13, 14, and 15, 1861, and the Journal of the Second Convention of the People of Northwestern Virginia at Wheeling, Which Assembled, June 11, 1861, and Continued in Session until June 25; Adjourned until August 6th, 1861; Reassembled on That Date, and Continued in Session until August 21st, When It Adjourned Sine Die* (Charleston, WV: News-Mail Company Public Printers, 1909), 224 and 225. Carlile's speech is in Lewis, *How West Virginia Was Made*, 310–312. McGregor wrote that "no sectional alignment was maintained. The Panhandle counties were just as likely to be found in opposition to division as the delegates from the counties further south." James Clyde McGregor, *The Disruption of Virginia* (New York: Macmillan, 1922), 243. For Boreman's concluding remarks, see Lewis, *How West Virginia Was Made*, 301. For Camp Carlile, see Snell, *West Virginia and the Civil War*, 31 and 83. Two sources exist for the pivotal vote that give different figures. Lewis's *How West Virginia Was Made*, 295, says the tally was 48–27. The *Journal of the Convention Assembled at Wheeling on the 11th of June 1861* (Wheeling, WV: Daily Press Book and Job Office, 1861), gives 50–28. While the numbers are too small to make any difference, I must agree with Curry that researchers ought to use the *Journal*. The convention authorized it at the time, while Lewis compiled his decades later from the newspapers. See Richard Orr Curry, *A House Divided: Statehood Politics and the Copperhead Movement in West Virginia* (Pittsburgh: University of Pittsburgh Press, 1964), 79–85, 168–169.

13. Curry, *House Divided*, 149–150; *Wheeling Daily Intelligencer*, November 5, 1861.

14. I derived these figures by comparing "Delegates to the Constitutional Convention," State of Convenience, https://archive.wvculture.org/history/statehood/delegatescc.html, and US Department of the Interior, Census Office, Manuscript Census Schedules, Harrison, Kanawha and Ohio counties, Virginia, Schedules 1 (Free Population) and 2 (Slave Population) for the Seventh (1850) and Eighth (1860) Census (hereafter cited as Census Sample); see also Charles H. Ambler, "The Makers of West Virginia," *West Virginia History* 2, no. 4 (July 1941): 267–278.

15. Charles Henry Ambler and Festus Summers, *West Virginia: The Mountain State*, 2nd ed. (Englewood Cliffs, NJ: Prentice Hall, 1958), 229–238; Curry, *House Divided*, 86–99; Otis Rice and Stephen W. Brown, *West Virginia: A History*, 2nd ed. (Lexington: University Press of Kentucky, 1993), 140–146; John E. Stealey III, *West Virginia's Civil War–Era Constitution: Loyal Revolution, Confederate Counter-Revolution, and the Constitution of 1872* (Kent, OH: Kent State University Press, 2013), 72–106; *Wheeling Daily Intelligencer*, November 12, 1861.

16. Hagar to Pierpont, July 30, 1861, Pierpont Papers, LVA, reel 5828, 510 and 511; "Debates and Proceedings of the First Constitutional Convention of West Virginia, November 30, 1861," State of Convenience, https://archive.wvculture.org/history/statehood/cc113061.html; *Wheeling Daily Intelligencer*, December 7, 1861. See also Michael B. Graham, *The Coal River Valley in the Civil War: West Virginia Mountains, 1861* (Charleston, SC: History Press, 2014).

17. Curry, *House Divided*, 90–99.

18. "Debates and Proceedings of the First Constitutional Convention of West Virginia,

December 3, 1861," State of Convenience, https://archive.wvculture.org/history/statehood/cc120361.html.

19. "Debates and Proceedings of the First Constitutional Convention of West Virginia, December 5, 1861," State of Convenience, https://archive.wvculture.org/history/statehood/cc120561.html. Brown was remarkably prescient. Former Confederate Henry M. Mathews of Greenbrier County became West Virginia's governor in 1877.

20. "Debates and Proceedings of the First Constitutional Convention of West Virginia, December 7, 1861," State of Convenience, https://archive.wvculture.org/history/statehood/cc120761.html; Curry, *House Divided*, 87. More recently, West Virginia state senator Charles S. Trump IV suggested implementing this plan by adding Frederick County, Virginia, to his state. The proposal went nowhere fast. See Eric J. Wittenberg, Edmund A. Sargus Jr., and Penny L. Barrick, *Seceding from Secession: The Civil War, Politics, and the Creation of West Virginia* (Eldorado Hills, CA: Savas Beatie, 2020), 244–248.

21. "Debates and Proceedings of the First Constitutional Convention of West Virginia, December 14, 1861," State of Convenience, https://archive.wvculture.org/history/statehood/cc121461.html; "Debates and Proceedings of the First Constitutional Convention of West Virginia, December 18, 1861," State of Convenience, https://archive.wvculture.org/history/statehood/cc121861.html.

22. "Debates and Proceedings of the First Constitutional Convention of West Virginia, December 2, 1861," State of Convenience, https://archive.wvculture.org/history/statehood/cc120261.html; "Debates and Proceedings of the First Constitutional Convention of West Virginia, January 7, 1862," State of Convenience, https://archive.wvculture.org/history/statehood/cc010762.html; "Debates and Proceedings of the First Constitutional Convention of West Virginia, January 17, 1862," State of Convenience, https://archive.wvculture.org/history/statehood/cc011762.html.

23. "Debates and Proceedings of the First Constitutional Convention of West Virginia, January 27, 1862," State of Convenience, https://archive.wvculture.org/history/statehood/cc012762.html.

24. Ambler and Summers, *West Virginia*, 235; Rice and Brown, *West Virginia*, 145; "Debates and Proceedings of the First Constitutional Convention of West Virginia, February 3, 1862," State of Convenience, https://archive.wvculture.org/history/statehood/cc020362.html.

25. Granville Davisson Hall, *The Rending of Virginia: A History* (1902; repr., Knoxville: University of Tennessee Press, 2000), 443 and 448. This book contains more than Hall's notes on the West Virginia statehood movement. It contains numerous other hard-to-find sources such as the Battelle tract.

26. "Debates and Proceedings of the First Constitutional Convention of West Virginia, February 12, 1862," State of Convenience, https://archive.wvculture.org/history/statehood/cc021262.html; Curry, *House Divided*, 91.

27. "Debates and Proceedings of the First Constitutional Convention of West Virginia, February 12, 1862," State of Convenience, https://archive.wvculture.org/history/statehood/cc021262.html. Battelle meant that Stuart and others were absent at the time he spoke. Stuart voted on both measures.

28. "Debates and Proceedings of the First Constitutional Convention of West Virginia, February 13, 1862," State of Convenience, https://archive.wvculture.org/history/statehood/cc021362.html; *Wheeling Daily Intelligencer*, February 15, 1862. There is

220　/　Notes to Pages 114–121

a minor discrepancy in the number of delegates between these two ballots. A total of 47 (24 for tabling and 23 against) delegates voted on February 12, but 48 participated in the next one. The minutes cite Edward Mahon of Jackson County as both absent and present. Other absentees include James W. Paxton of Ohio County, Waitman T. Willey of Monongalia County, and William Walker of Wyoming County. Of those, Paxton voted in the negative on February 12, while the remainder did not. What exactly happened here is unclear from the sources, but it had no appreciable impact on the event.

29. "Debates and Proceedings of the First Constitutional Convention of West Virginia, February 18, 1862," State of Convenience, https://archive.wvculture.org/history /statehood/cc021862.html.

30. *Wheeling Daily Intelligencer*, February 21, 1862, February 25, 1862, March 5, 1862, and March 3, 1862.

31. Abraham Lincoln, "Annual Message to Congress," December 3, 1861, in *Collected Works of Abraham Lincoln*, ed. Roy P. Basler (New Brunswick, NJ: Rutgers University Press, 1953), 5:36–53. The specific quote is on 48–50.

CHAPTER 5: THE RADICAL PHASE OF THE WEST VIRGINIA STATEHOOD MOVEMENT, MARCH 1862–JUNE 1863

1. Rutherford B. Hayes to Eliakim P. Scammon, May 4, 1862, in US War Department, *The War of the Rebellion: A Compilation of Official Records of the Union and Confederate Armies* (Washington, DC: Government Printing Office, 1880), series 1, 51, pt. 1, 599–600. Hayes's diary reprints this document except for one thing: his diary reported 6 a.m., while the *Official Records* record it as 1 a.m. See *Diary and Letters of Rutherford Birchard Hayes: Nineteenth President of the United States*, ed. Charles Richard Williams (Columbus: Ohio State Archaeological and Historical Society, 1922), 2:248–249. According to the 1860 Census Schedules for Kanawha County, Moses Ward was the first person to appear on the list, while William C. Blaine compiled it; James Oakes, *Freedom National: The Destruction of Slavery in the United States, 1861–1865* (New York: Norton, 2013), 293–300.

2. Oakes, *Freedom National*, 293–300; Elizabeth Varon, *Armies of Deliverance: A New History of the Civil War* (New York: Oxford University Press, 2019), 199 and 301.

3. Edward McPherson, *The Political History of the United States during the Great Rebellion*, 2nd ed. (Washington, DC: Philip and Solomons, 1865), 209–213.

4. *Wheeling Daily Intelligencer*, March 11, 1862, and March 10, 1862.

5. *Wheeling Daily Intelligencer*, March 24, 1862, April 1, 1862, and April 3, 1862.

6. *Wheeling Daily Intelligencer*, April 11, 1862 (Guyandotte), April 23, 1862 (results).

7. *Wheeling Daily Intelligencer*, February 21, 1862, and April 3, 1862. For more on John J. Davis, the head of a prominent West Virginia political family, including son John W. Davis, who ran for president in 1924, see his letters to his fiancée in *West Virginia: Documents in the History of a Rural Industrial State*, ed. Ronald L. Lewis and John C. Hennen Jr. (Dubuque, IA: Kendall/Hunt, 1991), 119–123.

8. Benjamin H. Smith to Pierpont, March 6, 1862, reel 5836, Francis M. Pierpont Executive Papers, 1861–1865, box 1, folder 2, Library of Virginia (hereafter cited as Pierpont Papers, LVA).

9. Green Slack to Pierpont, May 24, 1862, AR1722, box 6, Pierpont-Samuels Papers, West Virginia State Archives, Charleston.

Notes to Pages 122–131 / 221

10. *Kanawha Republican*, n.d., reprinted in *Wheeling Daily Intelligencer*, June 21, 1862.

11. Benjamin H. Smith to Pierpont, July 16, 1862, box 7, folder 1, Pierpont Papers, LVA. Noyes "Plus" Rand served as an officer in the Kanawha Riflemen. His first name was also his mother's maiden name, indicating that the Rands and the Noyeses, and by extension the family of Benjamin H. Smith, were related.

12. Union Club of Charleston Petition to Pierpont, August 19, 1862, box 7, folder 6, Pierpont Papers, LVA, emphasis original.

13. Petitioners to Pierpont, August 19, 1862, box 7, folder 6, Pierpont Papers, LVA. This document is the cover letter for numerous individual petitions dated June 2.

14. The full title is "An Appeal of the People of West Virginia to Congress, Suggesting for the Consideration of Members Material Facts; Accepting the 'Nation's Proposal' for the Gradual Abolishment of Slavery, and Asking That Body to Give Its Consent to the Erection and Admission of the New State into the Union at Its Present Session." It was dated May 22, 1862, but appeared on the front page of the *Wheeling Daily Intelligencer* on June 7. George Ellis Moore cites it in his "Slavery as a Factor in the Formation of West Virginia," *West Virginia History* 18, no. 1 (October 1956): 77–78. Richard Orr Curry cites it in his *A House Divided: Statehood Politics and the Copperhead Movement in West Virginia* (Pittsburgh: University of Pittsburgh Press, 1964), 98–99. Granville Parker reprinted it in full in his *The Formation of the State of West Virginia and Other Incidents of the Late Civil War* (Wellsburg, WV: Glass & Sons, 1875), 123–134.

15. US Congress, *Congressional Globe*, 37th Cong., 2nd Sess., 1862, 2414–2418 (hereafter cited as *Cong. Globe*).

16. *Cong. Globe*, 37th Cong, 2nd Sess., 1862, 2941–2942.

17. *Cong. Globe*, 37th Cong., 2nd Sess., 1862, 3038.

18. *Cong. Globe*, 37th Cong., 2nd Sess., 1862, 3308, 3315. See also Hans L. Trefousse, *Benjamin Franklin Wade: Radical Republican from Ohio* (New York: Twayne, 1963), 193, and Woods, "Mountaineers Becoming Free."

19. McPherson, *Political History of the United States*, 214–220.

20. *Cong. Globe*, 37th Cong., 2nd Sess., 3313–3320.

21. *Wheeling Daily Intelligencer*, July 17, July 19, July 21, July 25, and July 29, 1862.

22. Van Winkle to Willey, June 7, 1862, Waitman T. Willey Papers, West Virginia and Regional History Collection, Morgantown, WV (hereafter cited as Willey Papers, WVRHC); *Clarksburg National Telegraph*, June 13, 1862. Carlile's Indianapolis speech, July 30, 1862, is quoted from Curry, *House Divided*, 117–118. On October 23, 1862, John Hall, the president of the Constitutional Convention, shot and killed Mason County editor Lewis Wetzel over some critical stories in the *Point Pleasant Register*. This does not appear to have been a radical versus conservative political matter, as the *Intelligencer* stated two days later. *Wheeling Daily Intelligencer*, October 25, 1862.

23. James M. McPherson, *Battle Cry of Freedom: The Civil War Era* (New York: Ballantine, 1988), 511–545; for Camp Carlile, see Mark A. Snell, *West Virginia and the Civil War: Mountaineers Are Always Free* (Charleston, SC: History Press, 2011), 83.

24. Glenn David Brasher, *The Peninsular Campaign and the Necessity for Emancipation: African Americans and the Fight for Freedom* (Chapel Hill: University of North Carolina Press, 2014); Abraham Lincoln, "Emancipation Proclamation," in *Collected Works of Abraham Lincoln*, ed. Roy P. Basler (New Brunswick, NJ: Rutgers University Press, 1953), 6:28–31.

222 / Notes to Pages 131–140

25. William C. Harris, *Lincoln and the Union Governors* (Carbondale: Southern Illinois University, 2013), 59–61; Stephen D. Engle, *Gathering to Save a Nation: Lincoln and the Union's War Governors* (Chapel Hill: University of North Carolina Press, 2016), 214–238; Charles H. Ambler, *Francis H. Pierpont: Union War Governor of Virginia and Father of West Virginia* (Chapel Hill: University of North Carolina Press, 1937), 155–156.

26. Reynolds, William Clark, Diary, 1862, Civil War Collection, West Virginia State Archives. See also William Wessels, *Born to Be a Soldier: The Military Career of William Wing Loring of St. Augustine, Florida* (Fort Worth: Texas Christian University Press, 1971).

27. Terry Lowry, *22nd Virginia Infantry* (Lexington, VA: H. E. Howard, 1985), 37. See also his *The Battle of Charleston and the 1862 Kanawha Valley Campaign* (Charleston, WV: 35th Star, 2016).

28. George Ellis Moore, *A Banner in the Hills: West Virginia's Statehood* (New York: Appleton-Century-Crofts, 1963), 171.

29. Reynolds Diary.

30. Lowry, *22nd Virginia Infantry*, 38.

31. *Guerilla* (Charleston, VA), September 29, 1862.

32. Quoted from Roy Bird Cook, "The Civil War Comes to Charleston," *West Virginia History* 23, no. 2 (January 1962): 160.

33. *Guerilla* (Charleston, VA), September 29, 1862.

34. *Guerilla* (Charleston, VA), September 29, 1862.

35. *Richmond Daily Dispatch*, October 2, 1862, cited 19,000 bushels had been left behind by the retreating Union troops.

36. G. Slack to Pierpont, October 19, 1862, box 9, folder 1, Pierpont Papers, LVA.

37. *Fairmont National*, August 1, 1863.

38. G. Slack to Pierpont, October 19, 1862, box 9, folder 1, Pierpont Papers, LVA. The parenthetical sentence and the underlining are in the original.

39. Benjamin H. Smith and Lewis Ruffner to Pierpont, November 8, 1862, box 9, folder 3, Pierpont Papers, LVA.

40. John E. Stealey, *The Antebellum Kanawha Salt Business and Western Markets* (Lexington: University Press of Kentucky, 1994), 184.

41. Green Slack to Pierpont, December 29, 1862, Pierpont/Samuels Papers, West Virginia State Archives, Charleston.

42. *Wheeling Daily Intelligencer*, January 23, 1863.

43. *Cong. Globe*, 37th Cong., 3rd Sess., 1862, 41–51.

44. *Cong. Globe*, 37th Cong., 3rd Sess., 1862, 54–59.

45. *Wheeling Daily Intelligencer*, December 11 and 15, 1862.

46. Orville Hickling Browning, *The Diary of Orville Hickling Browning*, ed. Theodore Calvin Pease and James G. Randall (Springfield: Trustees of the Illinois State Historical Library, 1925), 596; for the Lincoln quote, see Allan Nevins, *The War for the Union: Part 2: War Becomes Revolution, 1862–1863* (New York: Macmillan, 1960), 352; and Ambler, *Francis H. Pierpont*, 184–185.

47. William C. Harris, *Lincoln and the Border States: Preserving the Union* (Manhattan: University Press of Kansas, 2011), 189 and 206.

48. Eric J. Wittenberg, Edmund A. Sargus Jr., and Penny L. Barrick, *Seceding from Secession: The Civil War, Politics, and the Creation of West Virginia* (Eldorado Hills, CA: Savas Beatie, 2020), 194 (Stanton) and 189–90 (Blair).

Notes to Pages 140–149 / 223

49. "Granville Parker's Account of Jacob Beeson Blair's Role in Lincoln's Approval of the Statehood Bill," in Parker, *Formation of the State of West Virginia*, 185–186.
50. *Mrs. Samuel Crane, Mrs. Francis H. Pierpont, and Mrs. L.A. Hagans to Abraham Lincoln, Thursday, Congratulate Lincoln on Signing Bill That Admits West Virginia into Union*, January 1, 1863, Manuscript/Mixed Material, Abraham Lincoln Papers: Series 1, General Correspondence, 1833 to 1916, Library of Congress, Washington, DC, https://www.loc.gov/item/mal2087900/; *Wheeling Daily Intelligencer*, January 3, 1863; F. N. Boney, *John Letcher of Virginia: The Story of Virginia's Civil War Governor* (Tuscaloosa: University of Alabama Press, 1966), 178.
51. *Wheeling Daily Intelligencer*, January 14, 1863.
52. *Wheeling Daily Intelligencer*, January 31, 1863.
53. *Wheeling Daily Intelligencer*, February 5, 1863.
54. Clemens to Pierpont, March 7, 1863, reel 5847, images 577 and 578; Pierpont Papers, LVA.
55. "Debates and Proceedings of the First Constitutional Convention of West Virginia, February 12, 1863," State of Convenience, https://archive.wvculture.org/history/statehood/cc021263.html.
56. "Debates and Proceedings of the First Constitutional Convention of West Virginia, February 13, 1863," State of Convenience, https://archive.wvculture.org/history/statehood/cc021363.html; "Debates and Proceedings of the First Constitutional Convention of West Virginia, February 16, 1863," State of Convenience, https://archive.wvculture.org/history/statehood/cc021663.html; Granville Davisson Hall, *The Rending of Virginia: A History* (1902; repr., Knoxville: University of Tennessee Press, 2000), 502.
57. "Debates and Proceedings of the First Constitutional Convention of West Virginia, February 17, 1863," State of Convenience, https://archive.wvculture.org/history/statehood/cc021763.html. The same website has an image of the voting record approving of the new constitution. The record shows fifty-four aye votes and six scratched off. Two of them, from Stephen M. Handsley of Raleigh and Job Robinson of Calhoun, are listed as absent in the above convention minutes. The remaining four abstained from the vote: Johanis P. Hoback of McDowell, James W. Paxton of Ohio, Benjamin H. Smith of Kanawha but representing Nicholas this time instead of Logan, and strangely Willey of Monongalia. See "Vote of Delegates on Revised Constitution," State of Convenience, https://archive.wvculture.org/History/statehood/ccvote.html.
58. Linda Fluharty, "12th West Virginia Infantry," http://www.lindapages.com/wvcw/12wvi/12-northcott.htm.
59. *Wheeling Daily Intelligencer*, March 16, 1863; Curry, *House Divided*, 129; see also his appendix for county returns in the referendum, 150–151; Darrell L. Collins, *The Jones-Imboden Raid: The Confederate Attempt to Destroy the Baltimore and Ohio Railroad and Retake West Virginia* (Jefferson, NC: McFarland, 2007).
60. Chester Hubbard to Willey, May 2, 1862, Willey Papers, WVRHC.

CHAPTER 6: WEST VIRGINIA UNDER RADICAL RULE, JUNE 1863–DECEMBER 1869

1. *Wheeling Daily Intelligencer*, June 22, 1863.
2. John E. Stealey III, *West Virginia's Civil War–Era Constitution: Loyal Revolution,*

224　／　Notes to Pages 150–157

Confederate Counter-Revolution, and the Constitution of 1872 (Kent, OH: Kent State University Press, 2013).

3. Stealey, *West Virginia's Civil War–Era Constitution*, 111; Mathew Holt et al. to Boremen [*sic*], September 3, 1863, box 7, Boreman Papers, West Virginia Dept. of Archives and History, Charleston, quoted in "The Bushwhacker's War: Insurgency and Counter-insurgency in West Virginia," ed. Richard O. Curry and F. Gerald Ham, *Civil War History* 10, no. 4 (December 1964): 431–432; Terry Lowry, *Last Sleep: The Battle of Droop Mountain, November 6, 1863* (Charleston, WV: Pictorial Histories, 1996); and Kenneth W. Noe, *Southwestern Virginia's Railroad* (Urbana: University of Illinois Press, 1994), 130. See also David W. Mellot and Mark A. Snell, *The Seventh West Virginia Infantry: An Embattled Union Regiment from the Civil War's Most Divided State* (Lawrence: University Press of Kansas, 2019).

4. *Wheeling Daily Intelligencer*, October 9, 1863, and October 20, 1863; *Morgantown Monitor*, October 23, 1863. Willey later wrote a history of the statehood movement that repeats the same story as Lang, Hall, and Ambler. See William P. Willey, *An Inside View of the Formation of the State of West Virginia* (Wheeling, WV: News Company Publishing Company and W. P. Willey, 1901).

5. Stealey, 110; "An Act Concerning Oaths and Affirmations, Passed November 16, 1863," in *West Virginia: Documents in the History of a Rural Industrial State*, ed. Ronald L. Lewis and John C. Hennen Jr. (Dubuque, IA: Kendall/Hunt, 1991), 134.

6. Law Order Books, Clarksburg and Wheeling Courts, Record Group 21, Records of the US District Court for Northern District of West Virginia, and Law Order Book, Charleston Court, Record Group 21, Records of the US District Court for the Southern District of West Virginia, National Archives and Record Administration Mid-Atlantic Branch, Philadelphia.

7. *Wheeling Daily Intelligencer*, February 22, 1864.

8. Forrest Talbott, "Some Legislative and Legal Aspects of the Negro Question in West Virginia during the Civil War and Reconstruction, Part 1," *West Virginia History* 24, no. 1 (October 1962): 18–19. The federal Department of War accredited between 196 and 212 African American soldiers from West Virginia during the Civil War. They enlisted in the Forty-Fifth United States Colored Troops in September 1864 at Camp William Penn near Philadelphia. These limited numbers precluded the Union Army from establishing a base for them in West Virginia. This contrasts with Kentucky's experience, where its trained thousands of Black soldiers at Camp Nelson. In the process, it undermined slavery in that pivotal border state and drove it toward more conservative rule. See Caleb Brownfield, "African American West Virginians in the Civil War: The 45th USCT" (Carter G. Woodson Project, Marshall University, n.d.), https://www.marshall.edu/woodson-dev/african-american-west-virginians-in-the-civil-war-the-45th-usct/.

9. *Wheeling Daily Intelligencer,* January 21, 1864.

10. *Wheeling Daily Register*. July 10, 1865.

11. *Morgantown Weekly Post*, October 15, 1864; *Wheeling Daily Intelligencer*, October 27, 1864; and *West Virginia Journal*, October 28, 1864, and November 2, 1864.

12. Otis Rice and Stephen W. Brown, *West Virginia: A History*, 2nd ed. (Lexington: University Press of Kentucky, 1993), 155.

13. *Wheeling Daily Intelligencer*, November 9, 1864, and November 10, 1864; *West Virginia Journal*, November 16, 1864.

14. US Congress, *Congressional Globe*, 37th Cong., 2nd Sess., 1862, 2414–2418, Senate,

38th Cong., 1st Sess., 1864, 1490; House, 38th Cong., 1st Sess., 1864, 2995; House, 38th Cong., 2nd Sess., 1865, 531. See also Shelton Winston, "West Virginia's First Delegation to Congress," *West Virginia History* 29, no. 4 (July 1968): 274–277.

15. *Wheeling Daily Intelligencer*, January 16, 1865; *West Virginia Journal*, January 27, 1865.

16. The proceedings of the House debate were published in *Wheeling Daily Intelligencer*, January 31, 1865, and February 1, 1865; the Senate debate appeared in *Wheeling Daily Intelligencer*, February 4, 1865; Kenneth R. Bailey, *Alleged Evil Genius: The Life and Times of Judge James H. Ferguson* (Charleston, WV: Quarrier Press, 2006), 29–30.

17. Milton Geofsky, "Reconstruction in West Virginia, Pt 1," *West Virginia History* 6, no. 4 (July 1945): 300–302; Stealey, *West Virginia's Civil War–Era Constitution*, 107–126; Randall S. Gooden, "The Completion of a Revolution: West Virginia from Statehood through Reconstruction" (PhD diss., West Virginia University, 1995); *Wheeling Daily Intelligencer*, February 14, 1865; *Wheeling Daily Register*, May 14, 1865.

18. *Wheeling Daily Intelligencer*, April 17, 1865; *Wheeling Daily Register*, April 17, 1865; *Morgantown Weekly Post*, May 20, 1865; *Clarksburg Weekly National Telegraph*, April 28, 1865.

19. *Wheeling Daily Intelligencer*, May 9, 1865; Arthur Boreman to James Boreman, May 12, 1865, Arthur I. Boreman Papers, West Virginia and Regional History Collection, Morgantown (WVRHC); R. J. McCandlish to Jonathan M. Bennett, May 30, 1865, Jonathan M. Bennett Papers, WVRHC; *Wheeling Daily Intelligencer*, July 3, 1865.

20. Geofsky, "Reconstruction in West Virginia, Pt 1," 300, 303–305.

21. Kanawha County Court Records, reel KAN-214, section 1865–22, no date but believed to be early November 1865, WVRHC; *Wheeling Daily Intelligencer*, November 28, 1865. The *West Virginia Journal* of November 8, 1865, published Polsley's decision in full, covering the whole front page and one column on the second, and even more in their November 15 issue; *Parkersburg Weekly Times*, November 25, 1865, *Wheeling Daily Register*, December 21, 1865.

22. Stealey, *West Virginia's Civil War–Era Constitution*, 117–118; Donald R. McVeigh, "Charles James Faulkner: Reluctant Rebel" (PhD diss., West Virginia University, 1954), 146–148; see also Eric J. Wittenberg, Edmund A. Sargus Jr., and Penny L. Barrick, *Seceding from Secession: The Civil War, Politics, and the Creation of West Virginia* (Eldorado Hills, CA: Savas Beatie, 2020), 143–180, 216–233.

23. Daniel Lamb to Gideon D. Camden, April 17, 1866, Gideon Camden Papers, WVRHC, quoted in Richard O. Curry, "A Reappraisal of Statehood Politics of West Virginia," *Journal of Southern History* 28, no. 4 (November 1962): 421; *Wheeling Daily Register*, April 24, 1866; *Wheeling Daily Intelligencer*, April 30, 1866; *Lewisburg Times*, May 12, 1866.

24. Stealey, *West Virginia's Civil War–Era Constitution*, 123–127; Geofsky, "Reconstruction in West Virginia, Pt 1," 303–305; table of electoral returns is on *Wheeling Daily Intelligencer*, July 11, 1866, and May 25, 1866; *Wheeling Daily Register*, May 31, 1866.

25. *Wheeling Daily Register*, August 27, 1866.

26. *Wheeling Daily Register*, October 5, 1866; *Wheeling Daily Intelligencer*, October 25, 1866.

226 / Notes to Pages 165–172

27. *Wheeling Daily Register*, October 15, 1866; *Wheeling Daily Intelligencer*, December 21, 1866.

28. *Wheeling Daily Intelligencer*, January 16, 1867; Boreman to County Boards of Registration, Township Registrars and Supervisors and Inspectors of Election, March 13, 1867, Arthur I. Boreman Executive Papers, State Dept. of Archives and History, Charleston, WV, quoted in Richard Orr Curry, "Crisis Politics in West Virginia, 1861–1870," in *Radicalism, Racism, and Party Realignment: The Border States during Reconstruction,* ed. Richard Orr Curry (Baltimore: Johns Hopkins University Press, 1969), 93–94.

29. *Wheeling Daily Intelligencer*, April 2, 1867; "Department of Free Schools, Report of the Superintendent of Free Schools, 1867," in Lewis and Hennen, *West Virginia: Documents,* 144–148; James (John) Edmund Stealey III, "The Freedmen's Bureau in West Virginia," *West Virginia History* 39, nos. 2–3 (January/April 1978): 99–142. See also John E. Stealey, ed., "Report on the Freedmen's Bureau Operations in West Virginia: Agents in the Eastern Panhandle," *West Virginia History* 42, nos. 1–2 (Fall 1980–Winter 1981): 94–129; and John Edmund Stealey III, ed., "Reports on the Freedmen's Bureau District Officers on Tours and Surveys in West Virginia," *West Virginia History* 43, no. 2 (Winter 1982): 145–155. In 2011, Professor Stealey told me that those articles contain every document in the National Archives file on the matter.

30. *Wheeling Daily Register*, January 17 and 18, 1867, and July 24, 1868.

31. Charles L. Wagandt, "Redemption or Reaction?—Maryland in the Post–Civil War Years," and William E. Parrish, "Reconstruction Politics in Missouri, 1865–1870," in *Radicalism, Racism, and Party Realignment: The Border States in Reconstruction,* ed. Richard O. Curry (Baltimore: Johns Hopkins University Press, 1969), 146–187 (Maryland) and 1–37 (Missouri).

32. *Wheeling Daily Intelligencer*, April 10, 1867, and April 22, 1867; *Wheeling Daily Register*, April 12, 1867.

33. *Wheeling Daily Register*, December 16, 1867 (full election returns); *Wheeling Daily Intelligencer*, October 24, 1867; *Wheeling Daily Register*, October 18, 1867; *Greenbrier Independent*, October 31, 1867. Each of these county names comes from the rulers of the time. The radicals formed Mineral County by cutting off the Unionist northern half of largely secessionist Hardy County. They also named Lincoln and Grant counties after the great Union heroes. When conservatives redeemed the state in 1870, they named Summers County in the following year after George W. Summers, one of their heroes. See Stephen G. Smith, "Secession, War, and Rebirth: The Civil War in West Virginia's South Branch Valley of the Potomac" (master's thesis, West Virginia University, 2000).

34. *Wheeling Daily Intelligencer*, January 22, 1868; *Wheeling Daily Register*, January 25, 1868.

35. O. S. Long and W. L. Wilson, "Reconstruction in West Virginia," in Hilary Abner Herbert et al., *Why the Solid South or Reconstruction and its Results* (Baltimore: R. H. Woodward, 1890), 280, quoted in Geofsky, "Reconstruction in West Virginia, Pt 1," 323–324. The book is a compilation of conservative essays on Reconstruction in the southern states. The *Greenbrier Independent* dedicated numerous columns over Caldwell's actions and fate, such as in its issues on August 14 and 21, 1869.

36. *Wheeling Daily Register*, March 2, 1868; *Wheeling Daily Intelligencer*, March 7, 1868.

37. Michael Les Benedict, *The Impeachment and Trial of Andrew Johnson* (New York:

Norton, 1973), 178; *Wheeling Daily Intelligencer*, May 18, 1868; *Wheeling Daily Register*, May 15, 1868.

38. George Wesley Atkinson and Alvaro Franklin Gibbens, *Prominent Men of West Virginia* (Wheeling, WV: W. L. Callin, 1890), 948; *Wheeling Daily Intelligencer*, August 26, 1868; *Wheeling Daily Register*, October 15, 1868; *Greenbrier Independent*, October 10, 1868.

39. *Wheeling Daily Register*, December 15, 1868 (election returns).

40. *Wheeling Daily Intelligencer*, January 20, 1869; February 2, 1869; February 22, 1869; *Wheeling Daily Register*, March 2, 1869; *Wheeling Daily Intelligencer*, March 3, 1869; *Greenbrier Independent*, July 2, 1870.

41. *Wheeling Daily Intelligencer*, May 12, 1869, May 21, 1869, and June 11, 1869; *Wheeling Daily Register*, May 13, 1869.

42. *Wheeling Daily Intelligencer*, May 28, 1867, and May 13, 1869; *Wheeling Daily Register*, June 16, 1869.

43. *Parkersburg State Journal*, September 22, 1869; *Wheeling Daily Intelligencer*, September 24, 1869, September 27, 1869, and October 4, 1869; *Wheeling Daily Register*, September 8, 1869; and *Wheeling Daily Intelligencer*, November 5, 1869.

EPILOGUE: WEST VIRGINIA'S REDEMPTION, 1870–1872

1. "Governor Stevenson Proposes Removal of Restrictions on Former Confederates," in *West Virginia: Documents in the History of a Rural Industrial State*, ed. Ronald L. Lewis and John C. Hennen Jr. (Dubuque, IA: Kendall/Hunt, 1991), 148–150; Randall S. Gooden, "The Completion of a Revolution: West Virginia from Statehood through Reconstruction" (PhD diss., West Virginia University, 1995); John E. Stealey III, *West Virginia's Civil War–Era Constitution: Loyal Revolution, Confederate Counter-Revolution, and the Constitution of 1872* (Kent, OH: Kent State University Press, 2013), 189.

2. Stealey, *West Virginia's Civil War–Era Constitution*, 175; "The Flick Amendment," in Lewis and Hennen, *West Virginia: Documents*, 148; Charles H. Ambler, *Francis H. Pierpont: Union War Governor of Virginia and Father of West Virginia* (Chapel Hill: University of North Carolina Press, 1937), 342–343.

3. Milton Geofsky, "Reconstruction in West Virginia, Pt 1," *West Virginia History* 6, no. 4 (July 1945): 345–349; Stealey, *West Virginia's Civil War–Era Constitution*, 214–224.

4. Stealey, *West Virginia's Civil War–Era Constitution*, 202, 685, and 236; *Wheeling Daily Intelligencer*, June 25, 1870.

5. Stealey, *West Virginia's Civil War–Era Constitution*, 239, 258–261.

6. Stealey, *West Virginia's Civil War–Era Constitution*, 270–321; *Wheeling Daily Intelligencer*, April 28, 1871.

7. William S. Laidley, *History of Charleston and Kanawha County, West Virginia, and Representative Citizens* (Chicago: Richmond-Arnold, 1911), 926–930; Stealey, *West Virginia's Civil War–Era Constitution*, 356–364.

8. Stealey, *West Virginia's Civil War–Era Constitution*, 712–724.

Index

abolition, 182, 186–88; as prewar political issue, 45, 47–49, 54–55, 59; in secession crisis, 70, 72, 79; in conservative phase of statehood movement, 94, 111; in radical phase of statehood movement, 118, 119, 126, 127, 137, 145; its legacies in West Virginia, 152, 158, 178. *See also* African Americans; emancipation; slavery

Act to Define and Contain Certain Conspiracies [June 1861], 100

African Americans, 5, 181, 183, 184, 185; in antebellum northwestern Virginia, 56; role in secession crisis, 78, 104; in debates on new state constitution, 111, 113, 119; escapes from bondage during Civil War, 125, 126; place in statehood movement, 142, 143, 146; status in new state, 148, 154, 160, 165–66, 169–71, 175–77. *See also* abolition; emancipation; slavery

Akerman, Amos, 180

Alabama, 69

alcohol, 109, 165

Alexandria, Virginia, 87

Alkire, W. S., 180

Allegheny County, Maryland, 61

Altoona Conference, 131

Ambler, Charles Henry: 1850s and, 39, 58, 60, 62; internal improvements and, 17; role in West Virginia history, 2–3, 5; Scots-Irish thesis and, 10; secession crisis and, 63, 73, 88; slavery and, 20; statehood movement and, 92, 103

Ambler, William M., 67

Ambler-Curry Thesis: 1850s and, 39–40; internal improvements, 13; place in

literature, 3–5, 7, 9, 185, 188; Scots-Irish culture and, 10; secession and, 63, 65, 70, 73, 90; statehood movement and, 92, 117

American Party. *See* Know-Nothings

"An Appeal to the People of West Virginia to Congress" [pamphlet May 1862], 123–24, 125, 189–99. *See also* Parker, Granville

Annapolis, Maryland, 75

Appomattox Court House, 159, 161, 170, 172, 184

Arizona, 69

Arkansas, 65, 75, 168

Atkinson, John H., 158

Atlanta, Georgia, 153

Atlantic Ocean, 90

Augusta County, 49

Austin, Dr., 120

Averell, William, 150

Bagby, Lucy, 26

Baker, Lewis: 1872 convention and, 182; Boreman administration and, 171, 173–76; imprisoned by federal authorities, 153

Baltimore, Maryland, 51, 75

Baltimore and Ohio Railroad, 13, 86, 87

Banks, Nathaniel, 153

Barbour County, 4, 31, 72, 86, 170

Bartley, Mordecai, 14

Bates, Edward, 101, 138, 143

Bath County, Virginia, 106

Battelle, Gordon, 105, 106, 143; antislavery views of, 108, 109–15

Beale, J. H. M., 47, 79

Beale, Richard L. T., 35

Bedford County, Virginia, 56

Bell, John, 61

Bennett, Jonathan M., 161, 182
Benton, Thomas Hart, 169
Berkeley County, 41, 108, 124, 162, 163, 167
Berlin, George, 74
Blaine, William C., 117, 220n1
Blair, Jacob, 94, 118, 128, 136, 138, 139, 157
Blair, Montgomery, 138
Bond, Hugh Lennox, 180
Boone County, 108
Booth, John Wilkes, 160
border states, 6; and secession crisis, 63, 83, 85, 90, 94; and emancipation, 116–19, 124–25, 127–30, 139, 140, 146; and redemption, 167, 172, 177–79, 185 188
Boreman, Arthur Ingram: biography and prewar career, 31, 44, 63; in statehood movement, 63, 101; as governor, 147–53, 158–62, 165–66, 169–73; as senator, 175, 176–77
Boston, Massachusetts, 176
Botetourt County, Virginia, 13
Botts, John Minor, 34, 35
Bouldin, Wood, 67
Brady, S., 26, 29
Branch, Thomas, 70
Braxton County, 102, 182
Brazil, 37
Breckinridge, John, 61, 84
Brooke County, 15, 22, 84, 119
Brown, James H., 103–4, 106, 109, 112–14, 120, 144
Brown, John, 40, 58, 68, 87, 96, 186
Brown, William Gay: and 1850 Virginia convention, 33, 35–36, 37; in secession crisis, 67, 70; role in West Virginia statehood movement, 94, 107, 112; as congressman, 118, 128, 136, 138–39, 150, 157; and slavery, 67, 70, 94, 118, 128, 138–39, 157
Browning, Orville, 138
Bruce, James C., 67
Brumfield, William, 113
Buchanan, James, 50, 54
Buchanan County, Virginia, 107
Buckhannon, Upshur County, 43

Bull Run, First Battle of, 89
Bull Run, Second Battle of, 130
Butler, Benjamin, 86
Burdett, John S., 80
Burley, James, 158

Cabell County: Marshall University and, 4; 1850 constitutional convention and, 33, 35; Ceredo Colony and, 53; West Virginia constitutional convention and, 107, 119; Granville Parker and, 123; Albert Gallatin Jenkins and, 54, 107; postwar unrest in, 173
Caldwell, Elbert, 113
Caldwell, George W., 76, 125, 147
Caldwell, Joseph W. (aka "Old Scratch"), 171, 180, 226n35
Calhoun, John C., 162
Calhoun County, 22, 102
Camden, Gideon D., 163
Camden, Johnson N., 172
Cameron, Simon, 76
Campbell, Alexander, 54
Campbell, Alexander, Jr., 22
Campbell, Archibald W., 54, 56, 59, 138, 151
Campbell County, Kentucky, 61
Camp Carlile (later Camp Willey), 102, 130
Camp Chase, Ohio, 100
Camp Willey (previously Camp Carlile), 130
Canada, 68
Canals, 12–13
Caperton, Allen T., 71, 72
Carlile, John Snider: resistance to secession, 74–78, 213n24; Second Wheeling Convention, 87–88; slave ownership of, 27, 31, 67–69; suggests statehood, 63, 80–84; and 1850 Virginia Constitutional Convention, 33–35, 44, 46, 51–52, 62; and conservative phase of statehood movement, 92–94, 101, 110, 115; and radical phase of statehood movement, 118, 125–30, 137, 142–43, 150, 156; and *Clarksburg National Telegraph*, 142, 145

Index / 231

Carnifex Ferry, Battle of, 96
Casey, Samuel L., 128, 137
Cass, Lewis, 40
census, 80, 102
Ceredo Colony, 40, 53, 58, 62, 186
Chapline, Henry, 29
Chase, Salmon P., 138, 139
Cheat River, 11
Cincinnati, Ohio, 11, 61, 86
Chambliss, John R., 35, 36
Charleston, Kanawha County, 32, 86–87,
    161; Confederate occupation of
    (1862), 131–35; Constitutional
    Convention of 1872 in, 181–83;
    federal district court in, 100, 151;
    slavery and, 32, 117
Cheat Mountain, Battle of, 96
Cincinnati, Ohio, 54, 133
Civil War, American, 185, 188
Clarksburg, Harrison County, 32, 56, 96,
    137; and secession, 76, 78, 85, 100;
    federal district court in, 100, 151
Clarkson, John N., 28, 98, 151
Clay, Cassius M., 169
Clemens, Sherrard: antebellum career of,
    51, 55, 67; duel with O. Jennings
    Wise, 143, 211n26; slave ownership
    by, 26, 31; statehood movement and,
    74–75
Clements, Andrew J., 128, 137
Colfax, Schuyler, 136
colonization, 59
Columbus, Kentucky, 93
Compromise of 1850, 39, 54
Confederate States of America, 6, 183,
    186; military role of, 92–93, 96,
    102–3, 124, 130, 132–34, 143;
    northwestern Virginia and, 79, 82,
    85, 89, 142, 146; West Virginia and
    returning Confederates, 142, 143,
    146, 150–53, 158, 160–64, 167–68,
    172, 176–77, 179
Confiscation Acts: First (1861), 94;
    Second (1862), 94, 150
Congress, United States: 1848 elections
    to, 41; 1854 elections to, 44–45;
    1856 elections to, 48, 51; northwest-
    ern Virginia in, 82, 88, 94;

emancipation efforts of, 118,
    124–27, 135–37, 156
Constitution, US: antebellum views of,
    45, 50; secession crisis and, 63, 82;
    and West Virginia statehood
    movement, 104–5; reorganized
    government fulfilling constitutional
    obligation to authorize West Virginia
    statehood, 124, 138–39; rights of
    slaveholders under Sixth Amend-
    ment, 144; postwar views of, 151,
    164, 180
Constitution, Virginia: tensions caused
    by, 9, 14, 16; Henry Wise and, 87;
    slavery and, 92; treason clauses used
    in West Virginia constitution, 108;
    role in West Virginia statehood,
    186–87
Constitution, West Virginia (1863–72):
    slavery and, 92; drafting of, 103, 115,
    119; adding Willey Amendment to,
    144, 146; township systems and, 153;
    conservative attacks on, 165, 179–80
Constitution, West Virginia (1872–Pres-
    ent), 179
constitutional amendments: Thirteenth,
    156–57, 158, 174; Fourteenth, 166,
    167–68, 170, 173, 174; Fifteenth,
    174, 175, 176, 177, 180, 181; West
    Virginia, 163, 179, 181, 182
Constitutional Union Party, 61
Conway, Martin, 136
conventions: Virginia 1825, 15; Virginia
    1829–30, 15–19, 104; Virginia 1851,
    9, 33–36, 184; Virginia Constitu-
    tional Convention (March to
    November 1861), 65, 66, 78, 80, 90,
    103; First Wheeling Convention (May
    13–15, 1861), 63, 80–81, 87, 124,
    180, 183; Second Wheeling Conven-
    tion, 1st Session (June 11–17, 1861),
    82, 86–88, 107, 124, 180, 183;
    Second Wheeling Convention, 2nd
    Session (August 1861), 100, 113,
    183; Virginia 1816, 15; West Virginia
    Constitutional Convention
    (November 1861–February 1862),
    93, 102–15, 127, 152, 183, 186;

conventions (*continued*)

West Virginia Constitutional Convention (February 1863), 142, 183; West Virginia Constitutional Convention (1872), 179, 182–85

Cooper, William P.: as editor of *Cooper's Clarksburg Register*, 41, 43–44, 47, 56; as delegate to Virginia Constitutional Convention 1861, 74, 78; as delegate to West Virginia Constitutional Convention 1872, 182

Cooper's Clarksburg Register: proslavery views of, 41, 45, 47, 49, 50, 55; flight of editor to Richmond, 74, 78; place in redemption, 182

Crane, Mrs. Samuel, 142

Crittenden, John J., 136

CSS *Shenandoah*, 159

Cumberland, Maryland, 12

Cummins v. Missouri, 168–69

Curry, Richard Orr: West Virginia history and, 3–4, 37; northwestern Virginia in the 1850s and, 37; secession crisis and, 62, 84; statehood movement and, 92, 103, 105, 108, 119, 129, 145; and source material, 218n12

Davis, Garrett, 128

Davis, Hector, 35

Davis, Henry Winter, 168

Davis, Jefferson, 79, 96, 156, 159

Davis, John J., 120, 220n7

Davisson, Granville, 26

Dayton, Spencer, 182

Declaration of Independence, 34

"Declaration of the People of Virginia Represented in Convention at Wheeling" [June 1861], 88

Delaware: as border state, 5–7, 93, 115, 185; voting patterns in the 1850s and, 41, 45, 51, 61–62; secession crisis and, 64–65, 73, 75, 85, 90; slavery and emancipation and, 22, 116, 118, 128, 131, 139, 146, 157, 167, 174; Conservative rule over, 148, 153–54, 158, 167, 172, 174, 177

Democratic Party (federal): in northwestern Virginia, 30; electoral fortunes in the 1850s and, 40, 43–45, 47–51, 54, 56, 58, 60, 62, 210n47; emancipation policies of, 154–56

Democratic Party of West Virginia (aka Conservatives), 145; 1866 state election ("The White Man's Party"), 165; 1867 state election, 169–70; 1868 state election, 72–173; 1869 state election and Fifteenth Amendment, 175–78; 1870 and redemption, 179–82, 184–85

Denison, William, 85, 87

Dering, Henry, 110, 112

Dew, Thomas, 17

Dille, John, 113, 114

Dinwiddie County, Virginia, 18

Diss Debar, Jacob, 176

Dixon, Archibald, 83

Doddridge, Philip, 15–17, 36

Doddridge County, 106, 109, 183

Donnally, Lewis F., 30

Douglas Stephen A., 54, 61, 84

Douglass, Frederick, 55, 56, 169

Drake, Charles, 171

Dred Scott Decision, 54

Droop Mountain, Battle of, 150

Dueling, 109

Dunnington, Mr., 51

Early, Jubal, 73

Eastern Panhandle of West Virginia, 155

Eastern Shore of Virginia, 97, 118, 136, 137

Echols, John, 133

education, 111, 166, 167, 170

Elder, Thomas, 92

elections, federal: congressional election of 1849, 41; congressional election of 1854, 43–45; congressional election of 1857, 51–53, 58; presidential election of 1848, 40–41; presidential election of 1852, 42; presidential election of 1856, 48–51; presidential election of 1860, 60–61, 63; presidential election of 1864, 154, 156; presidential election of 1868, 172–73

elections, Virginia: 1830 constitutional plebiscite, 15–17; 1850

Index / 233

constitutional plebiscite, 37–38; 1851 gubernatorial election, 38–39, 45; 1855 state election, 44–45; 1859 state election, 57–58; 1861 convention election, 64–65; 1861 secession reference plebiscite (May 23), 79, 82, 83–84
elections, West Virginia: October 1861 separation referendum, 102, 105; April 1862 constitution referendum, 119–20; April 1862 gradual emancipation ballot, 119–20; February 1863 referendum on Willey Amendment, 145; May 1866 constitutional amendment, 164; October 1866 state election, 165; October 1867 state election, 169; October 1868 state elections, 172–73; November 1868 federal elections, 172–73; October 1869 state election, 176–77, 182; April 1871 Flick Amendment referendum, 182–83; 1871 August Constitutional Convention election, 183; August 1872 constitutional referendum, 184
emancipation, 4–6, 116, 183, 185, 187–88; antebellum approaches to, 17, 35; rejection by statehood movement, 94–96, 104–5, 111; embrace by statehood movement, 119–20, 124–25, 130, 137, 140, 143, 145; role in early statehood politics, 152, 153, 154, 157, 177. *See also* abolition; African Americans; slavery
Emancipation Proclamation, 131, 133, 139, 146, 150
Egypt, 105
Ewing, Thomas, 99
Ex Parte Garland, 168–69, 171

Fairmont, Marion County, 77, 175
Fairfax County, Virginia, 30, 87
Faulkner, Charles J., 41, 162, 163, 184
Fauquier County, Virginia, 35
Fayette County, 11, 74, 79, 184
Federal District Court for Western Virginia, 100, 151

Ferguson, James Harvey, 33, 157–58, 159
Field, John W., 98
Fillmore, Millard, 49, 50
Fisher, George, 116, 128
Fisher, Miers, 70
Fitzhugh, Henry, 132–33
Fleming, Aretas B., 159
Flick, William Henry Harrison, 179–80
Flick Amendment, 179, 181, 182
Florida, 96
Flournoy, Thomas, 44
Floyd, John B., 96, 131
Foreman, Mason, 26, 28
Fort Milroy, 96
Fortress Monroe, 86
France, 55, 162
Franklin County, Virginia, 73
Frederick, Maryland, 75
Frederick County, Virginia, 108, 124
Fredericksburg, Battle of, 137, 138
Free Soil Party, 41, 43
Freedman's Bureau, 167, 175, 177
Frémont, John C., 50, 94
Fry, James H., 30
Fugitive Slave Act, 45

Gallipolis, Ohio, 11
Georgia, 65, 69, 96
Gillespie, Henry L., 74
Gilmer County, 66, 150
Goode, Thomas F., 73
Goff, David, 181
Goff, Nathan, 180
Goff, Waldo, 29, 80
Goggin, William, 56, 58
Goochland County, Virginia, 34
Goshorn, William and James, 26, 100
Grant, Ulysses S., 153, 159, 164, 172, 173, 175
Grant County, 170, 183, 226n33
Great Britain, 94
Great Kanawha River, 11, 87
Greeley, Horace, 169, 175
Greenbrier County, antebellum meeting in, 32; Civil War and, 79, 132; role in statehood movement, 102–3, 107–8;

234 / Index

Greenbrier County (*continued*)
redemption and, 161, 164, 166, 168
Greensville County, Virginia, 35
guerrillas: threats to railroads, 87;
military threat to statehood movement, 92, 103, 107, 130, 146; role in
redemption, 148–49, 150, 155
Guthrie, James, 83
Guyandotte, 11, 77, 96, 120

Hagans, Mrs. Lucian A., 142
Hagar, Robert, 104–5, 107–9, 111–13,
115
Haiti, 59
Hale, John P. (New Hampshire senator),
126
Hale, John P. (Kanawha County business-
man), 134, 150, 151, 183
Hall, Cyrus, 72
Hall, Ephraim B., 111, 112
Hall, Granville Davisson: views on West
Virginia's creation, 1, 147; secretary
to constitutional convention, 144,
215n35; editor of *Wheeling Daily
Intelligencer*, 164, 169, 171–72,
174–76, 182
Hall, John, 113, 120, 221n22
Hall, Leonard S., 72
Hampshire County, 4, 96, 108, 184
Hampton Roads, Virginia, 77
Hancock County: slavery and, 21;
secession crisis and, 84; role in
Wheeling Conventions and, 92, 102,
114; redemption and, 164
Handsley, Stephen M., 223n57
Harding, Richard W., 29
Harlow, Benjamin, 170, 173
Hardy County, 108, 183, 226n33
Harpers Ferry, 40, 58, 59, 68, 77, 167
Harrison County: slavery and slavehold-
ing in, 22–33; antebellum politics of,
38, 40, 45, 49; secession crisis in, 70,
74, 78, 84; statehood movement and,
100–2, 108, 110, 120; in West
Virginia, 164, 167, 183
Harrison, Nathaniel, 168
Harrison, Thomas W., 108
Harrison, William, 29, 31

Hayes, Rutherford B., 98, 102, 117
Haymond, Alpheus, 74
Haymond, Daniel, 158
Haymond, Hiram, 113
Haymond, Luther, 29, 181
Haymond, Thomas, 41
Helper, Hinton Rowan, 32
Henderson, John B., 128, 171
Henrico County, Virginia, 34, 72
Hervey, James, 113
Hicks, Thomas, 83
Hindman, William, 171, 172
Hoback, Johanis P., 223n57
Hoge, James W., 67
Holcombe, James, 69
Holden, Charles, 30
Hubbard, Chester, 145–46, 147, 165, 171,
214n34
Hunter, David, 153
Huntington, Cabell County, 2
Huttonsville, Randolph County, 89

Illinois, 41, 45, 51, 62, 65, 93
impeachment, 169, 171–72
Indiana, 41, 45, 51, 62, 65, 85, 93, 96,
136
Indianapolis, Indiana, 129
internal improvements: role in West
Virginia's formation, 10–11, 124,
147, 183, 186; role in Constitutional
Convention, 92, 103, 109–10, 112,
115; new state's quest for, 170
Ironton, Ohio, 11

Jackson, Andrew, 30
Jackson, John G., 9, 38
Jackson, John G., Jr.: runaway slaves and,
14; secession crisis and, 63, 80, 83,
215n35; opposition to emancipation,
145, 215n35; as judge in US district
court, 100, 151, 180
Jackson, Thomas J. "Stonewall," 96, 131,
162
Jackson County, 72
Jacob, John Jeremiah, 181
James River, 39, 130
Jefferson, Thomas, 59, 69, 162
Jefferson City, Missouri, 75

Jefferson County, 4, 108, 124, 163, 167, 184

Jenkins, Albert Gallatin, 51, 52, 54, 107, 157

Johnson, Andrew, 154, 160, 165, 169, 171

Johnston, Joseph, 29, 37, 45, 77

Kanawha County: slavery and slaveholding in, 21–33, 117, 146; antebellum politics of, 40, 52; secession and, 84, 87, 90, 96; federal court in, 100; statehood movement and, 97–98, 102, 104, 106, 110, 120–22; in West Virginia, 165, 167

Kanawha County Salt Business, 4, 11, 28, 121

Kanawha Salines, 131

Kanawha Valley: internal improvements and, 12; antebellum politics of, 62; statehood movement and, 80, 110, 112, 155, 157; military operations in, 86–87, 96, 130–31, 133; redemption and, 176

Kanawha River, 108

Kansas, 40, 55, 90, 136

Kansas-Nebraska Act, 45, 49, 54

Kelley, Benjamin F., 86

Kelley, Isaac, 26

Kennedy, Anthony, 128

Kent County, Delaware, 61

Kenton County, Kentucky, 61

Kentucky: as border state, 5–7, 22; antebellum politics, 41, 45, 51, 58, 61–62; secession and, 64, 65, 75, 83, 90, 93, 96, 115; emancipation and, 118, 128, 139, 146, 148, 153–54, 157–58; military events in, 82, 130–32; postwar politics, 167, 172, 177, 185–86

Kidwell, Zedekiah, 48

Kinchloe, Daniel, 29

Kingwood, Preston County, 97

Kitchen, Bethuel, 171

Know-Nothings: northwestern Virginia elections and, 40, 43–45, 48, 50–52, 62, 76, 79–80, 186. See also Fillmore, Millard

Laidley, James M., 30

Laidley, John, 120

Laidley, Richard Q., 131

Lamb, Daniel, 29, 104, 158, 163

Lane, James H., 126

Lang, Theodore, 1, 147

Leake, Walter Daniel, 34

Leavens, Charles, 98

Lecompton Constitution of Kansas, 54, 55

Lee, George H., 27, 29

Lee, Robert E., 59, 96, 130, 131, 159

Leigh, Benjamin Watkins (aka Appomattox), 17

Letcher, John A.: elected as Virginia governor, 56, 57, 58; Virginia Constitutional Convention and, 65; alliance with Confederacy, 77–79, 87, 89–90, 124; and West Virginia's statehood, 136, 142

"let-ups," 174, 176, 179. See also Republicans or Radicals (West Virginia)

Lewis, Charles, 29, 101

Lewis, John D., 28, 30

Lewis, John E., 98

Lewisburg, Greenbrier County, 32, 79, 166

Lewis County, 99

Lexington, Virginia, 56

Little Kanawha River, 11

Lincoln, Abraham: election of, 60–64, 67; and northwestern Virginia, 63, 76, 85, 90, 99, 115; emancipation in, 92, 138–41, 146, 186–87; and border states, 73–75, 78, 80, 93–94, 116, 213n24; border state emancipation plan, 117–19, 124, 127–28, 131, 133, 138–41; and West Virginia statehood, 148, 154–56; death of, 159–60

Lincoln County, 170, 226n33

Logan County, 21, 103, 182

Loring, William W., 96, 131, 132, 133

Louisiana, 65, 69, 131, 153

Louisville, Kentucky, 61

Lower or Deep South, 63, 64, 65, 69, 186

Macbeth (Shakespeare), 5

Madison, James, 9, 15

Mahon, Edward, 220n28
Mann, Andrew, 103
Marshall, John, 15
Marshall County, 80, 114, 183
Monroe, James, 15
Maxwell, Abner, 16
Marietta, Ohio, 11, 13
Marines, United States, 59
Marion County: antebellum politics of, 31, 41, 43, 61; secession crisis and, 65, 74; statehood movement and, 101, 137; postwar period and redemption, 173, 175, 184
Maryland, 5–8, 22, 185, 186, 187; antebellum politics of, 41, 45, 51, 58, 61, 62; and secession, 64–65, 75, 80, 83, 85, 90; as border state, 93, 115; emancipation, 118, 130–32, 139, 146; redemption of, 148, 167, 169, 172, 174, 177
Massachusetts, 43
Mason County, 47, 79, 133
Mason, James M., 66
Matthews, Henry W., 161
Maynard, Horace, 128, 136, 137
McCandlish, R. J., 161
McClellan, George B., 130, 154–56, 215n40; military operations in northwestern Virginia, 85–86, 89, 95, 124
McClure, Rev. J. T., 147
McComas, David, 98
McComas, Elisha, 35
McCullough, Samuel, 25
McDowell County, 21, 102, 107, 108, 182
McElwee, John, 180
McGrew, James C., 74, 75
Mecklenburg County, Virginia, 73
Mercer County, 102, 107, 108, 164
Mexico, 33, 36, 39, 40, 96
Michigan, 41
military units, 159
military units, Confederate: Charleston Sharpshooters, 79; Coal River Rifles, 79; Kanawha Riflemen, later the Twenty-Second Virginia, 79, 122, 131–32, 134; Shriver Greys, 79; Wise Legion, 87, 96

military units, Union: Army of Virginia, 130; Eighth West Virginia Volunteer Infantry Regiment, 135; First Delaware Infantry Regiment, 73; First Virginia Volunteer Infantry Regiment, 73, 79; First Separate Brigade, 161; Forty-Fifth United States Colored Infantry, 224n8; Fourth West Virginia Infantry, 145, 150; Seventh West Virginia Infantry, 150; Sixth West Virginia Cavalry, 147; Third West Virginia Infantry, 119; Twenty-Third Ohio Volunteers, 117
Mineral County, 170, 226n33
Minnesota, 128
Minor, Abia, 38
Mississippi, 69, 88
Mississippi River, 18
Missouri, 5–8, 22, 181, 185, 186, 187; antebellum politics of, 41, 45, 51, 58, 61; secession and, 62, 64, 65, 75, 85, 90; as border state, 93, 94, 96, 115; emancipation and, 118, 128, 131, 139, 146; radical rule of, 148, 153, 157, 158; redemption of, 167, 171, 174, 175, 177
Monongalia County: antebellum politics of, 31, 34, 48, 53, 56; military enlistments in, 4; statehood movement and, 80, 110, 120
Monongahela River, 11
Moore, William D., 79
Monroe County, 71, 107–8, 164, 166, 170, 181
Montgomery, Alabama, 172
Morgan County, 108, 164
Morgantown, Monongalia County, 2, 13, 85, 167, 170
Morris, D. S., 79
Morton, Jeremiah, 67
Mason County, 83
Moss, C. D., 78

Napoleon III, 55
National Road, 12
nativity, 18–19, 51, 80, 81, 88, 155, 171. *See also* Scots-Irish heritage

Nelson, Dr. J. L., 180
New Albany, Indiana, 11
New Castle County, Delaware, 61
New England, 136
New Hampshire, 41
New Jersey, 154
Newlin, Cyrus, 181
Newlon, Charles W., 217n9
Newman, Alexander, 41
New Mexico, 69
New Orleans, Louisiana, 11
newspapers: *Barbour Jeffersonian*, 76; *Buckhannon Advocate*, 169; *Parkersburg Gazette* (later *Parkersburg Gazette and Courier*), 14, 37, 41, 104; *Clarksburg Enquirer*, 16; *Clarksburg National Telegraph*, 129, 142, 145, 156, 160; *Clarksburg Weekly Campaign*, 57; *Clarksburg Telegraph*, 115; *Fairmont True Virginian*, 48, 53, 54, 71; *Fairmont National*, 134; *Greenbrier Independent*, 170, 173, 174, 226n35; *The Guerilla* (Charleston, Virginia), 132–33; *Kanawha Republican*, 33, 41, 53, 66, 156; *Lewisburg Times*, 164; *Mason County Journal*, 176; *Middlebourne Plain Dealer*, 119; *Morgantown American Union*, 48, 49; *Morgantown Monitor*, 150; *Morgantown Star*, 64, 65; *Morgantown Weekly Post*, 154, 156, 160; *New York Post*, 109; *Parkersburg Gazette*, 182; *Parkersburg News*, 57, 59; *Parkersburg State Journal*, 176; *Parkersburg Times*, 175; *Parkersburg Weekly Times*, 162; *Point Pleasant Register*, 174, 221n22; *Wellsburg Herald*, 41, 48, 60, 84, 124, 125, 129, 152; *West Virginia Journal*, 154, 156, 157; *Wheeling Argus*, 42, 44, 55; *Wheeling Compiler*, 16; *Wheeling Daily Union*, 59; *Wheeling Gazette*, 16, 41, 44, 45, 47, 57; *Wheeling Press*, 103; *Wheeling Times*, 42; *Virginia Patriot* (Taylor County), 79. See also *Cooper's Clarksburg Register*; *Star of the Kanawha Valley*; *Wheeling Daily Intelligencer*; *Wheeling Daily Register*
Newton, Enos W., 42, 156

New York, 43
Nicholas County, 79, 102
Nicolay, John G., 76
Noell, John W., 128, 136, 137
Norfolk City, Virginia, 34, 77
North or non-slaveholding states, 64, 66, 69, 75, 78, 93
North Carolina, 65, 75, 159
Northampton County, Virginia, 15
Northcott, R. S., 142
Northern Panhandle: and statehood movement, 87, 102, 110, 112, 119; and 1864 election, 154–56
Norton, E. M., 138

officeholding, 28–30, 88, 92, 97, 99, 104, 115, 122, 124, 162, 183
Ohio (state), 3, 13, 65–66, 80, 109, 119; elections in, 41, 45, 51, 58, 62; secession and, 65, 79, 80, 85; Civil War and, 93, 96, 150
Ohio County, 4, 183; slavery and slaveholding in, 21–33; antebellum politics of, 40–41, 50, 61; secession, 80, 101, 104–5, 119; statehood movement, 145, 154, 158, 164; in West Virginia, 169–70
Ohio River, 11, 13, 18, 39, 65, 72, 85, 96, 132
Ohio University, 31
Old Line Whigs, 49, 56
Opposition, 56, 57, 58

Pannell, Alex, 26
Parker, Granville, 109, 113, 123–24. *See also* "An Appeal to the People of West Virginia to Congress"
Parkersburg, Wood County, 11, 13, 14, 54, 63, 75, 85, 90, 145, 172, 180, 181
Patrick, Spicer, 30, 42, 67, 98, 154, 158
Patton, Ebenezer, 100
Patton, George S., 151
Patton, Willis, 120–21
Paxton, J.W., 138, 220n28, 223n57
Pearce, James, 128
Peck, Daniel, 158
Pendleton, J. H., 41
Pendleton County, 108

Peninsular Campaign, 124, 131
Pennsylvania, 3, 13, 104, 109;
    elections in, 41, 43, 45, 51, 58, 62;
    secession and, 65–66, 80, 96; Civil
    War and, 119, 131, 150
Perryville, Battle of, 130
Petersburg, Battle of, 159
Philippi, Barbour County, 12, 86, 89
Phillips, Wendell, 130
Piedmont Region of Virginia, 33, 38,
    64
Pierce, Franklin, 41, 49
Pierpont, Francis Harrison: antebel-
    lum career, 31; statehood
    movement and, 80, 88–89,
    133–34, 136, 138; governor of
    restored government of Virginia,
    97–99, 117, 121–22, 131, 143,
    147
Pierpont, Julia, 142
Pierpont, Frank P., 97
Pittsburgh, Pennsylvania, 11
Pleasants, John Hampden, 209n39
Pleasants County, 22, 33n39, 50, 72,
    210n47
Pocahontas County, 107, 108, 150,
    164
Point Pleasant, Mason County, 133
Polk, Leonidas, 93, 96
Polsley, Daniel, 162, 171, 174
Pomeroy, Joseph S., 112
Pope, John, 130
Potomac River, 39
Powell, John, 109, 111, 112
Powell, Lazarus, 128
Powhatan Hotel, 74
Preston, William Ballard, 17, 73
Preston County, 33, 61, 70, 74, 97,
    107
Price, Samuel, 161
Price, Sterling, 96, 161
proscriptions: and radical rule in West
    Virginia, 147, 151, 159, 162–63;
    amendment to state constitution,
    conservative attempts to
    overturn, 163–66, 169–71,
    179–80, 184, 187
Putnam County, 86, 161

Quarrier, William A., 162, 163

railroads, 42–43, 58, 68, 130, 178;
    Baltimore and Ohio, 13; Pennsylvania
    Railroad, 13, 27
Raleigh County, 74, 108
Rand, William J., 121–23
Rand, Noyes, 122, 131, 221n11
Randolph, George Wythe, 69
Randolph County, 89, 170, 181
Reconstruction, 148, 165, 167, 170, 177,
    181
reorganized or restored government of
    Virginia, 63; establishment of, 63, 88,
    97–98, 122–24, 162; and West
    Virginia statehood movement, 92,
    94, 102, 118–19, 138–42, 143, 147;
    and emancipation, 125, 136, 138–42;
    legality debates over, 101, 136, 139
"Report on State and Federal Relations"
    [May 15, 1861], 82
Republicans (federal party), 4, 186;
    antebellum influence on northwest-
    ern Virginia, 42–43, 49–50, 54, 58,
    60, 62; in secession crisis, 63, 66, 71,
    73, 75–76, 92; wartime policies of,
    92, 100, 148; emancipation and,
    124–28, 130, 142, 157, 166, 170,
    175; postwar politics of, 148, 157,
    166, 170, 175, 186
Republicans or Radicals (West Virginia),
    5, 165, 168–70, 173–81, 183, 184
Reynolds, William Clark, 131, 132
Rhode Island, 137
Rice, Henry M., 128
Richardson, Mr., 143
Richmond, Virginia: internal improve-
    ments and, 13; 1850 constitutional
    convention in, 33, 35; 1860 constitu-
    tional convention in, 66–73, 80, 82;
    military events in, 77, 89, 96, 159,
    172; West Virginia's statehood and,
    142
Richmond Junto, 32, 35
Rich Mountain, Battle of, 89
Ritchie, A. F., 97, 101
Ritchie, Thomas, 32–33
Ritchie County, 33, 72, 114, 129, 209n39

Roane County, 83
Robinson, Job, 223n57
Robinson, Mary, 27
Romney, Battle of, 96
Rosecrans, William S., 90, 94–96, 102
Ross, Mr. (Ohio County), 143
Ruffner, Charles, 30
Ruffner, David, 27
Ruffner, Henry, 3–4, 57, 58, 108, 110. *See also* Ruffner Pamphlet
Ruffner, James, 27
Ruffner, Lewis: West Virginia statehood and, 86, 88, 103, 110, 112; relations with conservative Unionists, 133–35
Ruffner Pamphlet [1847], 3–4, 31–32, 58
Ruffner, Hale, and Company, 135
Rundle, Jonathan, 47, 78, 160

Sabine County, Louisiana, 22
Scots-Irish heritage, 10, 80, 186. *See also* nativity
Scott, Robert Eden, 35
Scott, Robert G., 33
Scott, Winfield, 41, 85
secession: northwestern Virginia's vote on, 74; regional support and opposition to, 63, 68, 80, 84, 91; Kanawha County's battles with, 122–23
Second Party System, 30, 39, 43
Segar, Joseph, 94, 118, 136, 137
Senate, United States, 124, 125, 135, 156–57, 171–72
Seven Days Battles, 130
Seward, William Henry, 138, 139, 143
Seymour, Horatio, 72
Shakespeare, William, 5
Sheffield, William P., 137
Shenandoah Valley of Virginia: antebellum Virginia and, 36, 38, 39, 57, 58; secession and, 64, 71; West Virginia statehood movement and, 108, 125; military events in, 153, 159
Sherman, William T., 99, 153, 159
Shriver, William W., 29
Sinsel, Harman, 109, 112
Sisson, James, 28
Sissonville, Kanawha County, 28

Slack, Green, 86, 121, 124, 133, 134, 135
Slack, Greenbury, 97, 99
Slack, Hedgeman, 135
Slack, John Sr., 97–98, 99, 121, 124, 133
slavery, 3–4, 6, 8, 9, 39; place in northwestern Virginia's social structure, 9–10, 13–14, 18–33, 38, 47–48; as issue in antebellum Virginia's intrastate relations, 14–18, 43, 57–60, 64–72, 80–82, 86–88, 90–91; role in conservative phase of statehood movement, 93, 96, 101, 103–4, 108–10, 112; role in radical phase of statehood movement, 117, 118, 125, 126, 128, 139, 146; legacies in the new state, 148, 151, 156, 157, 158, 159, 172, 174, 177, 178, 184, 185, 186, 187. *See also* abolition; African Americans; emancipation
slaveholders: historical role of, 3–4; antebellum influence on northwestern Virginia, 18–33, 36; defense of slavery in 1850s, 47, 48, 53, 57; secession crisis and, 63, 67, 70, 72; protection of in constitutional convention, 103, 104; radical turn against, 124; resurgence in redemption, 183, 185, 187
Smith, Augustine J., 29
Smith, Benjamin H., 30, 86, 162; as United States Attorney for Virginia, 99, 100, 121, 134–35; and West Virginia statehood movement, 103, 113, 223n57; relations with Kanawha County Unionists, 99, 121–23, 134–35, 221n11; conservative candidate for governor, 165–66
Smith, "Captain" Bill, 170
Smith, Daniel, 30
Smith, Edward C., 6–7
Smith, Isaac Noyes, 99, 134, 150, 151
soldiers, 4, 79, 80, 85, 99, 115
South Carolina, 35, 63, 69, 72, 73, 96, 156, 159
Southampton County, Virginia, 17
southwestern Virginia, 13, 38, 108, 125
Sperry, Carlos A., 180–81

240 / Index

Star of the Kanawha Valley (later
Kanawha Valley Star): proslavery
views of, 41, 47, 48, 50, 52, 53, 57,
59; secessionist views of, 78, 79;
postwar return of editor, 160
state capital (West Virginia issue), 166,
170, 181, 182
Stevens, Thaddeus, 143
Stuart, Chapman, 106, 108, 109, 111,
112, 113, 144, 145
Staunton to Parkersburg Road, 12
Stanton, Edwin M., 138, 139, 171
steamboats, 11
Steenrod, Daniel, 25
Stephenson, Kenner B., 161
Stevenson, William E., 172, 173, 176,
178, 179
Storer College, 167, 173
Strother, James F., 41
Strum, Jesse Phillip, 217n9
St. Louis, Missouri, 11, 61, 169
Surghnor, Tom, 76
Swearingen, Eli B., 41
suffrage, 9, 14–16, 38, 124, 147, 185
Summers, George William, 30, 162;
and 1830 convention, 17–18; and
1850 convention, 33, 37; in 1850
gubernatorial election, 37–38, 45;
and 1861 secession convention,
67, 69, 75; and West Virginia
statehood movement, 75, 86–87
Summers County, 170, 226n33
Summers, Lewis, 30
Sumner, Charles, 125, 126, 128, 143
Supreme Court, US, 163, 168–69, 173
Sweeny, Robert, 145

Tanner, James, 29
taxation: in 1850 constitutional
convention, 36; and 1860
constitutional convention, 64, 66,
70–72, 78, 90, 92; and West
Virginia statehood movement,
110, 115, 124, 147; in 1872
constitutional convention, 183
Taylor County, 66, 97, 129
Taylor, Oliver L., 41
Taylor, Zachary, 40

Tennessee, 61; secession crisis and, 65,
75; and emancipation, 118,
127–28, 131, 136, 153, 157;
wartime experiences of, 174–76
Tenth Legion, 32
Tenure of Office Act, 171
Texas, 65
Thayer, Eli, 53, 62
Thomas, Benjamin, 137
Thompson, George W., 97
Thompson, J. J., 161
Thompson, R. A., 30
Tidewater region of Virginia, 33, 38,
39, 64
Tompkins, Christopher, 86–87
"To the People of North-Western
Virginia" [May 25, 1861], 84
township system, 109, 112, 115,
152–53, 163, 184
Trumbull, Lyman, 126
Tucker County, 120, 170
Turner, Franklin, 72
Turner, Nat, 17, 73
Tygart River, 11
Tyler County, 31, 119

Union Club of Charleston (Kanawha
County), 122–23
Unionists, 84, 86, 88, 162, 187–88;
conservatives, and conservative
phase of statehood movement,
117, 120–22, 124, 125, 130, 136,
140, 142–43, 146; and radical
phase of statehood movement,
148, 150, 151, 152, 153, 154, 159,
160, 161, 163, 171, 173; radicals,
and radical phase of statehood
movement, 120–23, 124, 125, 140,
146; and radical rule of the state
1863–1872, 148, 150, 151, 152,
154, 160, 163, 171, 172, 173
United States of America (federal
government): and conservative phase
of West Virginia statehood movement, 82, 93, 96, 97, 99, 107, 115;
and radical phase of West Virginia
statehood movement, 117, 121, 122,
128, 147; and the new state of West

Virginia, 148, 150, 152, 160, 161, 163, 177
United States or Union Army or Navy, 89, 93, 96, 115, 136, 170, 186
United State Supreme Court, 163, 168–69, 173
Uniontown, Pennsylvania, 14
Upper South, 63, 186
Upshur, Abel, 15–16
Upshur County, 43, 50, 51, 74, 119, 120

Vallandingham, Clement, 170
Van Bibber, Adna, 14
Van Winkle, Peter Goodwin: service in 1850 constitutional convention, 33; service in West Virginia constitutional convention, 109, 111, 112; and emancipation, 129; as US senator from West Virginia, 151, 156, 171
Vance, Cyrus, 29–30
Vance, John C., 120
Vicksburg, Mississippi, 133, 145
Virginia: antebellum intrastate relations of, 14–18, 30–33, 39, 41, 44, 54, 58; secession crisis and, 63, 65, 66, 67, 70, 71, 73, 78, 79, 82, 89, 90; and West Virginia statehood movement, 96, 100, 130, 136, 146; and West Virginia, 151, 152, 153, 162, 166, 172, 185
Virginia Capes, 86
Virginia State Fencibles, 59
Viva Voce voting method, 106–7

Wade, Benjamin, 126, 143
Walker, Frederick, 133
Walker, William, 220n28
Ward, Moses, 117, 220n1
War of 1812, 34
Washington, Booker T., 4
Washington, D.C.: as federal capital, 45, 75, 78, 86, 126–27, 130; emancipation in, 94, 118
Washington, John Augustus, 96
Watts, Samuel, 34
Wayne County, 4, 14, 53, 82, 120, 176, 182
Webster, Daniel, 39, 62, 84

Webster County, 21, 62, 102
Welch, James, 30
Welles, Gideon, 138
West, James G., 100–1
West Fork River, 11
western territories of the United States, 118, 127
Westmoreland County, Virginia, 35
West Virginia: as northwestern Virginia (to 1863), 39–40, 51, 61, 62; secession crisis and, 63, 64, 69, 72, 73, 75, 76, 79, 83, 84, 86, 88, 90, 91, 92, 214n34; slavery in, 9–10, 14–38; statehood movement (1861–1863), 5, 7, 16–17, 39, 64, 65, 83, 86, 88, 90, 91, 92, 96, 101–3, 110, 116–19, 124, 125, 127–29, 131, 136, 137, 138, 139, 140, 142–3, 145, 155, 186; statehood and its aftermath (1863–1872), 147–48, 151, 152, 156, 160, 162, 163, 164, 165, 168, 171, 172, 173, 175, 177, 179, 184, 185
West Virginia House of Delegates: moves against slavery, 152, 157–58; election to, 154; proscriptions and, 159, 169; education and, 167, 177; Fourteenth Amendment and, 167, 177; Fifteenth Amendment and, 174, 177; and redemption, 181, 183
West Virginia Independence Hall (formerly Federal Customs House), 80–81, 116
West Virginia Senate: abolishing slavery and ratifying Thirteenth Amendment, 157–58; proscriptions and, 163; Fourteenth Amendment, 167; elections to, 169, 182; and Fifteenth Amendment, 174, 177
West Virginia State Court System: changes made in West Virginia constitutional convention, 92, 109, 115; enforcing proscriptions, 151, 153, 162, 163, 165, 171; redemption of in 1872 constitutional convention, 180, 184
West Virginia University, 167, 170, 173

242 / Index

Wetzel, Lewis, 221n22
Wetzel County, 4, 100, 119, 155, 156
Whaley, Kieran V., 94, 118, 136, 157
Wheat, James, 81–82, 144
Wheeling, Ohio County, 4; economy and
population, 10–13; slavery in, 19,
25–26, 29; antebellum politics of,
18–19, 42, 48, 51, 55, 59, 60;
secession and, 76, 77, 78, 79, 85, 86;
statehood movement and, 63, 80, 87,
88, 100, 102–3, 119, 124, 130, 136,
137, 142, 145; in West Virginia, 147,
151, 154–55, 156, 167, 169
Wheeling Athenaeum, 100
Wheeling Daily Intelligencer, 4, 40; place in
antebellum northwestern Virginia,
41–44, 49, 53–55, 58–60, 62; and
secession crisis, 62, 65, 71, 79; and
conservative phase of statehood
movement, 102–4, 109, 113, 114;
and radical phase of statehood
movement, on emancipation,
119–20, 124–25, 137; and Carlile,
129; on conservative Unionists, 135;
on statehood, 140, 142–3, 145; and
West Virginia's radical administration (1863–1869), wartime opposition to conservative Unionists, 147,
150, 154; and Thirteenth Amendment, 156–57, 159; on death of
Lincoln, 160; opposed to conservatives and former rebels holding
offices, 162, 165, 166–67, 169–70,
172, 174, 175; on redemption, 182,
183; anti-slavery views of, 4, 42, 44,
59–60, 103–4, 109, 114, 119, 142;
and Know-Nothing Party, 44
Wheeling Daily Register: wartime
opposition to radicals, 153, 157, 159,
160; on postwar proscriptions, 162,
164, 169; on Boreman and the
radicals, 165, 170–71, 173, 175–76;
on African Americans, 168, 169, 174,
175–76

Whig Party, 30, 31, 40, 44, 45, 48, 62
Wickham, William C., 72
Willey, Waitman Thomas: early life and
career to 1861, 31, 33, 34, 36–37,
56; slaveholding and, 33, 67–70, 80,
82, 110, 112; in secession crisis, 69,
72, 74, 78; and statehood movement, 80, 82, 84, 94–95, 105, 107,
110, 112, 118, 130, 143, 220n28,
223n57; in Congress, 124–29,
138–39, 143; and West Virginia,
147, 150, 156–57, 172, 183
Willey, William P., 150, 224n4
Willey Amendment, 118; Willey
introduces to Congress, 124–27;
Senate vote on, 137; conservative
opposition to, 142; state constitutional convention debates on,
144–46; role in the new state, 152,
155, 180
William, Elisha, 121
Wilson, Benjamin, 70, 74, 78
Wilson, Robert, 128
Wilson's Creek, Battle of, 93
Winchester to Parkersburg Road, 12
Wise, Henry S.: in 1850 constitutional
convention, 37; as governor, 44, 45;
in 1861 Virginia constitutional
convention, 72; as Confederate
general, 87, 96, 131
Wise, O. Jennings, 143, 211n26
Wise County, Virginia, 107
Wood County: secession crisis and, 63;
First Wheeling Convention and, 80;
at West Virginia constitutional
convention, 110; opposition to
emancipation, 145; postwar politics
of, 164, 172, 176
Woods, Samuel, 72
Wyatt, Matthew P., 98
Wyoming County, 102, 108, 164
Wythe County, Virginia, 96

Zane, Mary L., 25